Whitestein Series in Software Agent Technologies

[illegible]

[illegible]

About Whitestein Technologies

[illegible]

www.whitestein.com

Whitestein Series in Software Agent Technologies

This series reports new developments in agent-based software technologies and agent-oriented software engineering methodologies, with particular emphasis on applications in various scientific and industrial areas. It includes research level monographs, polished notes arising from research and industrial projects, outstanding PhD theses, and proceedings of focused meetings and conferences. The series aims at promoting advanced research as well as at facilitating know-how transfer to industrial use.

About Whitestein Technologies

Whitestein Technologies AG was founded in 1999 with the mission to become a leading provider of advanced software agent technologies, products, solutions, and services for various applications and industries. Whitestein Technologies strongly believes that software agent technologies, in combination with other leading-edge technologies like web services and mobile wireless computing, will enable attractive opportunities for the design and the implementation of a new generation of distributed information systems and network infrastructures.

www.whitestein.com

Ontologies for Agents: Theory and Experiences

Valentina Tamma
Stephen Cranefield
Timothy W. Finin
Steven Willmott
Editors

Birkhäuser Verlag
Basel · Boston · Berlin

Editors:

Valentina Tamma
University of Liverpool
Agent Applications,
Research and Technology Group
Department of Computer Science
Chadwick Building
Liverpool L69 7ZF
Great Britain

Stephen Cranefield
University of Otago
Department of Information Science
PO Box 56
Dunedin
New Zealand

Timothy W. Finin
University of Maryland
329 Information Technology and Engineering
Baltimore County
1000 Hilltop Circle
Baltimore MD 21250
USA

Steven Willmott
Universitat Politècnica de Catalunya (UPC)
Dept. Llenguatges i Sistemes Informatics
Modul C5, 211b
Campus Nord
08034 Barcelona
Spain

2000 Mathematical Subject Classification 68T35, 68U35, 94A99, 94C99

A CIP catalogue record for this book is available from the
Library of Congress, Washington D.C., USA

Bibliographic information published by Die Deutsche Bibliothek
Die Deutsche Bibliothek lists this publication in the Deutsche Nationalbibliografie;
detailed bibliographic data is available in the Internet at <http://dnb.ddb.de>.

ISBN 3-7643-7237-0 Birkhäuser Verlag, Basel – Boston – Berlin

Part of Springer Science+Business Media
Cover design: Micha Lotrovsky, CH-4106 Therwil, Switzerland
Printed on acid-free paper produced from chlorine-free pulp. TCF ∞
Printed in Germany
ISBN-10: 3-7643-7237-0
ISBN-13: 978-3-7643-7237-8

9 8 7 6 5 4 3 2 1

www.birkhauser.ch

Contents

Foreword

There is a growing interest in the use of ontologies for multi-agent system applications. On the one hand, the agent paradigm is successfully employed in those applications where autonomous, loosely-coupled, heterogeneous, and distributed systems need to interoperate in order to achieve a common goal. On the other hand, ontologies have established themselves as a powerful tool to enable knowledge sharing, and a growing number of applications have benefited from the use of ontologies as a means to achieve semantic interoperability among heterogeneous, distributed systems.

In principle ontologies and agents are a match made in heaven, that has failed to happen. What makes a simple piece of software an *agent* is its ability to communicate in a "social" environment, to make autonomous decisions, and to be proactive on behalf of its user. Communication ultimately depends on understanding the goals, preferences, and constraints posed by the user. Autonomy is the ability to perform a task with little or no user intervention, while proactiveness involves acting autonomously with no need for user prompting. Communication, but also autonomy and proactiveness, depend on knowledge. The ability to communicate depends on understanding the syntax (terms and structure) and the semantics of a language. Ontologies provide the terms used to describe a domain and the semantics associated with them. In addition, ontologies are often complemented by some logical rules that constrain the meaning assigned to the terms. These constraints are represented by inference rules that can be used by agents to perform the reasoning on which autonomy and proactiveness are based.

In practice, the application areas of these technologies often overlap, for example: e-commerce, intelligent information integration, and web services. Increasingly, the multi-agent systems and ontology research communities are seeking to work together to solve common problems. A key focus to this joint working is emerging in ideas for the semantic web. Both ontologies and agent technologies are central to the semantic web, and their combined use will enable the sharing of heterogeneous, autonomous knowledge sources in a scalable, adaptable and extensible manner.

This volume collects the most significant papers of the AAMAS 2002 and AAMAS 2003 workshop on ontologies for agent system, and the EKAW 2002 workshop on ontologies for multi-agent systems. The workshops were taking different perspectives to the topic of using ontologies in the framework of a multi-agent system. On the one hand, there is the knowledge modelling perspective; *i.e.* how ontologies should be modelled and represented in order to be effectively used in agent systems. On the other hand, there is the agent perspective; what kind of capabilities should be exhibited by an agent in order to make use of ontological knowledge and to perform efficient reasoning with it.

The volume aims at providing a comprehensive review of the diverse efforts covering the gap existing between these perspectives. The papers cover a wide range of topics but can mainly be grouped in three categories: modelling principles for building and reasoning with ontologies for agents, semantic interoperability between different agents, and applications of ontologies in agent systems.

Modelling ontologies entails dealing with the problems of building ontologies, and establishing ontological commitment. Semantic interoperability includes reasoning with ontological knowledge that agents may use to proactively overcome differences in their conceptualisation of the world, and applications of ontologies concern real life examples of how ontologies can be used in agents.

For what concerns modelling and representing ontologies, Cranefield and colleagues in their first contribution propose to reduce the degree of human interpretation currently necessary to understand an interaction protocol, by describing at an abstract level the required agent actions that must be 'plugged into' the protocol for it to be executed. In particular, this can be done by designing and publishing ontologies describing the input and output data that are processed during the protocol's execution, together with the actions and decisions that the agents must perform.
Nodine and Fowler concentrate on ontological commitment, or the agreement to have applications and users conform to a common domain understanding, as encapsulated in one or more shared ontologies. They present their experiences in building ontology-based agent systems in multiple domains and illustrate the problems arising when a new application aims to locate and conform to some existing ontology or ontologies within its domain. The authors propose guidelines for ontology development and evolution, which should facilitate ontology reuse that may underpin a *usage model* for ontologies; one that enables the application designer to reuse ontological concepts from multiple ontologies in a more flexible manner, while retaining the essentially good properties of ontology sharing and reuse.
Pazienza and Vindigni also concentrate on ontological commitment, and in particular, on the lack of a shared knowledge model that can be assumed as a default *ontological commitment.* They propose a communication model based on the use of natural language, that predicates a strong separation among terms and concepts. In order to support the proposed communication model, the authors present a novel agent architecture able to deal with possible linguistic ambiguities by focusing on the conversational level.

An important part of this volume is devoted to approaches aimed at finding an ontological model that is shared by all the agents composing a system. These approaches become particularly important when agents commit to heterogenous ontologies. Dou and colleagues present an approach to ontology translation, one of the hardest problems agents must cope with. In their approach, the merging of two related ontologies is obtained by taking the union of the terms and the axioms defining them. Bridging axioms are added, not only as bridges between terms in two related ontologies, but also to make this merge into a completely new ontology, which can subsequently be merged with other ontologies. Translation is implemented using an inference engine (OntoEngine), running in either a demand-driven (backward chaining or data-driven (forward chaining) mode.

Leen-Kiat Soh contribution describes a multiagent framework for collaborative understanding of distributed ontologies. The framework aims to investigate and identify how agents collaborate to understand each other under resource constraints and operational setups, and to examine how agents manage and share their distributed ontologies triggered by various queries. To facilitate collaborative understanding, each agent maintains an ontology and a translation table with other agents or neighbors.
In Lister and colleagues, the authors address the problem of semantic interoperability on the web, and present their research experiments suggesting that as yet unaddressed issues should be considered; such as reconciling implicit ontologies, evolving ontologies, and task-oriented analysis. The authors consider the role of semantic interoperation in multi-agent systems, and describe strategies for achieving it via the ROADMAP methodology.
Stuckenschmidt and colleagues concentrate on the problem of answering queries over multiple data sources in a dynamic environment, where it is no longer realistic to assume that the involved data sources act as if they were a single (virtual) source, modelled as a global schema. In their contribution, they propose an alternative approach where they replace the role of a single virtual data source schema with a peer-to-peer approach relying on limited, shared (or overlapping) vocabularies between peer agents.
Chris van Aart and colleagues present an approach to agent communication, based on message content ontologies that specify the meaning and intention of messages. By committing to a shared ontology, several agents can reach an agreement on different agent communication languages.

With respect to applications, Annamalai and Sterling investigate the possibility for agent systems aiding with collaboration among Experimental High-Energy Physics (EHEP) physicists. They argue that a necessary component is an agreed scientific domain ontology, which must include concepts that rely on mathematical formulae involving other domain concepts, such as energy and momentum. In this work, previous efforts on representing mathematical expressions are adapted to produce a set of representational primitives and supporting definitions for modelling complex mathematical relations.
Chen and colleagues investigate the use of ontologies in a multi-agent system providing brokering services for pervasive computing. Cranefield and colleagues, in their second contribution, propose the use of a UML profile for ontology modelling, to represent an ontology for travel booking services, and automatically derive an object-oriented content language for this domain. This content language is then used to encode example messages for a simple travel booking scenario, and it is shown how this approach to agent communication allows messages to be created and analysed using a convenient object-oriented, agent-specific application programmer interface. Dickinson and Wooldridge present a belief-desire-intention (BDI) approach to the problem of developing an agent-assisted travel scenario, and ask what role ontologies would have in supporting the agent's activity. To

this end, their contribution discusses the Nuin agent platform, and illustrates various ways in which ontology reasoning supports BDI-oriented problem solving and communications by the agents in the system.
Sashima and colleagues focus on the problem of achieving coordination in ubiquitous computing, and in particular. bridging the coordination gap separating devices, services, and humans. They propose an agent-based coordination framework for ubiquitous computing to solve this human-centered service coordination issue.
Zimmerman and colleagues present agent-based supply chain monitoring system for tracking orders, in which communication is enabled through the definition of a shared ontology. The paper discusses the design of the ontology and its use for inter-agent communication is illustrated with the help of AUML models of the agent-interactions in the supply chain monitoring system.

Valentina Tamma

Valentina Tamma
Department of Computer Science
University of Liverpool
Chadwick Building
L69 7ZF Liverpool
Great Britain
e-mail: V.A.M.Tamma@csc.liv.ac.uk

Stephen Cranefield
Department of Information Science
University of Otago
Dunedin
New Zealand
e-mail: scranefield@infoscience.otago.ac.nz

Timothy W. Finin
Information Technology and Engineering
Baltimore County
Baltimore
USA
e-mail: finin@cs.umbc.edu

Steven Willmott
Dept. Llenguatges i Sistemes Informatics
Universitat Politecnica
Barcelona
Spain
e-mail: steve@lsi.upc.es

Ontologies for Interaction Protocols

Stephen Cranefield, Martin Purvis, Mariusz Nowostawski and Peter Hwang

Abstract. In this paper we propose reducing the degree of human interpretation currently necessary to understand an interaction protocol by describing at an abstract level the required agent actions that must be 'plugged into' the protocol for it to be executed. In particular, this can be done by designing and publishing ontologies describing the input and output data that are processed during the protocol's execution together with the actions and decisions that the agents must perform. An agent (or agent developer) that has previously defined mappings between the internal agent code and the actions and decisions in an ontology would then be able to interpret any interaction protocol that is defined with reference to that ontology. The discussion is based on the use of Coloured Petri Nets to represent interaction protocols and the Unified Modeling Language (UML) for ontology modelling. An alternative approach using Agent UML (AUML) is also outlined.

1. Introduction

Agent communication languages (ACLs) such as the Knowledge Query and Manipulation Language (KQML) [11] and the Foundation for Intelligent Physical Agents (FIPA) ACL [15] are based on the concept of agents interacting with each other by exchanging messages that specify the desired 'performative' (inform, request, etc.) and a declarative representation of the content of the message. Societies of agents cooperate to collectively perform tasks by entering into conversations—sequences of messages that may be as simple as request/response pairs or may represent complex negotiations. In order to allow agents to enter into these conversations without having prior knowledge of the implementation details of other agents, the concepts of agent conversation policies [17] and interaction protocols have emerged[1]. These are descriptions of standard patterns of interaction between

[1]Some authors treat these terms as synonymous, while others [13] make a distinction between them in terms of the type and generality of the representation formalism used.

two or more agents. They constrain the possible sequences of messages that can be sent amongst a set of agents to form a conversation of a particular type. An agent initiating a conversation with others can indicate the interaction protocol it wishes to follow, and the recipient (if it knows the protocol) then knows how the conversation is expected to progress. A number of interaction protocols have been defined, in particular as part of the FIPA standardisation process [16].

The specification of the individual messages comprising an interaction protocol is necessarily loose: usually only the message performative, sender and receiver are described. This is because an interaction protocol is a generic description of a pattern of interaction. The actual contents of messages will vary from one execution of the protocol to the next. Furthermore, the local actions performed and the decisions made by agents, although they may be related to the future execution of the protocol, are traditionally either not represented explicitly (e.g. in an Agent UML sequence diagram representation [28]) or are represented purely as labelled 'black boxes' (e.g. in a Petri net representation [5]).

In this paper we argue that the traditional models of interaction protocols are suitable only as specifications to guide human developers in their implementation of multi-agent systems, and even then often contain a high degree of ambiguity in their intended interpretation. Here we are not referring to the necessity for an interaction protocol to have formal semantics (although that is an important issue). Rather, we see a need for techniques that allow the designers of interaction protocols to indicate their intentions unambiguously so that a) other humans can interpret the protocols without confusion, and b) software agents can interpret protocols for the purposes of generating conversations. Ideally, an agent would be able to download an interaction protocol previously unknown to it, work out where and how to 'plug in' to the protocol its own code for message processing and for domain-specific decision making, and begin using that protocol to interact with other agents.

We propose reducing the degree of human interpretation currently necessary to understand an interaction protocol by describing at an abstract level the required agent actions that must be plugged into the protocol for it to be executed. In particular, this can be done by designing and publishing ontologies describing the input and output data that are processed during the protocol's execution together with the actions and decisions that the agents must perform. An agent (or agent developer) that has previously defined mappings between the internal agent code and the actions and decisions in an ontology would then be able to interpret any interaction protocol that is defined with reference to that ontology.

For example, consider a protocol describing some style of auction. Inherent in this protocol are the concepts of a bid and response and the actions of evaluating a bid (with several possible outcomes). There are also some generic operations related to any interaction protocol such as the parsing of a message to check that it has a particular performative and that its content can be understood by the agent in the current conversational context, and the creation of a message.

In the next section, we motivate our work by discussing an example: the FIPA Request Interaction Protocol, as specified by FIPA using Agent UML (AUML). This specification lacks a number of important details that would be required for an agent to use the protocol without additional human interpretation. In Section 3 we illustrate how a more detailed model of this interaction protocol can be defined using a coloured Petri net, and explain the role that an ontology plays in the definition. Section 4 then presents two approaches to defining the internal operations that an agent must implement in order to play a particular role in an interaction protocol. In Section 5 we return to consider the use of AUML for interaction protocol modelling, due to the current effort underway in FIPA to enhance and fully specify the language. We give an overview of our recent work on the development of an agent conversation controller that directly interprets AUML sequence diagrams, based on techniques similar to those discussed in Sections 3 and 4 in the context of coloured Petri nets. Section 6 concludes the paper.

2. Example: the FIPA Request Interaction Protocol

Figure 1 shows the FIPA Request Interaction Protocol[2] [14] using AUML [28]. This protocol defines a simple interaction between two agents. One agent plays the Initiator role and sends a request for an action to be performed to another agent which plays the Participant role. The protocol illustrates that there are three alternative responses that the participant can make after receiving the request: it can refuse or agree to the request or it may signal that it did not understand the request message. If it agreed, it subsequently sends a second response: a message indicating that its attempt to fulfil the request action failed, a message signalling that the action has been performed, or a message containing the result of performing the requested action.

There are some aspects of this protocol that are not specified. For example, it is not specified that each of the `not-understood`, `agree` and `refuse` messages should contain part of the original request in their content tuple, along with an additional proposition (representing respectively an error message, a precondition for the action to be performed, and a reason for refusal). To make the specification more precise there needs to be a way of annotating the protocol with constraints on the contents of the messages and the relationships between them. These constraints would need to be expressed in terms of a vocabulary relating to the structure of messages, i.e. an ontology for messages.

Furthermore, the underlying *intention* of this protocol is not explicitly specified. In order to customise this protocol to a particular domain, a request initiator agent must 'plug in' domain-specific procedures at six different points: the handling of `not-understood`, `refuse` and `failure` messages, analysing an `agree`

[2]The figure shows Version F of the protocol. Since this paper was written a more recent version of the protocol has been released by FIPA and promoted to standard status. The new version has removed the `not-understood` message and made the `agree` message optional.

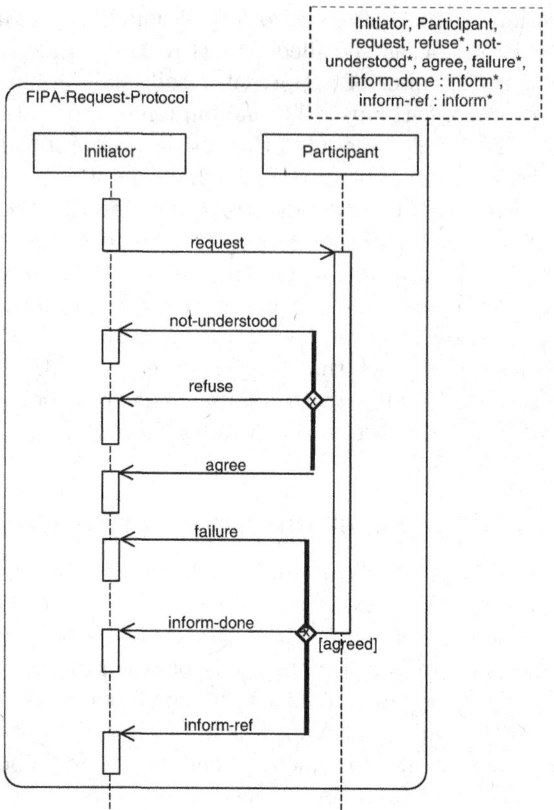

FIGURE 1. The FIPA Request Interaction Protocol defined using AUML

message to check if a precondition is specified by the participant, and the handling of the two different types of response that indicate the action was successfully performed. Similarly, there are three pieces of domain-specific functionality that an agent wishing to play the role of participant must supply: the parsing of the action being requested (possibly resulting in a failure to understand the message), choosing whether to agree to the request, and the choice between an `inform-done` response or an `inform-ref` message describing the action's result. We believe that an interaction protocol is not completely specified until the interface between the domain-specific agent-supplied code and the generic interaction protocol is defined. Clearly, interaction protocols should remain as generic as possible, making no commitment to any particular agent platform or implementation language. Thus the specification of this interface should be in terms of a programming-language independent representation. Furthermore, the agent operations related to a particular protocol will be related to the types of entity involved in the execution of that protocol, e.g. the notion of a bid in a 'call for proposals' protocol. This model of protocol-related concepts and the operations that act on them is an ontology that needs to be supplied along with the interaction protocol to give it a full specification.

3. A Coloured Petri Net approach

The discussion above was based on an analysis of an interaction protocol expressed as an AUML sequence diagram. However, the version of AUML used in the current FIPA standards has some shortcomings for further investigation of these ideas. First, this version of AUML is underspecified and the intended interpretation of an AUML sequence diagram is not always clear. Second, there are no graphical editors that directly support the use of AUML. Finally, these AUML sequence diagrams do not have a way of explicitly modelling the internal actions of agents[3]—which are exactly the points of the protocol at which we need to attach annotations refering to an ontology. We therefore adopted an alternative modelling language for our initial research in this area: coloured Petri nets.

Petri Nets [24] are a formalism and associated graphical notation for modelling dynamic systems. The state of the system is represented by *places* (denoted by hollow circles) that can contain *tokens* (denoted by symbols inside the places). The possible ways that the system can evolve are modelled by defining *transitions* that have input and output arcs (denoted by arrows) connected to places. The system dynamics can be enacted non-deterministically by determining which transitions are *enabled* by the presence of tokens in the input places, selecting one and *firing* it, which results in tokens being removed from its input places and new tokens being generated and placed in its output places.

Coloured Petri nets (CPNs) [18] are an elaboration of ordinary Petri nets. In a coloured Petri net, each place is associated with a 'colour', which is a type (although the theory of CPNs is independent of the choice of type system). Places can contain a multiset of tokens of their declared type. Each input arc to a transition is annotated with an expression (possibly containing variables) that represents a multiset of tokens. For a transition to be enabled, it must be possible to match the expression on each input arc to a sub-multiset of the tokens in the associated input place. This may involve binding variables. In addition, a Boolean expression associated with the transition (its *guard*) must evaluate to true, taking into account the variable bindings. When a transition is fired, the matching tokens are removed from the input places and multiset expressions annotating the output arcs are evaluated to generate the new tokens to be placed in the output places. If the expression on an output arc evaluates to the empty multiset then no tokens are placed in the connected place.

[3]UML activity diagrams have this capability and can be used on their own or in conjunction with sequence diagrams to specify the internal agent processing [28, 20].

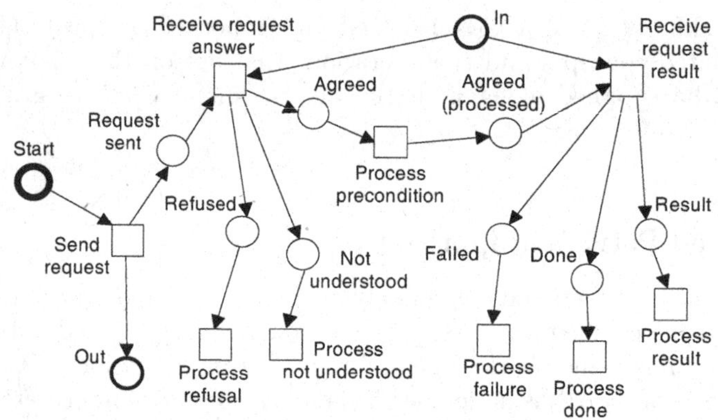

FIGURE 2. The Initiator role for the Request protocol as a CPN (outline only)

The coloured Petri net formalism provides a powerful technique for defining system dynamics and has previously been proposed for use in modelling interaction protocols [5, 19]. In this paper we take a different approach from our previous work [26, 25, 31] in the application of CPNs to interaction protocol modelling. We choose to model each side of the conversation (a *role*) using a separate CPN (we have also discussed this approach elsewhere [34, 35, 33, 32], and a variety of approaches have been used by other researchers [30, 23, 21]). Figure 2 shows an overview of the net for the Initiator role of the FIPA Request protocol (the 'colours' of places, the arc inscriptions and the initial distribution of tokens are not shown). In the figure, places are represented by circles and transitions are represented by squares. No tokens are shown. The places labelled In and Out are *fusion* places: they are shared between all nets for the roles the agent can play (in any interaction protocol). The agent's messaging system places tokens representing received messages in the In place and removes tokens from the Out place (these represent outgoing messages) and sends the corresponding messages.

The fully detailed version of this Petri net encodes the following process. The Initiator begins the conversation by sending a request with its `reply-with` parameter set to a particular value. When an answer with a matching `in-reply-to` parameter value is received, the Receive request answer transition is enabled and can subsequently fire at the agent's discretion. This transition generates a single token that is placed in one of the Agreed, Refused or Not understood places, depending on the communicative act of the reply (the remaining two output arcs each generate an empty multiset of tokens, i.e. no tokens are placed in their output places). In the case that the other agent agreed to the request, another message is subsequently expected from that agent, containing the result of the requested action. This is handled by the right hand side of the net in a similar fashion.

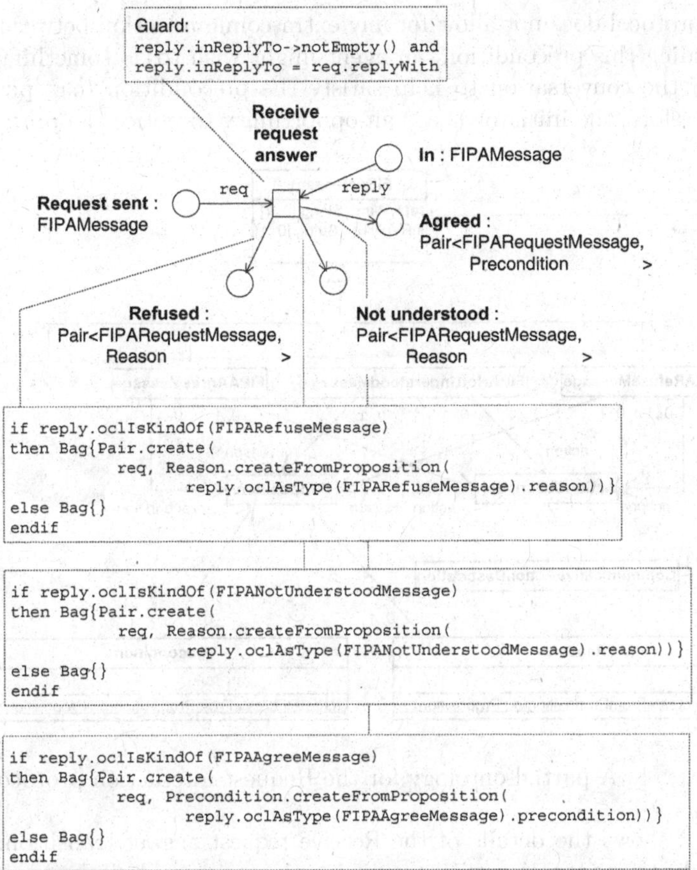
Guard:
reply.inReplyTo->notEmpty() and
reply.inReplyTo = req.replyWith
Receive
request
answer
In : FIPAMessage
req
reply
Request sent : FIPAMessage
Agreed : Pair<FIPARequestMessage, Precondition >
Refused : Pair<FIPARequestMessage, Reason >
Not understood : Pair<FIPARequestMessage, Reason >
if reply.oclIsKindOf(FIPARefuseMessage)
then Bag{Pair.create(
req, Reason.createFromProposition(
reply.oclAsType(FIPARefuseMessage).reason))}
else Bag{}
endif
if reply.oclIsKindOf(FIPANotUnderstoodMessage)
then Bag{Pair.create(
req, Reason.createFromProposition(
reply.oclAsType(FIPANotUnderstoodMessage).reason))}
else Bag{}
endif
if reply.oclIsKindOf(FIPAAgreeMessage)
then Bag{Pair.create(
req, Precondition.createFromProposition(
reply.oclAsType(FIPAAgreeMessage).precondition))}
else Bag{}
endif

FIGURE 3. Details of the 'Receive request answer' transition

In this Petri net we have included transitions that correspond to internal actions of the agent, such as those labelled Process refusal and Process not understood. These are not part of the protocol when it is viewed in the pure sense of simply being a definition of the possible sequences of messages that can be exchanged. However, we believe these 'internal' transitions communicate the underlying intent of the protocol: there are a number of points at which the agent must invoke particular types of computation to internalise and/or react to the different states that can occur. In the example shown, most of these internal transitions occur after the final states of the protocol. However, this is not necessarily the case, e.g. the Process precondition transition gives the agent a chance to reason about the precondition that may be specified by the other agent when it agrees to the request. This precondition must become true before the other agent will fulfil the request (in the simple case it can just be the expression `true`). Although the Request interaction protocol does not allow for any extra communication between the two agents regarding this precondition, an agent might wish to do something outside the scope of the conversation to help satisfy the precondition (e.g. perform an action). Therefore, the initiator needs an opportunity to notice the precondition.

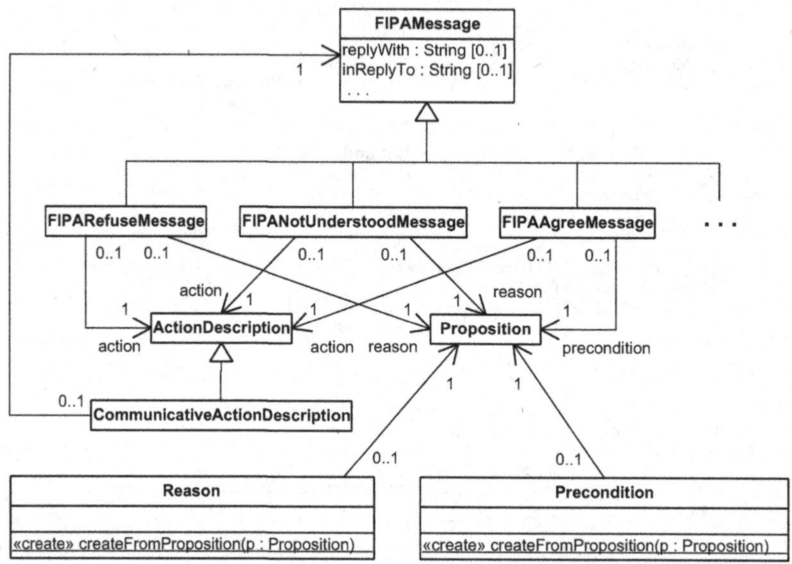

FIGURE 4. A partial ontology for the Request interaction protocol

Figure 3 shows the details of the Receive request answer transition. This is where we make the connection with ontologies: the types used as place colours and within arc expressions are concepts in an associated ontology (a portion of which is shown in Figure 4). We use the object-oriented Unified Modeling Language (UML) [3] to represent the ontology and UML's associated Object Constraint Language (OCL) [36] as our expression language. For brevity, we adopt the convention that a variable `x` appearing on an input arc represents the singleton multiset `Bag{x}` (`Bag` is the OCL type corresponding to a multiset).

In the case of the Request protocol, the concepts that need to be defined in the associated ontology are message types. Figure 4 therefore defines an inheritance hierarchy of FIPA ACL message types[4] (generalisation relationships are represented by arrows with triangular heads, while associations are represented by arrows with open heads). In addition, we have chosen to explicitly model the concepts of a reason and a precondition that are associated with the Request protocol. Within a FIPA ACL message these are both represented as propositions, but

[4]A more complex UML model for FIPA messages has been presented elsewhere [6], but that serves a different purpose. The model in this paper is not intended as an update of that previous work, but instead provides a different view of FIPA message types.

here the Reason and Precondition classes can be used (via their constructors) to achieve an additional level of interpretation of a proposition. Note that although the ontology is shown here as being a monolithic model, in practice some of the classes shown would be imported from a separate UML package.

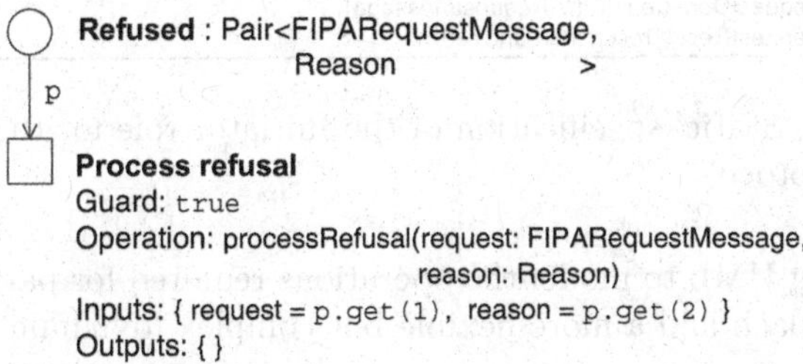

FIGURE 5. Details of the 'process request refusal' transition

In addition to the classes shown, the ontology is assumed to include a UML *class template* called Pair. A class template is a class that is defined in terms of one or more other classes, which are specified only as parameter names. When it is used (as in Figure 3) specific types must be supplied to instantiate the parameters. Pair represents a pair of elements with the type of each argument being the corresponding supplied parameter.

The arc expressions in Figure 3 use the operations oclIsKindOf and oclAsType. These are predefined OCL operations used for run-time type checking and type casting respectively.

4. Modelling Internal Agent Operations

In Figure 3, all processing represented by the transition is performed by the guard and the output arc expressions. This is not always the case. Consider the Process request refusal transition from Figure 2 (shown in detail in Figure 5). This represents the computation that an agent must do to react to the participant's refusal of the request. Although any future actions of the initiator agent are outside the scope of the Request protocol, in order for the protocol model to act as a standalone specification (without relying on implicit assumptions about the meaning of certain places) it should define the way in which the agent transfers information from the Petri net to its own internal processes. To support this, we optionally associate an *operation* with each transition, specifying the inputs to the operation as OCL expressions and providing a list of variables to which the outputs should be assigned (note that UML allows multiple output parameters in an operation). Figure 5 illustrates this for the Process request refusal transition.

The operations required to interface an agent with the CPN for a given role constitute part of the ontology for the protocol. In this section we describe two

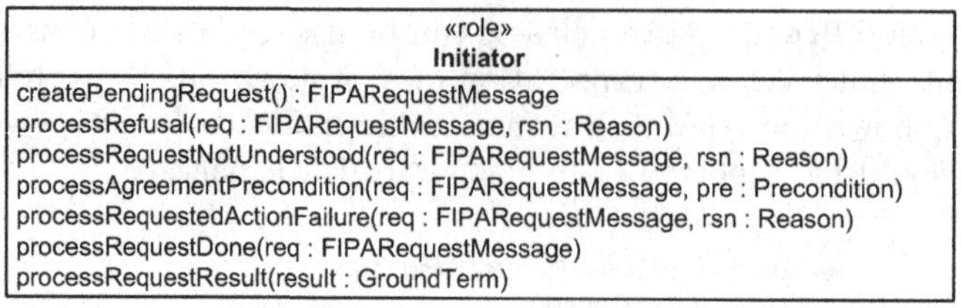

«role»
Initiator

createPendingRequest() : FIPARequestMessage
processRefusal(req : FIPARequestMessage, rsn : Reason)
processRequestNotUnderstood(req : FIPARequestMessage, rsn : Reason)
processAgreementPrecondition(req : FIPARequestMessage, pre : Precondition)
processRequestedActionFailure(req : FIPARequestMessage, rsn : Reason)
processRequestDone(req : FIPARequestMessage)
processRequestResult(result : GroundTerm)

FIGURE 6. 'Static' specification of the Initiator role for the Request protocol

approaches for using UML to model the operations required for particular roles: a simple 'static' approach and a more flexible but complex 'dynamic' approach.

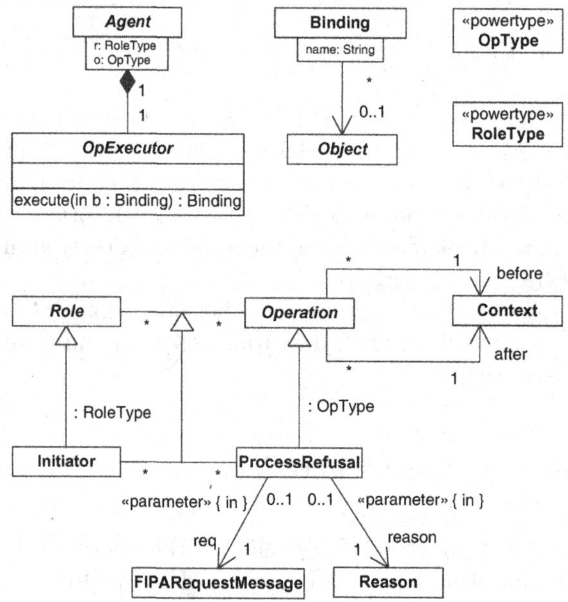

FIGURE 7. Specifying operations as first-class objects

4.1. The Static Approach

Figure 6 illustrates the static approach to including a role's operations in a UML ontology. This figure shows a class (annotated with the «role» stereotype) representing the role and containing all required operations. Although this looks like the specification of an application programmer interface rather than an ontology, it is not intended that an agent must implement operations with the same signatures as shown here. Instead an agent may be able to map these operations into those it does possess. To do this, the description of the role's required operations would need to include some information about their semantics, possibly using OCL pre- and postcondition expressions. This is a subject for future research.

The representation in Figure 6 does not model the operations required for a given role as first class objects in UML, but as features of a class representing the role. Although this has the benefit of simplicity, it has a number of shortcomings. Essentially it treats a role as an interface that an agent must implement if it wants to act in that role. We call this the static approach because it does not accommodate in a straightforward way the possibility of agents dynamically changing the roles they support. The UML object model does not allow classes (or agent types in this scenario) to change their set of implemented interfaces at run time. Also, the notation does not show graphically the relationships between the operations and the ontological concepts on which they depend.

4.2. The Dynamic Approach

Figure 7 shows an alternative approach that addresses the concerns raised above. The majority of the figure represents a base ontology containing classes to which a specific role ontology would make reference. Only the four classes at the bottom of the figure represent a specific ontology: a portion of the ontology for the Request interaction protocol.

Modelling both entities and the operations that act on them as first class objects is difficult to do in a straightforward way without departing from a "strict metamodelling architecture" where there is a firm distinction between instances and classes [1]. In this case, to allow the use of associations to define the types of operation arguments, each operation must be defined as a class. The abstract class `Operation` represents the concept of an operation that is associated with a role and which relates two contexts: the relevant local states of the world before and after the operation is performed. Particular operations are modelled as subclasses of `Operation` with their input and output arguments represented by associations labelled with the UML stereotype «parameter» and one of the Boolean 'tagged values' `in` or `out`

If operations are classes, we need to consider what their instances are. The answer is that the instances represent snapshots of the operation's execution in different contexts and with different arguments, in the same way that a mathematical function can be regarded as the set of all the points on its graph. However, the operation class only serves as a description of the operation: it will not be instantiated by an agent. Instead we model an agent as containing a collection of `OpExecutor` objects, each being an instance of some class that implements an operation. These objects are indexed by role and operation (this is shown using UML's qualified association notation). Roles and operations are both modelled as classes, so the types for these association qualifiers must be powertypes of `Operation` and `Role`. A powertype is a class whose instances are all the subclasses of another class [22, Chapter 23].

To invoke an operation, an agent calls `execute` on an `OpExecutor` object. The arguments to this method must be completely generic, so a binding structure is provided as an argument. This maps the operation's argument names to objects. The operation returns another binding list specifying values for any output parameters.

5. AUML Revisited

Section 3 motivated our use of coloured Petri nets by discussing some shortcomings of AUML as used in the FIPA interaction protocols. Recently FIPA has formed the Modeling Technical Committee [12] which is developing a new version of AUML, based on UML 2.0 and various UML-inspired modelling notations that have been defined by researchers in the area of agent-based software engineering. To date, work has focussed on the graphical notation, with a metamodel to be developed later. In parallel with (and informed by) the FIPA work on notation, we have have undertaken a preliminary investigation of how interaction protocols can be represented by sequence diagrams in sufficient detail to allow them to be directly interpreted by agents (once the application-specific code has been 'plugged in' to the appropriate points in the protocol) [9]. This required developing a mechanism for specifying the connection between the contents of incoming messages, the parameters and results of agents' internal operations, and the contents of outgoing messages—similar to the technique presented in Section 4 for use with coloured Petri nets. We also developed a metamodel for AUML sequence diagrams (based on a subset of the UML 2.0 metamodel), and implemented a library[5] for the Opal agent platform [29] that allows an agent to read an interaction protocol sequence diagram encoded in the XMI format, plug in methods that correspond to the internal actions specified in the protocol, and take part in a conversation according to that protocol by directly interpreting the sequence diagram.

Figure 8 illustrates the sequence diagram notation handled by our tool. The rectangles appearing on the lifelines represent the operations performed by agents when processing incoming messages and generating responses. These are specified by an operation name (not shown in the figure) and *start* and *end constraints*, denoted by dog-eared rectangles. These constraints specify how the inputs and outputs of the operations are related to the contents of the messages and variables of the protocol. In general, we believe that OCL would be the apppropriate language for expressing these constraints. However, as our tool is based on the Eclipse Modelling Framework (EMF) [8], and an OCL interpreter for EMF [27] was not yet available at the time this work was done, we used Java statements (interpreted by BeanShell [2]) for our prototype AUML interpreter. Figure 9 shows the declaration of the inputs and outputs of the `createProposal` operation from Figure 8: the operation's inputs are the two expressions in the content of the incoming CFP message (an action description and a referential expression describing a property that any responding proposal should satisfy), and the outputs are the action the

[5]The current library is an early prototype that supports only two-party conversations and a subset of sequence diagram features.

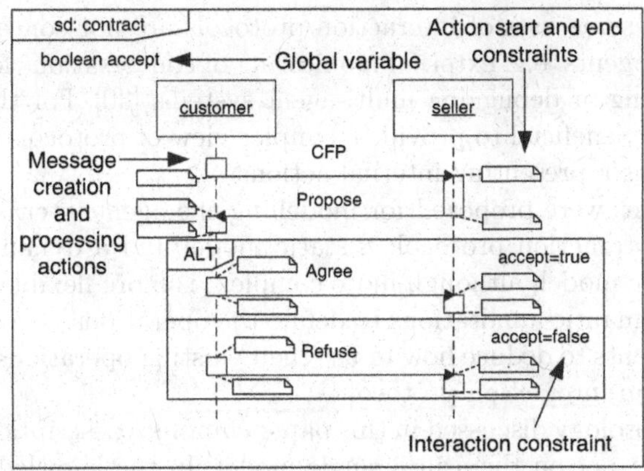

FIGURE 8. An executable AUML interaction protocol

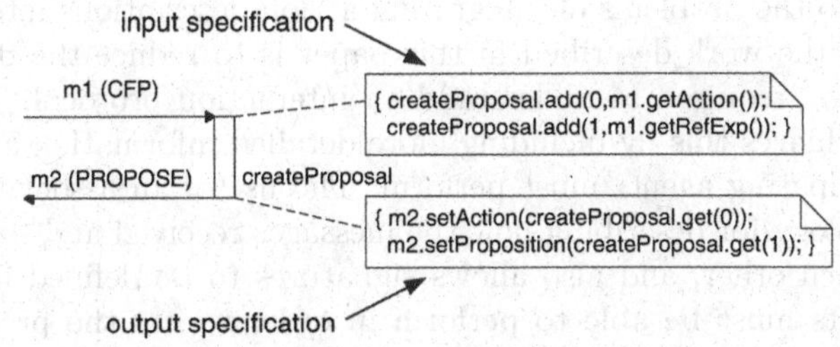

FIGURE 9. Declaring operation inputs and outputs in AUML

seller will propose to do (probably the same as that requested) and a proposition expressing the terms of the bid.

6. Conclusion

In this paper we have identified two weaknesses in traditional mechanisms for specifying agent interaction protocols: a lack of precision in defining the form of messages that are exchanged during the protocol and the relationships between them, and the lack of any explicit indication of where and how the protocol interfaces with an agent's internal computation. We have proposed the use of an ontology associated with a protocol to define the relevant concepts and the internal operations that an agent needs in order to partake in a conversation using that protocol, and have illustrated how this information can be represented in interaction protocols defined using coloured Petri nets and an extended version of AUML.

We note that some uses of interaction protocols are not concerned with the internal actions of agents, e.g. external monitoring of conversations for the purpose of compliance testing or debugging multi-agent systems [30]. For this type of application it may be beneficial to provide a simpler view of protocols that abstracts away the transitions representing internal actions.

Two techniques were proposed for modelling the agent internal actions necessary to use an interaction protocol: a static model and a dynamic model. We believe the dynamic model, although more complex, is more flexible and has more scope for adding semantic annotations to define the operations—an extension necessary to enable agents to deduce how to use their existing operations to implement those required by an interaction protocol.

The type of ontology discussed in this paper combines descriptions of concepts and operations that act on them in a single model. In the knowledge acquisition research community there has been considerable study of techniques for building libraries of reusable problem-solving methods, and work has been done on combining such libraries and ontologies in a single system [10]. This research may provide some insights into the problems of integrating action descriptions into ontologies.

The aim of the work described in this paper is to reduce the degree of human interpretation required to understand an interaction protocol. The solution proposed here achieves this by including more detailed information about the actions that participating agents must perform. The use of an associated ontology provides terminology for describing how the messages received and sent by agents are related to each other, and also allows signatures to be defined for the operations that agents must be able to perform in order to use the protocol for its intended purpose. These signatures provide a syntactic specification for the points in the protocol at which the agents must provide their own decision-making and information-processing code, and agent developers could use this to bind internal agent code to these points in the protocol. There is further work to be done to find ways of defining the meaning of these operations so that this binding can be performed on a semantic rather than syntactic basis. This will provide the ability for agents to engage in previously unknown interaction protocols by interpreting the specifications of the protocol and its associated ontologies.

References

[1] C. Atkinson and T. Kühne. Processes and products in a multi-level metamodelling architecture. *International Journal of Software Engineering and Knowledge Engineering*, 11(6):761–783, 2001.

[2] Beanshell: Lightweight scripting for Java. http://www.beanshell.org, 2003.

[3] Grady Booch, Ivar Jacobson, and James Rumbaugh. *The Unified Modeling Language User Guide.* Addison-Wesley, 1998.

[4] C. Castelfranchi and W. L. Johnson, editors. *Proceedings of the 1st International Joint Conference on Autonomous Agents and Multi-Agent Systems (AAMAS 2002).* ACM Press, 2002.

[5] R. Cost, Y. Chen, T. Finin, Y. Labrou, and Y. Peng. Using colored Petri nets for conversation modeling. In Dignum and Greaves [7], pages 178–192.

[6] S. Cranefield and M. Purvis. A UML profile and mapping for the generation of ontology-specific content languages. *Knowledge Engineering Review*, 17(1):21–39, 2002.

[7] F. Dignum and M. Greaves, editors. *Issues in Agent Communication*, volume 1916 of *Lecture Notes in Artificial Intelligence*. Springer, 2000.

[8] Eclipse modeling framework. http://www.eclipse.org/emf, 2004.

[9] L. Ehrler and S. Cranefield. Executing agent UML diagrams. In *Proceedings of the 3rd International Joint Conference on Autonomous Agents and Multi-Agent Systems (AAMAS 2004)*. ACM Press, 2004. To appear.

[10] D. Fensel, M. Crubezy, F. van Harmelen, and M. I. Horrocks. OIL & UPML: A unifying framework for the knowledge web. In *Proceedings of the Workshop on Applications of Ontologies and Problem-Solving Methods, 14th European Conference on Artificial Intelligence (ECAI 2000)*, 2000. http://delicias.dia.fi.upm.es/WORKSHOP/ECAI00/14.pdf.

[11] Tim Finin, Yannis Labrou, and James Mayfield. KQML as an agent communication language. In J. M. Bradshaw, editor, *Software Agents*. MIT Press, 1997. Also available at http://www.cs.umbc.edu/kqml/papers/kqmlacl.pdf.

[12] FIPA Modeling Technical Committee Web site. http://www.auml.org/auml/modelingtc, 2004.

[13] R. A. Flores and R. C. Kremer. To commit or not to commit: Modelling agent conversations for action. *Computational Intelligence*, 18(2):120–173, 2002.

[14] Foundation for Intelligent Physical Agents. FIPA request interaction protocol specification, version F. http://www.fipa.org/specs/fipa00026, 2001.

[15] Foundation for Intelligent Physical Agents. FIPA ACL message representation in string specification. http://www.fipa.org/specs/fipa00070, 2002.

[16] Foundation for Intelligent Physical Agents. FIPA interaction protocol library. http://www.fipa.org/repository/ips.html, 2002.

[17] M. Greaves, H. Holmback, and J. Bradshaw. What is a conversation policy? In Dignum and Greaves [7], pages 118–131.

[18] Kurt Jensen. *Coloured Petri Nets: Basic Concepts, Analysis Methods and Practical Use, Volume 1: Basic Concepts*. Monographs in Theoretical Computer Science. Springer, 1992.

[19] F. Lin, D. H. Norrie, Weiming Shen, and Rob Kremer. A schema-based approach to specifying conversation policies. In Dignum and Greaves [7], pages 193–204.

[20] J. Lind. Specifying agent interaction protocols with standard UML. In M. Wooldridge, G. Weiß, and P. Ciancarini, editors, *Agent-Oriented Software Engineering II*, volume 2222 of *Lecture Notes in Computer Science*, pages 136–147. Springer, 2002.

[21] S. Ling and S. W. Loke. A formal compositional model of multiagent interaction. In Castelfranchi and Johnson [4], pages 1052–1053.

[22] J. Martin and J. J. Odell. *Object-Oriented Methods: A Foundation*. Prentice Hall, Englewood Cliffs, NJ, UML edition, 1998.

[23] H. Mazouzi, Amal El Fallah Seghrouchni, and S. Haddad. Open protocol design for complex interactions in multi-agent systems. In Castelfranchi and Johnson [4], pages 517–526.

[24] T. Murata. Petri nets: Properties, analysis and applications. *Proceedings of the IEEE*, 77(4), 1989.

[25] M. Nowostawski, M. Purvis, and S. Cranefield. A layered approach for modelling agent conversations. In *Proceedings of the 2nd International Workshop on Infrastructure for Agents, MAS, and Scalable MAS, 5th International Conference on Autonomous Agents*, 2001. http://www.cs.cf.ac.uk/User/O.F.Rana/agents2001/papers/06_nowostawski_et_al.pdf.

[26] M. Nowostawski, M. Purvis, and S. Cranefield. Modelling and visualizing agent conversations. In *Proceedings of the Fifth International Conference on Autonomous Agents*, pages 234–235. ACM Press, 2001.

[27] Object constraint language library. http://www.cs.kent.ac.uk/projects/ocl, 2003.

[28] J. J. Odell, H. Van Dyke Parunak, and B. Bauer. Representing agent interaction protocols in UML. In Paolo Ciancarini and Michael Wooldridge, editors, *Agent-Oriented Software Engineering*, volume 1957 of *Lecture Notes in Computer Science*, pages 121–140. Springer, 2001. (Draft version at http://www.auml.org/auml/working/Odell-AOSE2000.pdf).

[29] Opal agent platform. http://sourceforge.net/projects/nzdis, 2004.

[30] D. Poutakidis, L. Padgham, and M. Winikoff. Debugging multi-agent systems using design artifacts: the case of interaction protocols. In Castelfranchi and Johnson [4], pages 960–967.

[31] M. Purvis, S. Cranefield, M. Nowostawski, and D. Carter. Opal: A multi-level infrastructure for agent-oriented software development. Discussion Paper 2002/01, Department of Information Science, University of Otago, PO Box 56, Dunedin, New Zealand, 2002. http://www.otago.ac.nz/informationscience/publctns/complete/papers/dp2002-01.pdf.gz.

[32] M. Purvis, M. Nowostawski, S. Cranefield, and M. Oliveira. Multi-agent interaction technology for peer-to-peer computing in electronic trading environments. In G. Moro, C. Sartori, and M. Singh, editors, *Proceedings of the 2nd International Workshop on Agents and Peer-to-Peer Computing, 2nd International Joint Conference on Autonomous Agents and Multiagent Systems*, pages 103–114, 2003.

[33] M. Purvis, M. Nowostawski, M. Oliveira, and S. Cranefield. Multi-agent interaction protocols for e-business. In *Proceedings of the 2003 IEEE/WIC International Conference on Intelligent Agent Technology (IAT 2003)*, pages 318–324. IEEE Press, 2003.

[34] M. K. Purvis, S. J. S. Cranefield, M. Nowostawski, and M. A. Purvis. Multi-agent system interaction protocols in a dynamically changing environment. In T. Wagner, G. Vouros, and S. Smith, editors, *Proceedings of the Workshop – Toward an Application Science: MAS Problem Spaces and their Implications to Achieving Globally Coherent Behavior, 1st International Joint Conference on Autonomous Agents and Multi-Agent Systems*, 2002.

[35] M. K. Purvis, P. Hwang, M. A. Purvis, S. J. Cranefield, and M. Schievink. Interaction protocols for a network of environmental problem solvers. In *Proceedings of*

the 2002 iEMSs International Meeting: Integrated Assessment and Decision Support (iEMSs 2002), volume 3, pages 318–323. The International Environmental Modelling and Software Society, 2002. http://www.iemss.org/iemss2002/proceedings/pdf/volume%20tre/214_purvis.pdf.

[36] J. B. Warmer and A. G. Kleppe. *The Object Constraint Language: Getting your models ready for MDA*. Addison-Wesley, 2nd edition, 2003.

Stephen Cranefield, Martin Purvis, Mariusz Nowostawski
Department of Information Science
University of Otago
PO Box 56
Dunedin, New Zealand
e-mail: {scranefield,mpurvis,mnowostawski}@infoscience.otago.ac.nz

Peter Hwang
Knowledge Engineering and Discovery Research Institute
AUT Technology Park, 581-585 Great South Road
Penrose, Auckland, New Zealand
e-mail: peter.hwang@aut.ac.nz

On the Impact of Ontological Commitment

Marian H. Nodine and Jerry Fowler

Abstract. Ontological commitment, or the agreement to have your applications and users conform to a common domain understanding as encapsulated in one or more shared ontologies, is a noble goal and essential for open agent systems. Our experiences building ontology-based agent systems in multiple domains have shown us that the intention for a new application to locate and conform to some existing ontology or ontologies within its domain has many impediments to its success. For instance, the goals of the designer of a domain ontology include developing a complete and comprehensive domain description; however, the application developer may only require a small fragment of that ontology. Multiple applications that conform to the ontology may, in fact, use completely orthogonal fragments of the ontology, and not be able to interact at all. Users may insist on importing into the ontology sets of terms that are neither logically consistent nor easily modelable.

With these issues in mind, we propose here some guidelines for ontology development and evolution that should facilitate ontology reuse. These guidelines could underpin a *usage model* for ontologies; one that enables the application designer to reuse ontological concepts from multiple ontologies in a more flexible manner, while retaining the essentially good properties of ontology sharing and reuse. These guidelines affect both the design and use of ontology-based applications, as well as the way applications advertise themselves to other agents with which they may interoperate.

Mathematics Subject Classification (2000). 68U35 Information Systems.

Keywords. Ontologies, ontological commitment.

1. Introduction

The goal of knowledge representation is to make explicit the semantics of a particular domain of interest for the purposes of sharing the knowledge among humans and computer artifacts. Sowa [21] subdivides knowledge representation into categories:

EDEN was funded jointly by the DOD, DOE and EPA.

Logic provides the formal structure and rules of inference.
Ontology defines the kinds of things that exist in the application domain.
Computation supports the applications that distinguish knowledge representation from pure philosophy."

There is a strong relationship between some specific ontology and the logical rules and computational artifacts that use that ontology, in that when they communicate among themselves, they have some level of assurance that the same terms have the same meanings to all. However, this use requires that the logical rules and the computational artifacts have explicit linkages with the ontology; often in the form of hard-coding the ontological terms into the rules and/or the application code itself.

In an agent-based system, common ontologies specify the ontological commitments of a set of participating agents [10]. An ontological commitment is an agreement to use a vocabulary in a way that is consistent with an ontology. An agent or human committed to an ontology understands (some subset of) the ontology and agrees to use it in a manner consistent with the semantics of the ontology. Agents and humans committed to the same ontology can share knowledge among themselves with some confidence that they share an underlying understanding of what is being said. Commitment to common, shared ontologies facilitates openness in an agent-based system.

We examine the conflicting requirements and goals of ontology designers, ontology-committed applications, and ontology-aware users, and their respective impact on the problem of ontology commitment and reuse. This conflict is evident, but unresolved, in the guide for the OWL Web Ontology Language [24], which states at one point, "... the development of an ontology should be firmly driven by the intended usage", and at another, "in order for ontologies to have the maximum impact, they need to be widely shared". The first statement implies that application designers and users need to have an impact on the development of an ontology, and the second implies that application designers and users should use pre-existing ontologies, which were designed without considering their needs. As ontological sharing and reuse increases, the gap between the ontology designers and the ontology users grows larger.

Our goal is to analyze what issues inhibit reuse and to propose strategies for facilitating reuse. In particular, we consider the problem of reuse of ontologies whose specification is complete, for applications whose requirements were not considered during the design of the ontology. This problem is not addressed in the ontology design methodologies summarized in [8]. We develop guidelines and approaches for agents to use existing ontologies in a more flexible manner.

We seek to relate the issues to real issues we have encountered within the context of one of our applications, EDEN [5]. EDEN is an agent-based system developed for the purpose of inter-organizational sharing of environmental data collected, stored and monitored by multiple government agencies and non-government scientists spread throughout the US and Europe, and relating information from these disparate data sources and schemas at a semantic level as needed by the users. EDEN uses ontologies to represent the semantics of the underlying information in several large, diverse production databases to populate those ontologies with instances.

2. Ontological Commitment

Because ontologies are meant to facilitate sharing and reuse of knowledge, it is important that the ontology and its collection of users (both human and agent) align themselves to a shared view of the domain during the process of designing and evolving the ontology for that domain. However, many existing ontologies have been developed either by designers attempting to characterize a domain (with no real computational applications that use them) or by application developers to support individual applications (with no real sharing of the ontology with other applications). The plethora of existing ontologies argues that many concepts are already represented within some ontology, so reuse of these ontologies, increasing the ontological commitment level, is now feasible. For example, some ontologies such as the Unified Medical Language System (UMLS) Metathesaurus [14] have achieved a higher level of commitment.

There are several issues that impede this sharing and knowledge. First are issues related to the conflicting goals and objectives of ontology definers, ontology-committed applications, and users of such applications. Second are issues of the mutual conflict between ontological commitment and ontological evolution. Third are issues of conceptual mismatches between ontologies and the applications and users that use them. Unfortunately, these issues stem from fundamental issues and characteristics of the problem of sharing ontologies so broadly. We discuss the first two issues in the remainder of this section, and the third (which has a more evident impact on the application designers and users) in a later section, "Impedance Mismatch".

2.1. Conflict: Definer, Application, User

The commitment to ontologies is hampered by the conflicting goals of ontology definers, developers of ontology-committed applications and ontology-committed application users, and often by the confusion of users and definers over the demands of ontology-committed applications. Here, we use the adjective "ontology-committed" to mean that something purports to use the terms in the ontology(-ies) in a manner consistent with its (their) definitions.

The goal of the *ontology designer*, working towards maximizing the usefulness of his ontology to a wide variety of applications, is to completely characterize a particular domain at the semantic level. The ontology designer needs expertise in knowledge representation and in the domain of the ontology. His intent is to develop a comprehensive and up-to-date ontology, with a broad set of acceptable terms. His job is hampered by the fact that the different domain experts have different viewpoints of the domain, and these viewpoints must be reconciled within the ontology itself, placing pressure on the designer either to take a commonly agreed-upon but consistent subset of the domain, or to attempt to placate everyone by including everything. The likely result is either the ontology will express concepts at a higher level than can be used effectively by an application that seeks to attach suitable labels to real data, or the terminology within the ontology will not be logically consistent and thus will not be easy to incorporate into an application.

The goal of the *application designer* is to use the ontology to support an application. The application designer has expertise in building applications, especially within given domains. His intent is to develop an efficient and useful application. It is likely that the application will not cover the whole domain; conversely, it may span multiple domains. Also, application designers need to focus on some issues that are unimportant to the ontology designer. For instance, a failure to take sufficient care of value representation issues in the ontology may force the application designer to code this information directly into the application, even though it is really domain-related knowledge. For example, within the Environmental Data Registry [1], it was difficult to relate measurements of chemicals between different representations because the measurement ontology was "well understood," and often explicit in the data representations themselves. Even terms such as "milligrams per kilogram" were sometimes represented inconsistently in text fields. This posed a problem in extracting values for computation in this "well understood" measurement system.

The desire of the *application user* is to be able to do his job well and easily. Application users have expertise in their own jobs and potentially in the domain of the application, but may have minimal understanding of knowledge representation or application design issues. Typical users want an understandable, natural, easy-to-use interface to the application that facilitates their work. This implies that they want the scope of the ontology restricted to the exact area within the domain that they are specifically concerned with. Another issue is that a user may have a comfortable vocabulary of domain-related terms that do not map well to the ontology representation model, to the domain model that the ontology developer had in mind or to the needs of the application itself.

2.2. Conflict: Commitment, Evolution

A second hampering factor when considering ontological commitment itself is the fact that ontological commitment impedes ontology evolution, and vice versa. Yet, both of these are necessary for an ontology to be successful. As Mark Tuttle et.al. say, "if you don't use it, it won't improve, if you don't improve it, it won't get used." [22]. In other words, use brings out the need to change, change is required for continued use.

As stated before, a measure of ontological commitment is the number of agents and humans that are committed to using the ontology. Each of these committed entities has made the effort to learn the ontology and to use its concepts in a manner consistent with their definition. However, the ontology itself may have problems, or may be incomplete in some aspect, or not reflect changes in the domain itself. In these situations, it becomes desirable at some point to evolve the ontology, providing an updated version. Initially, there is no real commitment to the updated version; rather, the entities committed to the old ontology must explicitly learn the new ontology, and adapt to the changes therein. This leads to the observation that, *as commitment to an ontology rises, so does the level of effort required to accommodate an evolutionary step.*

To put this more concretely, assume that an ontology has n applications that are ontologically committed to it. Each change in the ontology is likely to cause subsequent changes in the applications; thus, the one change will result in up to n application changes. Some of these may be easier, and some harder, but the impact is widespread. Making the further assumption that each application has, on average, m users, then the single ontology change has the prospect of additionally impacting mn users. The application designer may be able to shield the user from these changes, however.

Development of an application represents a strong degree of ontological commitment. The incorporation of an ontology into an application may require specific coding with respect to the ontology, so application developers tend not to appreciate it when the ontology evolves. This tends to discourage users from employing the precision they need to express their views of the data in an application. In EDEN, the first version of our ontology easily evolved into the second, because there were only three small database fragments and a single user view in the initial demonstration. As the complexity of the user interface increased to make multiple views possible, and as we added larger, more complex resources, the task of evolving the ontology from version two to version three became more demanding due simply to the numbers of agents impacted.

3. Setting: The EDEN Application

The examples of this paper are set within the context of the Environmental Data Exchange Network (EDEN) application. application. EDEN is a joint effort of the Environmental Protection Agency (EPA), Department of Defense (DOD), and Department of Energy (DOE) along with the European Environment Agency (EEA) whose goal is to develop ontology-based methods of sharing data. Among the ongoing efforts coming out of EDEN have been the Open Forum on Metadata Registries and the EDEN for Inland Water project of the European Community 5th Research Framework [12].

An important early component of EDEN, and the work from which we gained our experience, was the EDEN Demonstration System, an application of the InfoSleuth agent system [18] that used software agents to provide ontology-based integration of data from several databases of varying sizes, schemas, database management system software, and location. Included were resource agents that wrapped small locally mounted MS-Access database files, flat file databases served via HTTP, a moderate-sized Sybase database, and several very large Oracle databases, no two of which shared the same schema, and which were scattered across a half-dozen states.

Agents in the EDEN system communicated over an application domain relating to hazardous waste measurement and remediation, using a global domain ontology that had roughly two dozen concepts relating physical facilities with the locations of contaminated sites within their boundaries, the chemical contaminants that appeared at those sites, the measurements and the methods used to measure levels of compounds, and remediation projects at those sites and the technologies used in remediation. At one end of the EDEN agent community stood a User Agent whose task was to translate a query from a user's local ontology into the global ontology and then translate results from the global ontology back into the user's ontology. Similarly, at the other end of the agent community stood Resource Agents whose task was to translate from the global ontology into the resource's local ontology and then translate results back. Both User and Resource Agents made use of a Value Mapping Agent to provide conversions for instances of concepts between local value domains and the canonical global value domains used in the EDEN ontology.

While the EDEN ontology was limited in scope, the EDEN application itself was targeted towards a diversity of users spread across multiple agencies, each with their own ontologies and terminologies. The EDEN application itself was a forcing factor, encouraging this diverse community to converge on a common ontology so that they could share information. Thus, it serves as an abundant source of good examples for the issues we address.

4. Impedance Mismatch and its Consequences

By analogy with electrical systems, we use the term "impedance mismatch" to refer to circumstances in which conflicts between two ontologies, or between ontology and data, decrease the efficiency of an application that seeks to convey information in terms of ontologies. There are several areas where impedance mismatches crop up. This problem has been studied extensively within the heterogeneous database community in much greater depth than we present here [13, 16].

All of these issues conspire to make ontology sharing challenging. Some are manifested in the purely logical realm of relationships between ontologies, some in the realm of human-computer interaction, and some in the social environment of human political interaction. The first of these, terminology mismatch, is a declared target of the creation and development of ontologies, and is therefore easily addressed within the abstract world of the ontology developer, but frequently leads to friction during application development between developers and the user community. Others have straightforward logical resolutions that have significant computational demands in implementation, while still others affect the application developer's ability to resolve ontology conflict at all.

Terminology mismatch: This occurs either in the situation when different sets of users use the same term for different concepts, or in the situation when the term best suited to the user is already present in the ontology with a different meaning. The latter form of terminology mismatch can cause subtle difficulties to ontology developers, in that necessary concepts are sometimes omitted because the lexical terms needed to express them in human language are all present in other usages. In this situation, the meaning for the term already established in the ontology effectively trumps the new usage. For instance, the UMLS set of Semantic Relations was slow to develop the concept of genetic relationship because the terms parent and child existed for their use in logical tree structures.

With respect to the first situation, as an example we note that many terminology disagreements in the EDEN application resulted from the use of the same lexical term by different members of the application user community. For instance, what the EPA refers to as a "site" the DOD calls a "facility." What the EPA calls an "operable unit" (a specific location contained in an EPA "site") the DOD calls a "site." We initially thought that we could address this by synonymy, masking the preferred lexical term for one concept behind an application-level lexical mapping for one user group or the other. However, the term, "site," eventually became a controversial term that had to be avoided altogether in the ontology. Since the whole purpose of the application was to facilitate communication between these different user communities, we were compelled to resolve the problem in the ontology itself, by choosing a lexically distinct term, "eden_site," for the ontology, and adding mappings for each of the user communities, for political reasons.

Computationally, at a minimum, this kind of terminology mismatch demands extra layers of mapping during communication between users who require special terminology adaptation and agents that must necessarily use the terms of the application ontology itself to communicate. Once the political controversy in EDEN was resolved, the application was able to address this in a straightforward manner by lexical mappings in the user interface and the resource wrappers.

Uneven concept granularity: Some ontologies and other dictionaries have been developed with a focus on one particular aspect of a target domain. This aspect was well-developed and well-tested, but other aspects of the same domain were ignored. As a result, merging two such ontologies is likely to lead to differences in granularity between terms of the two.

For instance, most of the resources upon which the EDEN ontology was designed had very strong and detailed concepts relating to concentrations of specific contaminant compounds in hazardous waste sites on land and in bodies of water within the confines of a single region; another small experimental resource addressing the Basel Convention on transboundary shipment of contaminants was more concerned with quantities and broad classes of contaminants as they crossed territorial boundaries. This produced an almost orthogonal set of relationships for contaminants, measures, and locations.

Concept granularity mismatch often manifests itself in situations where the same physical sources of data have users with different perspectives. Several of the systems that were to be integrated in EDEN had been created to support scientific investigation into the application of remediation techniques. One of the goals of EDEN, however, was to provide a way of reconciling different agencies' views of data for the purpose of meeting statutory reporting requirements. This management goal had a very different purpose and perspective from the scientific one. A critical consequence was that the management model tended to oversimplify the characterization of a site, reducing the concept of "observed_contamination" to a site-wide average of contamination using a shallow ontology of contaminated media, while the scientific viewpoint demanded a more rigorous determination of such factors as soil structure, slope, water table (over time), and plume shape and motion in which the concept of average concentration made little sense. Reconciling these views involved more than just computation.

A prime example of granularity mismatch that had an enormous impact on feasibility of a computation occurred in a scenario in which we wished to ask the question, "What chemical contaminants are observed in the 'eden_sites' in a particular city and state?" Our data domain encompassed, at the extremes, one very small and simple database (ITT) designed to track remediation techniques and their application at a small set of "eden_sites," and one very large and complex database (OR) designed to monitor numerous kinds of environmental pollution and track remediation projects at many different points within a single "eden_site." The ITT data model simply listed contaminants per "eden_site." The OR data model listed numerous observations of detailed physical and chemical assays for many different specific compounds in several media at several depths for hundreds of monitoring locations in its single "eden_site."

The simple-minded query joins a constraint on the "eden_site" concept with the entire contents of the "observed_contamination" concept. ITT would return a handful of rows relevant to the constrained "eden_site" and its few hundred rows for "observed_contamination." Meanwhile, when the database behind OR was not busy, and the Internet permitted the timely return of large volumes of data, this query would return around a million rows of data related to "observed_contamination," and (for a majority of the queries) no data for the constrained "eden_site." The multi-resource query agent would then join on the constrained "eden_site." usually eliminating all the rows returned by OR. However, when OR's database was at all loaded, or bandwidth was scarce along the Internet route involved, the OR agent would time out or fail because of inadequate temporary space. The fact that most times the final answer was coincidentally correct concealed the egregious abuse of the OR resource from the user.

This situation forced us to remove the offending OR resource from the available query set, or to restrict queries over these concepts to constrain one or more other concepts as well, such as medium of contamination, contaminant, and concentration. The undesirable result of this was to make it trivially easy to overconstrain the query and receive no matching results.

Our long-awaited solution to this problem was to give the multi-resource query agent the capability of performing a distributed semi-join in which the identifiers that matched the constraint on "eden_site" were resolved and delivered as constraints on "observed_contamination." When this was implemented, the query agent now delivered, OR was immediately able to return an empty set to the queries for which it had no data relevant to the concept, and the query returned with an appropriate response time. Suddenly a whole range of queries of which this is but one example, were transformed from infeasible due to granularity mismatch into feasible queries that promised interesting answers.

Concept modeling mismatch: Some applications and information sources model individual concepts differently from others, thus it was hard to develop a single ontological concept that would relate well to all the ways it could be represented. For instance, the concept of a set of measurements of observed contaminant levels could be represented in the ontology and/or the data itself either with a class of measurement vectors, with one instance per observation, or a class of measurements, with one instance per measurement type per observation, specialized on measurement type. In some representations, a sampling point was specified as a geographic location further refined by depth; in others, a sampling point was a geographic location, and samples for measurement were taken along a vector of depths.

Another interesting issue in these measurements was reconciling what a value near zero meant, since the measurement's precision depended not only on what assay was performed but also on what equipment was used. A sample that reads "below detectable levels" on one apparatus might register a precise non-zero reading on a more refined piece of equipment. Yet this level of distinction, crucial though it might be to a scientific investigation, would be lost in comparison with another resource for which presence of the contaminant is all that is indicated.

In another dimension, the scientifically precise characterization may be of little importance at the level of policy making and triage of hazardous conditions, where proximity of the contaminated site to human habitation and the physical states of its contaminants may be a much more important factor in a decision than its precise concentration.

A computational impact of modeling mismatch that we experienced involved relating remediation technologies to contaminants, with the hope of providing a catalog of suitable technologies. The ITT resource sought to do this explicitly. In attempting to emulate this behavior by speculatively associating remediation technologies applied at "eden_sites" to the contaminants found there, we found ourselves traversing a query path, from technology to site to contaminant, that proved to yield infeasible queries for reasons essentially similar to the granularity mismatch discussion above.

Value representation mismatch: Many ontologies we have found do not even consider the representation of the values of the attributes in the instances of a concept, a requirement for many applications. For instance, it would be easy to say that "area" was a floating point number; therefore setting its range as the range of positive numbers. In EDEN, however, it should be no surprise that the Americans expressed area using English measure, while the Europeans (including the English) used metric measure. The application needed to know in which unit the value in a particular instance of the area is represented, and how the units relate. These concepts should therefore exist in the domain ontology.

In a more complex example, one information source in the EDEN application had "soil" as one of the media that could be polluted; but a second had "topsoil" and "subsoil" as separate concepts. A third site had multiple, more fine-grained classifications for soil. These did not all map easily onto any single ontological representation for soil, as mapping between the different concepts required additional knowledge (e.g. the depth of the soil), and sometimes was lossy (e.g. if everything was just mapped to "soil").

Attempting to resolve these differences in value representations led us to a series of design decisions that stood up well in retrospect. We identified three classes of value-mapping problem: general ones for which a global solution is appropriate because the map is of central importance to the domain, and will be susceptible to change over time, such as names, abbreviations, and boundaries of countries of the world; general ones that amount to computations of unchanging accepted truths, such as conversion of grams to kilograms; and particular ones of application to a single agent or set of agents, such as a preferred set of lexical terms for a given user. The first of these, the global class, we handled by creating a specialized value mapping agent that could handle either singular mapping requests or bulk requests to change entire columns of a data set from one value-domain to another. The remaining two we handled (within the value-mapping library) by invocation of the appropriate routines.

This approach resulted in an increase in response time of about 30% on our usual set of queries, because the original user query, each extracted database query, each non-null result set, and the final result-set delivered to the user all were likely to require a call to the same value mapping agent. However, the resulting improvement in flexibility of the system (a query for contamination in "soil" no longer returned null from the resource that identified soil with the letter "S" or the one that supported "topsoil" and "subsoil"), and the increased adaptability of being able to modify the mappings in a single location, were invaluable. The deployment of the value mapping agent, however, uncovered the following category, application mismatch.

Application mismatch: In certain cases, existing functional applications provide a direct and useful ontological structure from which another application can extract the information desired by its user community, but at a computational cost that needs to addressed in the implementation. An example of practical impact in the EDEN system was the design of value mapping across conceptual domains. The Environmental Data Registers (EDR) [1] had an ontological model entirely adaptable to the needs of EDEN, but the implementation of its value domain model was fully normalized. This produced response times that were suitable for lookup and mapping of individual terms, which was the original application. In EDEN, on the other hand, the goal was to use the EDR for large-scale term conversions for multiple columns of entire tables. The performance of the database used to implement this mapping was completely inadequate when only a handful of agents performed simultaneous mapping requests during a multi-resource query (analysis of the SQL query used to perform this mapping on an Oracle database yielded a query plan that required roughly 300 lines to print). To obtain tolerable performance, we were compelled to revise the ontology of the conceptual domain to support a flatter, non-normal data structure.

We made no attempt to characterize the computational complexity of the two different approaches; however, we observed in practice that a distributed query that involved requests made by a half-dozen agents to a single value mapping agent would either time out (independently of timeout interval) at the user agent or return partial results (depending on the timing of Internet-bound queries) when using the original application's ontological model — whereas when using our adapted non-normalized model, we saw complete results reliably returned.

The unfortunate but clear conclusion is that real-world data management issues must intrude even into ontology development when dealing with the large scales of data that many integrated applications require.

5. Ontology Development Issues

For ontological commitment to become real, ontology designers, application designers and users within a domain need all to be attracted to the same ontology. This affects not only the original design, but also the process of evolving the ontology. However, because of the issues of impedance mismatch discussed in the previous section, there also needs to be a nimble methodology for incorporating, excluding and supplementing standard ontological information into more application-oriented ontologies. This allows for the application designer to maintain appropriate tradeoffs between the responsibility of ontological commitment and the requirements of the application.

5.1. Design and Representation

Ideally, the design and representation of an ontology should be done in collaboration with users and applications; the applications then can incorporate the ontology as designed, and the users can validate the concepts, relationships and axioms that they access in the ontology via the application. These interrelationships are shown in Figure 1.

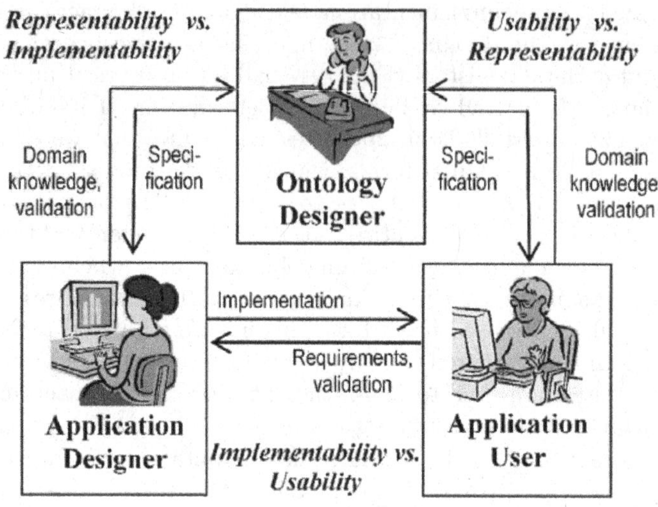

FIGURE 1. Ontological Interactions

Partly because of the desire to maximize ontological commitment, it is normally the goal of the ontology designer to represent the domain as completely as possible. Ontologies such as UMLS or environmental thesauri such as the General Multilingual Environmental Thesaurus (GEMET) [20] or the Terminology Reference System (TRS) [2] provide a broad base for discourse over their relative domains, medicine and the environment. Their definition has largely been driven, not by the implementors of the computer systems that use the ontologies, but rather by the practitioners within the domain itself. Practically, this can have significant effects on computational complexity.

5.2. Evolution and Versioning

As application developers develop applications using ontologies, and users use those applications, they identify weaknesses, missing concepts, and different issues that need to be addressed. For instance, when we developed our initial environmental ontology, some of the users who were used to the terminology in GEMET requested that we evolve our own ontology to be consistent with GEMET, or otherwise incorporate its terms. This request mandated an incorporation of that ontology into the environmental ontology. Once this incorporation was complete, all agents had to be adapted to the new ontology (this required a varying amount of effort depending on how closely the agent was hardwired to the ontology). Some of the users who were not used to the GEMET terminology also had to learn it. Thus, the evolution of the ontology caused much work for both users and developers. One could envision that the evolution of an ontology that has a higher level of ontological commitment, such as UMLS, could get very complex.

Clearly, the evolution of an ontology to a new version must be done carefully and collaboratively, involving the same types of as were involved in the original design. This indicates a slower, more coarse-grained type of evolution, which in turn affects the contents of the ontology.

An ontology may contain several types of information useful to the domain that it represents. These include:

- Concepts/classes, their attributes, and the types of representations their attributes can take.
- Relationships between concepts, including subclassing, synonyms, and containment.
- Axioms and functions over those concepts.
- Instances of those concepts the relationships between them, and axioms over the instances.

The first three of these are referred to as the *schema information* (also known as the conceptual model or meta-knowledge) and the last is referred to the *instance knowledge*.

Experience has shown us that instances, because they represent changing objects in the real world, tend to evolve much faster than the concepts themselves. Because of this, it is easier to factor the ontology into two pieces, the schema and the instances. Within the EDEN application, the environmental ontology itself only contained schema-level domain information, and we populated the schema using information from different environmental databases. Because the agents themselves naturally were written only against the schema concepts, and the schema-level ontology information evolved more slowly, ontology evolution did not create as significant a problem as it could have. This experience has carried over into numerous other applications developed using the InfoSleuth agent system [18, 5]; thus, we recommend this factoring unless the instance information is guaranteed to be stable (e.g., constants).

Ontological representation systems maintain this natural factoring between schema and instances, including OIL [19] and OWL [24]. OKBC [17] clearly distinguishes between schema and instances in its own vocabulary. Therefore, there is no real barrier to this factoring approach.

6. Compositional Ontologies

Given that the best approach to ontology design and use is a collaborative one among ontology designers, application developers and users, let us now turn our attention to the issue of reuse. Consider an application developer, developing an application to fulfill some of the needs of a specific class of users in a given application domain. The developer has decided to reuse as much already-defined ontological information as he can within his application, tagging the imported concepts back to the ontologies from which they were taken to facilitate the process of evolving the application within the ontology. Unfortunately, up to this point the application

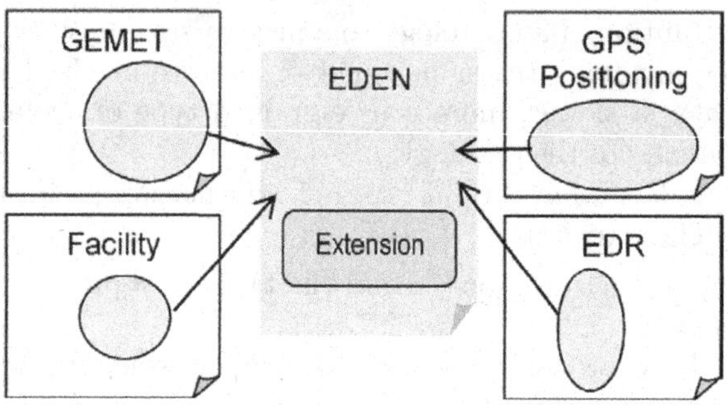

FIGURE 2. A Compositional Ontology

developer has had no input whatsoever into the ontological design, though he has been working closely with the prospective application users. Thus, the necessary collaboration between the ontology designer, the application developer and the users is missing in this situation. Furthermore, the users input into the application design is much more direct than that of the ontology designer. The result often is that there is no good existing ontological "match" to the application and/or its users.

Our experiences with our own ontology-based agent applications has led us to the following observations:

1. Reusing ontologies is necessary for acceptance by domain specialists, but many mature ontologies specify a lot more than current agent systems can actually use.
2. Most of the applications we have developed require concepts from multiple ontologies.
3. Most of the applications that we have developed require some concepts defined in no ontologies, because of mismatch issues.

In order to facilitate reuse, we have designed our applications to use a compositional notion of ontologies, where we select concepts from different ontologies as needed, and supplement the result with any new concepts that we cannot locate elsewhere. This leads us to support three operations over ontologies themselves, which we term subset, compose and extend, as shown in Figure 2.

6.1. Subset

Agents are frequently coded as specialists, understanding a focused subset of the domain itself. For example, an agent that is interfacing with information repositories on environmental remediation techniques would not necessarily understand the information related to companies and their responsibilities for cleaning up specific toxic waste sites; yet the scope of the domain encompasses both areas. These agents need not incorporate entire ontologies; in fact, this may not even be possible for lightweight agents using large ontologies. Standards such as FIPA [7] allow agents to advertise the ontologies they understand, However, such an advertisement may be misleading to other agents if the agent only understands a subset of the ontology, in that two agents advertising the same ontology may in fact understand orthogonal subsets of the ontology, rendering communication impossible.

Furthermore, too much ontology information may confuse users. As a practical matter, users of several of our agent applications including EDEN were confused by the presence of ontological terms for which no agent had advertised any knowledge. The presence of the term implied to them that they should be able to extract information (other than definition and ontological relationships) relevant to the term. That no agent had advertised the term was an unsatisfying explanation. Because of this, the agents themselves that implement the ontology must be careful how they present themselves to their users.

We define this subsetting using *ontological fragments*. An ontological fragment consists of:

- The name of the ontology.
- The classes or entities in the ontology that are supported within the application, and their superclasses.
- Constraints on those classes including such things as ranges of values allowed for specific slots.
- The axioms that reference the supported classes/ attributes.

The fragment can be expressed as a set of constraints over the classes and attributes. As an example from the EDEN system, each agent that provided a wrapper for a data resource advertised only a fraction of the domain ontology – precisely that portion for which it could provide data instances. In some cases, a wrapper agent advertised only a fraction of the slots of a class, and further placed semantic constraints on the content of the slots based on knowledge of the data instances about which it could report. In other cases, an agent might fill a slot with a static value from the canonical data representation for that slot. For example, because there was no record in a particular remediation database for land use, one of the attributes of a site, certain government database wrappers returned the generic value "Federal Facility" which was one of the values used in other databases.

Another decision that needs to be made on any system is whether a request for everything matching a query should return an empty set if an agent does not advertise all elements of a class, or should return nulls for the unadvertised elements. This provoked strong disagreement on our team between those who felt that the former was algebraically preferable and those who felt that the latter was more intuitive to users already intimidated by the challenge of understanding the nature of the results produced by a dynamic distributed information system. The disagreement was resolved to favor users over beauty.

6.2. Compose

Another issue that is brought about by ontological commitment is the issue that an agent often requires access to terms from multiple ontologies. There exist a growing number of useful and public ontologies, and it often seems more appropriate to pick and choose terms from those ontologies than to build a new one from scratch, with just the terms that you need for your ontology. The result is a virtual ontology that imports fragments of other ontologies, into some sort of unified and useful whole. For example, within the EDEN application the diverse ways of representing values relating to various concepts such as chemical or geographic identifiers made it necessary to compose the domain ontology incorporating terminology from the field of hazardous waste pollution and remediation with the EDR ontology for value representation.

The ability to compose ontologies has an immediate benefit in modular ontology design. For instance, if you look within the EDR tags, there are tags relating to location (street address, postal code) as well as geographic (latitude and longitude). These tags are not specific to the environmental domain, but are shared among other domains such as address books and GPS positioning systems. Furthermore, such structures seem relatively stable. This indicates that it may be much more useful to have, say, a single ontology for geographic positions, their representations, and the relationships between them that can be incorporated into environmental applications as well as those in other domains.

Many existing ontological languages provide a primitive form of composition by allowing ontologies to import other ontologies, and providing namespaces or name resolution policies for accessing terms and concepts in these imported ontologies. Importing is a similar notion to composition, but has some drawbacks that composition does not have – because composition works in conjunction with subsetting. These drawbacks include the following:

1. Controlling the size and quality of the resulting ontology may be difficult. For instance, the imported ontology may be very large, yet the importing ontology may only require a few terms from it. As a result, the importing ontology may end up to be far more complex than is required.
2. Importing is a transitive operation. That is, if ontology A imports ontology B, and ontology B imports ontology C, then the concepts available through ontology A include those of ontologies B and C as well. This can propagate in a relatively unconstrained manner, especially in open ontological systems such as is anticipated by OWL [24]. Such importation can also lead to importation of axioms, and will affect the size and complexity of any rule sets being reasoned over. Therefore, it is desirable to be able to control and truncate these chains of importation.
3. It is possible for ontologies to reference each other cyclically. For example, a "soil" ontology on soil types may reference geographic areas; a "geography" ontology on geographic areas may reference sites of pollution in different

areas, and a "pollutants" ontology may reference soil types when describing how pollutants spread under different conditions. This circularity causes problems if imports of ontologies are processed naively. One way of resolving this is to union the ontologies involved in the cycle, rather than naively following include statements, as was done in Ontolingua [6].

Composition used in conjunction with subsetting helps address these issues. For the first issue, the solution is to import only the subset of the imported ontology that is needed by the importing ontology. To address the second issue, the subset of the imported ontology can be truncated to avoid transitive references to other ontologies, as appropriate. Thus, the impact of the transitivity can be minimized. For the third issue, using composition in conjunction with subsetting makes it possible to refine and avoid many circularities, as long as the included parts of the different ontologies do not in and of themselves form a cycle.

6.3. Extend

Unfortunately, applications frequently need to incorporate concepts that are not represented in any ontology, or they may need to "glue" concepts from different ontologies together using new concepts. Thus, it is not sufficient to compose subsets of ontologies; frequently it is necessary also to add some new concepts. For example, within the setting of our EDEN application, the domain ontologies covered the concepts for which users wanted to retrieve information; for instance, they enabled the user to answer questions such as, "What toxic waste sites are within 10 miles of Houston, TX?" However, the agent-based system that supported the application also was able to ask higher- level, more abstract questions such as "Are the number of toxic waste sites within 10 miles of Houston increasing faster than they can be remediated?" These higher-level questions used concepts present neither in the domain ontology, nor in any other ontology available at the time.

The important issue with extension is to do it in a manner that will not create further problems later. There are two ways to extend an ontology; extensions that are safe and can easily be incorporated into other applications, and extensions that are unsafe and should eventually be agreed upon and then folded back by consensus into the ontology. We define safe and unsafe extensions with respect to the permissible definitional changes to the underlying ontology(-ies). A safe extension can be characterized as follows:

Safe extension: an extension incorporating existing concepts from one or more ontologies, where any new concepts are defined axiomatically against the existing concepts in such a way that instances of the new concepts can be determined computationally from instances of the existing concepts. The transformation axioms must be invertible; the conversion of any instance between its view in the existing concept(s) and its view in the new concept must be lossless in both directions.

Safe extensions are "safe" primarily because they can be shared among the agents easily, simply by sharing the axioms that allow for conversion from the existing classes to the extended classes. We note that new concepts within such a safe extension cannot have new attributes that would need to be present in any instance of that concept, as this would violate the lossless conversion property. So, for example, "milliliters per liter" would be a safe extension for a concept if the concepts "liquid" and "parts per million" were already present in the ontology being extended.

In contrast, unsafe extensions are "unsafe" because they are harder to share with other agents, as the other agents may not maintain the information necessary to populate instances of the unsafe classes. For example, adding a new concept, "Water pollutant" with a new property, "concentration" would not be a safe extension if there were no concept of containing medium in the original ontology. Other agents, committed to the ontology, may not have the information necessary to provide a concentration for each pollutant they have, or may have different ways of modeling the concept of how badly the pollutant is contaminating the water.

Because unsafe extensions allow agents to instantiate classes that have been extended unsafely and thus cannot easily be shared; these extensions limit the openness of the agent. However, unsafe extensions are sometimes necessary; for instance, they are often required to deal with some of the impedance mismatch issues discussed earlier. Allowing unsafe extensions increases the possibility that different agents will create divergent extensions to the ontology, and become incompatible with one another. Therefore, unsafe extensions should be treated with caution. One approach is to limit such extensions to those that are monotonic [10] – not requiring modifications to existing ontological elements. Idealistically, the need for specific unsafe extensions should be propagated to the ontology designers, who can determine whether or not there is a consensus on the need for the particular extension, and whether they should be incorporated into the next version.

6.4. An Example

Figure 3 shows a fragment of an example compositional environmental ontology closely related to the one we used in the EDEN application. This ontology used subsets of the GPS and Measurement ontologies, composed together with a fragment of the environmental ontology. The necessary concepts for this particular application span all three ontologies. The gray boxes indicate the three ontologies, and the white boxes within indicate the classes taken from the individual ontology into the compositional ontology. Note that the attributes from the "Sampling Point" class refer to concepts in the other ontologies.

7. Implementation Issues

Given that we allow the operations of subsetting, composition and (safe) extension over ontologies within an agent system, the agents themselves need to be able to represent exactly what combination they are committed to, in order to ensure that they do not mislead others with respect to their capabilities.

There are three issues with representation and implementation. The first is that the agent needs to be able to represent internally the full set of details on how the ontology fragments it is using fit together. This can be done with

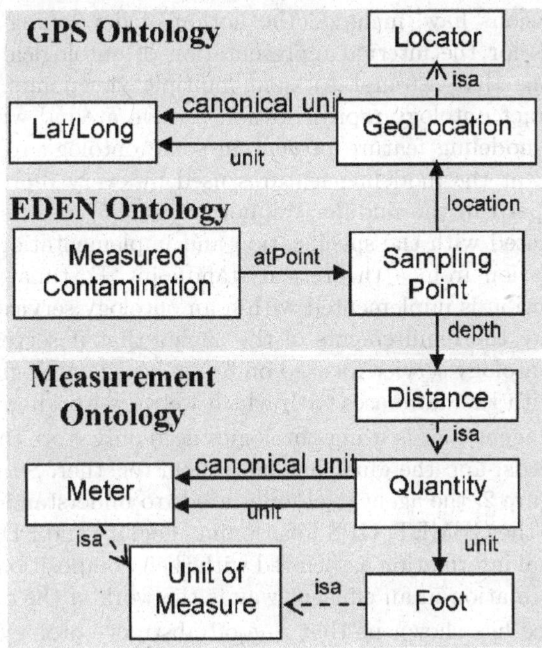

FIGURE 3. A part of the EDEN compositional ontology.

a suitable abstract ontology representation. Secondly, the agent must be able to converse in some detail with other agents about the parts of the ontologies that they understand. This must be done using a suitable exchange representation. Thirdly, messages should be able to represent the ontology fragments that the message covers. While we do not discuss this third issue in this paper, we note that representing ontology fragments in an ACL requires a more specific ontology field within the agent communication language.

7.1. Internal Representation

Internally, an agent needs to understand in detail the specific schema-level knowledge to which it is committed. This understanding may be complicated by the fact that ontological knowledge may be represented using many different representational models; for instance, there are subject-verb-object models such as DAML [4] and OWL [24], frame-oriented models such as OKBC [17], and object-oriented models such as UML [9, 3]. These all differ in key issues such as whether or not attributes are first-class objects, whether or not multiple inheritance is allowed, and how strongly-typed classes must be. Further complicating this, if the operations of subsetting, composition and extension are used, a single application may look into a set of ontologies whose underlying ontological models may diverge.

Recent discussions have included the notion of developing abstract ontology representations for the internal representation of ontological knowledge. As with all applications that attempt to span multiple viewpoints, key choices in specifying an abstract ontology representation revolve around whether it should incorporate every modeling feature present in some ontology representation, or it should only look at the modeling features used by every representation, or it should take some path in the middle. Wilmott et.al. [25] discuss in depth some of the issues associated with the specification and implementation of an abstract ontology representation from a theoretical standpoint. Fortunately, an abstract ontology representation is implemented within an ontology service, and thus only needs to incorporate the requirements of the agents that it serves. In the InfoSleuth system, our ontology service focused on frame-based ontologies, as they were most compatible with the databases with which we were working.

Internally, an agent that is using ontologies need only store the subsets of the ontology that it needs, and the glue that puts them together. So, for instance, in the ontology of Figure 2, the agent itself only needs to understand the concepts in the shaded areas of the GEMET, GPS Positioning, Facility and EDR ontologies, as well as the additional information associated with their composition and extension. Managing this information in an efficient way is the work of the ontology service.

Our experience has shown us that a good abstract ontology representation and a good ontology service are essential to cope with the incorporation of existing ontologies and their evolutionary steps. The abstract ontology representation engenders a unified methodology by which the agent can absorb existing ontology information and its particular use within the application. Agent implementors then use the ontologies in a more declarative and less hard-wired manner, which in turn facilitates the incorporation of new ontological information.

7.2. External Representation

Agents need to be able to share which parts of the different ontologies that they use or require, and how they put them together, with their other collaborating agents. This happens when the agent advertises its capabilities to another agent, when an agent is looking to locate another agent that can help it with some task, or when agents are negotiating over who is responsible for what subtasks. We have identified three basic ways that ontologies may be adapted dynamically: subsetting, composition, and extension:

Subsetting: The notion of subsetting an ontology is not reflected in the definition of the ontology itself, but rather in artifacts related to the use of the ontology. For example, fragments may be advertised from one agent to another, so that agents can inform other agents within their community of their exact capabilities. Alternatively, an application may be supported at the user end by an agent that interfaces with the user, ensuring that the user is presented only with the fragments of the ontology that are supported within the underlying agent community. Any user interfaces can then be tailored to the ontology fragment.

Composition: As with subsetting, composition should be specified at the time of use, however, there are some representational difficulties at this point. While subsetting can be defined as a set of axioms that overlays a single ontology, composition spans multiple ontologies and thus presents different representational challenges. For instance, a composition may wish to state that the values of the "LatitudeMeasure" slot for the "FacilityIdentification" in the EDR may be understood by the agent as represented in the "LatLongCoordinate" units defined in the "GPS Coordinates" ontology. In EDEN, we defined a geographic location as comprising a (selectable) coordinate scheme and a coordinate value.

OKBC [17] and OWL [24] present different challenges with respect to composition. Within OKBC, composition must be done by explicitly importing the component ontologies. Existing tools do not necessarily facilitate importing ontologies from remote locations, or ones that are represented in different languages (e.g., DAML). The resulting new ontology, even if it can be defined is a potentially huge superset of what is actually needed by the agent. Furthermore, it may be difficult to relate the terms in the new ontology back to the ontologies that it imported, and so to re-relate terms imported from the same ontology into two such composed ontologies. OWL, on the other hand, uses namespaces to facilitate the combination of ontologies and the relating of concepts among multiple ontologies. Due to the open nature of OWL ontologies, namespaces are explicitly rooted in URLs; thus, tracing the pedigree of the different elements in the ontology is not difficult. however, OWL suffers from a potentially severe problem with bounding ontology size due to the combination of the ease and the transitive nature of ontology importing, and the lack of an ability to subset or truncate unneeded concepts.

Extension: Safe extensions by definition should be able to be specified in terms of logical axioms over existing concepts in the ontology. While axioms are strongly considered among ontology designers, many ontology exchange languages hardly consider them at all; for instance, DAML+OIL at the moment has no good foundation for representing axioms and is thus unsuitable for exchanging knowledge concerning safe extensions. In EDEN, we prepared a number of ad hoc lexical translation processes to translate between an old version and an extended version of the ontology. This did not yield a reusable method.

8. Conclusions

Ontological commitment is the decision by a particular group of applications or users within an application domain to use the terms defined in a given ontology. High ontological commitment occurs when many users and/or applications within an application domain commit to sharing the same vocabulary of concepts, meanings and relationships defined within a specific ontology. Ontological commitment to a common set of ontologies is a key feature to provide for openness in an agent system, as it provides a common vocabulary over which agents can converse.

This paper focused mainly on two areas relating to ontological commitment and use. The first area is the clash of goals between ontology definers, application developers and users. Ontology definers are concerned with the completeness and purity of their ontological design. Application developers are often concerned only with specific subsets of the ontology that relate directly to the application, and with application-specific representational and computational issues. Users are concerned mainly with sticking with known and familiar terminology and vocabularies, which may not be logically structured and therefore may not be amenable to being reformulated into computationally-accessible concepts. This clash is complicated by the widening gap between these groups – developers, for instance, may be using ontologies that are already well-established. Thus, while several good design paradigms involving ontology designers, application developers, and users, exist for initial ontology development [10, 8, 11], none of these seem to encompass these more long-term concerns. We recommend the development of an extended ontology lifecycle that fosters evolution. Components required to support this lifecycle should include long-term ontology design support, a widely-available feedback channel from developers and users back to designers, and an open forum for discussing issues and extensions to the ontology.

An application committed to reuse existing ontologies may encounter several difficulties, as search for the perfect ontology for the application – one that is acceptable to both the application and its users – is not necessarily fruitful. We described a compositional approach to ontological use. Compositional ontologies base themselves in existing ontologies as much as possible, using the operations of ontological subsetting, ontological composition and ontological extension to tailor them to the specific needs of the applications. Compositional ontologies fit well with the needs of the application, and the approach has the potential to raise the level of ontological commitment to existing ontologies. However, they require more sophisticated ontology- related exchanges among collaborating agents. In order to incorporate these compositional ontologies, further work needs to be done on the development of a more formal algebra to support the subset, compose and extend operations over ontologies (in contrast to our current ad-hoc methods). Visser and Cui [23] attacked a related problem of heterogeneous ontology structures, and this may provide further insight into this formal algebra. Also, Jannink et.al. [15] provide a set of algebraic concepts rooted in the notions of the *congruence* of an ontology with an application and the *similarity* of ontologies, which relate to this effort.

As a second task, we need to develop a methodology for ensuring the correctness and consistency of these compositional ontologies.

Many approaches to the representation and specification of ontologies exist; some common ones for the exchange of ontological information include OKBC, DAML+OIL, OWL and UML. Each of these has features amenable to their adoption as a means to exchange information on ontological components and extensions, though none cover all of the issues addressed in this paper. Therefore, the exchange of such information using these standards is still problematic.

References

[1] Environmental Protection Agency. EPA environmental data registry. http://www.epa.gov/edr, 2002.

[2] Environmental Protection Agency. EPA terminology reference system. http://www.epa.gov/trs/index.htm, 2002.

[3] S. Cranefield, S. Haustein, and M. Purvis. UML-based ontology modelling for software agents. In *Proceedings of the Workshop on Ontologies in Agent Systems, 5th International Conference on Autonomous Agents*, 2001. http://CEUR-WS.org/Vol-52/oas01-cranefield-1.pdf.

[4] DAML.org. The DAML agent markup language homepage. http://www.daml.org, 2003.

[5] Larry M. Deschaine, Richard S. Brice, and Marian H. Nodine. Use of InfoSleuth to coordinate information acquisition, tracking and analysis in complex applications. In *Proceedings of Advanced Simulation Technologies Conference*, April 2000.

[6] Adam Farquhar, Richard Fikes, and James Rice. Tools for assembling modular ontologies in ontolingua. In *Proceedings of the National Conference on Artificial Intelligence*, 1997.

[7] Foundation for Intelligent Physical Agents. Agent communication language specifications. http://www.fipa.org/repository/aclspecs.html, 2003.

[8] A. Gomez-Perez. Ontological engineering: A state of the art. *Expert Update*, 1999.

[9] Object Management Group. OMG unified modeling language specification, v. 1.3. http://www.omg.org/technology/documents/formal/unified_modeling_language.htm, 2000.

[10] T. R. Gruber. Translation approach to portable ontology specifications. *Knowledge Acquisition*, 5(2), 1993.

[11] M. Gruninger and M.S. Fox. Methodology for the design and evaluation of ontologies. In *Proceedings of the Workshop on Basic Ontological Issues and Knowledge Sharing*, 1995.

[12] Palle Haastrup et al. The environmental data exchange network for inland water, 2004. http://www.eden-iw.org/contents/home.html.

[13] J. Hammer and D. McLeod. An approach to resolving semantic heterogeneity in a federation of autonomous, heterogeneous database systems. *International Journal of Intelligent and Cooperative Information Systems*, 2(1), 1993.

[14] B. L. Humphreys et al. Assessing and enhancing the value of the umls knowledge sources. In *Proceedings of the 15th Annual Symposium on Computer Applications in Medical Care*, pages 78–82, November 1991.

[15] J. Jannink, P. Mitra, E. Neuhold, S. Pichai, R. Struder, and G. WIederhold. An algebra for semantic interoperation of semistructured data. In *Proceedings of the IEEE Knowledge and Data Engineering Exchange Workshop (KDEX '99)*, 1999.

[16] W. Kent. The many forms of a single fact. In *Proceedings of IEEE Computer Society International Conference*, 1998.

[17] SRI Knowledge Systems Laboratory. OKBC home page. http://www.ksl.stanford.edu/software/OKBC, 2002.

[18] Marian Nodine et al. Active information gathering in InfoSleuth. *International Journal of Cooperative Information Systems*, 9(1/2):3–28, 2000.

[19] Welcome to the OIL page. http://www.ontoknowledge.org/oil, 2002.

[20] European Topic Centre on Catalogue of Data Sources. General Multilingual Environmental Thesaurus. http://www.nu.niedersachsen.de/cds/etc-cds_neu/library/software.html, 2001.

[21] John F. Sowa. *Knowledge Representation.* Brooks/Cole, 2000.

[22] M. S. Tuttle et al. Merging terminologies. *Medinfo*, 8(1):162–166, 1995.

[23] Pepjin R. S. Visser and Zhan Cui. Heterogeneous ontology structures for distributed architectures. In *Proceedings of the ECAI-98 Workshop on Applications of Ontologies and Problem-Solving Methods*, pages 112–119, 1998.

[24] W3C. OWL web ontology language guide. http://www.w3.org/TR/2004/REC-owl-guide-20040210/, 2004.

[25] S. Willmott, I. Constantinescu, and M. Callisti. Multilingual agents: Ontologies, languages and abstractions. In *Proceedings of the First International Workshop on Ontologies in Agent Systems (Held in conjunction with Agents 2001)*, 2001.

Marian H. Nodine
Telcordia Technologies
106 E. 6th Street, Suite 415
Austin, TX 78701
USA
e-mail: `nodine@alum.mit.edu`

Jerry Fowler
Human Genome Sequencing Center
Baylor College of Medicine
One Baylor Plaza
Houston, TX 77030
USA
e-mail: `gfowler@acm.org`

Agent to Agent Talk: "Nobody There?" Supporting Agents Linguistic Communication

Maria Teresa Pazienza and Michele Vindigni

Abstract. World-Wide Web technologies and the vision of Semantic Web have pushed for adaptive SW applications to scale up information technologies to the Web, where information is organized following different underlying knowledge and/or presentation models. Interoperability among heterogeneous intelligent agents has become an important research topic in the context of distributed information systems. Communication among heterogeneous agents involves several dimensions. "Ontological commitment" on a shared knowledge model cannot be assumed as a default.

To overcome this problem, we will describe in this article a communication model that bases on the use of natural language. We will argue on main topics involved in using natural language to achieve semantic agreement in agents communication. The model foresees a strong separation among terms and concepts, this difference being often undervalued in the literature, where terms play the ambiguous role of both concept labels and of communication lexicon. For agents communicating through the language, lexical information embodies instead the possibility to "express" the underlying conceptualizations thus agreeing to a shared representation. We will examine in details the different layers involved in agents communication and we will focus on a the different roles played by each element. A novel agent architecture able to tackle with possible linguistic ambiguities by focusing on the conversational level will be deeply described. Three different agent typologies will be presented: Resource agents, embodying the target knowledge, Service agents, providing basic skills to support complex activities and control agents, supplying the structural knowledge of the task, with coordination and control capabilities. NL communication is supported by two dedicated Service agents: a Mediator, that will handle conceptual mismatches arising during communication, and a Translator, dealing with lexical misalignments due to different languages/idioms.

Keywords. Intelligent agents, NLP, semantic web, ontology sharing.

1. Introduction

The demand for World-Wide Web technologies and the vision of Semantic Web have pushed for researches on heterogeneous multi-agent systems able to exchange information in a distributed environment. Building more adaptive SW applications becomes a crucial issue to scale up information technologies to the Web, where information is organized following different underlying knowledge and/or presentation models. Several different architectures already exist that implement models of communities with at least two kinds of entities involved: information agents (providing access to information sources) and application agents (consumers of information for application specific tasks) [22, 25]. In such architectures, information providers are often built as (sometime complex) wrappers of the underlying sources into formats suitable for being exchanged (and reasoned over) by more sophisticated entities, with roles of knowledge mediators or information brokers.

The adoption of agent paradigm in web information systems aims to inherit concepts and techniques from agents theory that offers an high level of abstraction and suitable mechanisms to address conceptual modeling of complex issues as Knowledge representation and reasoning, communication, coordination and cooperation among heterogeneous and autonomous parties.

Agent theory [32] goes in the direction of developing entities with a suitable amount of both competencies and knowledge to autonomously interact with others. Multi-agents societies (MAS) [29] constitute the most advanced model for a dynamic and unstructured framework in which specialized agents could interact and communicate through messages.

Interoperability among agents is an important research topic for information systems, as most of them foresee widespread architectures involving heterogeneous entities, based on different knowledge models and presentation paradigms. As a consequence, it should be useful to introduce specific intelligent agents that could work jointly while interacting with document management systems, for finding, extracting and presenting relevant information whenever needed. In such a context cooperating entities will share their knowledge and exchange information, being able (at least) to communicate in any way. This pushes for heterogeneous agents able to share a language, domain related ontologies (conceptual structures) and cooperating to task resolution.

The goal of a complete "interoperability" suddenly revealed difficult to pursue due to the continue innovations in the market of tools and applications: looking at the current state of art, except for low-level protocols that are more standardized and accepted, each system speaks its own language, uses its own communication protocol and adopt its own ontology.

Despite a few standards have been introduced for supporting intelligent agents communication (KQML [11], FIPA-ACL [12]), they seem to spread very slowly in this area.

In our opinion, there is a main reason for such a lack of a common framework for information agents today: heterogeneous agents do not commit to one fundamental assumption of any software system. In traditional software, semantics entailed in interactions is well defined in programs since the design and, in any case, involved entities share communication language and knowledge representation model. As a straight example, let us consider a key identifier in a database table (something as a UserID). Its meaning is well agreed and shared between the database and the specific application that uses it. Thus when it appears in a query, its symbolic value (let it be, USR004517) is referring to something (an instance in the DB) that maintains its own identity through the whole system both for functional and for denotational purposes. The used symbol does not need to explicit its meaning, as its referential role is already agreed and well understood since design time.

On the contrary, if we consider heterogeneous entities in an agent community, symbols in the knowledge of individuals are no more implicitly referring to same concepts/instances and should carry by themselves their meaning. Identifiers cannot be simply shared as their semantics is not entailed by the communication. Such an aspect introduces further dimensions to the complexity of the communication: terminology mediation, ontology sharing, context disambiguation, etc. For different entities interacting on the web it is impossible to guarantee they share concept meanings either in an early design phase or during implementation. This is a major issue for sharing document contents, where recognition of texts and identification of values base heavily on a shared/common knowledge model. This aspect of agents communication is still neglected due to the difficulty in defining "a priori" the quality and quantity of needed background (i.e. widely agreed) knowledge. Nevertheless, as the ability to access autonomous and dynamic information currently on the Web is vital for an agent society, we have to deeply cover this matter.

It is clear that in each agent community, even the most "open" to new comers, a level of semantic agreement must exist to bridge (or at least narrow) the gap between proprietary knowledge representations in the different participating systems. Relevant question here is how to build intelligent components requiring a minimal amount of shared knowledge for participating in a cooperation, in order to minimize commitments the designers must "a priori" agree upon.

In this article we will examine in detail the different layers involved in agent communication and we will focus on a communication model that considers the different roles played by each element. In the next chapter we provide a short overview of different places where this gap can be seen. Section three describes a model for communication that explicitly reckon the role of the language. Section four describes a proposal for a novel agent architecture able to tackle with possible linguistic ambiguities focusing on the conversational level. Then in section five we conclude by highlighting further improvements on the described architecture for intelligent agent communication.

2. How many ways can we misunderstand?

Whatever the adopted representation formalism, communicating agents can be modelled as entities exchanging messages to transmit information. Complex interactions could be seen as conversation sequences, that is policies and protocols for routing messages with appropriate contents among two or more agents, each with a specific role.

This framework involves several layers where semantic agreement among participants should be enforced, while communication can fail at each of them. Starting from simple message exchange, and going bottom-up we can identify at least the following levels:

Transport levels: quite standardized through TCP or ISO/OSI stack protocols. Generally these layers are seen by agents through abstractions provided by application level protocols, even if nothing in theory inhibit from using directly them for communication purposes.

Application Level: Application level protocols provide the message passing framework for agent communication. Several standards exist here, like for instance HTTP, SMTP or even RMI and CORBA protocols. This is usually the lowest relevant level involved in agent communication, providing basic mechanisms to allow platform independency and message delivery.

Speech Acts: Speech act theory [26] provides a formal background for agent interaction defining a few performatives that define semantics of different communicative actions like *ask*, *tell*, *inform* etc. These constitute a methodological effort to identify a backbone as much declarative as possible for communicating intentions about exchanged messages. Two resulting standards emerged, KQML [11] and FIPA-ACL [12]. Though both of them address the same communication layer, they lightly differ in the syntax, strongly in semantics: the first is not committed to a particular Content Language (CL) with respect to the message content, while the latter assumes a specific Semantic Language (SL) for composing new structured primitives from the core language (see for instance, KIF [13]). Aim of a content language is to express the target information, while performatives expressed in the query language are used to inform about meaning of the operations that content should undergo. This layer is crucial to ensure that agents understand each other intentions. While the application layer provide a shared abstraction of the communication channel, this level guarantees an explicit understanding of (what to do with) the exchanged messages.

The layers introduced so far account for the "syntactic" dimension of the communication /footnoteSpeech Acts entail semantics about performatives not about content. Agreement on a coherent use of them is a necessary (but not sufficient) condition for the communication to take place in the community. Although fundamental, this does not guarantee that the communication will be successful at both semantic and pragmatic levels. These latter involve semantic agreement on contents, as well as conversation policies (i.e. modalities to route the information flow through the community) that could prove crucial issues in building intelligent web agents. Content languages provide a first level of standardization for encoding contents, while here the lack of a uniform standard is more evident.

The problem here is that even if two agents agree upon using the same content language, they still may not be able to understand each other due to different vocabularies or different ontologies. Semantic misunderstandings (similarly as what happens for people) add a overwhelming complexity to agent communication, are very difficult to recognize and require a lot of competencies and capabilities from agents side.

2.1. It's Greek to me: the role of language in agent communication

Whichever the content language of choice, the problem that heterogeneous agents willing to communicate face is directly tied to the lack of a total "ontological commitment", that is the implicit agreement to rely on the same knowledge model (or at least for the concepts involved in the communication). In the context of knowledge sharing we refer to ontology as the means for specifying a conceptualization. An ontology is a description of concepts and relationships: in ontologies, definitions associate entities in the universe of discourse to symbols that declare what they mean, while formal axioms constrain both the interpretation and the well-formed use of these symbols. A shared ontology embodies the vocabulary with which queries and assertions are exchanged among agents; conversely agents sharing a vocabulary need not to share a knowledge base; each one knows things the other does not, and an agent that commits to an ontology is not required to answer all queries that can be formulated in the shared vocabulary. A commitment to a common ontology is a guarantee of consistency, but not completeness, with respect to queries and assertions by using the vocabulary defined in the ontology. Ontologies are seen as a means for "real" semantic integration, but current approaches do not consider linguistic insights to an appropriate extent.

In case of a shared knowledge representation, agent communication should be totally effective, as reference to any concept could be realized by direct referring to related symbols in the ontology without misunderstanding or mistakes. This kind of agent could communicate with others in its internal language, being its knowledge organized exactly the same of all the others.

In real world applications, this is often unfeasible as agents have instead "local" world representations, on which they base their goals and their assumptions; for instance, a seller and a buyer could have very different views of a marketplace, perceiving the same reality with respect to their objectives: an income for the seller becomes a cost for the buyer and although being both situated in the same environment/domain, their knowledge models could greatly differ as reflecting their different behaviors; then, to communicate, they must agree upon some other sort of shared (or better, "conventional") representation to be transmitted to other partners.

Many researches in this area are devoted to tackle this problem by defining ontological frameworks sufficiently expressive to fit application specific needs while remaining representational neutral and general enough to span over a broad range of domains. While a number of results show well sound theories one can build upon, there is no general consensus neither towards a representational formalism neither on widely adopted so called "upper ontologies".

We approach here this problem with a strongly different perspective: we already showed that agents cannot assume "a priori" that concepts in their "minds" could be directly communicated to others (as most of the symbols an agent uses have no common semantics) [23]. However, if ontological commitment does not hold at all for an open agent community, agents willing to communicate can be effectively designed so that the subset of symbols they will use in the communication "maximizes" the expectations to be coherent with the rest of the community. Let's call such attitude "linguistic commitment" (opposite to OC). We strongly believe that shifting emphasis from a "common ontology" towards a "coherent terminology" helps to tackle the problem of communication basing the process on weaker assumptions that are more "at hands" for the community. Without a complete "a priori" agreement, natural language is the only representation tool to be used to carry semantics. Linguistic communication, both in human and agent societies, supports a common representation level and enables a synthetic transmission of the information: discourse participants use mutually understandable terms to build phrases in order to communicate propositions.

2.2. Mapping, merging and messing up with knowledge: different approaches to reconcile heterogeneity

A known symbol (i.e. a word in the agent language) denotes a concept for an agent. This concept is related to others in whatever structured representation the agent adopts for its own knowledge (whatever this be, a taxonomy, a semantic network, etc.). We usually assume as word meaning the position its concept has in the ontology, by means of its relations with the rest of the ontology. Nevertheless, the difference between word and concept has been often underestimated, as usually terms play both the roles of concept labels and communication vocabulary. As a consequence, all agents willing to communicate need much more than to share the same vocabulary. By making more explicit the semiotic separation among terms, concepts and domain referents, it allows for a better modeling of the communication process.

The goal of Semantic Web is to have data defined on the web and linked in a way that is explicitly interpretable by autonomous agents (rather than just being implicitly interpretable by humans). Ontologies may be considered as the way "to cut" reality in order to understand and process it. Reasoning with terms from deployed ontologies is important for the Semantic Web, but reasoning support is also extremely valuable at the ontology design phase, where it can be used to detect logically inconsistent classes and to discover implicit subclass relations.

Using ontologies for the Semantic Web requires rules governing proper interpretation of the structure, as formal representations and constraints (semantics or meanings), and content, as ontology ground terms.

However, what exists by now is a multitude of specific ontologies managed by local authorities. Several questions have still to be addressed. Who could be made responsible for their integration? Who could provide knowledge support for such an operation? Who could maintain consistency across several realizations of the same conceptualization? Who could be responsible of it during application life cycle?

There are several different approaches to the problem of how to define a mapping among concepts belonging to different knowledge bases. Three main groups can well represent the proposed solutions:

Manual Mapping: the research is focused on concept representation; this kind of approach is usually followed by database researchers, that emphasize the role of ontology as a scheme for the application knowledge base, where concepts are considered as data types; among others, we remember here the use of conditional rules [6], functions [7, 1], first order logics [16], declarative representations [14] where mappings themselves are organized in an ontology. Unfortunately, manual specification of mappings is an expensive and error prone task for real scale problems. Moreover, this approach requires one to define a mapping for each couple of involved ontologies, thus making difficult to scale up this approach when the number of involved ontologies increases; as an alternative a mapping between local ontologies and a general one is proposed in [18], but this require to agree upon a common general purpose knowledge layer.

Adoption of a Formal Theory as description layer: instead of building mappings in a bottom-up fashion (by integrating "local" resources), the resources themselves are built accordingly to common assumption that guarantees the overall consistence. This approach is followed by a number of systems aimed to help human experts during the integration of DB schemes [3, 20, 10].

Automatic Mapping: this is driven by the assumption that equivalent concepts in different ontologies must show similar observable properties; in this area, classical ML techniques have been adopted, to provide similarity measures with respect to a few relevant attributes, for instance:

- by identifying similar attributes, through the use of neural networks [21]
- by using relationships defined in a thesaurus and a measure of "semantic distance" [4];
- by activating an heuristic search on the candidate mappings among value tuples [8].

Although several works discuss different qualities of ontological mappings, they focus the analysis on the mapping itself. Among the others, we mention here [19], where the semantic distance of two concepts is defined by a tuple of their contexts, the values they assume over a domain, their relations, and the data base states. Their analysis produces a hierarchy of semantic nearness, ranging over equivalence, correlation, relevance, similarity and incompatibility.

The previously mentioned approaches could be resumed in two distinct trends with respect to the problem of knowledge sharing:

- all parts willing to interact must adhere to the same ontology. In such a framework, they could refer to shared concepts, being implicit a common semantics for the exchanged information. This solution provides a strict coupling for the system components, and doesn't ask for specific inferential capabilities to the involved participants. It becomes unfeasible for open architectures, where a common sharing of the conceptual model for the environment could not be forced at design time, and thus it could not be adopted in highly dynamic scenarios, as the Web is, where the information model is inherently heterogeneous.
- a set of correspondences across each involved ontology is defined either manually or automatically. Resulting mappings are used during the communication process by a third part when semantic translation is required: this kind of interaction foresees that an exhaustive analysis over the involved ontologies is carried on before the interaction starts.

Most of the analyzed approaches require either shared instances, or shared concepts, or shared relations among ontologies or schemas, manually defined or derivable by the use of a shared formalism.

This kind of assumptions strongly reduces the applicability of these methods in an open environment. To let autonomous agents working in a dynamic environment to interact, a more free approach is needed, with the less possible "a priori" constraints, able to derive them at run time according to the situation emerging from the interaction.

2.3. One for all and all for one: on the ambiguity among terms and concepts

Agents have indeed a "local" world representation; but for communication purposes, interacting partners have to "agree" upon some sort of shared (i.e. conventional) representation of concepts to be transmitted.

We believe that a deep semantic "agreement" is totally inconceivable in most agent applications. On the Web, interaction happens on asynchronous bases while needed information may be found on unknown unexpected sites. In such a framework, to avoid a complete failure, we should relax some functional requirements; agents (as humans do in new unknown environments) will base their interaction on a weaker "agreement": the language. Without a stronger "a priori" commitment, the use of the natural language could represent the only tool to carry on semantics in communication processes. Linguistic communication, in humans as well as in agents, brings in a common representation level and enables a synthetic transmission of the information: discourse participants use mutually understandable terms to build phrases in order to communicate propositions.

Also in very degraded frameworks (low level in language comprehension) communication could be successful at a certain extent. For example, as in human interactions, also in case of partners adopting different jargons, comprehension could happen at least at terminological level as well as at proper names level. Sharing this kind of linguistic knowledge will be enough for both comprehension of discourse topic and related levels of interest. Similar considerations could be done in an agent framework. The adoption of natural language as representation support introduces some further complexity in reasoning mechanisms. Nevertheless, a part the case of lack in any other kind of shared knowledge in which our linguistic choice becomes mandatory, our approach supports agents communication and reasoning on a wider number of not strictly predefined interactions.

2.4. A rose is a rose is a rose: symbols and meaning

Whichever the formalism to represent knowledge, we agree with John F. Sowa in [27] that "the primary connections are not in the bits and bytes that encode the signs, but in the minds of the people who interpret them. The goal of various metadata proposals is to make those mental connections explicit by tagging the data with more signs. Those metalevel signs by themselves have further interconnections, which can be tagged with "metametalevel" signs. But meaningless data cannot acquire meaning by being tagged with meaningless metadata. The ultimate source of meaning is the physical world and the agents who use signs to represent entities in the world and their intentions concerning them".

According to this statement, we could suppose a concept be completely specified only by an "interpretation function" that maps it to those real world entities it refers to, that is:

Definition 2.1. Given two concepts C_1 and C_2, we will say that they are *ideally equivalent* iff they conceptualize the same real world entities.

We use "ideal" to highlight that this kind of equivalence is never available to software agents. An ontology approximates the domain conceptualization in the designer mind, and thus a concept equivalence could not be formally verified inside the model, but only externally postulated. The entire ontology by itself represents the maximal degree of description an agent could provide for a concept: which relations are involved in, among which concepts, and so on. We will call the set of all these information the *ontological context* of a concept. In a real open framework we assume that different agents could adopt different ontologies, while sharing their linguistic knowledge (if any). The lexicon becomes the main tool to express concept semantics. Possible mappings between concepts in different ontologies are thus implicitly constrained to be linguistically plausible (that is, represented in a coherent way by shared terms) and to adopt lexical descriptions of ontological structural constraints. The most these descriptions will be similar, the greater will be the confidence in the similarity of the expressed concepts. We thus rewrite the equivalence definition 2.1:

Definition 2.2. Given two concepts C_1 and C_2, belonging respectively to agents A_1 and A_2, they are *equivalent with respect to* A_1 and A_2, when the lexical descriptions of their ontological contexts are the same.

This is the same that happens with people: a speaker trying to communicate an unknown concept to an hearer, will use other concepts to better define it, assuming language uncertainty to be localized, that is, that the probability of a misalignment between lexicon and ontology will decrease by increasing the number of words in the description. This is driven by the hypothesis that, if both participants know a term, both of the them use it to denote the same concept, that is:

Definition 2.3. If T is a term that denotes C_1 for agent A_1 and C_2 for agent A_2, then C_1 and C_2 are supposed to be equivalent for A_1 and A_2.

This is often referred as "one sense per domain" hypothesis [31], (i.e., in case of agents linguistically interacting on the same domain, used terms could unambiguously express concepts). When trying to apply this criterion in agent communication, two main problems are faced:

1. ontologies built for specific tasks couldn't have so much shared terms, or use morphological variants of the same word
2. either the involved agents could adopt broader ontologies, or the two domains could not totally overlap. This is the case, for instance, of agents devoted to information retrieval on the web, that will adopt a "general purpose" reference ontology, where a broad knowledge is expressed with unknown granularity

In these cases, the above assumption 2.3 doesn't hold, and we need a more restrictive rule to keep into account the new situation (that is the ambiguity of the lexical information). This suggests a new equivalence definition:

Definition 2.4. Given $T_1..T_n$ terms common to both A_1 and A_2 agent lexicons, if $T_1..T_n$ *univocally* denote concept C_1 for A_1 and C_2 for A_2, then C_1 and C_2 are supposed to be equivalent for A_1 and A_2.

In other words, a concept can be referred by a set of terms (synonyms): in case there is a subset of synonyms that univocally identifies a concept in both agent ontologies, then we suppose they are equivalent for the two agents. This rule extends the previous one, as in absence of polysemy, a single term will be sufficient to univocally identify a concept in both the ontologies.

It is emerging the role ontologies assume in agents communication. Let us discuss a little bit more on them.

3. Agent ontologies

Let us define an agent ontology O as the tuple $< C, T, R, L >$ where C is a set of concepts, T a set of language terms , R a set of relationships among concepts and $L : CxT$ the correspondence relation between terms and concepts.

Relations in R have structural meanings. Different kinds of semantic relationships could share the same meaning, as $IS-A$, $Ownership$, $Part-of$, $Reference$, etc: the correspondence between these relation types and the used relationships depends on the different domains [15]. To be able to rebuild portions of a concept ontological context, it is necessary that semantics of the involved relations is made explicit and agreed. In an ontology there are different kinds of relationships and while they all participate to structurally define a concept, their contribution could be different. For instance, $Part - of$ relationship that explains the structural formation of concepts (a brick is $part - of$ an house, a wheel is $part - of$ a car, etc,) has a denotational contribute greater than the generic $Related - to$, that doesn't clarify the correlation meaning. Unfortunately, the kind of relationships active in an ontology depends strongly on structure's production objective. In [5], from a study about 40 different ontologies derived from the shared Ontolingua Frame ontology [9], postulating the existence of 85 different relationships, only 58% of them is used at least one time in any ontology, and of these, less than 20% is used more than 10 times (and none in all the ontologies). [1]

The lack of standard representations makes difficult to assume relationships as shared features for a structural definition of the ontological context of a concept. This analysis shows as set of closed theories exist, that are not meant to be compared or expressed in an automatic way.

The only relation type broadly shared, even if sometime implicitly expressed in the ontology, or implemented by using different relationships, is taxonomic description. In most of the ontologies, a taxonomic hierarchy is structured as a tree, where any concept could have at least a single concept as its generalization. However, there are ontologies where multiple inheritance is allowed.

Luckily, a taxonomy is strongly definitory for concepts. It is the case of dictionaries, where a concept is defined in terms of its *genus* and its *differentia*, that are its direct super class, and the features that discriminate it from others belonging to the same genus. The existence of a shared taxonomy makes it possible to compare concepts by their positions in hierarchies: more these are similar, less will be the uncertainty on their equivalence.

3.1. Ontological similarity evaluation

A communication act could be seen as the activity of sending some information from a sender to a receiver (being this encoded as a message through a communication language) and decoded when received. Several components contribute at different degree in this process. The communication context of two agents (S in the role of a speaker/sender and H in the role of a hearer/receiver) could be sketched as being composed in a number of dimensions orthogonal to the communication flow [2] : these are, the sender *conceptual plane* $O(S)$, the sender *lexical plane* $V(S)$, the receiver *lexical plane* $V(H)$ and the receiver *conceptual plane* $O(H)$ (see Fig. 1).

[1] It is worth noticing how the preference for several relationships is often biased by the formalism of the adopted implementation framework: the relation $Subclass - of$ is used more often than $Superclass - of$ (that is not in the first twenty). Adding a new class to the ontology is easier in a top down than in a bottom up fashion, as new concepts are usually related to pre-existing relations by inheritance, and in most of the ontology editing tools this relation is implemented by a meta attribute in the child concept pointing to the parent class.

[2] We use here a geometrical representation as a metaphor to highlight the role the different components have in communication.

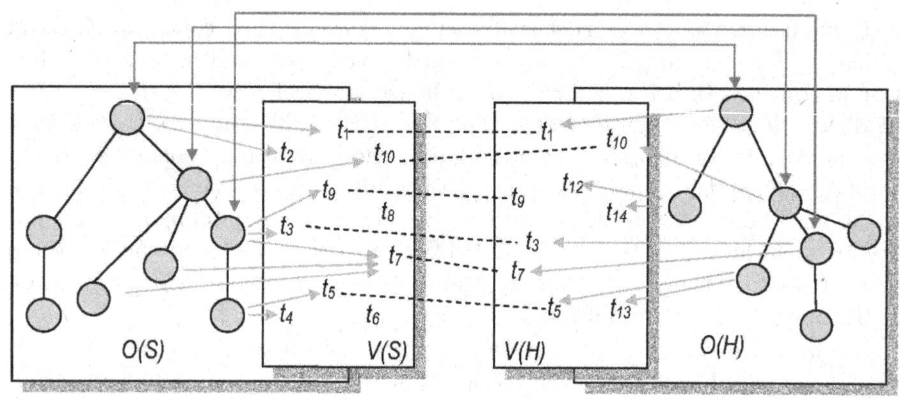

FIGURE 1. A graphical representation of the communication context

Conceptual planes $O(S)$ and $O(H)$ contain concepts C and relationships R: they are the "interior" components of agent minds, resulting from domain conceptualizations made by designers, and expressed in some logic formalism. Lexical planes $V(S)$ and $V(H)$ contain words of T agent lexicons. For (natural language) speaking agents, information in their lexicons represents the way they "express" underlying conceptualizations, thus a (weak) agreement to a shared formalism. Relation L among concepts and terms in the language correlates what the agent can represent in its mind with what it can express. This is represented in figure by light arrows, going from the conceptual plane to the lexical one. The mapping between lexicons $V(S)$ and $V(H)$ is shown by dashed lines, depicting the *linguistic equivalence* relation between the two agents terms: if S and H speak the same language, these lines represent the (partial) identity relation between symbols in $V(S)$ and $V(H)$; lines in the upper part of the figure point to the "true" mapping among agent concepts that in our hypothesis is unavailable to the communication. Agent S, willing to transmit a concept C to agent H, must go by first from its conceptual plane $O(S)$ through its lexical plane $V(S)$, then send some information to the hearer H that will map it to its lexical plane $V(H)$, and finally project it to its conceptual plane $O(H)$. This makes the communication complex, as in the general case, the relationship between different planes is not bijective, and each step can lead away from the target. As a consequence, it is often unfeasible a straight approach where an agent chooses a word in its lexicon as the message content; there is no guarantee that the receiving agent will be able to invert the encoding process to catch the right concept in its own ontology. In the following paragraphs we will use this model to make it clear the role the different components play in the communication process, trying to provide an accurate analysis of each of them.

3.1.1. Conceptual similarity among planes $O(S)$ and $O(H)$. Similarity among the conceptual planes is crucial for the communication. Topological differences could reveal deep differences in conceptualizations (and then in concept meaning, see

Fig. 2). Of course not all ontological misalignments imply conceptual misalignments (even if the opposite holds: different conceptualizations will have different models). Unfortunately, conceptual misalignments could not be directly derived in communication as direct mapping is unfeasible by hypothesis; anyway, it is useful for our analysis to characterize the different typologies that could emerge when comparing concepts in two ontologies.

Given two equivalent concepts C_S in $O(S)$ and C_H in $O(H)$, each of them is involved, more or less directly, in a few relationships with other concepts inside its own ontology. For sake of simplicity, let us consider only the subsumption relation class-subclass ($\sqsubseteq$). Let $C'_S \in O(S)$ be a concept subsumed by C_S, that is $C'_S \sqsubseteq C_S$. A number of cases could happen:

Equivalence: $\exists C'_H \in O(H) \mid C'_S \equiv C'_H \wedge C'_H \sqsubseteq C_H$, that is, there is a concept in $O(H)$ that is equivalent to C'_S and is subsumed by C_H. For instance, in both the ontologies there is a $<\mathit{dog}>$ concept and an $<\mathit{animal}>$ concept and $<\mathit{dog}> \sqsubseteq <\mathit{animal}>$ (as in case of Fig. 2-1).

Contradiction: $\exists C'_H \in O(H) \mid C'_S \equiv C'_H \wedge \neg(C'_H \sqsubseteq C_H)$, that is, the concept in $O(H)$ equivalent to C'_S is not reachable through the subsumption relation from C_H. For instance, both the ontologies have a concept for $<\mathit{circle}>$ and $<\mathit{polygon}>$, but one of them declares that $<\mathit{circle}> \sqsubseteq <\mathit{polygon}>$, whilst the other one does not. This reflects a deep difference in their conceptualization (as in case of Fig. 2-2).

Indetermination: $\forall C'_H \in O(H) \mid C'_H \not\equiv C'_S$ that is, there is no concept in $O(H)$ equivalent to C'_S. In this case ontologies are not in contradiction, simply $O(H)$ represents a different conceptualization that $O(S)$. For instance, both ontologies have $<\mathit{dog}>$ concept, but only one of them get the concept $<\mathit{mammal}>$ and the relation $<\mathit{dog}> \sqsubseteq <\mathit{mammal}>$; in this case there are two possibilities:

- *Compatibility*: $O(H)$ could admit the missing concept, that is the misalignment is at the aggregation level: concepts are represented with different granularity. With respect to the previous example, one of the ontologies contains the concept of $<\mathit{mammal}>$ as an intermediate level among $<\mathit{dog}>$ and $<\mathit{animal}>$, while the other one not (see Fig. 2-3a).
- *Incompatibility*: $O(H)$ description could not admit the missing concept, as it uses a different categorization for its concepts. This usually reflects differences in the properties considered to be salient for the generalization. For instance, having two different ontologies for animals, one organized around classes as mammal, bird, etc. and the other on their behavior as carnivore, herbivore, etc (as in Fig. 2-3b).

Semantic similarity measures based on evaluation of taxonomic links usually use distance metrics between compared concepts, with respect to nodes known as equivalent: shorter is the path between two nodes, greater is their similarity. Such an approach often assumes that taxonomic relations have uniform distances, while it doesn’t hold in the general case. In real world taxonomies, the “distance” covered

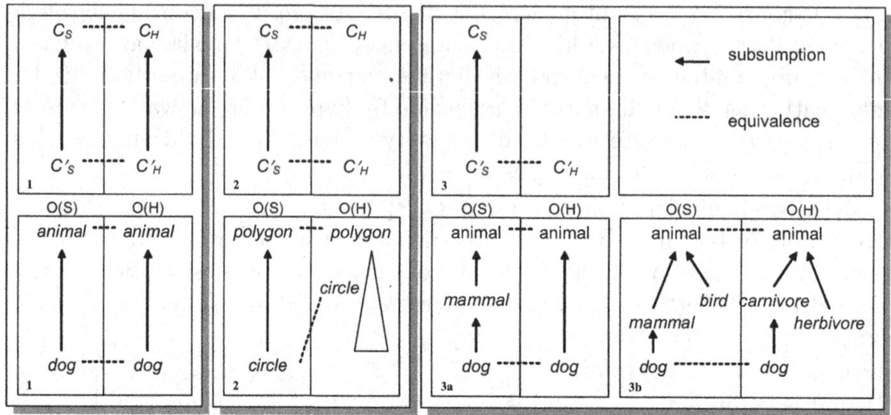

FIGURE 2. Topological differences in conceptual planes

by direct taxonomic relationships is roughly variable, as a few sub-taxonomies, for instance, tend to be more dense than others.

As the $IS - A$ relationship induces a partial ordering in concepts, a measure of the topological similarity of ontological contexts could be obtained by weighting shared constraints (as positive evidences), the contradicting constraints (as negative evidences) and indeterminate constraints over the two ontologies.

3.1.2. Lexical similarity among planes $V(S)$ and $V(H)$. Let us now take into account the role of the lexicon in communication process. To transmit information between a speaker and an hearer, it is necessary that a shared vocabulary exists and is adopted. Greater is the difference between speaker and hearer dictionaries, greater is the probability of term known to one agent and unknown to the other one (success in the communication tends to be zero).

A simple measure of similarity can be obtained as the average mutual coverage with respect to the number of words in each dictionary.

The set coverage is defined as a number ranging from 0 to 1. Two identical sets will have maximal coverage, which is 1, while disjoint sets will measure 0; in other cases coverage quantifies the set overlap. We define the coverage as:

Definition 3.1. Given a non-empty set X and a subset $Y \subset X$, the coverage σ of Y over X is the quotient of their cardinality, that is $|Y|/|X|$.

The common coverage of two non-empty sets will be then the average of the coverage of their intersection with respect to each of them. In our case:

Definition 3.2. If $V(S)$ and $V(H)$ are the speaker S and hearer H lexicons, then the lexical coverage $\sigma(V(S), V(H))$ is:

$$\sigma(V(S), V(H)) = \frac{1}{2}\frac{|V(S) \cap V(H)|}{|V(S)|} + \frac{1}{2}\frac{|V(S) \cap V(H)|}{|V(H)|}$$

where

$$\sigma(V(S), V(H)) = 0\, if\ V(S) = \oslash\ or\ V(H) = \oslash$$

Is agent lexicons significatively overlap (high σ values), this states that the set of symbols (i.e. language terms) they are using to communicate is sufficiently similar to expect their conceptual planes to be organized around the same concepts. Notice that lexical similarity does not guarantee by itslef that the communication will succeed but only reflects at which extent a language agreement exists "a priori".

3.1.3. Lexical expressivity. A strong similarity in conceptual and lexical planes is not sufficient to ensure communication to be successful. In fact by definition agents do not have an a priori knowledge of characteristics of the interacting agent's ontology as they don't know each other. As a consequence they will not use common internal representation language whilst they could. They will pass through the lexical level for communication purposes. The activation of this procedure could generate a failure. Let us do an exemplification; let us suppose that both the agent ontologies and their lexicons are exactly the same, but that they could use a single word only to express any concept (very poor lexical expressivity). Agent S will use the unique word it gets as lexicalization for communicating any concept. Even if H knows the word it can't disambiguate what it hears, as this extremely poor lexical expressivity does not allow to focus the right concept among all possible ones in its mind. The correct mapping between lexical and conceptual planes is fundamental for agents using lexicons for knowledge transmission. This motivates the adoption of a one-to-one correspondence between these planes realized in the majority of ontologies. For exemplification purposes in real application, it is generally considered concepts are represented in an ontology by only one lexicalization.In the web context a communication could be activated between any couple of agents, independently by the amount (if any) of ontology overlapping. In case of partial knowledge/dictionary sharing, several concepts will be cut-off as they could receive different lexicalizations. A richer set of terms increases the probability of concept comprehension by the receiver. Lexical redundancy could be seen as a magnifying factor for the lexical plane with respect to the concept plane.

Unfortunately it is not ever possible to extend the number of unambiguous lexicalizations for a concept; from a cognitive perspective, the creation of a new word is strictly related to the intention of explicitly specify a concept. However, distinct lexicalizations could denote the same concept in an ontology, if the underlying domain conceptualization makes no difference among referents they have in the real world. Lexical variety implies an implicit drawback : often a word could denote even totally different concepts. This phenomenon (namely, the word polysemy) could be seen as the opposite contraction of the lexical plane with respect to the concept plane; in this case distinct concepts in the conceptual plane partially overlap on the lexical one. Generally, these two phenomena are both present: lexical richness implies greater ambiguity.

A measure for linguistic expressivity for an agent A lexicon is obtained by assigning each word w a *weight* P, inversely proportional to its ambiguity:

$$P_A(w \in T_A) = \frac{1}{|Sense_A(w)|} \ with\ Sense_A(w) = \{c|(c,w) \in L_A\} \tag{3.1}$$

where $Sense_A(w)$ represents the set of (agent A) concepts associated to word w, (i.e. its different senses).

We then define the expressivity $Expr(c)$ of a concept c as the sum of the weights of each word that could express it, that is:

$$Expr(c \in C_A) = \sum_{w \in Words_A(c)} P_A(w)\ with\ Words_A(c) = \{w|(w,c) \in L_A\} \tag{3.2}$$

being $Words_A(c)$ the set of words that could express c. Low values of $Expr(c)$ denote poorly represented concepts in the lexicon, while high scores stand for richly expressed concepts.

Over the whole ontology of the agent A, we can define the expressivity of the lexicon T_A as the average expressivity of its concepts, that is:

$$\overline{Expr(T_A)} = \frac{\sum_{c \in C_A} Expr(c)}{|C_A|} \tag{3.3}$$

Notice that the expressivity could vary over the range $(0, +\infty)$, where an higher value stands for a "wider" dimension for the lexical plane with respect to the conceptual one.

3.1.4. Lexical-Semantic coherence. Basic assumption for the communication is the lexical-semantic coherence: source and destination use lexicons in a coherent way, by assigning words to concepts in a consistent approach. That is, if C_S is a concept in the conceptual plane $O(S)$ of a speaker agent S and w a word in $Words(C_S)$ we assume that the following rule holds:

$$if\ (\exists C_H \in O(H) \mid C_S \equiv C_H) \wedge w \in V(H)\ then\ C_H \in Sense_H(w) \tag{3.4}$$

that is: if there is a concept C_H in the H hearer's ontology equivalent to C_S and H knows the word w the speaker uses to represent C_S, than H too represents C_H by w. This means that if a concept C exists that is known by both S and H, then each word in their common vocabulary either expresses C for both of them, or doesn't express C at all. Lexical mismatches could happen when the hearer doesn't know the word w or the concept C_H (thus eventually using w to refer to other concepts). In real frameworks we could not guarantee that rule 3.4 globally holds. Exceptions to this rule represent situations in which agents use their vocabularies in an inconsistent way. In case of frequent inconsistencies, it becomes very difficult information exchange between the two agents.

If we think this exception to the rule 3.4 could usually hold, than the equivalence relation between the lexical planes must be considered as an accidental equivalence among strings belonging to two different languages. In this case the shared vocabulary could not convey any information.

The different factors we analyzed represent the natural dimensions along which the communication flows. We could distinguish between:

Endogenous factors, i.e. intrinsic conditions, that could be evaluated for each agent and represent its disposition towards the communication based on its cognitive model, that is its lexical espressivity.

Exogenous factors, i.e. contextual conditions, defined at communication time between participants, and embedded in the conceptual plane distance, the lexical distance and the lexical-semantic coherence; they represent properties emerging from the interaction much more than individual qualities.

4. Toward a linguistic agent society: a language-aware architecture

From the above analysis of our linguistic communication model it emerges that, even when supposing participants agree on a communication language (at least for what concerns grammar and protocol), it is possible for direct communication to fail at content level. This could happen in the following cases:

1. Hearer dictionary does not include the word used by the speaker; this could happen either in case the hearer adopts another word to express the same concept, or when speaker and hearer use different languages.
2. Hearer does not know a concept the other is speaking about, that is H knowledge does not contain a (unique) lexical representation for this concept;
3. Hearer maps the word into one or more different concepts while only one is known by the speaker; this happens with morphologically ambiguous words.

The need to bring into the communication more information to express a concept meaning requires the introduction of further communication capabilities. In a real world framework it is unrealistic to suppose that each agent willing to communicate could have these capabilities, as most of them could even not be aware of such issues. In fact it would require to both interacting agents the ability to manage several kinds knowledge as well as to infer an appropriate behavior while being in a heterogeneous and dynamical framework. An agent with the inferential abilities needed to deal with language ambiguities will gather several skills that will greatly increase both design and implementation complexity. Real applications need to access to different services and resources asynchronously while accomplishing several tasks: it is unfeasible to duplicate such competencies for each agent. Moreover, a key idea of any agent based distributed approach is to keep individuals simple and easy to maintain, to customize, and adapt. Another important aspect is that existing information services, (whose implementation, query language and communication channels are out of the control of user applications) could be easily integrated. In fact most of the existing Web information sources have been developed before the definition of agent technologies. As a consequence it seems more feasible to realize wrapper agents over these resources than directly to update them: this kind of agents simply interface information sources and consumers, providing uniform data access and view.

4.1. Agent Taxonomy

We defined an agent society with different specific competencies and in terms of the different functionalities they offer for the communication task. Among others, our main objective from an architectural point of view is to keep the resulting architecture independent from the application domain; three different agent "typologies" have been devised as sufficient for supporting language communication:

1. Resource agents, representing the ends of the communication channel. They own the knowledge target of the communication;
2. Service agents, owning the single functionalities to support complex linguistic activities (mainly represented by a Mediator and a Translator);
3. Coordinator agents, that supply structural knowledge of each task, and have coordination and control capabilities.

Whilst they all share the same structural paradigm, each of them exhibit specific design choices oriented to the task it is devoted to. In detail, splitting competencies between Service and Coordinator agents realizes a separation between tactical highly specialized problem-solving skills, and strategic knowledge on how to combine them to achieve a complex goal. In such a way, it is possible to dynamically recombine existing components to solve new problems, and dually, to upgrade single functionalities without having to redesign the entire system.

Main functionalities of a Coordinator agent relate to the ability:

- to identify Resource agents involved in the communication act,
- to identify Service agents to support communication,
- to manage the information flow among them.

From the application point of view the separation between functionalities and the consequent need to interact with a single agent hide the underlying complexity of the information retrieval activities and communication tasks: these are conceived to be the most frequent application environments to be met.

A Service agent has task specific capabilities. It will:

- be delegated by the Coordinator agent for the resolution of a specific task that will become its goal
- identify precise sub goals requiring information from Resource agents
- delegate to the Coordinator agent the task to effectively retrieve the needed information

A Resource agent will:

- support a transparent access to the underlying resource
- reply to system queries following agreed communication language and protocol

To realize these functionalities, agents must be endowed with appropriate knowledge and processing capabilities to manage it. Thus a Coordinator agent should at least embody the knowledge of the physical model of both Resource agent and Service agent distribution in the system, a model for the services involved in the communication task through the different situations (i.e. involved agents may have or not the same ontology, or the same language) and a communication protocol to interact with Resource and Service agents; a Service agent will know at least how to attain its goal, which additional information is needed, and a communication protocol to interact with the Coordinator agent.

Being at the lowest cognitive level, any Resource agent will know only the model of the data it owns, the procedures to answer to specific queries on its knowledge, and the communication protocol to interact with Coordinator agents.

In this context we focus on the issues related to the use of the natural language in the communication activity. Although the described architecture is meant to deal with a more general class of problems, we here refer only to the needs of a communication scenario. The reasoning skills could broadly vary in this framework: for instance, every resource could be represented as an agent with a basic set of skills, able at least to receive specific requests, to act in order to satisfy them, while Service agents (as described below) expose higher cognitive levels. These roles, according to the chosen organization, could be even implemented by a single agent: the proposed categorization holds for modelling purposes only.

The simplest agent organization foresees five different agents: two Resource agents, (a Speaker and a Hearer, willing to interact, i.e. communicate), two Service agents (a Mediator and a Translator agent providing the specific services required), and a Coordinator agent that will supervise all the different activities.

4.1.1. The Resource agents. As Resource agents, Speaker and Hearer are responsible for the management and the presentation of domain knowledge in their own resources. They alternate in the role of Sender and Receiver while information flow is managed by a Coordinator agent with which they interact. Nevertheless, domain knowledge and language knowledge are intrinsically different: though they use a communication language, agents are not necessarily aware of the language structure, neither they must be able to learn new words. Language could be seen as an unconscious phenomenon, as it is for people. Of course, people could in some measure reason about language, as their conscious knowledge includes some linguistic skill, but this does not apply for systems. They can't negotiate terminology or autonomously resolve communication failures, as this requires a shift in the discourse domain, from the content to the language level. An hearer agent knows how to reply to the queries it receives. When it does not understand the query, as for instance in case of adopted ambiguous terms, a deeper linguistic knowledge is required. If this knowledge could be successfully factorized externally from each single agent, this will greatly reduce the linguistic skills needed. More in detail, we suppose that knowledge of the underlying language model makes Resource agents able to reply to simple queries about:

- the lexical relation L between terms and concepts
- conceptual relations R among concepts

with no other assumptions on inference capabilities to correlate concepts in their ontologies.

4.1.2. The Mediator Agent. The Mediator agent carries on a mediation activity between actors, being able to understand the information the speaker wants to express as well as the way to present it to the hearer. He will narrow the gap existing between the information content of each lexicalization and its joint use, thus providing inferential contribution to the agents communication. The mediation activity overlaps in a transparent fashion the agent interaction. The Mediator agent is designed to act independently from a specific domain. We assume that he has no prior knowledge about the dialog topics , while it is focused on understanding which relationships exist between concepts involved in the communication as well as terms used to express them, without any assumption on the adopted internal knowledge representation formalisms. This working modality has been choosen for making the Mediator agent universally valid in any application domain. Its role consists in being able to activate the mediation process and manage it until successful completion.

Due to the fact the mediation activity is developed out of the speaking agents, the Mediator needs to work on a restricted view of the ontologies. Instead of duplicating, he builds a partial image of the involved parts, by querying agents about specific knowledge on terms and concepts, and dynamically compares the results in order to find a mapping for the target concept.

Let us to provide an example: two agents, say John and Mary, are talking together: during the dialog, John use the word α that Mary does not know. The Mediator could come in hand in finding a word known by Mary with the same meaning of α. To accomplish this, the Mediator must have some specific skills with respect to the reasoning: at least it must be able to judge if two concept are or not equivalent for the two involved agents. In practice, the Mediator will learn what John means by α, asking him other terms representing the same concept. If John could provide synonyms of the sense it is using, the Mediator could try to query Mary with these. In case she can identify a corresponding concept (for instance she knows a synonym β), then the mediation will succeed. But if, for instance, β is ambiguous for Mary, than the Mediator should learn more features of the concept John is expressing. John could explain to the Mediator that for him α is a γ. Mediator will ask them Mary if she knows meaning of γ, and so on. Conversation will go on until information from two participants will be enough to let the Mediator decide, with some "degree of confidence", a mapping among what John is speaking about and what Mary knows. By "degree of confidence" we mean that the Mediator offers its service to solve problems tied to the communication, not to the possible inconsistencies of the conceptualizations.

The mediation function is inspired by human behavior: if an hearer does not understand the meaning of a word, he asks for more details, firing sub-dialogue events, based on a sequence of query-answer, aimed to identify the target concept, or its position in the ontology: in this activity he will base also on the clues provided by synonyms, relations with other concepts, and so on. A positive aspect of this kind of mediation is that the analysis is framed into a local search space. In real world ontologies, big differences in the taxonomic structure already appear in the upper levels, making impossible a large-scale mapping between misaligned structures. Seeing the mediation activity as a terminological problem helps in understanding the analogies existing on the underlying models.

This view of the ontological mediation is based on minimal assumptions on the knowledge model the involved agent has: by adding more restrictive hypotheses on their introspection capabilities, it is possible to include in the same framework more sophisticated techniques. Reasoning about concept properties, attribute similarity and relations requires a deeper semantic agreement among participants that is out of the scope of this research. We stress here that, in absence of such agreements, what agents could expose about their ontologies is the lexical component, and thus we focus the mediation activity on this.

4.1.3. The Translator Agent. In case the interacting agents speak different languages, lexical misalignment are no more a local problem, but have to be dealt introducing a new entity, able to determine a mapping between terms in the two languages by an intelligent management of an extensive resource: the dictionary. For this reason, a Translator agent is foreseen in such a situation.

By "intelligent management" we mean that the Translator agent is expected to provide more than simple word-level translation according to the dictionary, but try to find the best "semantic" translation with respect to the sense under analysis, as a human usually does when translating something. Note that the problem of finding a translation in ontological mediation although quite similar to the classical machine-translation problem, exhibit some peculiarities due to the nature of the task: in fact, while machine translation approaches usually take into account the word context represented by the phrase the term is in, in our case the dialog participants have clear intentions to transmit specific senses, and thus could provide additional information on the ontological context of the word under analysis. This means for instance that the Translator agent could exploit the useful information provided by a set of synonyms in order to find the most appropriate translation or, depending on the underlying resource, try to match different senses in the dictionary against the ones the agent has.

We choose to localize the mediation and translation tasks in different entities to separate the reasoning mechanism of the mediation activity, that is essentially based on labelled graphs matching, and the translation, that is strictly tied to the amount and modalities of the information stored in the resource.

4.1.4. The Coordinator agent. In real environment the communication needs emerging in the dialog are unforeseen. It is necessary to add the third agent typology, aiming to coordinate the operations carried on by the Service agents. A Coordinator agent will then take in charge determining which interaction flow is necessary

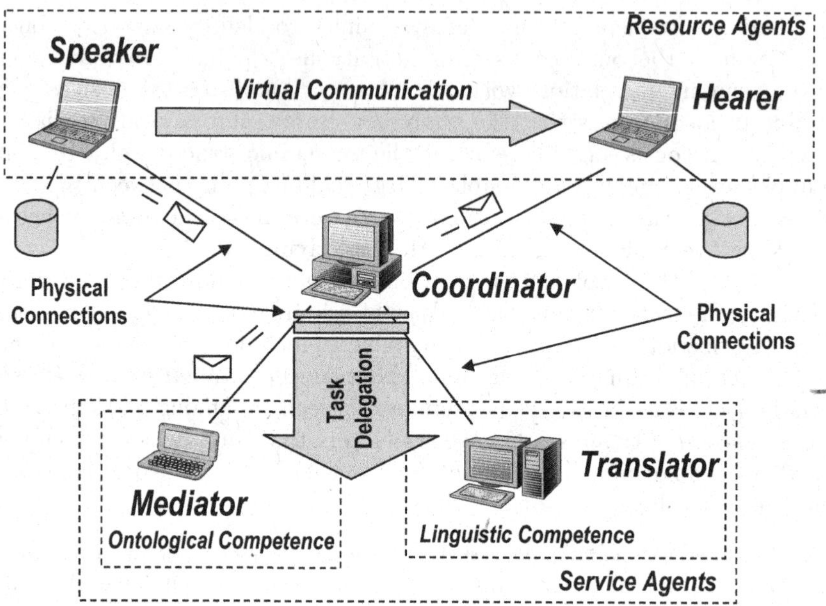

FIGURE 3. Schematic view of the agent architecture

to communicate an information, activating for each single task the required Service agents and supervising their activities. With respect to a Facilitator agent [30], a Coordinator agent could exhibit a number of extra capabilities, being responsible not only on the information/services routing (as the other does), but making its own plans on the way the information should be combined in the system and on which agents (capabilities) be involved in the process. This usefully decouples the local strategies, adopted by each single Service agent to solve its goals from the knowledge on how to combine its results with other parts in the system.

Given this framework, the communication scenario becomes the following: two agents willing to communicate will contact a Coordinator, declaring their own languages and ontologies, asking him to organize a meeting and to arbitrate the dialog. The Coordinator accepts the task and, if necessary, contacts another agent to support needed knowledge for completing the communication task. If the communication succeeds, the Coordinator will continue in its role of "message router"; in case during the meeting a misunderstanding happens, the Coordinator will involve one or more Mediators, by asking them to solve it. From the two interacting agents points of view, the Coordinator is performing all the activities. Task delegation to Mediators and Translators is thus hidden to the users, that will even ignore the need for these supplementary services.

4.2. Adaptive agent communication

After identification of agent classes (typologies), their functionalities and roles, it is now important to analyze in details how interactions may occur at a physical layer. The previously described architecture could be defined as a pool of cooperating agents that interact following two different modalities (see [24] for furhter details):

- an event-driven asynchronous communication based on a request/reply protocol
- a demand-driven synchronous communication based on direct queries.

Agents could adopt a message based communication language that is a simplified version of KQML [11] implementing only the most common performatives (ask-one, ask-all, tell, etc.). In this architecture, software agents owning information sources could freely communicate, through the interaction with a Coordinator agent, independently from their physical collocation on the network. Coordinator agents are responsible for finding suitable support agents to process a message, to forward requests to them, to translate responses for dialog participants and to transmit information needed for message building. Depending on the message type, the Coordinator agent will obtain a direct answer or will activate the procedures required to process it. The overall system is information oriented and implements several different functionalities. The agent architecture is structured in a number of layers that implement the different procedures needed for the communication, the reasoning and the internal knowledge storage and maintenance. The different interfaces among agents and the OS are built over TCP stack, that represent the basic layer needed to connect and speak with software agents through the underlying network and different OSs. The delivery and monitoring message components along with the agent connection listeners, are wrapped in. These listeners are owned by the Coordinator, that is responsible for a coherent activation of Service agent requests. Its knowledge base contains information on capabilities, languages and ontologies of each single agent: it dynamically decides upon the involved connections based on all these information. The Coordinator uses its KB to serve requests, that will involve one or more of the following actions:

1. Identification of an agent that could process the request
2. Request translation to be comprehensible for the receiving agent
3. Request decomposition into simpler ones, delegated to Service agents
4. Results combination in a response for the requesting agent

To compel with these requests, the Coordinator continually scans the network operations, waiting for a new agent connection, or an existing agent disconnection. Whenever it receives any one, it will activate the appropriate procedure. In the following, we briefly sketch the principal procedures involved either in the connection elaboration or in a request.

4.2.1. Processing agent connections. When a connection request is sent from an agent to the Coordinator agent, a communication channel will be setup between the two agents. Due to the communication protocol, the Coordinator waits for a registration message with agents personal data. Purpose of this message is to provide to the system an explicit characterization for connecting agents . A newcomer must inform the Coordinator with both its category, (providing a nickname to let all other agents in the system to logically address it in their messages), and the services it will expose to the community. The role each agent has in the system is defined on connection basis: this approach makes it possible for the same agent to assume time by time more than one role (for instance, nothing inhibits a Mediator to later perform as a Translator, or a Resource agent). For each role, the agent has to register to the Coordinator by declaring what kind services it will provide, thus allowing to build a dedicated communication channel for each specific role. The Coordinator records the link among name, role, connection and physical agents in a sort of directory service in its knowledge base, to be used later for message routing. Depending on the role, further information will be necessary: for instance, the Coordinator will be informed upon ontology and language the Resource agent will adopt, while a Translator will specify for which languages could be useful. These additional information is used both to decide run-time the dynamic information path, and to plan adequate support activities to be delegated to Service agents.

4.2.2. Processing agent requests. Due to the fact all agents are connected through the Coordinator, it is needed to guarantee a coherent information flow through the system. The Coordinator behavior becomes complex and structured related to the knowledge required for the communication task. For instance, let suppose an agent S is registered in the system, with a "speaker" (i.e. information sender) role. At a given time, S will send a request to communicate a concept to agent H. At that moment, the Coordinator must take a number of decisions: by accessing its knowledge base, it will check all pre-conditions that should be verified for making communication feasible. First of all, it will verify H is known to the system. If H is available, the Coordinator will match the information provided by S with respect to H capabilities to determine one of the following situations:

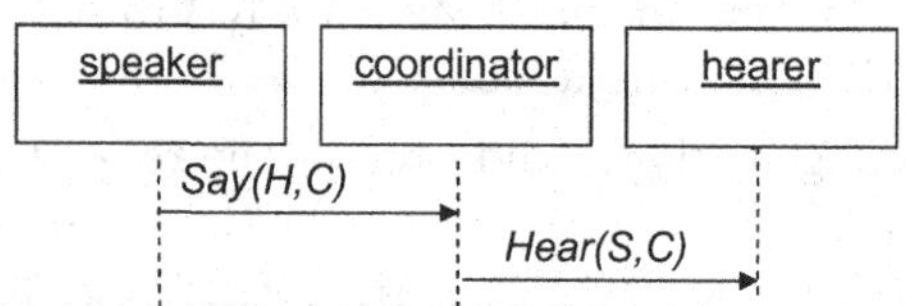

FIGURE 4. Communication acts in direct connection

a) both A and B use the same ontology: the A message will be directly transmitted to B, with only (eventual) syntactic translations of its structure (see Fig. 4, where we use $Say(H, C)$ to represent a communication activity aimed to transmit concept C to agent H. The message is translated to $Hear(S, C)$ to represent a logical translation performed by the Coordinator that leaves the content unmodified);
b) S and H refer to different ontologies while using the same language (see Fig. 5):

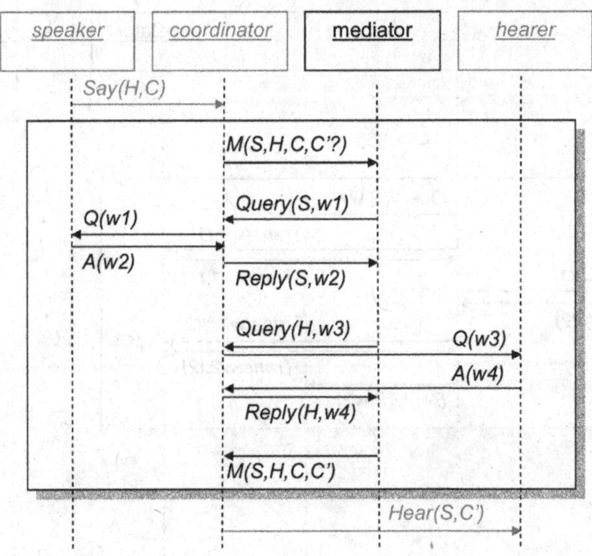

FIGURE 5. Mediated communication among agents

the Coordinator will verify the presence of a Mediator agent and if unavailable, S will be notified with an appropriate message; otherwise the Coordinator will build a suitable request for mediation (represented by $M(S, H, C, C'?)$, transmitting the concept under investigation plus S and H logical names. To be transparent, the Coordinator will behave, time by time, as speaker and as hearer, directly replying to the Mediator queries for further information (represented in figure by $Query(Agent, Info)$) if caching the required information, otherwise redirecting them to the appropriate agent (eventually syntactically translating them in the S and H languages, see $Q(Info)$ in figure). When the mediation activity ends, the Coordinator will collect responses from the Mediator (i.e. concept(s) C'_H equivalent to C_S), will update its knowledge base, and in case of success of the mediation, will send back the appropriate information to the hearer($Hear(S, C')$), finally notifying to the speakers the success of information delivery;

c) both involved parts adopt different ontologies and languages (see Fig. 6): the Coordinator will interleave the actions performed in b) with appropriate queries to a Translator agent. In fact, the mediation activity happens at symbol level, and further translations will be needed to present to the Mediator the requested information in a uniform language. For instance, if the Mediator uses H language, then each lexical information flowing through S would first be translated by the Translator agent (in figure 6, when the Mediator asks $w1$ to "S", the Coordinator sends the message $Trans(w1, t1?)$ to the Translator agent asking to translate it, then pass the translated query $Q(t1)$ to S, obtains its answer $A(t2)$, asks back the Translator for its service to bring $t2$ in a form the Mediator could

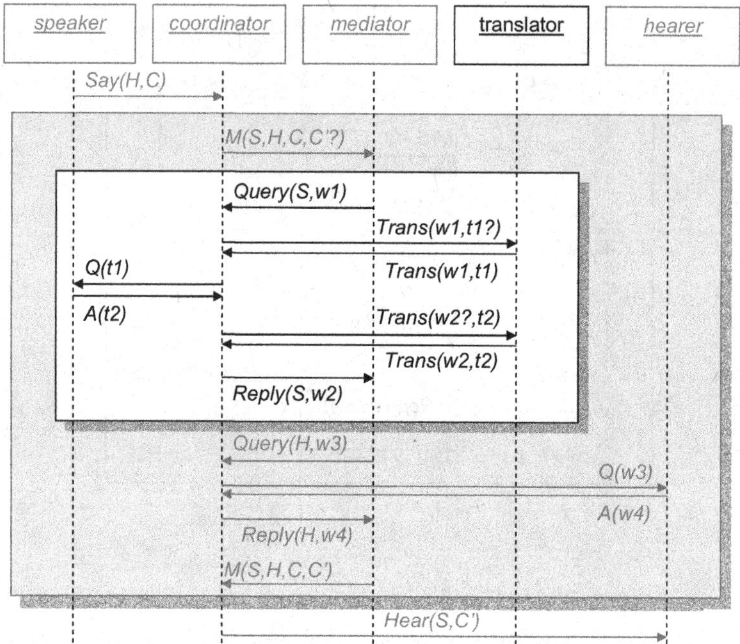

FIGURE 6. Translated and mediated commnuication

understand and redirect the translation $w2$ to the Mediator ($Reply(S, w2)$)). Depending on the intelligence of the Coordinator, some information could also be cached before querying for the Translator (for example, to maximize the translation accuracy, waiting for all the synonyms identifying a concept to be collected before querying a translation), thus improving the overall performance.

In case the needed information in each of previous a), b) or c) cases is already available in the Coordinator knowledge base, it could directly reply without involving further actions. This knowledge acquisition process is extremely important as, run-time, it could result in new linguistic resources "emerging" from the overall communication process, and eventually, to new Resource agents (it could be considered as a positive follow up). In a resource extraction context, we could adopt the same architectural framework by just specializing this process. It is feasible the Coordinator releases periodically the acquired knowledge in form of a new Resource agent, to maintain distinct as most as possible the identified functional roles in the communication system.

5. Conclusions

The real innovation of the web will be realized when agents will collect contents from multiple sources, process the information and exchange the results with other agents. Consumer and producer agents can reach a reciprocal understanding by sharing concepts from their ontologies, which provide the vocabulary needed for a wide spectrum communication. The structure and semantics of ontologies should make it easier to share, among an agents community, the document content meaning.

Web resources are accessible to agents surfing the web for performing useful tasks such as improved search and resources discovery, information bordering and information filtering.

A group of interacting agents could be seen as a small cooperative society requiring a shared language and communication channels in order to circulate ideas, knowledge and background assumptions: general abilities for language processing may be considered as part of the agent knowledge; differences in formal representation may be overcome by means of transposition - conversion mechanisms.

Agents act on behalf of humans, interacting with other agents. The new perspective of computing is re-centering on information rather than on processes, and in examining the nature of such information more closely. It will be required to understand what is to be represented to be used in computing, communication and so on. As whatever be the content of the communication, it is supported by specific linguistic expressions (surface representation and underlying structuring), these must be covered when leaving to agents authority in searching and extracting content in the context of document retrieval and information extraction activities. Such a specificity is not related to a general knowledge of the language, but requires information onto sub languages and domain related knowledge repositories.

A high level competence on language understanding is thus required as well as the ability to abstract concepts by their lexicalizations.

While several formalisms for expressing at some extent information contents exist, none is 1) expressive, 2) shared, 3) synthetic as the natural language. Formal languages, as XML, for document content representation are limited by the lack of an universal agreement on which categories should be assumed as a shared model and at what extent. Different domain conceptualizations are hardly compatible as different aspects emerging from knowledge bases strongly depend on the application tasks they have been written for [2]. As argued in [28] "Many of the ontologies for web objects ignore physical objects, processes, people, and their intentions. A typical example is SHOE (Simple HTML Ontology Extensions) [17], which has only four basic categories: String, Number, Date, and Truth. Those four categories, which are needed to describe the syntax of web data, cannot by themselves describe the semantics. Strings contain characters that represent statements that describe the world; numbers count and measure things; dates are time units tied to the rotation of the earth; and truth is a meta language term about the correspondence between a statement and the world. Those categories can only be defined in terms of the world, the people in the world, and the languages people use to talk about the world." Linguistic communication becomes the only solution in all situations where there is no explicit agreement among parts to coherently use a formal language, that is when the ontological agreement is missing.

However, the expressive power on natural language poses a number of issues in adopting a direct approach to the interpretation of meaning. Polysemy, morphological variants and synonymy require a linguistic expertise to deal with: even if almost natural for humans, they could seriously deceive computer systems. The proposed communication model substantiates the respective contributions of the different components involved in the communication process by introducing a novel communication scheme; adopting an explicit separation between the concept level where contents are organized and the lexical level where they are expressed by terms in a language helps in incrementally affording the communication problem: to encode a concept in a set of terms that will express the structural relationships among concepts in speaker mind, to find mappings among linguistic expressions in participant languages, to decode the linguistic information in the mind representation of the receiver. For both Information Extraction and communication purposes two different aspects need to be tightly integrated converging in a framework in which different autonomous systems could cooperate, while needed, for knowledge exchange. An intelligent agent based approach could be a suitable solution: definition of an agent society (to which belong members with different properties and abilities) would perform the task of knowledge communication (exchange of information on both a specific matter and the world) with a collective and individual gain. We based on these assumptions for defining our linguistic agents society that proved to be successful to support knowledge exchange in a large extent of situations ranging from an homogeneous and compatible to an only partially overlapping world model.

References

[1] M. Q. W. Baldonado. An interactive, structure-mediated approach to exploring information in a heterogeneous, distributed environment. *Ph.D. Dissertation, Stanford University*, 1997.

[2] Roberto Basili, Michele Vindigni, and Fabio Massimo Zanzotto. Integrating ontological and linguistic knowledge for conceptual information extraction. In *Proc. of the IEEE/WIC International Conference on Web Intelligence (WI'03)*, Halifax (Canada), 2003.

[3] R. J. Bayardo, Jr., W. Bohrer, R. Brice, A. Cichocki, J. Fowler, A. Helal, V. Kashyap, T. Ksiezyk, G. Martin, M. Nodine, M. Rashid, M. Rusinkiewicz, R. Shea, C. Unnikrishnan, A. Unruh, and D. Woelk. InfoSleuth: Agent-based semantic integration of information in open and dynamic environments. In *Proceedings of the ACM SIGMOD International Conference on Management of Data*, volume 26,2, pages 195–206, New York, 13–15 1997. ACM Press.

[4] S. Bergamaschi, S. Castano, S. di Vimercati, S. Montanari, and M. Vincini. An intelligent approach to information integration. In *Proc.s of the International Conference on Formal Ontology in Information Systems (FOIS'98)*, Trento, Italy, 1998.

[5] A. Campbell, H. Chalupsky, and S. Shapiro. Ontological mediation: An analysis. unpublished manuscript.

[6] C. K. Chang and H. García-Molina. Conjunctive constraint mapping for data translation. In *Proceedings of the Third ACM International Conference on Digital Libraries*, Pittsburgh, Pa., 1998. ACM Press, New York.

[7] S. Chawathe, H. Garcia-Molina, J. Hammer, K. Ireland, Y. Papakonstantinou, J. D. Ullman, and J. Widom. The TSIMMIS project: Integration of heterogeneous information sources. In *16th Meeting of the Information Processing Society of Japan*, pages 7–18, Tokyo, Japan, 1994.

[8] W. W. Cohen and H. Hirsh. Learning the CLASSIC description logic: Theoretical and experimental results. In *Principles of Knowledge Representation and Reasoning: Proceedings of the Fourth International Conference (KR94)*. Morgan Kaufmann, 1994.

[9] A. Farquhar, R. Fikes, and J. Rice. The ontolingua server: A tool for collaborative ontology construction. In *Technical report, Stanford KSL 96-26*, 1996.

[10] D. Fensel, S. Decker, M. Erdmann, and R. Studer. Ontobroker in a nutshell. In *European Conference on Digital Libraries*, pages 663–664, 1998.

[11] T. Finin, R. Fritzson, D. McKay, and R. McEntire. KQML as an Agent Communication Language. In N. Adam, B. Bhargava, and Y. Yesha, editors, *Proceedings of the 3rd International Conference on Information and Knowledge Management (CIKM'94)*, pages 456–463, Gaithersburg, MD, USA, 1994. ACM Press.

[12] Foundation for Intelligent Physical Agents. FIPA 97 specification part 2: Agent communication language, October 1997. Version 2.0.

[13] M. R. Genesereth and R. E. Fikes. Knowledge Interchange Format, Version 3.0 Reference Manual. Technical Report Logic-92-1, Computer Science Department, Stanford University, Stanford, CA, USA, June 1992.

[14] P. Gennari and J. Musen. Mappings for reuse in knowledge-based systems. In *11 th Workshop on Knowledge Acquisition, Modelling and Management KAW 98*, Banff, Canada, 1998.

[15] N. Guarino and R. Poli. Formal ontology in conceptual analysis and knowledge representation. In *Special issue of the International Journal of Human and Computer Studies, vol. 43 n. 5/6, Academic Press.*, 1995.

[16] R. V. Guha and Douglas B. Lenat. Enabling agents to work together. *Commun. ACM*, 37(7):126–142, 1994.

[17] J. Heflin, J. Hendler, and S. Luke. SHOE: A knowledge representation language for internet applications. Technical Report CS-TR-4078, 1999.

[18] R. Hull. Managing semantic heterogeneity in databases: a theoretical prospective. In *Proc. ACM Symposium on Principles of Databases (Invited Tutorial)*, pages 51–61, 1997.

[19] V. Kashyap and A. P. Sheth. Semantic and schematic similarities between database objects: A context-based approach. *VLDB Journal: Very Large Data Bases*, 5(4):276–304, 1996.

[20] C. A. Knoblock and J. L. Ambite. Agents for information gathering. In Jeffrey M. Bradshaw, editor, *Software Agents*, pages 347–374. AAAI Press / The MIT Press, 1997.

[21] W.S. Li. Knowledge gathering and matching in heterogeneous databases. In *AAAI Spring Symposium on Information Gathering*, 1995.

[22] M. T. Pazienza, A. Stellato, and M. Vindigni. Purchasing the web: an agent based e-retail system with multilingual knowledge. In *Proc. of the IEEE/WIC International Conference on Web Intelligence (WI'03)*, Halifax, Canada, 2003.

[23] M. T. Pazienza and M. Vindigni. Language-based agent communication. In *proceedings of EKAW02, 13th International Conference on Knowledge Engineering and Knowledge Management, OMAS Workshop on Ontologies for Multi-Agent Systems*, Siguenza, Spain, 2002.

[24] M. T. Pazienza and M. Vindigni. Agent Based Ontological Mediation in IE Systems. In *Lecture Notes in Artificial Intelligence LNAI 2700*, Springer Verlag, Berlin Heidelberg, 2003.

[25] M.T. Pazienza, A. Stellato, M. Vindigni, A. Valarokos, and V. Karkaletsis. Ontology integration in a multilingual e-retail system. In *HCI International 2003, 10th International Conference on Human-Computer Interaction*, Crete (Greece), 2003.

[26] J. R. Searle. *Speech Acts: An Essay in the Philosophy of Language.* Cambridge University Press, Cambridge, England, 1969.

[27] John F. Sowa. *Knowledge representation: logical, philosophical and computational foundations.* Brooks/Cole Publishing Co., 2000.

[28] John F. Sowa. Ontology, metadata, and semiotics. In *Proceedings of the Linguistic on Conceptual Structures*, pages 55–81. Springer-Verlag, 2000.

[29] Gerhard Weiss, editor. *Multiagent Systems: A Modern Approach to Distributed Artificial Intelligence.* The MIT Press, Cambridge, MA, USA, 1999.

[30] G. Wiederhold and M. R. Genesereth. The conceptual basis for mediation services. *IEEE Expert*, 12(5):38–47, 1997.

[31] W. Wilks. Senses and texts. In *N. Ide (ed.) special issue of Computers and the Humanities, 31(2).*, 1997.

[32] M. J. Wooldridge and N. R. Jennings. *Intelligent Agents - Theories, Architectures, and Languages*, volume 890 of *Lecture Notes in Artificial Intelligence.* Springer-Verlag: Heidelberg, Germany, 1995.

Maria Teresa Pazienza
University of Rome "Tor Vergata"
Dept. of Computer Science, Systems and Production
Via del Politecnico 1
Rome (Italy)
e-mail: `pazienza@info.uniroma2.it`

Michele Vindigni
University of Brescia
Dept. of Quantitative Methods
Via C.da S.ta Chiara 15
25125 Brescia (Italy)
e-mail: `vindigni@eco.unibs.it`

Ontology Translation by Ontology Merging and Automated Reasoning

Dejing Dou, Drew McDermott and Peishen Qi

Abstract. Ontology translation is one of the most difficult problems that web-based agents must cope with. An *ontology* is a formal specification of a vocabulary, including axioms relating its terms. Ontology translation is best thought of in terms of ontology merging. The merge of two related ontologies is obtained by taking the union of the terms and the axioms defining them. We add *bridging axioms* not only as "bridges" between terms in two related ontologies but also to make this merge into a complete new ontology for further merging with other ontologies. Translation is implemented using an inference engine (*OntoEngine*), running in either a demand-driven (backward-chaining) or data-driven (forward chaining) mode. We illustrate our method by describing its application in an online ontology translation system, *OntoMerge*, which translates a dataset in the DAML notation to a new DAML dataset that captures the same information, but in a different ontology. A uniform internal representation, *Web-PDDL* is used for representing merged ontologies and datasets for automated reasoning.

1. Introduction

"Semantic interoperability" is the problem of achieving communication between two agents that work in overlapping domains, even if they use different notations and vocabularies to describe them. We follow common practice in using the word *ontology* as a formal specification of a vocabulary, including axioms relating its terms. *Ontology translation* is a key element of the semantic-operability problem; we define it as the problem of translating datasets, queries, or theories expressed using one ontology into the vocabulary supported by another. As web-based agents rely more and more on logical notations for communication and reasoning, the problem of ontology translation will become more important. In this paper, we argue that the problem can be thought of as a deduction task, which can be solved

---

This research was supported by the DARPA/DAML program.

by relatively straightforward theorem-proving techniques. However, the deduction must make use of axioms supplied by human experts. We are developing tools for making it easier for experts to create these axioms, but, for the foreseeable future, there is no way to eliminate humans from the loop entirely.

Previous work on ontology translation has made use of two strategies. One is to translate a dataset (i.e., a collection of facts) to a vocabulary associated with one big, centralized ontology that serves as an interlingua. Ontolingua [29] is a typical example of this strategy. The problem with this idea is its assumption that there can be a global ontology covering all existing ontologies. Creating such a thing would require agreement among all ontology experts to write translators between their own ontologies and the global one. Even if in principle such harmony can be attained, in practice keeping all ontologies — including the new ones that come along every day — consistent with the One True Theory would be very difficult. If someone creates a simple, lightweight ontology for a particular domain, he may be interested in translating it to neighboring domains, but can't be bothered to think about how it fits into a grand unified theory of knowledge representation.

The other strategy is to do ontology translation directly from a dataset in a (source) ontology to a dataset in another (target) ontology, on a dataset-by-dataset basis, without the use of any kind of interlingua. OntoMorph [23] is a typical example of this strategy. XSLT, the XML Style Language Transformations system [27], is often used to write such translators. For practical purposes this sort of program can be very useful, but it tends to rely on special properties of the datasets to be translated, and doesn't address the question of producing a general-purpose translator that handles any dataset in a given notation.

In this paper we present the theory and algorithms underlying our online ontology translation system, *OntoMerge*, which is based on a new approach to the translation problem: ontology translation by ontology merging and automated reasoning. The *merge* of two related ontologies is obtained by taking the union of the terms and the axioms defining them, using XML namespaces to avoid name clashes. We then add *bridging axioms* that relate the terms in one ontology to the terms in the other through the terms in the merge. We develop one merged ontology not only as a "bridge" between two related ontologies but also as a new ontology for further merging with other ontologies in the ontology community.

Although ontology merging requires ontology experts' intervention and maintenance, automated reasoning by an inference engine (*OntoEngine*) can be conducted in the merged ontology in either a demand-driven mode (backward-chaining) or a data-driven (forward chaining) mode.

This paper is organized as follows: Section 2 gives a detailed description of our approach to ontology translation, with the focus on forward chaining. Section 3 presents OntoMerge, an online ontology translation service and its application to a real-world translation problem. Section 4 describes our recent work on backward chaining and on semiautomatic merging tools for generating the bridging axioms. Section 6 concludes the paper.

2. Our Approach

2.1. Uniform Internal Representation

As we have pointed out, past work in the area of ontology translation has usually mixed up syntactic translation and semantic translation. We think it is more enlightening to separate the two. If all ontologies and datasets can be expressed in terms of some uniform internal representation, we can focus on semantic operations involving this representation, and handle syntax by translating into and out of it. Although the users don't need to know the details of this internal representation, getting them right is important to make our program work. For web-based agents, the representation should contain the following elements:

1. A set of XML namespaces
2. A set of types related to namespaces.
3. A set of symbols, each with a namespace and a type.
4. A set of axioms involving the symbols.

Our language, called "*Web-PDDL*," is the AI plan-domain definition language PDDL augmented with XML namespaces and more flexible notations for axioms [38]. Like the original PDDL [36], Web-PDDL uses Lisp-like syntax and is a strongly typed first-order logic language. Here is an example, part of a bibliography ontology [6] written in Web-PDDL.

```
(define (domain yale_bib-ont)
        (:extends
           (uri "http://www.w3.org/2000/01/rdf-schema#"
                :prefix rdfs))
        (:requirement :existential-preconditions
                      :conditional-effects)
        (:types Publication - Obj
              Article Book Techreport Incollection
              Inproceedings - Publication
              Literal - @rdfs:Literal)
        (:predicates (author p - Publication a - Literal)
              .....
```

The DAML version of this ontology is at

`http://www.daml.org/ontologies/81`.

Assertions using this ontology are written in the usual Lisp style: `(author pub20 "Tom Jefferson")`, for instance. Quantifiers and other reserved words use a similar parenthesized syntax.

We write types starting with capital letters. A constant or variable is declared to be of a type T by writing "`x -` T." To make the namespace extensions work, we have broadened the syntax for expressing how one ontology ("domain") extends another. In the original PDDL, there was no specification of how domain names were associated with domain definitions. On the web, the natural way to make the association is to associate domains with URIs, so we replace simple domain names with `uri` expressions, which include a `:prefix` specification similar to XML namespace prefixes. With this new feature, we can add `@prefix:` to each term in a Web-PDDL file to declare its namespace (ontology); for instance, `@rdfs:Literal` means a type from the `rdfs` namespace. Symbols without a prefix come from the local namespace.

Types can be thought of as sets, but they are not first-class terms in the language. Types are associated with expressions as well as with objects, so that when a domain definition is loaded into memory the Web-PDDL system can check whether an expression's type is incompatible with its syntactic context. Catching such type errors early makes debugging knowledge bases much easier. Types cannot in general be identified with "classes" as that term is used in Owl and other description logics [19]. For one thing, to make type checking feasible, the sets denoted by two types must be disjoint unless one is a subtype of the other. Nonetheless, in this paper we assume that classes and types are equivalent, leaving until a later date the issue of when classes must be treated as unary predicates instead of types.

It is sometimes useful to state that an object `x` has type T, where T is a subtype of the type it was declared with. For this purpose one can use the pseudo-predicate `is`, writing `(is` T `x)`.

If someone wants to use our system with an external representation other than Web-PDDL, there must exist a translator between the two. We have provided such a translator, which we call *PDDOWL*[1] [12], for translating between Web-PDDL and DAML. Writing translators for other XML-based web languages would not be difficult. In the following sections, we will use Web-PDDL to describe our work on ontology merging and automated reasoning, and ignore the external representation.

2.2. Ontology Merging and Bridging Axioms

Once we have cleared away the syntactic differences, the ontology translation problem is just semantic translation from the internal representation of a dataset in the source ontology to the internal representation of a dataset in the target ontology. For the rest of this paper, we will use two alternative bibliography ontologies as a running example. These were developed as contributions to the DAML Ontology Library, and while they are both obviously derived from Bibtex terminology, different design decisions were made by the people who derived them. One was developed at Yale, and we have given it the prefix `yale_bib` [4]; the other was developed at CMU, and it gets the prefix `cmu_bib` [5]. Although neither of them is a realistically complex ontology, the semantic differences that arise among corresponding types, predicates and axioms in these two ontologies serve as good illustrations of what happens with larger examples.

For example, both ontologies have a type called `Article`, but `@cmu_bib:Article` and `@yale_bib:Article` mean two different things. In the `yale_bib` ontology,

[1] Formerly called PDDAML

`Article` is a type which is disjoint with other types such as `Inproceedings` and `Incollection`. Therefore, `@yale_bib:Article` only means those articles which were published in a journal. By contrast, `@cmu_bib:Article` includes all articles which were published in a journal, proceedings or collection.

Another example: both of these ontologies have a predicate called `booktitle`. In the `cmu_bib` ontology, `(booktitle ?b - Book ?bs - String)` means that `?b` is a `Book` and it has title `?bs` as String. In the `yale_bib` ontology, `(booktitle ?p - Publication ?pl - Literal)` means `?p` is an `Inproceedings` or an `Incollection`, and `?pl` is the title of the proceedings or collection which contains `?p`.

Here is how these distinctions would come up in the context of an ontology-translation problem. Suppose the source dataset uses the `yale_bib` ontology, and includes this fragment:

```
(:objects ... Jefferson76 - Inproceedings)
...
(:facts ... (booktitle Jefferson76
                       "Proc. Cont. Cong. 1") ...)
```

The translated dataset in the `cmu_bib` ontology would then have to include this:

```
(:objects ... Jefferson76 - Article
              proc301 - Proceedings)
...
(facts ... (inProceedings Jefferson76 proc301)
           (booktitle proc301 "Proc. Cont. Cong. 1")
           ...)
```

Note that we have had to introduce a new constant, `proc301`, to designate the proceedings that `Jefferson76` appears in. Such *skolem terms* [41] are necessary whenever the translation requires talking about an object that can't be identified with any existing object.

It is tempting to think of the translation problem as a problem of rewriting formulas from one vocabulary to another. The simplest version of this approach is to use forward-chaining rewrite rules. A more sophisticated version is to use lifting axioms [22], axioms of the form `(if p q)`, where `p` is expressed entirely in the source ontology and `q` entirely in the target ontology. Such an axiom could be used in either a forward or backward (demand-driven) way, but the key improvement is that the axiom is a *statement* that is true or false (hopefully true), not an ad-hoc rule. This is essentially the idea we will use, except that we do away with any restrictions on the form or the vocabulary of the rules, and we adopt the term "bridging axiom" for them. A *bridging axiom* is then any axiom at all that relates the terms of two or more ontologies. By looking for such axioms, we separate the problem of relating two vocabularies from the problem of translating a particular dataset. This makes dataset translation a slightly more difficult problem, but the flexibility and robustness we gain are well worth it.

Another antecedent of our research is the work on data integration by the database community. For a useful survey see [31]. The work closest to ours is that of [33], who use the term "helper model" to mean approximately what we mean by "merged ontology." One difference is that in their framework the bridging rules are thought of as metarules that link pairs of data sources, whereas we embed the rules in the merged ontology. However, the greatest difference is that for databases the key concerns are that inter-schema translations preserve soundness and completeness. In the context of the Semantic Web, while soundness is important, it is not clear even what completeness would mean. So we have adopted a more empirical approach, without trying to assure that all possible useful inferences are drawn. Because it is entirely possible that an ontology could introduce undecidable inference problems, it's not clear how we could do better than that.

Bridging axioms use vocabulary items from both the source and target ontologies, and in fact may make use of new symbols. We have to put these symbols somewhere, so we introduce the concept of the *merged ontology* for a set of *component ontologies*, defined as a new ontology that contains all the symbols of the components, plus whatever new ones are needed. (Namespaces ensure that the symbols don't get mixed up.)

We can now think of dataset translation this way: Take the dataset and treat it as being in the merged ontology covering the source and target. Draw conclusions from it. The bridging axioms make it possible to draw conclusions from premises some of which come from the source and some from the target, or to draw target-vocabulary conclusions from source-language premises, or vice versa. The inference process stops with conclusions whose symbols come entirely from the target vocabulary; we call these *target conclusions*. Other conclusions are used for further inference. In the end, only the target conclusions are retained; we call this *projecting* the conclusions into the target ontology. In some cases, backward chaining would be more economical than the forward-chain/project process, as we discuss in Section 4. In either case, the idea is to push inferences through the pattern

$$\text{source} \Leftrightarrow \text{merge} \Leftrightarrow \text{target}.$$

Getting back to our example of merging the `yale_bib` and `cmu_bib` ontologies, we suppose we are using a merged ontology with prefix `cyb_merge`. When one term (type or predicate) in the `yale_bib` ontology has no semantic difference with another term in the `cmu_bib` ontology, we just use a new term with the same meaning as the old ones, then add bridging axioms to express that these three terms are the same. It happens that (as far as we can tell), `@cmu_bib:Book` is the same type as `@yale_bib:Book`, so we can introduce a type `Book` in the `cyb_merge` ontology, and define it to mean the same as the other two. Because types are not objects, we cannot write an axiom such as `(= Book @cmu_bib:Book)`. (A term with no namespace prefix should be assumed to live in the merged ontology.) So we have to use a pseudo-predicate (or, perhaps, "meta-predicate") `T->` and write rules of the sort shown below. We call these *type-translation rules*:

```
(axioms:
        (T-> @cmu_bib:Book Book)
        (T-> @yale_bib:Book Book)
        ...)
```

The general form of a type-translation rule is

```
        (T-> type1 type2 [P])
```

which means "type1 is equivalent to type2, except that objects of type1 satisfy property P." We call P the *distinguisher* of type1 and type2. If P is omitted, it defaults to true. For instance, suppose ontologies ont-A and ont-B both use the type Animal, but ont-A uses it to mean "terrestrial animal." Then the type-translation rule would be

```
  (T-> @ont-A:Animal @ont-B:Animal (terrestrial x))
```

All other axioms can be stated in ordinary first-order logic. Consider the predicate title, declared as (title ?p - Publication ?t - String) in both the yale_bib and cmu_bib ontologies. We just reuse the same symbol in our cyb_merge ontology. The corresponding bridging axioms become:

```
     (forall (?p - Publication ?ts - String)
             (iff (@cmu_bib:title ?p ?ts)
                  (title ?p ?ts)))

     (forall (?p - Publication ?ts - String)
             (iff (@yale_bib:title ?p ?ts)
                  (title ?p ?ts)))
```

When one term (type or predicate) in the yale_bib ontology has a semantic difference from the related term in the cmu_bib ontology, the bridging axioms become more substantial. Sometimes the axioms reflect our decision that one of the component ontologies gets a concept closer to "right" than the other. In our example, we might decide that cmu_bib has a better notion of Article (a type). Then we add bridge axioms for Article, @cmu_bib:Article, and @yale_bib:Article:

```
     (T-> @yale_bib:Article Article
          (exists (?j - Journal ?s - Issue)
                  (and (issue ?s ?j)
                       (contains ?s x))))
```

The bridging axioms above mean the following: in the cyb_merge ontology, Article is the same type as @cmu_bib:Article, which we prefer. But it is a @yale_bib:Article if and only if it is contained in some Journal.

We also add bridge axioms for booktitle, for which we decide that yale_bib's predicate makes more sense. The axioms relate @cmu_bib:booktitle, @yale_bib:booktitle, and our new predicate thus:

```
     (forall (?a - Article ?tl - String)
             (iff (@yale_bib:booktitle ?a ?tl)
                  (booktitle ?a ?tl)))
```

```
(forall (?a - Article ?tl - String)
        (iff (booktitle ?a ?tl)
             (exists (?b - Book)
                     (and (contains ?b ?a)
                          (@cmu_bib:booktitle
                             ?b ?tl)))))
```

We make `booktitle` in the merged ontology be the same predicate as `@yale-_bib:booktitle`, and then declare that, if and only if `?a` is an `Article` with `booktitle ?tl`, there exists some `Book ?b` such that `?b` contains `?a` and `?b` has `@cmu:booktitle ?tl`.

The full version of the merge of the `cmu_bib` and `yale_bib` ontologies can be found at [8].

Given the merged ontology, any term in either component ontology can be mapped into a term or terms in the `cyb_merge ontology`, some terms in `cyb_merge` can be projected back into terms in `cmu_bib` and some into terms in `yale_bib`. When some datasets represented in the `yale_bib` ontology need to be translated into the datasets represented in the `cmu_bib` ontology, an automated reasoning system, such as a theorem prover, can do inference by using those bridging axioms to implement translation, as we explained above. We will explore the forward-chaining option in depth in the next section.

We should mention one additional advantage of merged ontologies compared to direct translation rules between two related ontologies. The merged ontology serves not only as a "bridge" between the two given related ontologies, but also as a new ontology for further merging. If `foo1_bib`, `foo2_bib`, `foo3_bib` ... come out, we can use `cyb_merge` as a starting point for building a merged ontology that covers them all, or we may prefer a more incremental strategy where we merge `foo1_bib` and `foo2_bib`, creating, say "`foo_1_2_merge`," which would be used for translating between these two, then merge it with `cyb_merge` if and when a need arises for translations involving components of both merged ontologies. Exactly how many merged ontologies one needs, and how to select the right one given a new translation problem, are open research questions. But the point to make here is that the number of merged ontologies one needs is unlikely to be as large as the number of rewrite-rule sets one would need under the direct-translation approach. If there are N ontologies that need to be translated into each other, the direct-translation approach requires $N(N-1)$ rule sets (assuming for simplicity that all pairwise combinations occur), which could be cut to $N(N-1)/2$ if the rules are bidirectional. Our approach requires on the order of N merged ontologies. Of course, the exact amount of work saved depends on the sizes of the overlaps among the component ontologies, and how these sizes change as they are merged, both of which are hard to predict.

2.3. Automated Reasoning

It is common assumed that theorem proving will always lead to combinatorial explosions. The desire to avoid it has led researchers to develop web languages, such as RDF and DAML, that look more like description logics [19] and not so much like predicate calculus, putting up with the awkwardness of description logics in hopes of reaping some benefit from their tractable computational properties. We reverse that decision by translating DAML back into predicate calculus and doing old-fashioned theorem proving on the resulting internal representation. Our rationale is that, based on the examples we have looked at, we are inclined to think most of the theorem-proving problems that arise during ontology translation, while not quite within the range of Datalog [44, 45], are not that difficult [37]. Our inference engine, called *OntoEngine*, is a special-purpose theorem prover optimized for these sorts of problems. When some dataset in one or several source ontologies are input, OntoEngine can do inference in the merged ontology, projecting the resulting conclusions into one or several target ontologies automatically.

A key component of OntoEngine is the indexing structure that allows it to find formulas to be used in inference. Figure 1 shows what this structure looks like. As ontologies and datasets are loaded into OntoEngine, their contents are stored into this structure, as are the results of inferences.

We use a combination of tree-based and table-based indexing. At the top level we discriminate on the basis of namespace prefixes. For each namespace, there is an *ontology node*. The facts stored in an ontology node are next discriminated by predicate. The resulting *Predicate node*s are then discriminated into five categories:

1. Predicate declarations
2. Positive literals (atomic formulas)
3. Negative literals (negated atomic formulas)
4. Implications with the predicate in the premise
5. Implications with the predicate in the conclusion

Predicate declarations are expressions such as `(title ?p - Publication ?tl - String)`. Positive literals and negative literals are facts such as `(title b1 "Robo Sapiens")` and `(not (title b1 "John Nash"))`.

All other formulas from bridging axioms except type translation rules are expressed as *implications* in INF (Implicative Normal Form):

$$P_1 \wedge \cdots \wedge P_j \cdots \wedge P_n \Rightarrow Q_1 \wedge \cdots \wedge Q_k \wedge \cdots \wedge Q_m$$

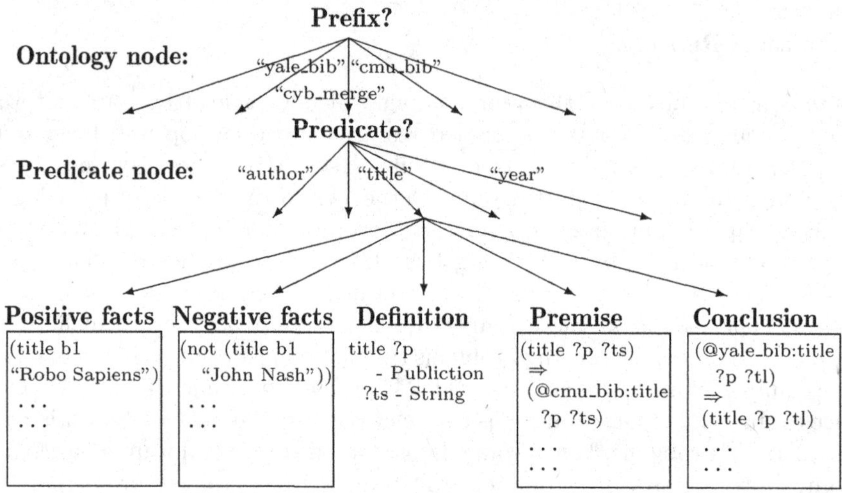

FIGURE 1. Indexing Structure for OntoEngine

where each P_i and Q_j is an atomic formula.[2] We use the word *clause* as a synonym for *implication.* The conjunction of P's we call the *premise* of the clause; the conjunction of Qs we call the *conclusion.*

In the indexing structure, the fourth and fifth categories are implications in which the predicate in question occurs in the premise or conclusion, respectively. (Of course, it could occur in both, in which case the formula would be indexed into both categories.)

So far, we have implemented a forward-chaining inference algorithm using the indexing structure of figure 1. The algorithm is shown in figure 2. In the procedure `Forwardchaining`, the phrase "best clause" needs some explanation. Theoretically, since we are drawing all possible inferences, it doesn't matter in what order we draw them. However, in our current version of the algorithm there are cases where doing the inferences in the wrong order would result in incompleteness. If clause 1 is

$$P_1 \Rightarrow Q_1 \wedge Q_2$$

and clause 2 is

$$P_2 \wedge Q_2 \Rightarrow Q_3$$

then our algorithm will fail to conclude Q_3 from P_1 and P_2 unless clause 1 runs first, because Q_2 has to be present for clause 2 to conclude Q_3. To compensate,

[2] An INF formula is equivalent to a set of one or more Horn clauses. A Horn clause is a disjunction of literals containing at most one positive literal [41]. Not all axioms can be expressed as Horn clauses, obviously, but it has been our empirical observation that bridging axioms mapping formulas to disjunctions "do not occur in nature." To some extent, this is because existing ontologies are written using relatively inexpressive languages, which leaves us in a slightly embarrassing position: If our advice that more expressive languages be used for ontologies is followed, then our current technique for doing ontology translation may turn out to be too weak.

we use a heuristic to try to ensure that we get as many conclusions as possible as early as possible. The heuristic is to choose the "best clause," defined as a weighted average:

$$W_1 \times \text{size of conclusion} - W_2 \times \text{size of premise}$$

The design of OntoEngine profitted from our study of KSL's JTP (Java Theorem Prover [10]). In the end we decided not to use JTP, but to develop our own prover, because JTP didn't contain some of the mechanisms we needed, especially type-constrained unification, while at the same time being oriented too strongly toward the traditional theorem-proving task.

3. Application: OntoMerge

We have embedded our deductive engine in an online ontology translation service called *OntoMerge* [11]. In addition to OntoEngine, OntoMerge uses PDDOWL [12] to translate into and out of the knowledge-representation language OWL [3]. OntoMerge serves as a semi-automated nexus for agents and humans to find ways of coping with notational differences, both syntactic and semantic, between ontologies. It accepts a dataset as a DAML file in the source ontology, and will respond with the dataset represented in the target ontology, also as a DAML file.

When receiving a DAML file, OntoMerge calls PDDOWL to translate it into a translation problem expressed as a Web-PDDL file which is input to online version of OntoEngine. To do anything useful, OntoEngine needs to retrieve a merged ontology from its library that covers the source and target ontologies. Such an ontology must be generated by human experts, and if no one has thought about this particular source/target pair, before, all OntoEngine can do is record the need for a new merger. (If enough such requests come in, the ontology experts may wake up and get to work.) Assuming a merged ontology exists, located typically at some URL, OntoEngine tries to load it in. If it is written in DAML or other Web language, OntoEngine first calls PDDOWL to translate it to Web-PDDL file, then loads it in. Finally, OntoEngine loads the dataset which needs to be translated in and processes those facts one by one until all possible inferences have been generated. To get a final output file in DAML, OntoMerge calls PDDOWL again to translate back to DAML the projection of the Web-PDDL dataset to the target vocabulary.

OntoMerge has worked well so far, although our experience is inevitably limited by the demand for our services. In addition to the toy example from the dataset in the `yale_bib` ontology to the dataset in the `cmu_bib` ontology, we have also run it to translate a dataset with more than 2300 facts about military information of Afghanistan using more than 10 ontologies into a dataset in the `map` ontology [15]. About 900 facts are related to the geographic features of Afghanistan in the `geonames` ontology [13] and its airports in the `airport` ontology [14]. We have merged the `geonames` ontology and the `airport` ontology with the `map` ontology. After OntoEngine loads the two merged ontologies

```
Procedure Process(facts)
    For each oneFact in facts Do
        Forwardchaining(oneFact)
```

```
Procedure Forwardchaining(fact)
    For each INF clause from corresponding Premise table in best-first order
        newFacts = Modus_Ponens(fact, clause)
        For each newFact in newFacts Do Forwardchaining(newFact)
```

```
Function Modus_Ponens(fact, clause) returns facts
  facts= empty set
  oneAtf = the corresponding AtomicFormula for fact in left-side of clause
  restAtfs = the remaining AtomicFormulas in left-side of clause
  substi = Unify(oneAtf, fact)
  If substi is not empty Then substitutions = Conj_match(substi, restAtfs)
  If substitutions is not empty
  Then newFacts = substituting right-side of clause with substitutions
  For each newFact in newFacts Do
      If newFact belongs to target ontology Then store it
      Else add it into facts which will be returned for further inference
  Return facts
```

```
Function Conj_match(substi, Atfs) return substitutions
  substitutions = substi
  If Atfs is empty Then return substitutions
  Get newAtfs by substituting Atfs with substi
  facts = the corresponding facts for FIRST (newAtfs)
  For each oneFact in facts do
      oneSubsti = Unify(FIRST(newAtfs), oneFact)
      If oneSubsti is not empty
      Then oneSubstis = Conj_match(oneSubsti, REST(newAtfs))
              add oneSubstis into substis
  If substis is not empty Then add substis into substitutions
  Else substitutions = empty set
  Return substitutions
```

FIGURE 2. The forward-chaining algorithm

Function Unify(*oneAtf*, *fact*) return substitutions
  For each *variable* from *oneAtf* and its corresponding *constant* from *fact* **Do**
    If Typecheck(*variable*, *constant*)
    Then add {*variable*/*constant*} to *substitutions*
  Return *substitutions*

Function Typecheck(*variable*, *constant*) return boolean
  match = false
  If *variable*'s type is same as or the super type of *constant*'s type
  Then *match* = true
  Else
    typeCons = type of *constant*
    fact = (is *typeCons* *constant*)
    Forwardchaining(*fact*)
    If exist *var*, (is *typeCons* *var*) is the only premise of some clause and
      variable's type is same as or the super type of *var*'s type
    Then *match* = true
  Return *match*

FIGURE 3. The forward-chaining algorithm (cont'd)

in, it can accept all 2300 facts and translate those 900 facts in the `geonames` and `airport` ontologies into about 450 facts in the `map` ontology in 5 seconds [3]. For each `@geonames:Feature` or each `@airport:Airport`, the bridging axioms in the merged ontologies will be used for inference to create a pair of skolem terms with types `@map:Point` and `@map:Location` in the fact like (`@map:location` *Location01 Point02*). The values of the `@geonames:longitude` (`@airport:longitude`) property and the `@geonames:latitude` (`@airport:latitude`) property for each `@geonames:Feature` (`@airport:Airport`) can be translated into the values of the `@map:longitude` property and the `@map:latitude` property for the corresponding `@map:Location`. The value of the `@airport:icaoCode` property for each `@airport:Airport` and the value of `@geonames:uniqueIdentifier` property for each `@geonames:Feature` can be translated into the values of `@map:label` property for the corresponding `@map:Point`. The reason that the translated dataset only has 450 facts is some facts in the `geonames` and `airport` ontologies can't be translated to any term in the the `map` ontology.

[3] After the submission of the original paper to EKAW02 OMAS workshop, we have improved the performance of OntoEngine. This performance is an order of magnitude better than that originally reported.

Prospective users should check out the OntoMerge website[4]. The website is designed to solicit descriptions of ontology-translation problems, even when OntoMerge can't solve them. However, we believe that in most cases we can develop a merged ontology within days that will translate any dataset from one of the ontologies in the merged set to another.

4. Recent Work

4.1. Backward Chaining

Although so far forward-chaining deduction has been sufficient for our needs, we recognize that backward chaining is also necessary. For example, suppose one agent has a query:

```
(and (father Fred ?x) (travel ?x ?y) (desti ?y "SF"))
```

which means "Did Fred's father travel to South Florida?" This query could be answered by another agent with its datasets in another ontology, which may have different meanings for `travel` or `desti`. In this case, the ontology-translation problem becomes the problem of answering the query in the target ontology with the datasets in the source ontology.

In addition, backward chaining may be necessary in the middle of forward chaining. For example, when OntoEngine is unifying the fact `(P c1)` with `(P ?x)` in the axiom:

$$(\texttt{P}\ ?\texttt{x}) \land (\texttt{member}\ ?\texttt{x}\ [\texttt{c1}, \texttt{c2}, \texttt{c3}]) \Rightarrow (\texttt{Q}\ ?\texttt{x})$$

it can't conclude `(Q c1)` unless it can verify that `c1` is a member of the list `[c1, c2, c3]`, and the only way to implement this deduction is by doing backward chaining.

We have embedded a backward-chaining reasoner into OntoEngine for querying through different ontologies. We have given a detailed example in [25] of reasoning using two different genealogy ontologies, one developed by Dynamics Research Corporation (DRC) [17] and one developed by BBN technologies [16]. The dataset is a set of several hundred facts expressed in the BBN genealogy; a typical query is "Who was the queen of Henry VI and what is date of their marriage?," and is expressed in the DRC genealogy,

A full treatment of backward chaining across ontologies would raise the issue of *query optimization*, which we have not focused on yet. There is a lot of work in this area, and we will cite just two references: [28, 18]. We intend to focus more on overcoming complicated semantic differences when querying through different ontologies.

4.2. Semiautomatic Tools for Ontology Merging

Our merging of two related ontologies is obtained by taking the union of the terms and the axioms defining them. We then add bridging axioms that relate the terms in one ontology to the terms in the other through the terms in the merge.

[4]http://cs-www.cs.yale.edu/homes/dvm/daml/ontology-translation.html

Semi-Automatic tools for generating bridging axioms. To generate these bridging axioms, we must first find out the correspondence between the concepts of two ontologies, which is the target of ontology mapping. In many cases, only humans can understand the complicated relationships that can hold between the mapped concepts. Generating these axioms must involve participation from humans, especially domain experts. You can't write bridging axioms between two medical-informatics ontologies without help from biologists.

The generation of an axiom will often be an interactive process. Domain experts keep on editing the axiom till they are satisfied with the relation expressed by it. Unfortunately, domain experts are usually not very good at the formal logic syntax that we use for the axioms. It is necessary for the axiom-generating tool to hide the logic behind the scenes whenever possible. Then domain experts can check and revise the axioms using the formalism they are familiar with, or even using natural-language expressions. So instead of seeing a logical fact representation such as

```
(booktitle Jefferson76 "Proc. Cont. Cong. 1")
```

they will see a sentence like: "The title of the book containing Jefferson76 is 'Proc. Cont. Cong. 1'," assuming that there is a natural-language template associated with the predicate `booktitle`:

```
(booktitle ?pub - Publication ?lit - String) =>
   ("the title of the book containing "
      (:np "publication" ?pub)
      "is " not?
      (:select ((is-var ?lit) => ("the string " ?lit))
               (=> "'" ?lit "'"))))
```

in which `:np` starts a noun phrase and `(is-var ?var)` checks whether `?var` is bound to a variable or a non-variable. The elements in the template are delimited by whitespace and parenthesis. The whole NL expression is the concatenation of the strings generated from each elements. It is not hard for domain experts to produce this kind of template for the predicates in their domain. The depth of the coverage is up to them. Any symbols without templates will be processed using default phrases.

We have developed a semi-automatic mapping tool and a template-based natural language generator, and embedded them into our axiom-generating system. Domain experts now can generate the INF format bridging axioms as specified in Section 2.3.

The following example shows how we generate the bridging axioms between the two `booktitle` predicates in the bibliography ontologies. The mapping tool can easily suggest a mapping between these two properties because they share the same name. Domain experts are aware that the semantic meaning of yale_bib's `booktitle` conforms to that of BibTex, and prefer it be copied into the merged ontology directly. However they also know that the semantic meaning of cmu_bib's `booktitle` is not quite the same. The suggested mapping can be corrected by adding another predicate `inProceedings` (or `inCollection`) to the cmu_bib side, along with appropriate NL templates. Then the domain experts can fill in the underlined slots with exemplar instances in the following two groups of natural language expressions, and try to make the whole expression denote the correct meaning.

> "the title of the book containing a publication is the string ?lit" ⟵ @yale_bib:booktitle
>
> **implies**
>
> "the title of a publication (a book) is the string ?lit" ⟵ @cmu_bib:booktitle
> (and | or | implies | implied by)
> 'a publication appears in the Proceedings ?proc" ⟵ @cmu_bib:inProceedings

An acceptable fill-in might be:

> "the title of the book containing Jefferson76 is the string 'Proc. Cont. Cong. 1'"
>
> **implies**
>
> "the title of Proc11 (a book) is the string 'Proc. Cont. Cong. 1'"
> and
> "Jefferson76 appears in Proc11"

Our axiom-generation system then tries to derive the axiom by generalization. It is not always simply a matter of replacing all the constants with variables and slapping universal quantifiers over them. In the example above, Proc11 shows up only on the right-hand side of the implication. It's possible that "Proc11" is a special constant that is part of the meaning of "booktitle." (The translation of `(chinese Lao)` in one ontology might be `(citizen Lao china)`. This indicates that the translation of `(chinese ?x)` is `(citizen ?x china)`, because `china` is a special constant that is part of the translation of `chinese`.) But in fact in deriving the proper axiom for translating `booktitle`, "Proc11" should be turned into an existential variable. Such choices must be made by the human users.

Consistency checking of the generated axioms will also alleviate the burdens on domain experts. For instance, in the final correct axiom, the type of the variable which takes the place of Jefferson76 should be narrowed down to `@yale_bib:InProceedings` from the much broader concept `Publication`, otherwise inconsistency would come up because the `cmu_bib:inProceedings` predicate won't hold for a `yale_bib:InCollection`.

5. Related work

Lots of research has been done on ontology mapping, including implemented systems named CUPID [34], GLUE [24] and CTX-Match [42]. Some existing systems do not recognize an explicit boundary between ontology mapping and ontology merging; these include Chimaera [39], PROMPT [40], FCA-Merge [43], and MOMIS [21]. The matching algorithms they used can be divided into two ways: ontology-based and instance-based. Instance-based approaches mainly exploit machine learning techniques to uncover the sematic relations among the concepts. Examples include GLUE and FCA-Merge. However, the situation we met in our ontology translation problem is that usually we just have two ontologies and data available in only one of them. Ontology-based approaches should be more applicable to such situations. Three levels of knowledge are utilized in locating the mappings: syntactic, structural and semantic matching. Syntactic matching focuses on the name similarity between nodes' labels, as in CUPID. Structural matching analysis the neighborhood of ontology nodes, as in PROMPT and Chimaera. Semantic matching tries to find the mapping between meanings of the concepts. Additional knowledge information like a pre-compiled thesaurus or WordNet [26] are usually used to find semantic mappings, as in CTX-Match.

However, most of the mapping tools can only find mappings with "subclassOf", "subpropertyOf" or "equivalent" relationships. The reason why it is hard to do anything better is that most current ontologies contain more types (i.e., classes) and predicates than axioms which relate these types and predicates. Many ontologies contain no axioms at all, even when it is obvious that their designers know more about the domain than subclass relationships. We expect that as ontology designers become more sophisticated, they will want, nay, will demand, the ability to include more axioms in what they design. Axiom-driven matching tools will go beyond those simple relationships, and try to find matches between ontologies that preserve the truth of the axioms on either side. For example, the two `booktitle` predicates in the yale_bib and cmu_bib bibliography ontologies share the same name, but any attempt to view one of them as a subproperty of the other will cause the axioms involving them to become untranslatable.

Ontology-mapping tools typically return a list of pairs of concepts, one from each source ontology.. The merging tools do return the merged ontology, but most of them consider merging only classes. All the properties in the original ontologies are copied into the merged one, unless they mean exactly the same thing. So a dataset in the source ontology can be transferred to the merged ontology, but still not in a form understandable by an agent using the target ontology. To solve the ontology-translation problem, we need a merged ontology in which the mappings are expressed as a set of bridging axioms which explain how those concepts in the original ontologies are related.

An approach similar to ours is presented in [35]; their MAFRA framework uses a semantic bridging ontology (SBO) to encode the mappings. An instance of SBO contains axiomatic rules that transform instances of a source entity to instances of target entity. This is not quite as general as our axioms, but in practice the difference is probably of little importance.

We should also compare our system with other programs for doing inference, rule-based or otherwise. There are by now an abundance of rule languages for manipulating RDF. Any query system can be made into a rule system by providing a notation for attaching an action to a query, such that the action is performed for each instance of the query retrieved, and by now there are dozens of query systems for RDF. (A good survey is [30].) Many of these systems could be adapted to suit our purposes. Indeed, OntoMerge incorporates some infrastructure code from the open-source Jena RDF-inference toolkit [9], and we could no doubt improve the performance of OntoMerge by borrowing further optimization techniques from other sources. However, no pre-existing inference engine did everything we needed our engine to do. In particular, most rule-based inference software does not do equality substitution, nor are existing packages sensitive to the goal of drawing inferences in a target ontology. Including these facilities means tinkering with the innards of an inference engine; it would be impossible or extremely awkward to use someone else's inference system as a black box whose output we filter.

The dominant pattern for inference on the semantic web involves description-logic notations such as OWL [19, 3]. There are several efficient inference systems available for such logics [32], many of which have been equipped with front ends for RDF. The term *description logic (DL)* covers a family of subsets of first-order logic with the following features:

- All predicates are unary or binary. Unary predicates are called *classes*, and binary predicates are called *roles*. The name "class" is used for unary predicates because it is often thought of as the set of all entities the predicate is true of.
- Class terms can be created by set-theoretic operations on existing classes, plus the use of *restrictions* such as $\exists role.class$, which is the class of objects x such that there is a y such that $class(y)$ and $role(x, y)$. E.g.,

  $$\texttt{(Person} \sqcap \exists \texttt{ has-child.Female)(Fred)}$$

  asserts that `Fred` is a person who has a female child.
- Role terms can be created (in some DLs) by taking inverses $(\cdot^{-1})$ and compositions of roles.
- Some DLs extend the basic framework by allowing axioms asserting that one class is a subset of or equal to another. Some allow classes to be recursively defined.
- The standard reasoning tasks performed by DL systems include
  - *classification*: determining whether an individual belongs to a class.
  - *subsumption*: determining whether one class is a subset of another.

One reason DLs have attracted a lot of attention is that for many of them the classification and subsumption tests are decidable. Variations in the expressiveness correspond to variations in computational complexity. However, DLs can't approach the expressiveness of first-order logic without giving up decidability and all those complexity analyses. The question, therefore, is how much expressiveness is needed for the ontology-translation task.

Unfortunately, there are two reasons why DLs fall short. One is that they lack a robust notion of forward chaining. They can be used for answering queries in merged ontologies, but not for translating datasets.

However, the more fundamental reason for the inadequacy of DLs is that even simple bridging axioms are difficult to express. Consider this axiom from section 2.2:

```
(forall (?a - Article ?tl - String)
        (iff (booktitle ?a ?tl)
             (exists (?b - Book)
                     (and (contains ?b ?a)
                          (@cmu_bib:booktitle
                               ?b ?tl)))))
```

Even though the axiom uses only types (a special case of classes) and binary predicates, it is impossible to express it as a standard DL axiom. The best we can do is something like this:

$$(\exists \texttt{booktitle}^{-1}.\texttt{Article}) \\ = \exists \texttt{@cmu\_bib:booktitle}^{-1}.\exists \texttt{contains}.\texttt{Article}$$

In English: "The strings that are booktitles of articles (in the merged ontology) are the strings that are booktitles (in the CMU ontology) of books that contain articles." This formula falls short because it doesn't *equate* the article corresponding to an article title on the left side of the axiom with the article corresponding to a containing book on the right side. To state that, we would need to use a very expressive DL that allowed equations of role compositions:

$$\texttt{booktitle} = \texttt{contains}^{-1} \circ \texttt{@cmu\_bib:booktitle}$$

However, in conjunction with other required expressivity enhancements, adding role-composition equations makes DLs undecidable [20], so we end up with a clumsy notation that may be no more efficient than first-order logic.

6. Conclusions

We have described a new approach to implement ontology translation by ontology merging and automated reasoning. Here are the main points we tried to make:

1. Ontology translation is best thought of in terms of *ontology merging.* The merge of two related ontologies is obtained by taking the union of the terms and the axioms defining them, then adding bridging axioms that relate the terms in one ontology to the terms in the other through the terms in the merge.
2. It is important to separate syntactic translation and semantic translation. If all ontologies and datasets can be expressed in terms of some uniform internal

representation, semantic translation can be implemented by automatic reasoning. For this to be feasible, the internal representation must be as flexible as possible. We believe that the language we use, Web-PDDL, has about the right degree of flexibility. Translating from other notations to Web-PDDL is performed by dialect-dependent modules. An example is our PDDOWL system, which transforms formulas in Web-PDDL to DAML, and back.

3. We have developed a special-purpose inference system, OntoEngine, for performing automated reasoning in merged ontologies for the purpose of ontology translation. The key features of OntoEngine are its indexing structures for managing multiple ontologies, its ability to do equality substitution, its mechanism for handling existential variables and skolem terms, control rules for ordering both forward and backward chaining operations, and the use of type- constrained unification.
4. We set up an ontology translation server, OntoMerge, to apply and validate our method. We hope OntoMerge can attract more ontology translation problem from other people and get their feedback, which will help our future work.
5. We designed a semi-automatic tool which can help generate the bridge axioms to merge ontologies. It provides a natural-language interface for domain experts, who are usually not good at logic formalism, to construct and edit the axioms.

References

[1] http://www.w3c.org/TR/wsdl

[2] http://www.daml.org

[3] http://www.w3.org/TR/owl-guide

[4] http://www.cs.yale.edu/homes/dvm/daml/ontologies/daml/yale_bib.daml

[5] http://www.daml.ri.cmu.edu/ont/homework/atlas-publications.daml

[6] http://cs-www.cs.yale.edu/homes/ddj/ontologies/yale_bib_ont.pddl

[7] http://cs-www.cs.yale.edu/homes/ddj/ontologies/cmu_atlas_publications.pddl

[8] http://cs-www.cs.yale.edu/homes/dvm/daml/ontologies/pddl/cmu_yale_bib_merge.pddl

[9] http://jena.sourceforge.net/tutorial/RDF_API/index.html

[10] http://www.ksl.stanford.edu/software/JTP

[11] http://cs-www.cs.yale.edu/homes/dvm/daml/ontology-translation.html

[12] http://cs-www.cs.yale.edu/homes/dvm/daml/pddl_daml_translator.html

[13] http://www.daml.org/2002/04/geonames/geonames-ont.daml

[14] http://www.daml.org/2001/10/html/airport-ont.daml

[15] http://www.daml.org/2001/06/map/map-ont.daml

[16] http://www.daml.org/2001/01/gedcom/gedcom.daml

[17] http://orlando.drc.com/daml/Ontology/Genealogy/3.1/Gentology-ont.daml

[18] S. Adali, K. Candan, Y. Papakonstantinou, and V. S. Subrahmanian. Query caching and optimization in distributed mediator systems. In *Proc. ACM SIGMOD Conf. on Management of Data*, pages 137–148, 1996.

[19] F. Baader, D. Calvanese, D. McGuinness, D. Nardi, and P. Patel-Schneider. *The Description Logic Handbook; Theory, Implementation, and Applications.* Cambridge University Press, 2003.

[20] F. Baader and W. Nutt. Basic description logics. In F. Baader, D. Calvanese, D. McGuinness, D. Nardi, and P. Patel-Schneider, editors, *The Description Logic Handbook; Theory, Implementation, and Applications*, pages 43–95. Cambridge University Press, 2003.

[21] D. Beneventano, S. Bergamaschi, F. Guerra, and M. Vincini. The MOMIS approach to information integration. In *ICEIS (1)*, pages 194–198, 2001.

[22] S. Buvac and R. Fikes. A declarative formalization of knowledge translation. In *Proceedings of the ACM CIKM: The 4th International Conference on Information and Knowledge Management*, 1995.

[23] H. Chalupsky. Ontomorph: A translation system for symbolic logic. In *Proc. Int'l. Con. on Principles of Knowledge Representation and Reasoning*, pages 471–482, 2000. San Francisco: Morgan Kaufmann.

[24] A. Doan, J. Madhavan, P. Domingos, and A. Halevy. Learning to map between ontologies on the semantic web. In *Proceedings of the World-Wide Web Conference (WWW-2002)*, 2002.

[25] D. Dou, D. McDermott, and P. Qi. Ontology translation on the semantic web. In *Proc. Int'l Conf. on Ontologies, Databases and Applications of SEmantics (ODBASE) 2003*, pages 952–969, 2003. LNCS 2888 Springer-Verlag.

[26] C. Fellbaum, editor. *WordNet: An Electronic Lexical Database.* MIT Press, 1998.

[27] Khun Lee Fung *XSLT: Working with XML and HTML.* Addison-Wesley 2001

[28] M. R. Genesereth, A. M. Keller, and O. M. Duschka. Infomaster: an information integration system. In *Proceedings of the ACM SIGMOD International Conference on Management of Data*, pages 539–542, 1997.

[29] T. Gruber. Ontolingua: A Translation Approach to Providing Portable Ontology Specifications. *Knowledge Acquisition* , 5(2):199–200, 1993.

[30] P. Haase, J. Broekstra, A. Eberhart, and R. Volz. A comparison of rdf query languages. In *Proceedings of the Third International Semantic Web Conference, Hiroshima, Japan, 2004.*, NOV 2004.

[31] A. Y. Halevy. Answering queries using views: A survey. *VLDB J* , 10(4):270–294, 2001.

[32] I. Horrocks and P. F. Patel-Schneider. FaCT and DLP. *Lecture Notes in Computer Science*, 1397:27, 1998.

[33] J. Madhavan, P. A. Bernstein, P. Domingos, and A. Halevy. Representing and Reasoning about Mappings between Domain Models. In *Proc. AAAI 2002*, 2002.

[34] J. Madhavan, P. A. Bernstein, and E. Rahm. Generic schema matching with cupid. In *Proc. 27th Int. Conf. on Very Large Data Bases (VLDB).*

[35] A. Maedche, B. Motik, N. Silva, and R. Volz. , mafra - a mapping framework for distributed ontologies. In *Proceedings of EKAW2002*, pages 235–250, 2002.

[36] D. McDermott. The Planning Domain Definition Language Manual. Technical Report 1165, Yale Computer Science, 1998. (CVC Report 98-003) Available at `ftp://ftp.cs.yale.edu/pub/mcdermott/software/pddl.tar.gz`.

[37] D. McDermott, M. Burstein, and D. Smith. Overcoming ontology mismatches in transactions with self-describing service agents. In *Proc. Semantic Web Working Symposium*, pages 285–302, 2001.

[38] D. McDermott and D. Dou. Representing Disjunction and Quantifiers in RDF. In *Proceedings of International semantic Web Conference 2002*, pages 250–263, 2002.

[39] D. McGuinness, R.Fikes, J.Rice, and S.Wilder. An Environment for Merging and Testing Large Ontologies. In *Proceedings of the Seventh International Conference on Principles of Knowledge Representation and Reasoning (KR2000)*, 2000.

[40] N. F. Noy and M. A. Musen. Prompt: Algorithm and tool for automated ontology merging and alignment. Technical Report 2000-0831, *Proc. AAAI* **17** Also available as Stanford SMI, 2000.

[41] S. Russell and P. Norvig. *Artificial Intelligence: A Modern Approach (2nd edition)*. Prentice Hall, 2002.

[42] L. Serafini, P. Bouquet, B. Magnini, and S. Zanobini. An algorithm for matching contextualized schemas via sat. In *Proc. CONTEX'03*, 2003.

[43] G. Stumme and A. Maedche. Ontology merging for federated ontologies on the semantic web. In *Proceedings of the International Workshop for Foundations of Models for Information Integration (FMII-2001)*, September 2001.

[44] Jeffrey D. Ullman *Principles of Database and Knowledge-Base Systems,* **1**. New York: Computer Science Press. 1988a

[45] Jeffrey D. Ullman *Principles of Database and Knowledge-Base Systems,* **2** New York: Computer Science Press 1988b

Dejing Dou
Department of Computer and Information Science
120 Deschutes Hall
University of Oregon
Eugene, OR 97403-1202
e-mail: `dou@cs.uoregon.edu`

Drew McDermott
Computer Science Department
Yale University
P.O. Box 208285
New Haven, CT 06520-8285
e-mail: `drew.mcdermott@yale.edu`

Peishen Qi
Computer Science Department
Yale University
P.O. Box 208285
New Haven, CT 06520-8285
e-mail: `peishen.qi@yale.edu`

Collaborative Understanding of Distributed Ontologies in a Multiagent Framework: Experiments on Operational Issues

Leen-Kiat Soh

Abstract. This chapter describes a set of experiments that uses a multiagent framework for collaborative understanding of distributed ontologies (CUDO). Our current focus is on the operational issues of such collaboration among the agents, with each agent managing an information database in a distributed information retrieval simulation. To facilitate collaborative understanding, each agent maintains an ontology and a translation table with other neighboring agents to map between each own concepts and the neighbors'. Based on an infrastructure prototype, our experiments have focused on how neighborhood profiling, the translation tables, and query experience impact the collaborative activities among the agents. The specific objectives of our analyses are to investigate (a) the recognition of useful neighbors for sharing queries, (b) the efficiency of query handling in different real-time scenarios and with different resource constraints (such as the number of threads and available translations), and (c) the effects of different concepts and query demands on collaborative understanding. Our results show that the different resource constraints influence the collaborative activities significantly and thus also impact how the agents learn of each others ontologies.

Keywords. Multiagent systems, distributed ontology learning, dynamic profiling.

1. Introduction

In the real world, where human agents are autonomous, distributed, and capable of individual learning, there are different languages. To communicate or collaborate, humans speaking different languages either learn a common language or use a translator. Learning a common language that is not a person's native tongue usually incurs additional effort on that person. On the other hand, speaking through a translator may not be always feasible and may be too costly. Similarly, in a multiagent environment, autonomous and distributed agents may encounter different events, gather different experiences, and learn different ontologies. To improve communication, these agents must be able to understand each other. Our research, called Collaborative Understanding of Distributed Ontologies (CUDO), is to investigate these issues in a multiagent system, in which each agent maintains an information database and the corresponding ontology. In this chapter, we investigate the role of operational issues in how these agents collaborate in a distributed information retrieval simulation.

Our CUDO research is motivated by our long-term research goals: (1) to promote understanding among agents of a community, thus reducing communication costs and inter-agent traffic, (2) to improve cooperation among neighbors of a community, thus enhancing the strength (productivity, effectiveness, efficiency) of a neighborhood and supporting the distributed effort of the community, (3) to encourage pluralism and decentralization within a multi-agent community - specialization of agents of a community since each agent can rely on its neighbors for tasks not covered by its capabilities, and (4) to enable collaborative learning to improve the throughput of the community, the intelligence in communication and task allocation, the self-organization within the community, and integrity of the community.

We originally proposed our CUDO framework in [1] where we identified two strategies with which an agent can learn to improve its ontology. First, users can teach them - by supplying a list of words and what the classifying concepts are for that list of words. Second, an agent can learn through its interactions with its neighbors. As a result, each agent learns its own concepts based on its experiences and specialties. When a new concept arrives, the agent needs to incorporate it into its ontology and its translation table. This is supported by three important components: conceptual learning, translation, and interpretation, with a Dempster-Shafer belief system [2].

Our current research focuses on developing and analyzing the operational components of our framework, applied to a document retrieval problem. Each agent interacts with a user who submits queries based on keywords. These keywords are known as concepts in the agents. The goal of this problem is satisfy as many queries as possible and as well as possible. An agent may turn to its neighbors for help. Thus, this collaboration facilitates the distributed ontology learning.

In this chapter, we report on our experiments applying a prototype infrastructure of CUDO in a distributed information retrieval simulation. The objective is to *understand how collaborative understanding of distributed ontologies is impacted by operational issues such as queries, the number of communication threads, the variability within the translation tables and so on.* Therefore, in this paper, we focus on the operational design of our infrastructure and the investigations on how neighborhood profiling, translation tables, and query experience influence the relationship among collaborative agents. Our experiments are aimed at studying (a) the learning of useful neighbors for sharing queries, (b) the efficiency of query handling in different real-time scenarios and with different resource constraints, and

(c) the effects of different ontological concepts and query demands on collaborative understanding.

Here is how we organize the following discussions. First, we briefly outline the methodology of our framework in Section 2. Then we describe our implementation. Note that though this chapter studies the operational issues in our experiments, we include the ontological components in both Sections 2 and 3. Subsequently, we discuss our experiments and results in Section 4. Finally, we conclude.

2. Framework

In our CUDO framework, the multiagent system is one in which agents can exchange queries and messages to learn about each other's ontology. To improve the communication and collaboration efficiency, agents determine whether some translation is worth learning, which neighbors to communicate to, how to handle and distribute queries, and how to plan for agent activities. The framework consists of two sets of components. The operational components allow the agents to work together in a multiagent system. The ontological components allow the agents to communicate and understand each other.

Our discussion here is related to [6]. In [6], however, the agents were not able to learn collaboratively in a multiagent system. Instead, the learning was conducted only between two agents via exchange of concepts (ontologies) where the agents were neither able to adapt to changes in concept definitions nor able to handle multiple assertions from different neighbors. Moreover, our framework addresses translation and interpretation of concepts, query processing and composition for collaboration among agents, and action planning based on traffic and agent activities, which indirectly control the learning rates of the agents.

In the following, we briefly introduce and describe the operational and ontological components of our framework. Interested users are referred to [1] and [3] for more details. Here we define the neighborhood of an agent as a subset of the multiagent system such that the agent is able to contact each of its neighbors. Neighborhoods are assumed to be overlapping.

2.1. Ontological Components

We represent an ontology item as a vector. Each vector consists of a concept and then a list of links describing that concept. Each agent maintains a set of such vectors and collectively such a set is known as the ontology of the agent. Note that here we refer a link to a URL address of an online document.

Each agent maintains a comprehensive translation table. Each table lists the concepts that the agent knows and maps them to the corresponding concepts of the neighboring agents. Each translation is accompanied with a credibility value. Table 1 shows an example. In the example, the agent has four neighbors. It knows of concepts such as "basketball" and "car". For "basketball", it is similar to N1's "NBA" with a credibility value of 2.1, N2's "Bball" with a credibility value of 1.0, and N4's "Basketball" with a credibility value of 3.4. However, it does not have a translation for "basketball" between itself and N3.

Concepts	**N1**	**N2**	**N3**	**N4**
basketball	*NBA 2.1*	*Bball 1.0*	*NIL*	Basketball 3.4
car	*NIL*	*Auto 2.1*	*Car 1.0*	*Move 1.0*
...				

TABLE 1. A translation table example.

In general, in the beginning, each agent has an empty translation table. At the birth of an agent, an agent learns from the users' submission (or queries). Then the agent learns about the relations it has with its neighbors through two functional occasions. First, when it queries another agent for certain knowledge or information. Second, when it receives a query from another agent. When an agent queries another agent for certain knowledge and if the queried agent responds positively with its own semantics, the querying agent will duly interpret it and update it in its translation table. When an agent receives a query from another agent, if it does not have a readily available and up-to-date translation, then the agent interprets the semantics that accompany the query. At the end of the interpretation, if the agent is able to recognize the semantics, it then reflects the learned mappings in the translation tables.

Note also that there is also the scalability issue to address. In a large-scale system with hundreds and thousands of agents and hundreds and thousands of concepts, for an agent to maintain a translation of that magnitude is not scalable. In our multiagent system, we make use of the notion of the neighborhood. An agent's neighborhood is a subset of the entire multiagent system such that the agent only considers the agents in its neighborhood when it tries to satisfy the queries received. Agents that are not in the neighborhood will not be approached; and thus the translation table can be reduced significantly in size. This neighborhood approach is feasible as each agent has the ability of relaying queries, allowing a query to be relayed eventually to an agent that knows about the queried concept, as every agent has a neighborhood and the neighborhoods overlap. This allows our design to address the scalability issue to some extent.

2.2. Operational Components

There are three important operational components: query processing, action planning, and query composition. Note that in our framework, an agent sends out a query to its neighbor when it needs to find some additional links (or links) to satisfy that query. Agents are required to compose queries when they relay or distribute queries to other agents. Finally, for the system to be effective, the action planning component of the agent decides how to distribute queries and learn about others ontologies based on the observed environmental properties such as the message traffic and the profile of the agent's neighborhood.

2.2.1. Query Processing. Each agent has a query processing module. This module accepts a query from the user, parses the query, and decides what to do with the query. A query is basically a composition of query's originator, the *search key* (or also known as the concept name), the request (in terms of the number of links desired), and the sender of the query. When an agent receives a query, it first matches the search key or concept name to its own ontology. If it finds a match, it proceeds to retrieve the links (or links) filed under that concept. If this number is greater than the desired number, then the query is satisfied. However, it is possible that the agent may encounter two other scenarios and each leads to collaboration with other agents or neighbors. First, the agent finds a match between the search key and its ontology but does not have enough links to satisfy the query. As a result, it needs to ask for help from other agents. Second, it is possible that the agent may not *recognize* the search key as it fails to find a match in its own ontology. This is when the agent needs to relay the query to other agents or to learn about the search key. The agent relays the query to another agent, say, b, when it finds a match for the search key in the *translation table* - that is, b knows about the search key. On the other hand, the agent will try to learn about the search key if it fails to find a match for the search key in the translation table. As will be discussed further in Section 3, the translation table of an agent is a matrix in which each cell represents a mapping between a concept of the agent and possibly a concept of a neighbor agent.

To identify the particular neighbors to ask for help, an agent makes use of two dynamically maintained knowledge bases. First, it uses its translation table. As alluded earlier in Section 2.2, in some cases, the mapping is NULL or empty when such a correspondence dose not exist. Each mapping is quantified by a confidence value, specifying how closely related the two concepts are. With this translation table, an agent can locate the appropriate neighbors for help. Second, it uses a neighborhood profile. A neighborhood profile is a record from the viewpoint of an agent of each of its neighbors, in terms of how helpful, useful, and responsive a neighbor has been in the past. This provides an operational aspect to the query processing.

Once an agent decides to help, it will compose a query or queries based on what its neighborhood profiler and translator have observed and learned so far. In general, issues such as specialties, personalities, and communication experiences of the neighboring agents determine how a query should be composed. The agent might want to send a query to a particular neighbor with high priority, or broadcast the query to every neighbor with low priority, or target a group of specialized neighbors, or ask for help from a helpful and knowledgeable agent. This decision making process is based on the observations that the agent has experienced and the lessons it has learned interacting with its neighbors. This approach enhances the cooperative efficiency and effectiveness between an agent and its neighbors, thus strengthening the collaboration within the system.

2.2.2. Action Planning. We will briefly discuss its activities here. An action planner monitors its environment to decide which course of actions to take: (1) offer help by adopting and relaying a query to other agents, (2) supply the necessary translation information and let the querying agent retrieves the knowledge itself, or (3) return a NULL response to terminate the query. Such a decision is based on two criteria observed from the environment and the priority of the query: (1) the activities the agent currently is engaged in provided by the activity monitor of the agent, and (2) the traffic situation among the agent and its neighbors provided by the traffic monitor of the agent. The query priority signifies the importance of the request to the querying agent.

2.2.3. Query Composition. When an agent decides to relay a query, it needs to compose the query fitting for its neighbors. The query composer refers to the neighborhood profiler to construct its queries. For every interaction between an agent and its neighbor, the success of the interaction, the accuracy of the translation, the usefulness of the knowledge and information, the responsiveness of the neighbor, and other inter-agent issues are logged and evaluated. Each criterion will be scored; the scores averaged; and all idly-linked neighbors ranked in terms of the average. The query composer thus constructs its queries based on the average: allocate higher requests to useful and helpful neighbors, for example. In short, the query composer decides how to allocate requests among the agent's neighbors based on the knowledge expertise as well as operational behavior of the neighbors that it has observed.

Query Acknowledgement. After a query is processed, the queried agent returns the result back to the querying agent. The querying agent has to acknowledge it. When the result is received, the incident will be recorded in the knowledge base regarding the neighborhood: (a) success of the interaction — based on the NULL, information, and knowledge typing if the response, (b) responsiveness of the neighbor — based on the elapsed time between query sent and response received, (c) nature of the query — concept categories, priority levels, originators, etc., and (d) log of activities and traffic observations. In general, conceptually, the knowledge base provides a library from which an agent can learn to compose better queries as the community evolves. This modification of knowledge maintains the ontologies, translation tables, and neighborhood profiles. Further, it could also compile statistics such as average, risk factor, friendliness factor, and success rate and records.

2.3. Agent Communication Language

Our agent communication language is rudimentary and only sufficiently functional to capture the various communication acts. It does not in particular follow a certain formal representation language such as DAML or OWL. The syntax is Lisp-based. For example, a query request that an agent receives is: (request <user ID> <concept name> <number of links desired>) where <user ID> is the user that posed the query, <concept name> is the search key, and <number of links desired>

is the number of links related to <concept name> that the user would like to have returned. A query relay that an agent *a* sends to another agent *b* has the following syntax: (relay <originator ID> <sender ID> <receiver ID> <query ID> <concept name> <number of links desired>) where (originator ID> and <sender ID> are the ID of agent *a*, and <receiver ID> of agent *b*, and <query ID> is the ID that agent a tags onto the original query that it received. Note that <originator ID> and <sender ID> will be different if the query is subsequently relayed again. When agent *b* returns the links, the message has the following syntax: (results <originator ID> <sender ID> <receiver ID> <query ID> <concept name> (<link 1> <link 2> ... <link N>)), where <sender ID> is agent *b*, and <receiver ID> is agent *a*, and (<link 1> <link 2> ... <link N>) is the list of links returned. A link is either a URL address of an online document or the pathname of a filed document. When agent *a* collects all returned results from its neighbors, it composes the final message to be returned to the user: (results <sender ID> <user ID> <concept name> (<link1> <link 2> ... <link N>)).

3. Methodology and Design

In this section, we describe the methodology and the current design of the operational components of an agent in the CUDO framework discussed in Section 2. As shown in Figure 1, an agent has nine important modules.

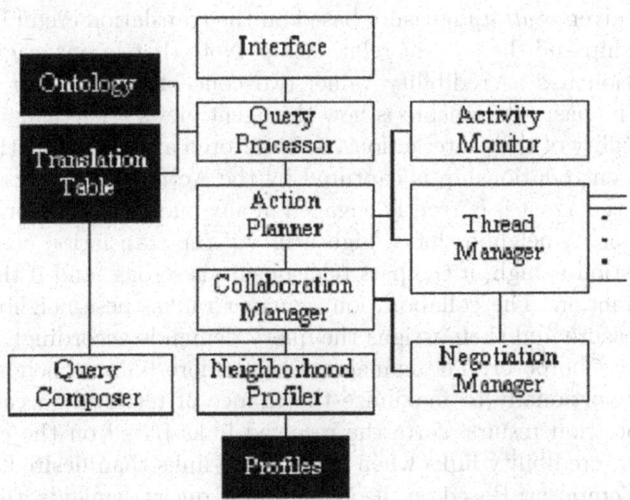

FIGURE 1. The current design of the operational components of an agent in our framework.

(1) **Interface:** This module interacts with the user to obtain queries and to provide queried results. Currently, we have (simulated) software users that automatically generate timed queries for our experiments. Each software user submits its queries through a socket connection with the interface.

(2) **Query Processor:** This module receives a query from the Interface module and processes it. It first checks the agent's ontology base. If the query matches one of the concepts in the ontology, the module retrieves the number of links available. If the query does not find a match in the ontology, the module examines its translation table. If there are available translations, that means a collaboration is possible.

(3) **Action Planner:** This module serves as the main reasoning component of the agent: (a) If the number of internal links satisfies the query, then the action planner simply provides those links to through the Interface module to the user; (b) otherwise, if the agent understands the query and finds available translations, it initiates its collaborative activities; (c) if the agent does not understand the query, it will relay the query to another agent; and (d) finally, if there are no available translations, the retrieval process stops and the agent reports back to the user. Whether a collaboration is feasible depends on the current status of the agent, as recorded by the Activity Monitor and Thread Manager modules. If the agent does not have enough resources for a collaboration, the retrieval process terminates.

(4) **Collaboration Manager:** When the action planner calls for a collaboration, this module takes over. The objective of this module is to form an appropriate group of neighboring agents to approach and distribute the query demands (link allocations) accordingly among them. To design such a collaboration plan, this module relies on the Neighborhood Profiler module, and the translation table. Each neighbor is given a *utility* measure based on the translation credibility value, the past relationship and the current relationship. Note that in our original thesis [1], each translation has a credibility value: two concepts are similar to only a certain degree. The past relationship is how the agent views a particular neighbor in terms of the quality of their interactions, as monitored and stored by the Profiler module. The current relationship is captured by the Activity Monitor module to indicate whether the agent is currently engaged in any query transactions with the particular neighbor. A neighbor has a high utility if the translation credibility of the query in question is high, if the past relationship is strong, and if there is not any current interaction. The collaboration manager ranks these neighbors based on the utility measure and then assigns the query demands accordingly, with the help of the Query Composer. The manager assigns more links to neighbors with higher utility proportionally to maximize the chance of retrieval success. It also collects the negotiation results, sorts the received links based on the credibility, and filters out low-credibility links when it has more links than desired.

(5) **Query Composer:** Based on the allocation of query demands, this module composes a specific query for each neighbor to be approached. As previously mentioned, each query is associated with a document or link demand that specifies the number of links desired. A query will also include the name of the originator and a

time stamp when it is first generated. If the query is based on a translation, then the translated concept name is used. If the agent does not recognize a concept and needs to relay a query it has received to a neighbor, it simply uses the queried concept directly.

(6) **Neighborhood Profiler:** The design of this module is based on our work in coalition formation [5]. The relationship is a composition of four basic numbers: *_numHelp* (the number of times the agent provides help to the neighbor), *_numSuccess* (the number of times the agent successfully solicits help from the neighbor), *_numRequestFrom* (the number of times the agent receives a request from the neighbor), and *_numRequestTo* (the number of times the agent initiates a request to the neighbor) [4]. Based on these numbers, we can derive helpfulness, usefulness, importance, and reliance of each neighbor, from the viewpoint of the agent.

(7) **Activity Monitor:** This module keeps track of the activities in a *job vector* — whether the agent is processing a query on its own, or negotiating with other neighbors for more links, or entertaining a request from a neighbor. Each *job* is described with a list of attributes such as the originator, the executor, the task description, the current status, and so on.

(8) **Thread Manager:** This module manages the threads of the agent. It is a low-level module that activates the threads, updates and monitors the thread activity.

(9) **Negotiation Manager:** This module manages the negotiation tasks. In our current design, the interaction between two agents does not involve negotiations as the two simply exchange information. However, our long-term plan views negotiation as an important part of interpreting ontologies (the act of mapping concepts between two agents) in a distributed environment. Negotiations that are too time consuming, stagnant, or no longer useful will be modified or aborted; negotiations that are successful will be learned; and so on. We will adapt our previous work in reflective negotiations [5] to distributed ontology in this framework.

Together with these nine operational components are three dynamic knowledge or data bases: ontology, translation table, and profiles. As discussed in Section 2, the profiles keep track of the relationships between the agent and its neighbors, updating the neighborhood parameters. The ontology is a *dictionary* listing the concepts that the agent knows. Each concept has a list of supporting links. Each agent also maintains a translation table that stores the mappings between what the agent knows and what its neighbors know. Each mapping is tagged with a credibility value.

4. Implementation

We have implemented all the nine modules of our agent as depicted in Figure 1 in C++. Each agent receives its user queries from a software user through a socket connection, and communicates with other agents through a central relay server module through socket connections as well. Each agent generates and maintains its neighborhood profile during runtime dynamically.

For our experiments, each agent is equipped with a translation table right from the start. Note that in our original CUDO framework [1], the entries in a translation table is learned over time based on the experience of each agent. Here, since we focus on the operational design of collaborative understanding of distributed ontologies, we assume that each agent has a translation table to begin with.

In addition, each agent is equipped with an ontology database. This database lists all the concept terms that an agent knows. For each concept, there is a list of links (or links) that are examples that illustrate the concept.

5. Discussion of Results

We have performed a comprehensive set of experiments to investigate the impact of operational factors on how agents collaborate. Ultimately, this investigation will give us insights as to how such resource-constrained collaborations affect how agents learn distributed ontologies. In this, we will first describe our experimental setup and then discuss the results.

5.1. Experimental Setup

Here is the setup of our experiments:

There are five agents supporting a software user each. All agents are neighbors and can communicate among themselves. All five agents and their threads are run on the same CPU.

Every agent has a unique set of nine concepts in its ontology. Each concept has five supporting links.

Each agent has a translation table where each cell of the table indicates the translation between a local concept and a foreign concept in a neighbor and the translation's credibility value. If a translation is not available, we use the symbol NIL.

For our distributed information retrieval simulation, each software user has a query configuration file. Thus, instead of manually submitting these queries, the software user simply reads them from the file and sends them to the corresponding agent. Each query in a configuration file has (a) a cycle number, (b) the queried concept name, and (c) the number of links desired. The cycle number indicates when the query will be submitted to the agent. Each configuration file has about 300 cycles, and two batches of queries. Both batches are the same with the only difference being the cycle numbers. This allows us to investigate whether the agents are able to improve in their response time in the second batch after having learned how to form collaborations better through neighborhood profiling in the first batch.

In the first batch of query scenarios, there are six segments of queries:

(1) Cycles 0-10: Each query that each agent receives asks for a different concept that the agent has in its ontology. Each agent is also able to satisfy the

query demand on its own, and thus does not need to collaborate in this segment. All queries across the users are submitted at the same cycles.

(2) Cycles 11-40: Each query that each agent receives asks for a different concept that the agent has in its ontology. Unlike Segment 1 above, each query has a query demand greater than what an agent can handle. Thus, in this segment, each agent needs to collaborate. All queries are submitted in a *staggered* manner. Agent 1 sees all its nine queries first; agent 2 sees all its queries next; and so on.

(3) Cycles 41-70: The queries here are set up similarly as those in Segment 2 above except that the number of links or links desired for every query is twice that in Segment 2. Thus, extensive collaborations are needed. Queries are also staggered in this segment.

(4) Cycles 71-80: In this segment, every agent does not recognize the queried concepts that it sees; that is, an agent does not have the queried concepts in its ontology. This forces each agent to relay the queries to other neighboring agents. Queries are *packed* — all agents see their queries at the same time — in this segment.

(5) Cycles 81-110: This segment is almost the same as Segment 4. The only difference is that the queries are staggered.

(6) Cycles 111-120: In this segment, two users query about concepts that their agents do not have in their respective ontologies, two users query about only some concepts that their agents do not have in their respective ontologies, and one user queries about concepts that its agent has in its ontology. The queried number of links is small and no negotiations are needed.

The second batch starts around Cycle 150, and repeats the above query scenarios. Figure 2 gives a brief overview of our query scenarios.

Our query scenarios are staggered or packed to investigate the response behaviors of the agents. Since the number of negotiation threads is limited for each agent, packed queries with high link demands may lead to only partial link retrievals. Our query scenarios also come with low and high link demands. Low link demands do not require or require fewer collaborations, while high link demands prompt the agents to plan for collaborative actions. Finally, an agent may or may not know some of the queried concepts. The agent's ontology specifies this knowledge. When an agent knows the queried concept, it has more options, approaching different neighbors for help. When it does not know the queried concept, then it shifts the responsibility to one of the neighbors, essentially making itself a relay station.

Given the above query scenarios, we further vary two sets of parameters: the number of negotiation threads and the credibility values in the translation tables. We vary the number of negotiation threads between 0 and 5. When the number is 0, the agents do not have collaborative capabilities since they cannot contact other agents. When the number is 5, an agent can simultaneously conduct 5 negotiations. Thus, this number directly impacts the resources that the agents have to collaborate to satisfy queries. This is relevant to *operational* constraints. There are also six sets of translation tables. In the first set, the credibility values

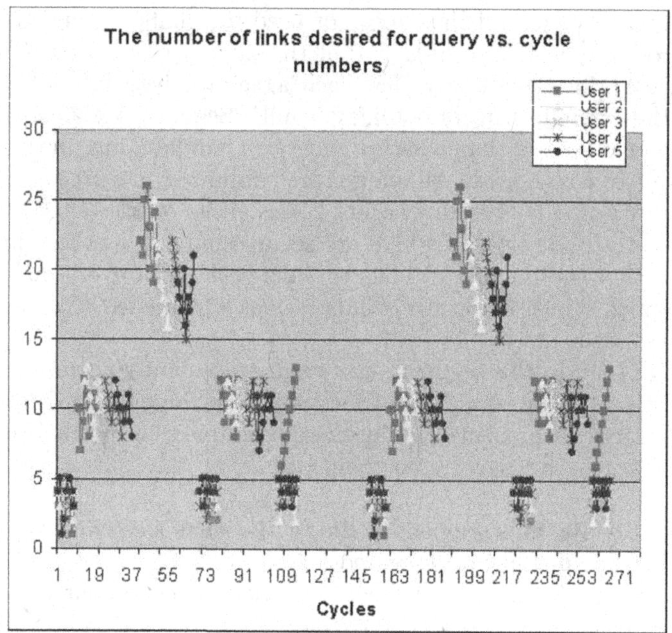

FIGURE 2. The number of links for the queries submitted by the software users to the agents for each cycle.

of all translations are above zero. In this situation, every concept that one agent knows has four translations. In the second set, one of the agents has what is termed as a "narrow ontology". That is, its translation table contains has numerous NIL translations (more than 50% of all table cells). In the third set, two agents have narrow ontologies. In the fourth set, three agents do; in the fifth set, four agents do; finally, all agents do. With these sets, we want to see how successful the agents are in satisfying high-demand queries when they are faced with varying degrees of *ontological* constraints; and how operational factors help alleviate these constraints.

Given the six different numbers of negotiation threads and six sets of translation tables, we carry out a total of 36 runs using the same set of query scenarios.

5.2. Parameters Collected

Our current experiments concentrate on two sets of parameters:

(1) **Neighborhood Profile Parameters:** For each neighbor, an agent collects parameters documenting the outcomes of their past interactions. These parameters are alluded to in Section 3, used in the computation of a neighbor's utility measure. Table 2 defines these parameters.

Parameters	Definitions
_numSuccess	The number of successful negotiations that the agent has initiated to neighbor *i*
_numHelp	The number of successful negotiations that the agent has received from the neighbor *i*
_numRequestTo	The total number of negotiations that the agent has initiated to the neighbor *i*
_numRequestFrom	The total number of negotiation requests that the agent has received from neighbor *i*
_successRate	*_numSuccess/_numRequestTo*
_helpRate	*_numHelp/_numRequestFrom*
_requestToRate	*_numRequestTo/_totalRequestTo* where *_totalRequestTo* is the sum of all negotiations that the agent has initiated
_requestFromRate	Presently this number is not updated, as our negotiation design does not incorporate the argumentative reasoning in [5]. However, we plan to re-visit this number in the future once the interpretation module is completed. This number tells the agent how much neighbor *i* relies on the agent

TABLE 2. Neighborhood profile parameters.

(2) **Query Result Parameters:** For each query, an agent collects parameters documenting the characteristics of the query and the query outcome. Table 3 links the definitions of these parameters.

Parameters	Definitions
_originator	The originator of the query, either from a software user (ID) or another agent
_cycle	The cycle ID when the query is first generated
_numLinksDesired	The number of links desired by the query
_numLinksRetrieved	The number of links retrieved at the end of the retrieval process and presented to the user, always smaller than *_numLinksDesired*
_conceptName	The query keyword
_successQuality	*numLinksRetrieved/numLinksDesired*
_duration	The actual elapsed time between the receipt of a query and the presentation of the query results to the user
_listLinks	The list of links retrieved and presented to the user at the end of the retrieval process

TABLE 3. Query result parameters.

5.3. Results

Our overall, long-term plan of analysis aims at analyzing the results at eight different levels. At level 0, we derive an overview of the correctness and assessment of the results. At level 1, we want to analyze the agents retrieval quality in the two batches of queries. At level 2, we aim to compare across the agents and see whether there are significant patterns. At level 3, we want to look into the retrieval results of each segment. Note that each segment has its unique set of characteristics as previously discussed in Section 5.1. At level 4, we want to investigate the role of the concepts. Some concepts may have few supporting links and some have many. At level 5, we will analyze the impact of different queries on the quality of the retrieved results. A query with a high-link demand may not necessary result in poorer results than one with a low-link demand. At level 6, we plan to examine closely the impact of the translation tables with narrow and wide ontologies, and how distributed ontology learning may help improve the tables for better query effectiveness. Finally, at level 7, we will study the operational impact of the threads as a constrained resource.

In this paper, we report on some in-depth level-0 analyses. Further, we present observations and discussions on other levels.

5.3.1. Level-0 Analysis. Figures 3-7 show the graphs of the *_successQuality* of each users queries vs. the number of threads. Here are some observations:

(1) The average *_successQuality* of a user's queries increases as expected when the number of threads increases. This is because for high-demand queries that call for collaborations, the agent has more resources (i.e., negotiation threads) to do so..

(2) The average *_successQuality* of a user's queries drops significantly whenever the corresponding agent has a narrow ontology. However, the drops are more significant when the number of threads is smaller. This indicates that the retrieval benefits from the collaborative distributed ontology design. When agents are able to collaborate more often, the *_successQuality* of a query is higher.

(3) Figure 8 shows the average *_successQuality* and standard deviation of all queries for each number of threads. As we can see, with a higher number of negotiation threads, queries are satisfied more successfully (high average values), and also more consistently (low standard deviation values).

(4) Figure 9 shows the average *_successQuality* for agents with narrow ontologies and those with non-narrow ones. Note that if agent *A1* does not have a translation for mapping its concept name *C1* to any of agent *A2*'s, that does not necessarily mean that *A2* does not have a translation mapping one of its concepts to *A1*'s concept name *C1*. This is by design as we ultimately aim to show how collaborative agents can learn new translations or refine old ones as they help each other in satisfying queries. As observed, the number of narrow ontologies does not impact the success quality. From the operational point of view, this was unexpected. When the number of narrow ontologies within the multiagent system increases, we expected that more agents would *relay* queries to their neighbor,

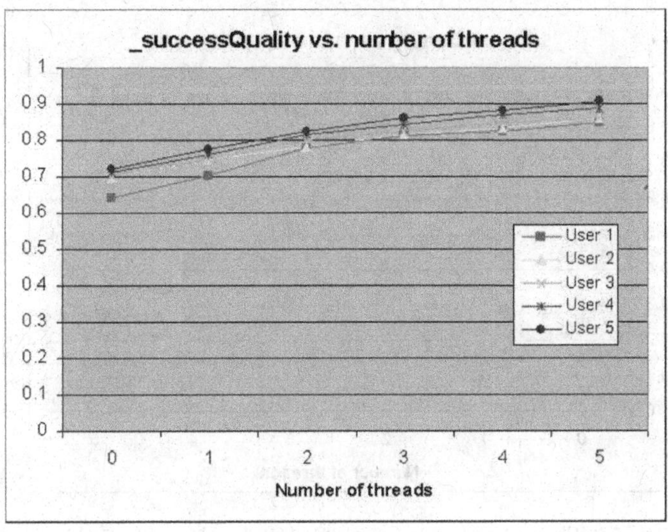

FIGURE 3. The average _successQuality_ value of each user's queries vs. the number of threads where no agents have narrow ontologies.

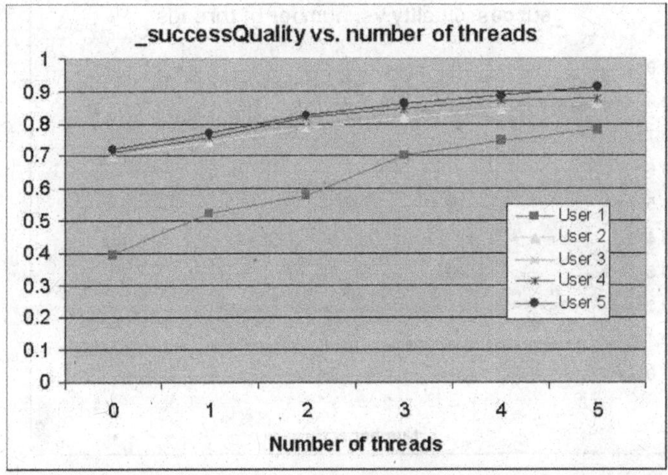

FIGURE 4. The average _successQuality_ value of each user's queries vs. the number of threads where agent 1 has narrow ontology.

and that would cause the negotiation threads to be used more frequently. We suspect that the agents' collaborative activities reduce the impact of having narrow ontologies.

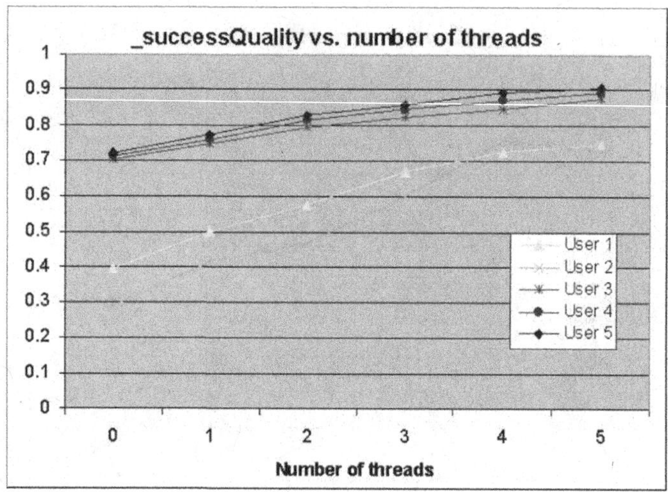

FIGURE 5. The average *_successQuality* value of each user's queries vs. the number of threads where agents 1 and 2 have narrow ontologies.

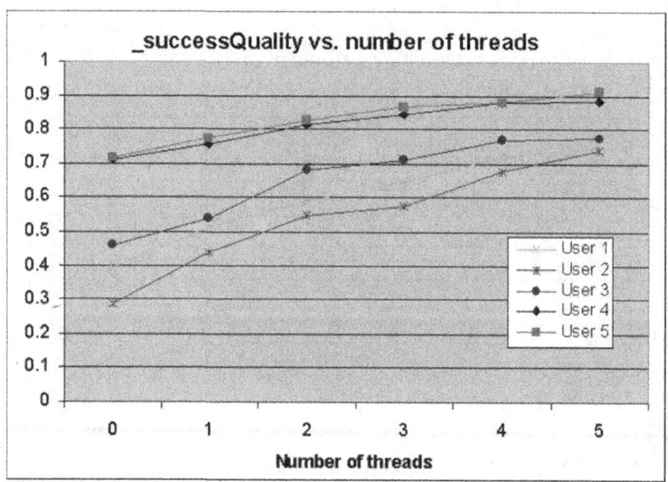

FIGURE 6. The average *_successQuality* value of each user's queries vs. the number of threads where agents 1, 2, and 3 have narrow ontologies.

(5) Figure 10 shows the average *_duration* (in seconds) for each query to be processed and presented back to software user 1 (by only agent 1), for different numbers of negotiation threads. As observed, when the number of threads

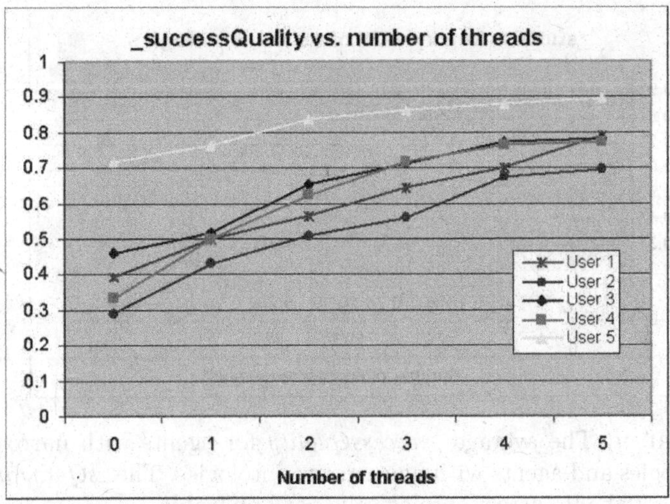

FIGURE 7. The average *_successQuality* value of each user's queries vs. the number of threads where agents 1, 2, and 3 have narrow ontologies.

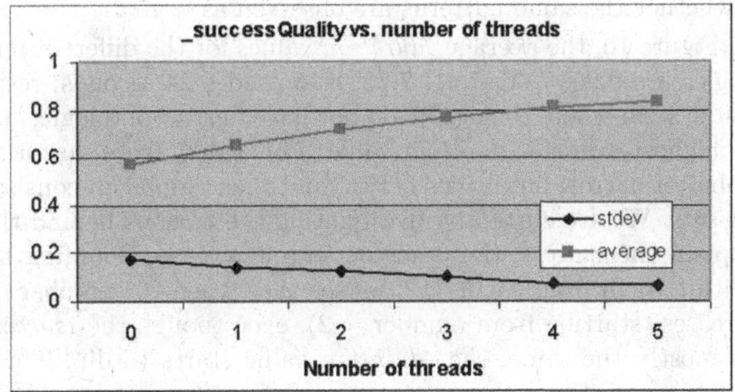

FIGURE 8. The average and standard deviation of the *_successQuality* for all users vs. the number of threads.

increases, it takes longer for a query to be responded to. This observation was not anticipated. However, upon further analysis, we realize the following. When an agent has more threads, not only it can approach more neighbors for help, but it also receives more requests for help from other agents. As a result, the agent manages more tasks and slows down its processes for retrieving and supplying results to the software users. This indicates an oversight in our design with regards to the efficiency of our implementation. We are currently reviewing our program code

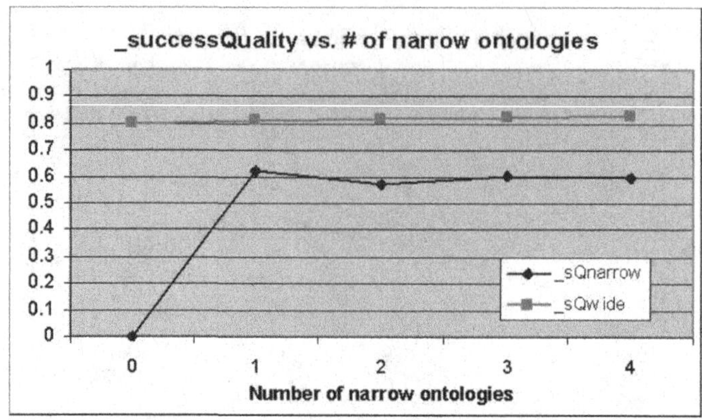

FIGURE 9. The average *_successQuality* for agents with narrow ontologies and agents with non-narrow ontologies. The *_sQnarrow* value for the 0 narrow ontologies is not applicable.

to pinpoint the places where we could optimize the multi-threaded programming portion. We will also perform the same analysis on all other software users and agents to see whether the same patterns are observed as well.

(6) From Figure 10, the average *_duration* values for the different numbers of narrow ontologies are 9.96, 7.66, 7.41, 7.73, 8.15, and 8.24 seconds, respectively. The multiagent system where the agents do not have narrow ontologies, unexpectedly, have the highest average *_duration* value. This value drops, has a minimum when the number of narrow ontologies is two, and then climbs up consistently for the next three sets. We are currently investigating the reasons behind this curve, to at least explain the data of the 0-narrow ontology case. Coupling the above observation with that in from Figure 12, we see that when the number of narrow ontologies increases (starting from number = 2), even though the *_successQuality* value remains mostly the same, the *_duration* value starts to dip. This clarifies somewhat our observations.

Figure 10 The average *_duration* for agent 1, for different numbers of threads, vs. the number of narrow ontologies.

(7) Figure 11 shows the average profile of agent 1 of its neighbors: *_numSuccess*, *_numHelp*, *_numRequestTo*, and *_numRequestFrom*. The values of *_numHelp* and *_numRequestFrom* are the same; that is, the *_helpRate* is 100%. For this agent 1, the number of times it has requested for help is smaller than the number of times it has entertained other agents requests. This indicates that the query scenarios tend to invoke collaborations, causing the originating agents to ask for help from many different neighbors. From the graph, we see that the agent approaches more neighbors for help as it has more negotiation threads. However, when the number of threads is 5, the rate levels off just a little, indicating that a convergence may

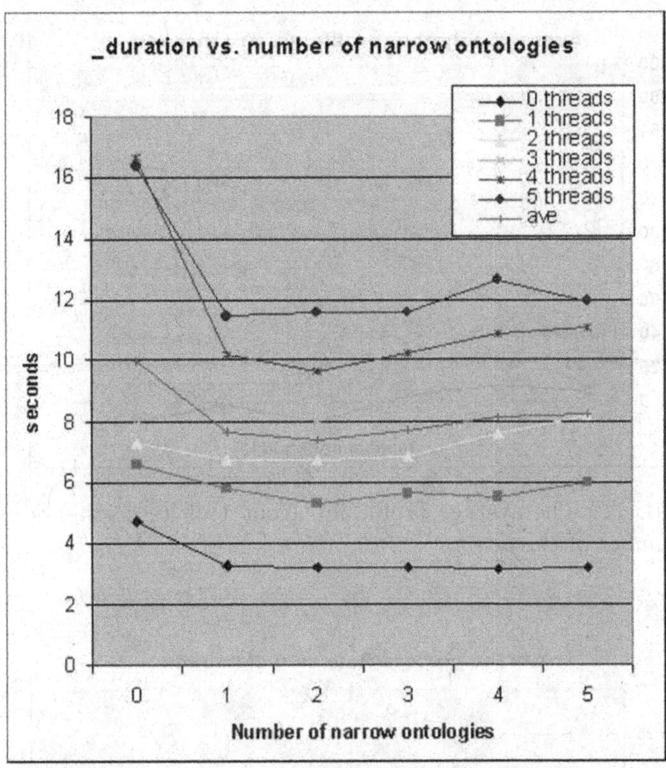

FIGURE 10. The average *_duration* for agent 1, for different numbers of threads, vs. the number of narrow ontologies.

occur when the number of threads is larger than 5. This means that in our current experimental setup, our link demand is still more than what the agents can handle.

(8) Figure 12 shows the average *_successRate* vs. the number of threads available. As observed, the agent is able to negotiate more successfully when the number of threads increases. This is expected since with more threads available, an agent is able to entertain more requests. Coupling this with Figure 13, we see that agent 1 is able to conduct *more* negotiations *more* successfully when the number of threads increases — more effectively and more efficiently. This is a good indicator that would help guide the design of distributed ontology learning in our work.

(9) Figure 13 shows the *_requestToRate* vs. the number of threads available. As observed, when the number of threads is 1, agent 1 relies on agent 2 (or N1) heavily. This is due to the fact that in the beginning of an agent, all neighbors are weighted very similarly; as a result, the agent will approach the first neighbor that it knows. However, as the number of threads increases, the agent is able to collaborate more with other neighbors. As a result, the reliance on N1 decreases significantly. Meanwhile, the reliance on the other three neighbors steadily increases.

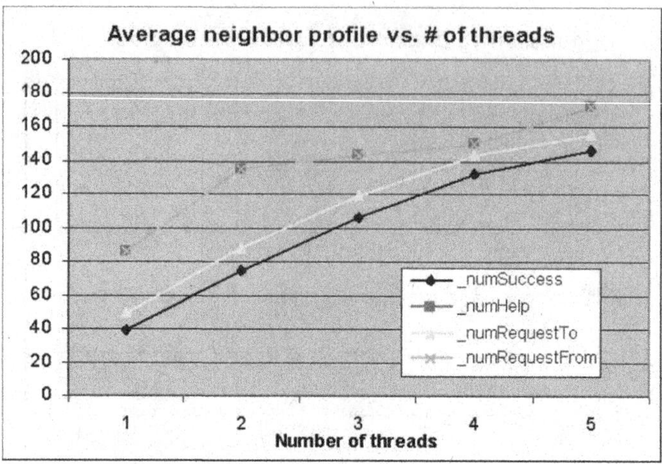

FIGURE 11. The average profile for agent 1 of its neighbors vs. the number of threads

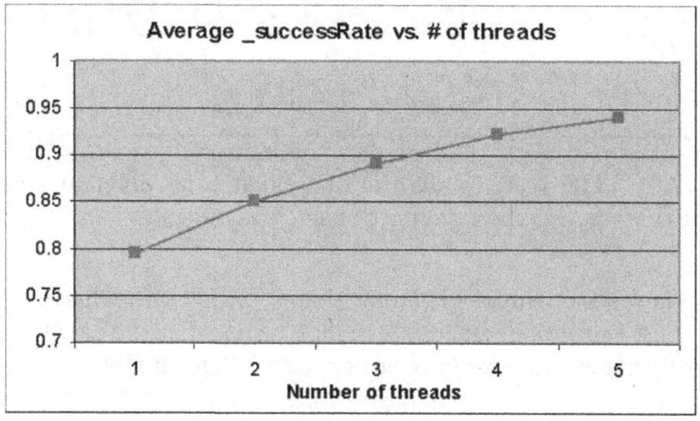

FIGURE 12. The average profile for agent 1 of its neighbors vs. the number of threads

This is a good lesson, as we now know that in order for the system to exhibit unintended bias favoring one neighbor over another, we need to have enough number of threads, laying the groundwork for the distributed ontology learning design of our work.

The *_requestToRate* from agent 1 to its neighbors, N1 (agent 2), N2 (agent 3), N3 (agent 4), and N4 (agent 5) vs. the number of threads.

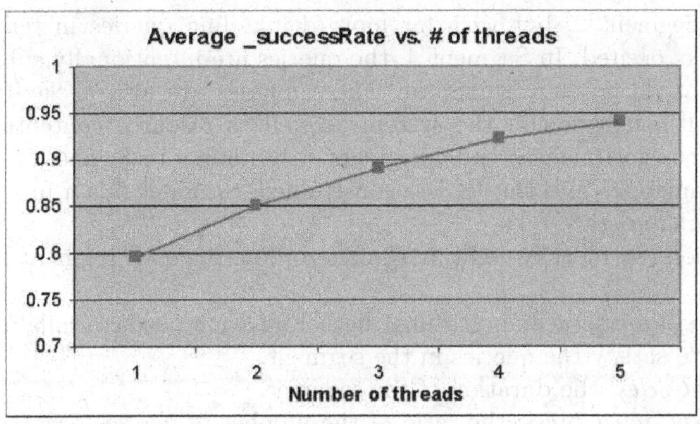

FIGURE 13. The *_requestToRate* from agent 1 to its neighbors, N1 (agent 2), N2 (agent 3), N3 (agent 4), and N4 (agent 5) vs. the number of threads.

5.3.2. Other Level Analysis. Level-1 Analysis: Batch Results

At this level, we want to investigate whether the agents are able to handle the second batch of queries (exactly the same with the first batch) better compared to the first batch. From the experiments, we observe that:

- The average *_successQuality* of the second batch is a little better than that of the first batch (0.85 vs. 0.81), more so when the number of agents with narrow ontology is high. This confirms that the ontological learning (translations) in the first batch helps the agents in the second batch.
- The average *_duration* values of the two batches are very similar (10.38 vs. 10.39 s). Thus, at least for our experiments, the ontological learning does not help reduce the average search time.

Level-2 Analysis: Neighborhood Profiles

At this level, we want to investigate how the neighbors affect the search result. Each agent maintains a profile of each of its neighbors, recording *_successRate*, *_helpRate*, and *_requestToRate.* Our preliminary analysis of the results indicates that an agent is able to locate its best neighbor eventually, striking a balance between operational quality and credibility of the translation. We are currently adding time constraints in another experiment to address partial successes. Results are forthcoming.

Level-3 Analysis: Segment Results

At this level, we want to investigate how the agents handle the different segments. Briefly, there are six segments in each batch of queries. Segment 1 is the least demanding in terms of the number of links or links desired for each query. Segment 2 consists of queries that each lead to an agent having to collaborate with its neighbors. Also, the queries are submitted in a staggered manner. Thus, the agents are not flooded with all their queries at the same time. Segment 3 is similar to Segment 2, but with far more demanding queries in terms of the number of links desired. In Segment 4, the queries are intentionally submitted to the agents that do not have links for. These queries are also packed to induce communication congestion in the system as well as resource contention within each agent for negotiation threads. Segment 5 is similar to Segment 4 but with staggered submissions and thus is less constrained. Segment 6 is a mixture of all the above characteristics.

In addition, we identify eight attributes to describe each segment (see Table 4):

(1) *_cooperationNeeded*: indicating whether an agent needs to collaborate with its neighbors to satisfy the queries in the segment.

(2) *_numCycles*: the duration of the segment.

(3) *_queryCompactness*: the ratio of the number of queries occurring at the same cycles to the total number of queries in the segment.

(4) *_queryDensity*: *_queryCompactness* normalized by *_numCycles*.

(5) *_aveNumLinks*: the average number of links desired per query in the segment.

(6) *_maxNumLinks*: the maximum number of links or desired links of a query in the segment.

(7) *_minNumLinks*: the minimum number of links or desired links of a query in the segment.

(8) *_knowledgeRatio*: the ratio of the number of queries submitted to the agents who know the requested concepts over the number of total queries in the segment.

In general, if a segment requires cooperation, with a larger number of queries for an agent, higher compactness, lower number of cycles, higher query density, and higher number of links desired per query, and lower knowledge ratio, then we expect the system to perform less successfully.

Seg	**cN**	**nC**	**qC**	**qD**	**aL**	**maL**	**miL**	**kR**
1	N	9	1	0.11	3	5	1	1
2	Y	27	0.8	0.03	10	12	7	1
3	Y	27	0.8	0.03	20	26	15	1
4	Y/N	9	1	0.11	4	5	2	0.02
5	Y	26	0.8	0.03	11	12	7	0.00
6	Y/N	9	1	0.11	5	13	2	0.54

TABLE 4. Description of the six different segments. Abbreviations: cN =_cooperationNeeded, nC =_numCycles, qC =_queryCompactness, qD =_queryDensity, aL =_aveNumLinks, maL =_maxNumLinks, miL =_minNumLinks, and kR =_knowledgeRatio.

From the experiments, we observe that:

- The average *_successQuality* values for segments 2 and 3 are similar given the same number of threads. The key difference between the two segments is the average number of links desired per query. So, we see that the average number of links desired does not directly impact the quality of the retrieval. It does impact the *_duration* value, however.
- The *_knowledgeRatio* value impacts the average *_successQuality* value: agents with higher *_knowledgeRatio* values achieve higher *_successQuality* values, especially when the number of threads is small (0 or 1). As the number of threads increases, the impact of *_knowledgeRatio* decreases. Also, as the number of agents with narrow ontology increases, the number of threads factors more significantly into the *_successQuality* values of the agents with low *_knowledgeRatio* values. In general, more agents having narrow ontology in the system does not affect their retrieval outcome if the knowledge ratio is high. However, when the knowledge ratio is low, both the number of threads and the number of agents having narrow ontology will impact greatly on the retrieval outcome.
- The impact of *_queryDensity* value of the segments on the query results is not expected. We expected that the *_successQuality* would be high when the *_queryDensity* was low. However, this is not the case. Actually, the segments with a high query density (1, 4, and 6) have significantly higher *_successQuality* than do the other segments. This indicates that the query density is not as important as other attributes in determining the retrieval quality. As future work, we will design further experiments with the same number of links desired per query but with different query density values to more clearly investigate the role of *_queryDensity* in *_successQuality*.
- The number of links desired per query impacts the retrieval results. As *_aveNumLinks* increases, *_successQuality* decreases given the same number of threads. Also, when the average number of links desired is large, it dominates the variance in the number of agents having narrow ontology in determining *_successQuality*.
- If the average number of links desired is kept the same for any two segments, the segment with a higher maximum number of links desired will yield worse query result. This is consistent even when the number of threads is varied.
- The *_successQuality* is less predictable when the agents have fewer threads. This indicates that when there are enough threads for the agents to communicate with, the retrieval results are more predictable — a key motivation for multiagent cooperation.
- The *_successQuality* is less predictable when there are more agents with narrow ontology. This may be a good sign. As each agent processes queries and learns, it updates its translation table, and thus it performs gradually better. We will investigate the convergence of this observation in the future.
- The average *_duration* increases the fastest for Segment 5 as the number of threads increases. Note that in this segment, the *_knowledgeRatio* value is zero. That is, all queries submitted are intentionally directed to the agents

who do not understand the queries, which result in many relays. Since an agent has to contact all known neighbors, the more threads it has, the more neighbors it contacts and that leads to the significant increase in *_duration*.
- The average *_duration* value is less predictable when the agents have fewer threads. This observation echoes the one regarding *_successQuality*. Also, when the number of threads is small, the average *_duration* value is more predictable if the system has more agents with narrow ontology. Overall, we see that the number of threads play a significant role in determining the average *_duration* value.

Level-5 Analysis: Individual Results

At this level, we compare the systems performance to the different groups of queries, based on the numbers of links desired. From the experiments, we observe that:

- The *_searchQuality* value decreases as the number of links desired increases. This is expected.
- In general, when the number of links desired is small, the average *_searchQuality* value increases as the number of negotiation threads increases. The reason for this observation is that an agent needs to contact its neighbors when it cannot provide a sufficient number of links. With more threads, the agent is able to ask for more help and that leads to more successes. However, if the environment is over-constrained (e.g., when a set of queries are packed in a short segment), the number of threads available for communication at any given time decreases and the benefit is not observed. Also, when the link demand is high, the *_searchQuality* values are similar in spite of the different numbers of negotiation threads. We see that the system saturates at this point.

6. Conclusions

We have described our work-in-progress with collaborative understanding of distributed ontologies in a multiagent framework, focusing on the operational components. We have outlined the methodology and design of our framework. The methodology involves building agents with key operational components to support ontological functions such as query processing, query composition, negotiation, and collaboration. We have also briefly discussed our implementation. We have focused mainly on our on-going experiments and study of operational issues. We have described our query scenarios, translation tables, and ontologies, as well as two key sets of parameters collected from our experiments: neighborhood profile and query result parameters. Our experiments have generated a lot of data that we are currently reviewing and investigating. We have reported on some preliminary analyses to give an overall assessment of our system's feasibility and correctness. In general, we see that the number of negotiation threads available to each agent in the system has a key role in determining the *_successQuality* of a query task, the average *_successRate* of a negotiation, and the degree of collaboration among agents. We also see that the number of "narrow" ontologies influences the agents' behaviors negligibly. We plan to look into this finding further. Our immediate future work includes (1) completing the 7 levels of analyses identified in this paper to analyze our infrastructure, (2) finishing the interpretation module to add complexity into the negotiation protocols, (3) studying the impact of learning in-depth, and (4) investigating the usefulness of the utility measure and its impact on the accuracy of translation. For the last item, remember that the utility measure of a neighbor is based on the credibility of the particular translation as well as the agents relationships. That means, even if a neighbor is very knowledgeable (with high credibility), an agent may not approach that neighbor for help if the *_successRate* is low. As a result, our distributed ontology learning may be biased towards how close two agents have collaborated, and factor in less importantly the actual accuracy of the translation. Thus, in a way, we are addressing a type of operational distributed ontology: agents learn ontologies that are useful and credible to them, instead of only learning ontologies that are highly credible to them.

Acknowledgement

The author would like to thank JingFei Xu for her programming and running the experiments for this project.

References

[1] Soh, L.-K. 2002. Multiagent, Distributed Ontology Learning, *Working Notes of the 2nd AAMAS OAS Workshop*, July, Bologna, Italy.

[2] Shafer, G. 1976. *A Mathematical Theory of Evidence*, Princeton, NJ: Princeton University Press.

[3] Soh, L.-K. 2002. A Mutliagent Framework for Collaborative Conceptual Learning Using a Dempster-Shafer Belief System, *Working Notes of AAAI Spring Symposium on Collaborative Learning Agents*, Stanford, CA, Mar 25-27, pp. 9-16.

[4] Soh, L.-K. and Tsatsoulis, C. 2002. Satisficing Coalition Formation among Agents, *Proceedings of AAMAAS02*, July, Bologna, Italy.

[5] Soh, L.-K. and Tsatsoulis, C. 2002. Reflective Negotiating Agents for Real-Time Multisensor Target Tracking, in *Proceedings of IJCAI'01*, Seattle, WA, Aug 6-11, pp. 1121-1127.

[6] Williams, A. B. and Tsatsoulis, C. 1999. Diverse Web Ontologies: What Intelligent Agents Must Teach to Each Other, *Working Notes of the AAAI Spring Symposium Series on Intelligent Agents in Cyberspace*, Stanford, CA, Mar 22-24, 115-120.

Leen-Kiat Soh
Computer Science and Engineering
University of Nebraska
256 Avery Hall
Lincoln, NE
(402) 472-6738
e-mail: lksoh@cse.unl.edu

Reconciling Implicit and Evolving Ontologies for Semantic Interoperability

Kendall Lister, Maia Hristozova and Leon Sterling

Abstract. This paper addresses current approaches to the goal of semantic interoperability on the web and presents new research directions. We critically discuss the existing approaches, including RDF, SHOE, PROMPT and Chimaera, and identify the most effective elements of each. In our opinion, the ability of these primarily closed solutions to succeed on a global web scale is limited. In general, a unilateral solution to the problem on a global level seems unlikely in the foreseeable future. We review and contrast our own research experiments AReXS and CASA and suggest that as yet unaddressed issues should be considered, such as reconciling implicit ontologies and evolving ontologies and task-oriented analysis. We also consider the role of semantic interoperation in multi-agent systems and describe strategies for achieving this via the ROADMAP methodology, with emphasis on building and assuring knowledge models.

Keywords. Ontology translation/mapping, Ontology maintenance/evolution, Data standardisation.

1. Introduction

The much talked about goal of building a new Internet that is comprehensible to machines as well as humans is generally considered to involve enhancing content and information sources with semantic markings and explicit ontologies. A number of approaches to this goal have been proposed, and these generally involve a new representation for semantically enriched data. Something that seems to be often overlooked, however, is that a single solution is unlikely to be usefully applicable to the entire world wide web. It is obvious that business needs are generally quite different to the needs of individuals, and that even within the business community different areas will require solutions of varying sophistication, accuracy and scale.

The widespread success of the world wide web and its underlying technologies, HTML and HTTP, has been due in no small part to their simplicity and ease of adoption. By providing a simple architecture that anyone could learn and use with minimal overhead, content flourished on the web. Other information technologies that arguably provided more effective methods for locating and retrieving data failed to take off in the same exponential way that the web did. Where the web infrastructure itself doesn't even contain the most rudimentary searching and resource location features, Gopher, WAIS and a large number of proprietary online databases that predated the world wide web all provided automated indexing, searching, hypertextuality and other information management capabilities. But despite their apparent advantages, all of these technologies were overtaken by the web. In fact, in many cases proprietary databases and indexes have had their interfaces replaced with web-based solutions, to the point that the actual technology is largely hidden. It is more than a coincidence that where the world wide web succeeded and grew to become a de facto standard, the more complex alternatives faltered and missed out on popular adoption.

Similarly, we consider that the next generation of semantically-capable global information infrastructure will necessarily be relatively simple in order to achieve the same scale of acceptance. That is not to say that sophisticated technologies have no place - on the contrary, they will be vital for the areas of industry that require them, and their advances will no doubt drive other research efforts even further. Also, the intelligent agents that roam this infrastructure will themselves be very sophisticated. However, there remains a fundamental role for simple, flexible and adaptive technologies that do not demand strict adherence to formal standards and protocols and the development and publishing costs that follow. By leaving the majority of the intelligence for semantic comprehension in the interpreting applications rather than the medium itself, we will develop technologies that can operate in any information environment, not just those that are sophisticated and semantically enhanced. There is no suggestion that semantically rich environments are not useful and desirable, but it is not practical to expect the entirety, or even the majority, of the information landscape of the future to be uniformly structured, as current research seems to imagine.

2. Current projects toward a semantic web

Discussions of the problems of semantic operability on the web have a tendency to become discussions of the problem of managing and integrating ontologies. The reasons for this are not obscure: ontologies are widely regarded as a critical element of the next generation of data integration solutions, and the world wide web is a heterogeneous environment in which foreign data (and therefore ontologies) are regularly juxtaposed. What is less clear is how such data can be combined. A number of new technologies have been proposed that extend or replace existing web technologies; prominent among these are RDF, SHOE, PROMPT and Chimaera. However, these tools and techniques either require adoption of a specific standard for ontology representation (RDF [1], SHOE [6, 7]) or are only semi-automated reconciliation solutions (PROMPT [20], Chimaera [18]). In fact, even the ontology representation standards such as RDF and SHOE appear to require manual construction of the new intersection ontologies that provide mappings between different ontologies.

Each of these tools and technologies has been well described by their authors and developers, and the purpose of this paper is not to repeat the existing descriptions. Each development attempts to overcome the heterogeneity of the web, but they all suffer common problems. For example, although Chimaera successfully addresses the issue of managing different ontologies by reconciling them, it is still a tool that requires manual manipulation and human decision-making. Similarly, PROMPT also is only semi-automatic.

RDF provides a transportable way of expressing information, but the schema itself is separated from the information. Thus maintenance is difficult, as if the data changes the schema must be changed as well to maintain consistency. This problem will be faced by any implementation that uses an explicit representation of ontology. RDF appears to provide a useful medium for expressing data and metadata, and further layers such as DAML+OIL [8, 19] increase the opportunities for reasoning about the data contained in a document based on its accompanying meta-data. But each ontology must still be constructed either in isolation from other ontologies (in which case reconciling information sources faces all the problems discussed in the introduction to this paper), or the ontology developer must find and look inside external ontologies to choose which to extend. Since this implies that the other ontologies are well-formed and available, there is hardly a need for reconciliation - this paper is concerned with situations in which two (or more) existing information sources are to be brought together. It is not clear that RDF or DAML+OIL can assist with this task.

The biggest disadvantage of SHOE is lack of central management. Because of its flexibility, many different users can create new or extend existing ontologies to annotate the data, which makes it difficult for agents and humans to query this data. As mentioned regarding RDF and DAML+OIL, agents must be aware of the many existing ontologies, and SHOE still does not solve the problem of automatically reconciling diversity. Thus results from a query may remain incomplete or mismatched because the agent is not able to find all the relevant data. Further, SHOE does not yet support a wide range of ontology formats.

Since the previous version of this article was published, OWL, or Web Ontology Language, has received a great deal of attention and effort. Supported and endorsed by the World Wide Web Consortium (W3C), OWL is a revision of DAML+OIL, extended to include, among other features, relations between classes, cardinality, equality, characteristics of properties and enumerated classes [26]. OWL provides a means to tag and mark entities mentioned in web pages, connecting them to ontologies for definition, and relating them to other entities for reasoning and deduction. The motivation behind the development of OWL is to provide a language to support the Semantic Web, discussion of which is beyond the scope of this article (see the W3C web site [25] for information). OWL comes in three versions which differ in complexity, trading expressiveness and syntactic freedom for computability and decidability.

As a language for declaring entities' types by reference to web-accessible ontologies, and reasoning about these entities, OWL is a strong candidate for a de facto standard for on-line communication. If all information publishers could be convinced to develop ontologies for their content and mark it accordingly, and their ontologies could be meaningfully integrated or at least reconciled consistently, then the Semantic Web effort will succeed and the technologies to be presented in this article will no longer be necessary. As yet, this has not happened, nor does it seem likely in the immediate future. Further, there is an enormous body of information both on- and off-line that will probably never be marked with OWL or other ontological meta-data, unless this could be done automatically.

3. Reconciling implicit ontologies

Most data on the Internet today appears without any explicit ontology. To integrate data that has no accompanying explicit ontological representation requires either that formal ontologies be constructed for each data source, manually or automatically, or that the conceptual and semantic correspondences between elements in the data be recognised or deduced directly, without resorting to an explicit representation of the ontology. The former process at first seems to be the more reasonable, as it mirrors the intuitive process a person would be likely to define if asked to plan the task (see [17] for a detailed analysis of task-based contexts). However, we suggest that the latter process is in fact closer to the actual approach a person would take when given two data sources and asked to reconcile them. Furthermore, the first method introduces several of the most troublesome ontology management issues, namely constructing accurate and usable ontologies, choosing a representation, and then aligning different ontologies. If the two ontologies are developed together, some of the difficulties of the development can be stepped over as the engineer juggles and reconciles concepts and relationships as they go, but such a synergy certainly cannot scale far beyond two data sources at a time. In reality it is often desirable to compare and contrast data from multiple sources, such as a variety of on-line book stores. One objective of our research into ontological reconciliation is to automate the process as much as possible so that any solutions are eventually globally deployable.

Another important benefit of an automated, lightweight approach to ontological reconciliation is that it makes whatever technology is deployed very adaptable to changes in the data environment. If an intelligent agent is tasked with retrieving prices of books from three major on-line book stores, traditional ontology development and management approaches require that an engineer assess the data sources and construct mapping ontologies between them. If the companies publishing their stock data does not supply a well-formatted ontology along with the shopping data, the engineer also has to construct three individual ontologies before any mapping can even be considered. If a fourth source of on-line books becomes available, the engineer is required again to construct either another mapping ontology to align the new source and the existing mapping ontologies, or the process must begin again from scratch. Of course, if the intelligent agent has its own ontology for the domain of books sales (which is likely, if it has been designed to search and report on data of this type), it is only necessary for the engineer to construct maps between this ontology and each data source. But each time one of the companies changes their data representation the engineer is again required to manually intervene, unless the company provides sufficient hooks in their ontology for backward compatibility. In the low margin world of on-line commerce, this is hardly likely to be considered a cost-effective effort even though technologies such as SHOE deliberately support this [6]. An automated solution is obviously preferable to one that requires human supervision, and we suggest that in most end-user applications, the required accuracy is generally not high enough to demand heavyweight tools and processes. Additionally, a well-designed user interface could allow the user to touch up the results of the automatic reconciliation on-the-fly, thus harnessing the intelligence of the user for effectively no cost.

4. Practical reconciliation

The bulk of this paper discusses two recent projects that have produced promising results for alternative approaches to ontological reconciliation. Elements of this analysis were originally published in [15] but have been significantly updated here to illustrate the practical possibilities for implementing the ideas presented in the first part of this paper. The projects described here are a progression from earlier work [23, 24]. The two approaches to ontological reconciliation described in this section are lightweight and suitable for inclusion in intelligent software agents, particularly information agents which are required to deal with varied and uncertain information sources and formats. Neither approach is tied to a particular ontology representation language, indeed AReXS does not use explicit formal ontologies at all. Rather than the more abstract exercise of aligning hand-crafted ontologies, these two approaches deal with semi-structured information as it tends to occur in practice. Where CASA uses knowledge units to interpret an information source and AReXS constructs example-based assumptions of semantic equivalence, our most recent work is a combination of these approaches called ROADMAT[1] which has demonstrated improved results and will be described in future publications.

4.1. CASA

Classified Advertisement Search Agent (CASA) is an information agent that searches on-line advertisements to assist users in finding a range of information including

[1] ROADMAT has been developed by Gillian Tee as part of her honours thesis in the Intelligent Agent Lab.

rental properties and used cars [3, 4]. It was built as a prototype[2] to evaluate the principle of increasing the effectiveness and flexibility of information agents while reducing their development cost by separating their knowledge from their architecture, and discriminating between different classes of knowledge in order to maximise the reusability of constructed knowledge bases. CASA is able to learn how to interpret new HTML documents, by recognising and understanding both the content of the documents and their structure. It also represents a framework for building knowledge-based information agents that are able to assimilate new knowledge easily, without requiring re-implementation or redundant development of the core agent infrastructure.

CASA classifies knowledge into three categories: general knowledge, domain-specific knowledge and site or source specific knowledge. Each category is independent from the others, and multiple instances of each category can exist. This segregation of knowledge by practical use is markedly different to the usual approach of capturing and representing all high-level knowledge in a formal hierarchy or graph and ignoring low-level knowledge. It provides more seamless integration of different types of knowledge, as well as discriminating between knowledge that is likely to be common across heterogeneous data sources, and knowledge that is likely to change. This increases the effectiveness of an information agent equipped with such knowledge, as it does not approach a new data source empty handed, but armed with the ability to make assumptions and deduce correspondences between the new data and sources with which it is familiar.

General knowledge gives a software agent enough information to understand and operate in its environment. General knowledge is knowledge that is true for all information sources, and is independent of specific domains and sites. The set of general knowledge developed for CASA describes on-line web documents, and includes knowledge of the components that make up an HTML document such as what are tables, paragraphs and lines, as well as knowledge of what a web page is and how one can be accessed.

Domain-specific knowledge provides an information agent with a basic understanding of the area in which it is required to work. This knowledge is true for a particular field and is independent of site or source specifics. For the case of university services, domain knowledge would generally include the concepts of students, lectures, theatres, semesters, professors and subjects, as well as ontological relationships such as the idea that students take classes, classes cover particular topics and occur at certain times during the week at certain locations, and that particular subjects make up a course. Because domain knowledge is independent of site-specific knowledge, it can be re-used across numerous sites and should remain useful into the future.

Site-specific knowledge is true for a particular information source only. Site knowledge is specific and unique, but necessary for negotiating the contents of a particular information source; it provides a means of understanding the basic

[2]CASA was built by Sharon Gao as part of her doctoral thesis in the Intelligent Agent Lab.

data that comprise an information source, for a particular representation. Continuing the university web site example, site-specific knowledge might encode the particular pattern or format in which a certain institution presents a description of a unit of teaching, or of a degree, including information such as table structures, knowledge unit sequences and marker text that locates certain classes of information.

The three categories of knowledge that CASA manages provide different levels of operational assistance for the information agent. General knowledge enables an agent to act and interact in a particular environment, providing the basis for navigation and perception and giving the agent a means by which to internalise its input. Site-specific knowledge permits an agent to assimilate and process information from a particular source, which is a necessary ability if the agent is to perform useful tasks. Domain-specific knowledge sits between general and site-specific knowledge, giving a conceptual framework through which an agent can reconcile information from different sources. Domain-specific knowledge can also assist an agent to negotiate unfamiliar information sources for which it has no site-specific knowledge. Domain knowledge can be used in conjunction with general knowledge to analyse a site's conventions and representations and to attempt to synthesise the site knowledge necessary to utilise the new information source. Because domain knowledge is not tied to a particular representation, it can be adapted and applied to a variety of different sites or data sources, significantly reducing development time for information agents.

A significant benefit of classifying knowledge into categories is that knowledge can be more readily reused and incorporated into other agents. Compartmentalising knowledge allows agents to teach each other about new information sources or even new knowledge domains. Domain knowledge is reusable by design, and general knowledge is similarly useful. Given the modular approach to information agent construction presented in CASA, once an agent has been taught about a certain domain of knowledge, that knowledge can be applied to a variety of environments just as easily as it can a variety of sites. By plugging in a different general knowledge base, a web-based information agent could easily become an SQL- or XML-based information agent, with the cost of redevelopment greatly reduced by the re-applicability of the domain knowledge base. It also seems quite feasible for an information agent to be armed with a variety of general knowledge bases permitting it to work in multiple environments as appropriate, or even at the same time, utilising its knowledge as applicable both to process recognised information and to interpret and negotiate unfamiliar conceptual representations.

The knowledge categories also enabled a limited amount of learning within CASA. Within the domain knowledge structure CASA was able to add to knowledge units; for example, a real estate instance of CASA learned suburb names for location of properties described in advertisements and the going rates for properties to enable it to understand the meaning of terms such as "cheap". It also learnt the site-specific knowledge required to interpret HTML table structures automatically without training data. This learning protected CASA from the evolution of form that inevitably occurs in on-line information sources, allowing it to adapt to unstated ontological changes.

4.2. AReXS

AReXS (Automatic Reconciliation of XML Structures) is an application[3] that reconciles heterogeneous data sources presented in XML documents. It aligns data sources according to their implicit ontological structure. It is able to reconcile differences of expression and representation across XML documents from heterogeneous sources without any predefined knowledge or human intervention [15]. It achieves this by identifying XML elements whose meanings are similar enough to be considered equivalent. AReXS requires no knowledge or experience of the domain in which it works, and indeed is completely domain independent. It uses Example-Based Frame Matching (EBFM) [9] and is able to achieve very high recall with modest precision on real world data collected from commercial web sites. By requiring no domain knowledge, AReXS is suitable for application to any field; its success relies on its ability to identify and resolve the differences in representation that result from sourcing data from a multi-cultural environment.

AReXS does not fit into the traditional mould of an ontology management tool, as it does not use any type of formal ontology representation. Instead, it more closely mimics the intuitive process that a person is likely to follow when tasked with aligning multiple structured data sources. In formal terms, AReXS attempts to automatically resolve the problems of synonymy and polysemy that are significant hurdles to semantic interoperability [14, 15, 16].

For example, a pair of XML documents from different sources, both describing services offered by universities, might contain elements named SUBJECT and UNIT respectively. If the two elements happen to both signify self-contained units of course work, an agent with no prior domain experience or knowledge will have little hope of realising this. AReXS resolves this discontinuity by considering the values of instances of the elements as well as the element names, deriving confidence in a match from similarities in either comparison. If one document contains the statement `<SUBJECT>Introductory Programming</SUBJECT>` and another contains a similar statement `<UNIT>Introduction to Programming </UNIT>`, AReXS is able to consider the possibility that the two elements `SUBJECT` and `UNIT` are in this context signifying the same concept. If further correspondences could be found between other instances of these same elements, the confidence of a conceptual match would increase.

AReXS works by analysing two XML structures and identifying matching elements, generating a map of equivalence between concepts represented in the two documents. It is important to note that no formal representation of such concepts is attempted - rather, it is assumed that elements represent concepts, and that the equivalence of two elements can be deduced based on similarities between instances of both elements. As a metaphor, AReXS works in much the

[3]The original AReXS system was built by Dominic Hou as part of his honours thesis in the Intelligent Agent Lab.

same way that two people who do not share a common language might teach each other by pointing at objects and saying the names that each person's language gives to that object.

Identification of conceptual equivalence is based on a consideration of lexicographical similarity between both the names and the contents of XML tags in each document. Matches are then assessed to deduce structural similarities between documents from different sources. By repeating this search for semiotic correspondence across other pairs of elements generated from the contents of the XML documents under consideration, AReXS is able to build a local context for data and then use this context to reconcile the ontological differences between XML documents.

To establish the extent of the context shared by pairs of documents, the AReXS engine uses the Character-Based Best Match algorithm [21] to evaluate textual similarity between the names and contents of elements. Such a string based comparison works well to filter out simple manifestations of local cultures; for example, one university web site may choose to include the identification number of a subject in the name of the subject while another may not, opting instead to have a second element containing a numeric identification code for each unit. While AReXS will not be able to realise that the number in the name of a subject from one university corresponds to the numeric unit code from another, it will generally conclude from the similarity of the names that units and subjects are conceptually compatible in this context.

Applying a textual similarity analysis on real data is likely to generate a large number of candidate concepts that may or may not contribute to the local context of the data. AReXS increases its confidence in a candidate for equivalence depending on the uniqueness of the matches between element pairs. The uniqueness function described by [9] is used to establish the likelihood of a textual match between elements actually revealing a shared, unique concept, based on the principle that the more common a concept is across significantly different elements, the less rich the concept is and thus the less there is to be gained from considering it as part of the data context.

The results of tests based on sample real world data from web sites including amazon.com, angusandrobertson.com.au, barnesandnoble.com and borders.com show that AReXS is capable of accurately identifying conceptually equivalent elements based on both the element names and sample instances of the elements. These web sites were chosen as useful examples for two reasons. Firstly, they are live, international representatives of the types of data source with which people desire to interact (and in fact already do interact) on a regular but casual basis, and secondly they provide data that by its nature is open to subjective decisions during the process of choosing a logical representation. The casual nature of the interaction that people generally have with sites such as these is important, as discussed earlier in this paper. Since AReXS has been tailored to process XML formatted input, the raw data from the sampled web sites was encoded into XML by hand. Although much care was taken not to add any information or structure to the data that might spoil the experiments, extracting relatively free data from web sites and converting it to a structured form is not the focus of the AReXS prototype please refer to the next section on CASA to see how this extraction can be automated.

The AReXS algorithms allow identification of concept matches regardless of the ordering of concepts or elements, and its consideration of both names and values of elements allows it to identify equivalences even if one of the name or the value is absent (e.g. `<>John Cole</>` matches `<AUTHOR>John Cole</AUTHOR>`); in other words, AReXS is tolerant of inconsistent data. An element name might well be missing if the XML data has been automatically generated from another source, as happened during the construction of the test input for these experiments - it was not possible to identify from the sample web sites exactly what the intended name of a particular element was, so rather than make one up, the element tag name was left blank. Admittedly, this left the XML documents malformed, but substituting dummy element names would solve this and would actually allow AReXS to cope with more than one missing element name in each data source. The AReXS engine has also demonstrated partial success in identifying many-to-one conceptual equivalences, which can occur in situations like that described earlier in which multiple concepts are represented by multiple elements in one data source but only one element in the other data source.

Although AReXS only supports reconciling pairs of data sources, the EBFM algorithm on which it is based provides for comparison of multiple sources and so extending AReXS to support this feature is feasible. While AReXS is partially able to recognise many-to-one equivalences, it will require further work to actually capitalise on this recognition. Finally, the principles implemented in AReXS could quite readily be adapted to allow the extension of data structures based on identification of concept matches within element names or values. Drawing on the example described earlier of university service descriptions, if one information source presents automobile data with an element of the form <*make_model*>Mitsubishi Magna</*make_model*> and a second source opts for two elements <*make*>Mitsubishi</*make*> and <*model*>Magna</*model*>, it is possible to see that a software agent could use analysis techniques similar to those implemented in AReXS to realise that both elements from the second source are encoded within a single element of the first source.

New results in reconciliation

Since this work was first published, the capabilities of the AReXS engine have been further examined. The domain of second-hand car advertisements was chosen for a series of experiments, which will be briefly discussed here. Classified advertisements are one of the more popular and successful use that people have found for the Internet so far, probably due to the fact that they leverage the Internet's strengths, being convenient communication and information retrieval, while avoiding it's weaknesses by conducting actual transactions off-line - although auction sites are also popular on the Internet, for high-value items such as cars, classified advertisement sites tend to act more like match-makers than brokers,

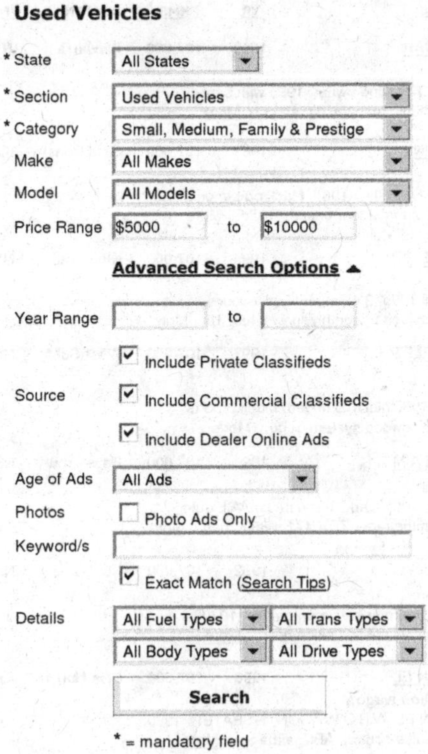

FIGURE 1. Search interface for Autotrader

bringing together interested sellers and buyers who then meet and make their own arrangements. Five popular web sites were chosen:

- Autotrader (*www.autotrader.com.au*)
- Autoweb (*www.autoweb.com.au*)
- Carsales (*www.carsales.com.au*)
- Drive (*www.drive.com.au*)
- Ebay (*www.ebay.com.au*)

The search function of each site, an example of which is shown in Figure 1, was used to collect 100 current entries, creating a database of 500 car descriptions. The web sites typically presented the car descriptions in the form of tables, like that shown in Figure 2. This data was then parsed by custom written information agents to create pseudo-XML documents (it was not necessary to conform strictly

SAVE	PHOTO	MAKE & MODEL	YR	KMS	REGION	STATE	PRICE	SELLER
		**NISSAN PULSAR** **manual** Nissan Pulsar Q Second owner, 1993 with service history, 107000kms, manual, air, steer,... More	**1993**	**107,000**	**Illawarra**	**NSW**	**$7,800**	**Private**
Fresh		NISSAN SKYLINE manual coupe Nissan Skyline R31 Gts-x 1987, black purple pearl, 5sp manual, 107,000kms, 2door coupe, RB20... More	1987	107,000	Gold Coast	QLD	$8,000	Private
		NISSAN BLUEBIRD manual Nissan Bluebird 1995, 2.4L manual, all options, 107000kms, serviced 6 monthly, new tyres, 10... More	1995	107,000	Nth Shore	NSW	$7,850	Private
Fresh		TOYOTA STARLET Toyota Starlet 1997 black, 5 speed, mags, sports exhaust, tints, Kenwood system, rego... More	1997	107,000	West Subs	NSW	$8,500	Private
Fresh		HOLDEN ACCLAIM automatic sedan Holden Acclaim 1996 Dark Green sedan V6L auto, 107000kms, 4 mths rego, ZDV-471, $8000 neg... More	1996	107,000	Hawkesbury	NSW	$8,000	Private
Fresh		VOLVO 850 automatic sedan Volvo 850 1992 maroon sedan automatic, 107000kms, 12 mths rego, Volvo service since new,... More	1992	107,000	Nth Shore	NSW	$9,950	Private
		FORD FALCON EL **automatic station wagon** FORD FALCON EL, AUTO WAGON, 6-SEATER. 1996, 107,000kms, cruise control, ABS, airbags,... More	**1996**	**107,000**	**Bris Metro**	**QLD**	**$9,500**	**Private**

FIGURE 2. Car descriptions presented by Autotrader

to the XML standard for our purposes). The descriptions of cars were thereby transformed into documents of the form:

<Autotrader>
<car>
<make_model>Toyota Corolla SECA</make_model>
<yr>1993</yr>
<kms>140,000</kms>
<price>$9,995</price>
<state>WA</state>
<media>?</media>
<dealer></dealer>
</car>
</Autotrader>

The data presented by the classified advertisement web sites was not always in the form of a simple table - Figures 3, 4 and 5 show different styles of presentation.

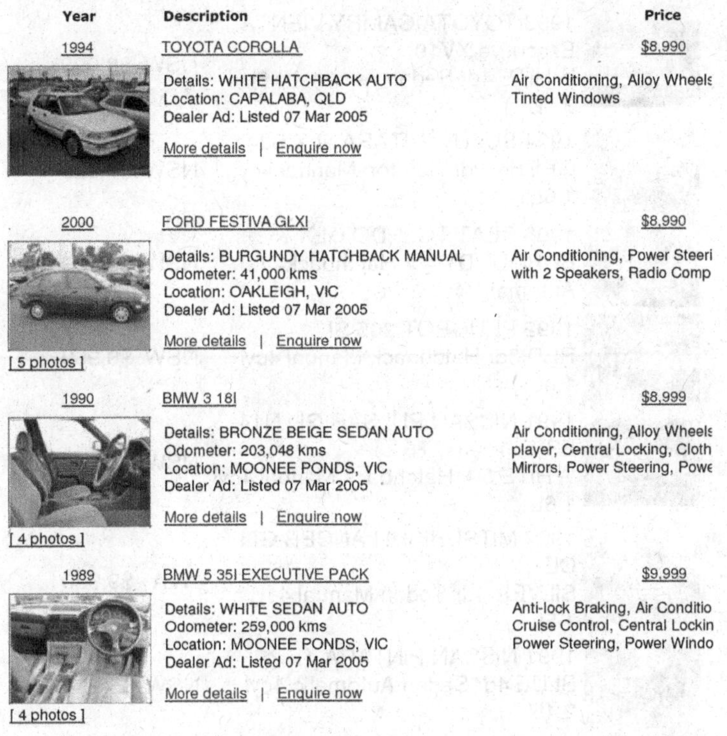

FIGURE 3. Car descriptions presented by Autoweb

Regardless, the use of task-oriented information agents to extract the required data from the web pages made collecting the data into a consistent form quite simple. Attempting to create a single information agent to parse all five web sites would have taken significantly longer than this more direct approach.

Where possible, the markup tag names were taken directly from the original source data. Each of the five sets of car descriptions were paired and given to AReXS to reconcile, producing a collection of mappings between fields based on any evidence that AReXS could find to claim conceptual correspondences between

1993 TOYOTA CAMRY VIENTA
Executive XV10
WHITE 4dr Sedan Automatic 6cyl
3.0L
NSW $8,999
1994 SUZUKI VITARA JLX SJ413
GREEN 2dr Hardtop Manual 4cyl
1.6L
NSW $7,999
1996 SEAT TOLEDO GLX
BURGUNDY 4dr Hatchback
Automatic 4cyl 2.0L
NSW $9,999
1992 PEUGEOT 205 SI
RED 3dr Hatchback Manual 4cyl
1.6L
NSW $8,999
1991 NISSAN PULSAR GLi N14
ES
WHITE 5dr Hatchback Manual 4cyl
1.6L
NSW $6,999
1997 MITSUBISHI LANCER GLi
CE
SILVER 4dr Sedan Manual 4cyl
1.5L
WA $9,990
1991 NISSAN PINTARA Ti
BLUE 4dr Sedan Automatic 4cyl
2.4L
NSW $5,999
1996 MITSUBISHI MIRAGE CE
RED 3dr Hatchback Manual 4cyl
1.5L
NSW $9,999

FIGURE 4. Car descriptions presented by Carsales

the sets. For example, the data from Autotrader was compared with with that from Autoweb:

Source Autotrader.xml
<make_model>Subaru Liberty GX</make_model>
<yr>1993</yr>
<kms></kms>
<price>$9,990</price>
<state>VIC</state>
<dealer>Eastern Vehicle</dealer>

Source Autoweb.xml
<year>1989</year>
<description>FORD FALCON</description>
<price>$5,990</price>
<body_type>WAGON</body_type>
<colour>YELLOW</colour>
<location>OAKLEIGH, VIC</location>

The original form of the data for these two web sites can be seen in Figures 2 and 3. These two representations are quite tabular and it is very easy to read a

Compare	Item Title	PayPal	Price	Bids	Time Left ▲
Featured Items					
	PONTIAC TRANSAM 1980- STUNNER!!! GREAT PRICE!!		**AU $12,000.00**	-	14h 49m
	TOYOTA LANDCRUISER 78 SERIES 11 SEAT TROOPCARRIER SUPERB OFF ROAD OR GENERAL VEHICLE FOR CAMPING, TOWING,		**AU $34,900.00**	-	17h 23m
	BMW 525i. 1989 sedan		AU $10,000.00 Buy It Now		21h 19m
	1968 XTGT FALCON		**AU $25,000.00** AU $37,000.00 Buy It Now	1	1d 00h 56m
	Chevrolet Trail Blazer 2000 Luxury 4WD/SUV 54,000 KLMS Rare US Chevrolet Luxury SUV, Converted to Right Hand D		**AU $29,500.00**	-	1d 02h 29m

FIGURE 5. Car descriptions presented by Ebay

schema or ontology for the data directly from the column headings[4]. Other web sites did not present such a straight forward format, notably those in Figures 4 and 5.

For a person, a quick glance at the sample records is enough to identify two direct field matches, *yr* with *year* and *price* with *price*. Relying solely on the field names, *make_model* might not be expected to encode the same meaning as *description*, but the sample contents of these two fields suggest that there may in fact be a correlation. AReXS proposed the following mapping between these two data sources:

[4]For reasons related to printing, some of the figures in this article had to be updated; some of the web sites involved had changed their design since the original analysis was performed and consequently look slightly different. Although none of the changes were significant, the reader may notice minor differences in field names and contents

Slot 0 [*year*]	↔	Slot 1 [*yr*]	: 0.99965
Slot 1 [*description*]	↔	Slot 0 [*make_model*]	: 0.99996
Slot 2 [*price*]	↔	Slot 2 [*kms*]	: 0.81160
Slot 2 [*price*]	↔	Slot 3 [*price*]	: 0.99962
Slot 3 [*body_type*]	↔	Slot 0 [*make_model*]	: 0.41018
Slot 5 [*location*]	↔	Slot 0 [*make_model*]	: 0.02155

Comparing the automated results with our expectations, the correlation between *year* and *yr* has been convincingly detected, as has that between *price* and *price*. Further, as predicted based on the field content, a strong correspondence has also been identified between *description* and *make_model*. These are the three strong content-based concept matches. However, a number of other weaker correspondences are suggested, and these are just as interesting as the strong matches. Based on the example data, there is a moderate correlation between *price* values and *kms* values. This is understandable, as the Character-Based Best Match string comparison algorithm focuses on pairs on characters within the strings being compared, and since both *price* and *kms* are actually numbers, there is naturally a high coincidental correspondence - numbers have a small alphabet and so exhibit much less variation than alphanumeric strings. The CBBM algorithm is further confused by the fact that for second-hand cars, the distance travelled will generally be in the order of 100,000 kilometres and the asked sale price will be in the order of 10,000 dollars, thus there is almost no difference in the lengths of the strings that represent these numbers. It seems very likely that the only reason that the correspondence between *price* and *kms* was not stronger is the '$' dollar sign present in the *price* fields.

AReXS also reported a weak correspondence between *body_type* and *make_model*. Examining the sample date reveals that the people who entered the data occasionally include words such as 'sedan' or 'wagon' in the *make_model* field, which seems natural enough. This highlights the fact that even in natural language communication between people, ontological differences arise - some car owners obviously believe that the concept of a car's make and model includes it's body type, whereas others believe that that information belongs elsewhere. Some probably would have included it in a separate field if one had been offered, but lacking such a field decided to attach the information to the most appropriate available field. We also believe that the lexicographic nature of the CBBM comparison algorithm contributed to the weak correspondence between *body_type* and *make_model* - these fields contain natural language words which inherently contain common substrings. Similarly, we explain the slight correspondence between *location* and *make_model* as merely the result of linguistic coincidence.

In many cases, the unexpected results were as interesting as the expected ones, and revealed potential methods for improving the AReXS functionality. For example, both the Autotrader site and the Drive site included in their car descriptions fields labelled *colour*. Typical contents of these fields were *white*, *yellow* and so on. Intuitively, these fields should have been among the easiest for AReXS to match, and yet on 100 records from each site it was only confident enough to rate them with a correspondence of 0.71911. It seems likely that a string comparison algorithm working on a word basis rather than a character-pair basis as the used CBBM algorithm does would be more appropriate for such data, yet it is not clear how an information agent should make a decision like this. Perhaps colour should be regarded as a basic concept that all information agents should know (general knowledge, in knowledge classification scheme implemented in CASA), or at least ones dealing with cars (domain knowledge, as per CASA). Similarly, although prices and numbers look similar, they generally shouldn't be considered for conceptual equivalence just because they both consist mainly of digits. AReXS copes quite well with them, but tends to allow too much correspondence between them - some basic knowledge about types of data would surely improve its results.

Generally, it is our opinion that the techniques for enabling semantic interoperability used in AReXS complement other techniques such as explicit ontology-based approaches. Combining a variety of techniques should lead to a synergy that provides even better results. As identified earlier, seeding AReXS's reconciliation attempt with small domain- or task-specific ontologies should enhance its results. Other domain or general knowledge such as types of data would allow AReXS to explore the most likely matches first, increasing its efficiency greatly. Although we have not as yet conducted a comprehensive analysis, experiments with smaller sample sets have produced less consistent results as individual variations in the sample data have greater impact on the reconciliation process. Some data are clearly more easily reconciled than others; what is not yet clear and deserves further attention is how to identify how useful given data will be prior to reconciling.

4.3. Modifications to the AReXS algorithm

Two noteworthy modifications were made to the AReXS implementation of the EBFM algorithm, after running the initial experiments. The first of these was to remove uniqueness screening for fields in the input XML documents (referred to as slots and frames respectively by [9]). The EBFM algorithm screens input data records according to their uniqueness, that is, how different they are to all other input data. This was found to significantly reduce the ability identify semantic matches, as even what appeared to be strong correspondences were heavily penalised. In effect, fields such as vehicle prices had very little chance of being successfully reconciled because there was relatively little variance in the actual prices. We felt that similarity within a field in a single information source shouldn't reduce the value of matches between fields from different sources, and when we removed this restriction we found the results to be more in line with our expectations, and thus much more useful.

The second modification that we made was similar. We made the reward for matching contents of fields independent of the uniqueness of the match. The original EBFM algorithm devalues matches if they are common, whereas we found that this reduced the effectiveness of the reconciliation process. An example of the effect of removing this restriction was the following improvement in reconciling two information sources:

Reward tied to uniqueness of match:

Slot 0 [*make_model*]	↔	Slot 1 [*description*]	: 0.57109
Slot 3 [*price*]	↔	Slot 2 [*price*]	: 0.07830

Reward tied only to similarity of contents:

Slot 0 [*make_model*]	↔	Slot 1 [*description*]	: 0.99997
Slot 0 [*make_model*]	↔	Slot 3 [*body_type*]	: 0.41019
Slot 0 [*make_model*]	↔	Slot 5 [*location*]	: 0.02156
Slot 1 [*yr*]	↔	Slot 0 [*year*]	: 0.99965
Slot 2 [*kms*]	↔	Slot 2 [*price*]	: 0.81161
Slot 3 [*price*]	↔	Slot 2 [*price*]	: 0.99962

Certainly the number of false positive results has been increased, but they are well below the cut-off level at which a correspondence would be considered to be a semantic match (0.9 or greater seems to be a reasonable limit). The only real concern is the moderate correspondence between *kms* and *price*, but even this is not rated highly enough that presents a risk of being confused with other stronger matches. More importantly, the confidence of the matches between *make_model* and *description* and *price* and *price* has increased dramatically, and a further very strong correspondence has been identified between *yr* and *year*, bringing the overall result much closer to what we had expected based on our own understanding of the sample data.

5. Multi-agent systems: applied semantic interoperability

Multi-agent systems are an area in which multiple view-points and independent interpretations of data and events are increasingly becoming a topic of interest, particularly for multi-agent systems that are open and permit heterogeneity amongst their population. In such systems, it is inherently difficult to predict the information needs of individual agents, let alone which particular data representations they require. Although many proposed multi-agent systems enforce system-wide global ontologies, this is not always desirable or feasible.

Developing such systems reliably and predictably requires careful consideration of the structure of knowledge and responsibility within the system. Agent-oriented software engineering has emerged as an active area of research in the past several years to address the question of how to develop information agents systematically. The first complete methodology proposed to guide the process of developing a multi-agent system from analysis to design was Gaia [27]. According to Gaia, a multi-agent system is conceived as a computational organisation of agents, each playing specific roles in the organisation, and cooperating with each

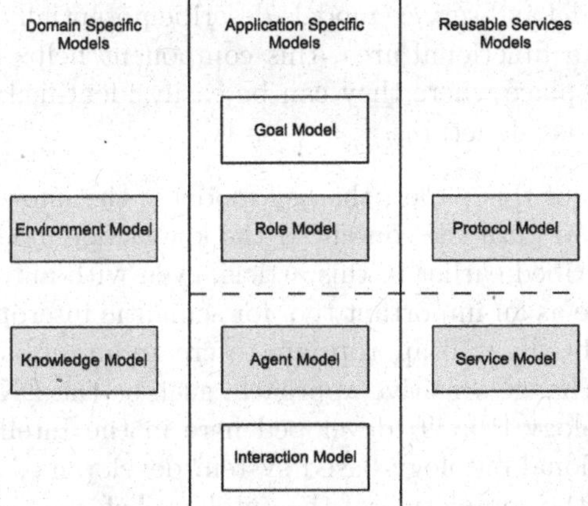

FIGURE 6. ROADMAP Models

other towards the achievement of a common application (i.e. organisational) goal. Several extensions of Gaia have been proposed including ROADMAP, as reported in [12, 13].

The ROADMAP methodology is to develop a series of models. It started as an attempt to extend the original version of Gaia with a dynamic role hierarchy as a way to deal with open agent systems, and included additional models to explicitly describe the agent environment and agent knowledge. From Gaia, ROADMAP inherits the organisational view on multi-agent systems, and basic definitions of roles, protocols, agents and services.

In ROADMAP, a system is viewed as an organisation of agents, consisting of a role hierarchy and an agent hierarchy. The role hierarchy is the specification of the system representing the correct behaviour of agents. The agent hierarchy is the implementation of the system, providing actual functionalities. The role hierarchy constrains the agent hierarchy in the same way as organisational structures, responsibilities and business procedures constrain individuals in a human organisation.

Figure 6 shows the structure of the ROADMAP models. The models are grouped into three categories:

- The environment model and the knowledge model contain reusable high-level domain information. This category of ROADMAP models provides a flexible framework whereby an agent can be conceptualised rather than being seen in terms of computer code.
- The goal model, role model, agent model and interaction model are application specific. This category of models provides for the definition of the agent as a coherent software structure that can meet the needs identified in the first category.

- The protocol model and service models describe potentially reusable software components. As a functional area, this component helps keep the reusable components in a place where they càn be easily identified and not confused with the conceptual structures.

For the purposes of this paper, the key model is the knowledge model. Any evolving ontology would form the content of the knowledge model in a web-based agent system. As described earlier in this article, even with automatic ontological reconciliation available as an important tool for semantic interoperability, in some situations it is undoubtedly still appropriate to create an ontology manually. We favour a lightweight, change-sensitive approach, such as the EXPLODE ontology development methodology [10, 11] developed here in the Intelligent Agent Laboratory. Unlike traditional ontology-based system development, where the entire system must wait for the completion of the ontology before it is possible to build intelligent agents, EXPLODE allows the development of the system to not depend on the ontology structure and thus to proceed safe in the knowledge that the final ontology will be built around both the application's domain knowledge and system's technical requirements. Thus significant implementation time can be saved, as the ontology and the software agents are treated as equal elements of the system. The EXPLODE methodology avoids the problems of ontology maintenance and integration by employing a multi-staged approach with frequent small releases and continuous integration. This approach extends our vision of lightweight ontological management to to situations that do require construction of an explicit ontology.

6. Conclusions and Future Directions

If one of the technologies described in this paper emerged as a unilateral favourite for knowledge representation and data integration, the Internet would quickly cease to be that unstructured wilderness that so many paper introductions claim it to be. Unfortunately, it seems unlikely that any single proposed solution will be widely accepted in the near future. Even if such an event occurred, it is doubtful that many smaller commercial and individual publishers of information would be willing to devote the time and effort required to comply with a standard that requires ontology development. If ontologies developed by leading academics require significant effort to be combined, aligned or otherwise reconciled, as they currently do even with the aid of computerised ontology management tools, how much more the millions of ontologies that would be thrown together by people who just want to get their in-formation on to the web? Ontology engineering is a complicated activity that, while it is clearly important and will definitely play a major role in some areas of information integration, seems likely to always bring overheads that make it unattractive to many publishers, particularly those who move in the global, heterogeneous public space of the Internet. We are proposing and developing technologies and methodologies that cope with heterogeneity and change in information sources by performing implicit ontological reconciliation.

However, it would be a shame to ignore the much work being done to provide information sources with meta-data in the form of explicit ontologies and schema. One important direction for the future development of the tools and algorithms described in this paper is the combination of systems that consider implicit ontologies with ones that understand explicit meta-data. Since we are effectively advocating a multi-level and decentralised approach to semantic interoperability, it is natural to imagine solutions that combine a variety of strategies, each with its own strengths and weaknesses. Although the AReXS project requires no domain knowledge at all, there is no reason to restrict ourselves to this; if domain or any other relevant knowledge is available then of course it should be harnessed. It seems intuitive that, for example, the uninformed reconciliation done by AReXS could be significantly enhanced by using the knowledge contained in any supplied ontology, schema or DTD as an advantageous starting point for the reconciliation effort. Thesaurus projects such as WordNet [2] can provide ready-made synonym tables, enabling the space of possible concept matches that must be searched to be greatly reduced, or at least for the most interesting and profitable areas to be searched first. Basic grammatical or formatting knowledge could be similarly employed, as could lists or ontologies of manufacturers and products. Similarly, the instance-based approach employed by AReXS could augment current approaches to merging and reconciling structured ontologies, particularly if instances or exemplars are include along with concepts, as is the case in the popular ontology editing tool Protégé [5].

The approaches and methods that we have presented here address the issue of semantic interoperability in lightweight, flexible, adaptive, reusable and intelligent ways. In the future we intend to expand these approaches, strengthening the tools available for the creation, distribution and maintenance of smart information processing tools that work with information and people the way they are, rather than requiring that people and information alter their respective practices and forms to suit technology.

Acknowledgements

The projects described in this article were supported by ARC Discovery Project DP0209297, Multi-Ontologies meet UML: Improving the Software Engineering of Multi-Agent Systems, which was folded into the ARC Special Research Centre of Excellence, CE0348177, for Perceptive and Intelligent Machines in Complex Environments.

The authors owe great thanks to Dominic Hou, Sharon Gao, Gillian Tee, Thomas Juan and our colleagues in the Intelligent Agent Laboratory at the Department of Computer Science and Software Engineering at The University of Melbourne.

References

[1] Decker, S., Erdman, M., Fensel, D., Studer, R. *Ontobroker: Ontology-based Access to Distributed and Semi-Structured Information.* R. Meersman et al. (eds), Semantic Issues in Multimedia Systems, Kluwer Academic Publishers, Netherlands, 1999.

[2] Fellbaum, C. (ed.) *WordNet: An Electronic Lexical Database.* MIT Press, Cambridge, America, 1998.

[3] Gao, X., Sterling, L. *A Methodology for Building Information Agents.* In Y. Yang, M. Li, A. Ellis (eds), Web Technologies and Applications, pp 43-52, International Academic Publishers, 1998.

[4] Gao, X., Sterling, L. *Semi-structured Data Extraction from Heterogeneous Sources.* In D. Schwartz, M. Divitini, T. Bratjevik (eds), Internet-based Knowledge Management and Organizational Memories, pp 83-102, Idea Group Publishing, 2000.

[5] Gennari, J., Musen, M. A., Fergerson, R. W., Grosso, W. E., Crubézy, M., Eriksson, H., Noy, N. F., Tu, S. W. *The Evolution of Protégé: An Environment for Knowledge-Based Systems Development.* Stanford University, Technical Report SMI-2002-0943, 2002.

[6] Heflin, J., Hendler, J. *Semantic Interoperability on the Web.* In Proceedings of Extreme Markup Languages 2000, Graphic Communications Association, Alexandria, America, 2000.

[7] Heflin, J., Hendler, J. *Dynamic Ontologies on the Web.* In Proceedings of the Seventeenth National Conference on Artificial Intelligence, Menlo Park, America, 2000.

[8] Hendler, J., McGuinness, D. L. *The DARPA Agent Markup Language.* In IEEE Intelligent Systems, Vol. 15, No. 6, November/December, pp 67-73, 2000.

[9] Ikeda, Y., Itoh, F., and Ueda, T. *Example-based Frame Mapping for Heterogeneous Information Agents.* In Proceedings of the International Conference on Multi-Agent Systems, Paris, France, 1998.

[10] Hristozova, M. *EXPLODE: Extreme Programming for Lightweight Ontology Development.* Master of Engineering thesis, Department of Computer Science and Software Engineering, The University of Melbourne, 2003.

[11] Hristozova, M., Sterling, L. *An eXtreme Method for Developing Lightweight Ontologies.* In S. Cranefield, T. Finin, S. Willmott (eds), Proceedings of the Workshop on Ontologies in Agent Systems, First International Joint Conference on Autonomous Agents and Multi-Agent Systems, CEUR Workshop Series, 2002.

[12] Juan, T., Pearce, P., Sterling, L. *ROADMAP: Extending the Gaia Methodology for Complex Open Systems.* In Proceedings of the First International Joint Conference on Autonomous Agents and Multi-Agent Systems, Bologna, Italy, 2002.

[13] Juan, T., Sterling, L. *The ROADMAP Meta-model for Intelligent Adaptive Multi-Agent Systems in Open Environments.* In Proceedings of the Fourth International

Workshop on Agent Oriented Software Engineering, Second International Joint Conference on Autonomous Agents and Multi-Agent Systems, Springer-Verlag Lecture Notes in Computer Science, Vol. 2935, 2003.

[14] Klein, M. *Supporting evolving ontologies on the Internet.* In Proceedings of the EDBT 2002 PhD Workshop, Prague, Czech Republic, 2002.

[15] Lister, K., Sterling, L. *Agents in a Multi-Cultural World: Towards Ontological Reconciliation.* In M. Stumptner, D. Corbett, M. Brooks (eds), Advances in Artificial Intelligence, Proceedings of the Fourteenth Australian Joint Conference on Artificial Intelligence, Springer-Verlag Lecture Notes in Artificial Intelligence, Vol. 2256, pp 321-332, 2001.

[16] Lister, K., Sterling, L. *Tasks as Context for Intelligent Agents.* In Proceedings of the IEEE/WIC International Conference on Intelligent Agent Technology, Halifax, Canada, 2003.

[17] Lister, K., Sterling, L. *Reconciling Ontological Differences for Intelligent Agents.* In P. Bouquet (ed), Meaning Negotiation, AAAI Technical Report WS-02-09, Eighteenth National Conference on Artificial Intelligence, Edmonton, Canada, 2002.

[18] McGuinness, D., Fikes, R., Rice, J., Wilder, S. *An Environment for Merging and Testing Large Ontologies.* In Proceedings of the Seventh International Conference on Principles of Knowledge Representation and Reasoning, Breckenridge, America, 2000.

[19] McGuinness, D. L., Fikes, R., Hendler, J., Stein, L. A. *DAML+OIL: An Ontology Language for the Semantic Web.* In IEEE Intelligent Systems, Vol. 17, No. 5, September/October, 2002.

[20] Noy, F., Musen, N. *An Algorithm for Merging and Aligning Ontologies: Automation and Tool Support.* In Proceedings of the Workshop on Ontology Management at the Sixteenth National Conference on Artificial Intelligence, Orlando, America, 1999.

[21] Sato, S. *CTM: An example-based translation aid system.* In Proceedings of the Fifteenth International Conference on Computational Linguistics, Nantes, France, 1992.

[22] Steels, L. *Self-Organising Vocabularies.* C. Langton, T. Shimohara (eds), Artificial Life V: Proceedings of the Fifth International Conference on the Synthesis and Simulation of Living Systems, Nara, Japan, 1996.

[23] Sterling, L. *A Knowledge-Biased Approach to Information Agents.* In Proceedings of the International Workshop on Information Integration and Web-based Applications and Services, Yogyakarta, Indonesia, 1999.

[24] Sterling, L. *On Finding Needles in WWW Haystacks.* In Sattar, A. (ed.), Advanced Topics in AI, Proceedings of the Tenth Australian Joint Conference on Artificial Intelligence, Springer-Verlag Lecture Notes in Artificial Intelligence, Vol. 1342, pp 25-36, 1997.

[25] World Wide Web Consortium. `www.w3c.org`. World Wide Web Consortium web site, 2004

[26] Web Ontology Language (OWL). `www.w3c.org/2004/OWL`. World Wide Web Consortium web site, 2004

[27] Wooldridge, M., Jennings, N. R., Kinny, D. *The Gaia Methodology for Agent-Oriented Analysis and Design.* In Journal of Autonomous Agents and Multi-Agent Systems, 3(3):285-312, 2000.

Kendall Lister, Maia Hristozova and Leon Sterling
Intelligent Agent Laboratory
Department of Computer Science and Software Engineering
The University of Melbourne
Australia
e-mail: `krl@cs.mu.oz.au`
`majah@cs.mu.oz.au`
`leon@cs.mu.oz.au`

Query Processing in Ontology-Based Peer-to-Peer Systems

Heiner Stuckenschmidt, Frank van Harmelen and Fausto Giunchiglia

Abstract. The unstructured, heterogeneous and dynamic nature of the Web poses a new challenge to query-answering over multiple data sources. The so-called Semantic Web aims at providing more and semantically richer structures in terms of ontologies and meta-data. A problem that remains is the combined use of heterogeneous sources. In a dynamic environment, it is no longer realistic to assume that the involved data sources act as if they were a single (virtual) source, modelled as a global schema, as is done in classical data integration approaches. In this paper, we propose an alternative approach where we replace the role of a single virtual data source schema with a peer-to-peer approach relying on limited shared (or: overlapping) vocabularies between peers. Since overlaps between vocabularies of peers will be limited and the dynamic nature of the system prohibits the design of accurate mappings, query processing will have to be approximate. We provide a formal model for such approximate query processing based on limited shared vocabularies between peers, and we show how the quality of the approximation can be adjusted in a gradual manner. The result is a flexible architecture for query-processing in heterogenous and dynamic environments, based on a formal foundation. We present the approach and discuss it on the basis of a case study.

Keywords: Semantic web, methods and formalisms for knowledge sharing, knowledge-based mediation architectures

1. Introduction

1.1. Semantic Web and Peer-to-Peer

The approach to query-processing that we present in this paper is strongly motivated by the peer-to-peer (P2P) architecture [12] that we expect for the Semantic Web. In this section we will argue why we expect the Semantic Web to have such a peer-to-peer architecture.

When we look at the current World Wide Web, we see in fact a mixed architecture, that is partly client/server-based, and partly P2P. On the one hand, each node in the network can directly address every other node in the network in a single, flat, world-wide address space, giving it the structure typical of many P2P networks. On the other hand, in practice there is currently a strong asymmetry between nodes in this address space that act as content-servers, and nodes that act as clients. Recent estimates indicate the presence of 50 million web-servers, but as many as 150 million clients. On the scale of the World Wide Web, any form of centralization would create immediate bottlenecks, in terms of network throughput and server capacity.

This need for a flat, non-server-centered architecture will be even stronger on the Semantic Web. Of course, the same physical load-balancing arguments hold as on the current Web, but the Semantic Web adds a new argument in favor of a P2P-style argument. On the Semantic Web, any server-centered architecture will not only create physical bottlenecks, but as communication relies on the use of ontologies will also create *semantic bottlenecks*. Since the semantics of information will be explicit (or at least: more explicit) on the Semantic Web, any single server will in a way "impose" a particular semantic view on all its clients. This will have undesirable consequences, both in terms of the pluriformity of the available information, as well as in terms of the size of the central ontology that such information-servers would have to maintain.

Instead, a P2P-style architecture will be able to avoid both the physical and the semantic bottlenecks. Different semantic views, expressed in terms of different ontologies, will be provided by many peers in a flat network of peers, each employing their own local, small ontology. Of course, this increased flexibility comes at a price: such "different semantic views, in terms of different ontologies" creates a significant data-integration problem: how will these peers be able to communicate if they do not share the same view on their data? In the remainder of this paper, we propose an approach where the communication between peers relies on a limited shared vocabulary between them. This replaces the role of the single virtual database schema that is the traditional basis for solving data integration problems.

In the following, we will briefly point to existing work on integration of heterogeneous databases, and we will see that this work is predominantly based on the notion of a global schema that is connected to the heterogeneous schemas to be integrated. Subsequently, we argue why this traditional approach is no longer viable in a peer-to-peer style network as the Semantic Web will be. The remainder of the paper will then be devoted to describing our proposal for such new approaches that will enable us to do query processing in a peer-to-peer setting without the need for global integrating schemas.

1.2. The Need for New Approaches

The problem of integrating heterogeneous database schemas [10] has been addressed by many researchers.

The integration is normally done using a global schema that is connected to the heterogeneous schemas to be integrated by a number of views. We can distinguish two general approaches [7]:

- *Global-As-View:* In the global-as-view approach every relation in the global schema is defined as a view over the different schemas to be integrated.
- *Local-As-View:* In the local-as-view approach, views are used to define the schemas of local information sources in terms of the global one.

The benefits of using explicit semantic models, i.e. ontologies, has been recognized in many approaches. A survey of approaches using ontologies is provided by [19]. Description logics have been proven to be a useful formalism for specifying and reasoning about semantic models [3] to support information integration. It has been shown that results from the database area provide solutions for the integration of semi-structured information (see e.g. [1]).

However, some peculiar characteristics of P2P networks and, in particular, the fact that they are characterized by strong dynamics, require the development of new solutions, which substantially extend the current data integration technology. This issue has been discussed in length in [5]. We report here only the main ideas. Consider the situation where John, a person living in Toronto, is described in the database F of his family doctor, and also in the database H of the hospital where he once received medical treatment.

Example: John goes to another country, for instance Trentino in Italy. Unluckily, here he has an accident; he breaks a leg, and he must get medical aid. The medical office has its own database M which now needs to query H for the purpose of retrieving previous treatment details. Furthermore, a new record from M should appear in F. However the acquaintance between M and F does not need to be maintained for ever, since the two databases will probably not need to coordinate again.

1.2.1. Dropping the global schema. In situations like that described in the example, the design and development of data integration mechanisms for randomly acquainted databases which may need to communicate only a few times, becomes impractical. In particular, it makes little sense to speak of a global schema [7], as we cannot think of a set of P2P databases just as an implementation of a single virtual database (this being the assumption which motivates the definition of a global schema). It is no longer possible to see the global schema as a view of the local database (global-as-view approach) or, vice versa, the local databases as views of the global database (local-as-view approach). For instance, we can no longer assume that there is a unique universe, containing all the elements of the single databases, but rather many overlapping domains. From a foundational point of view, any theory developed under the assumption of a global schema, and under the implicit assumption that the global schema is fixed, prevents us from the studying the dynamics of a P2P network. As far as we know, in the data integration literature, these two assumptions have never been relieved, see for instance [7, 10]. As a consequence, the problem handling heterogeneous information sources becomes a coordination task that reoccurs whenever two peers want to cooperate.

1.2.2. Good enough answers. In a P2P network, it becomes hard to maintain high quality answers to queries, for instance the fact that data can flow among the databases preserving soundness and completeness. In this context, soundness means that the data provided by the local databases satisfy the global schema (but they are not necessarily complete, some of them can get lost in the coordination). Completeness has the dual meaning. In the data integration literature, completeness is often given up, still maintaining the request of soundness. In a P2P environment, it will be possible to have completeness and soundness only in limit cases, for instance with low dynamics or simplified interaction among the databases.

One area where there will often be interest in getting very high quality data integration is the medical care domain. There are however many other application domains where this is not the case. One such example is tourism. This domain is not life critical, and in many cases the small dimension of a single business (e.g., hotels) does not justify big investments. Consider the following example.

Example: When planning his vacation in Trentino, John goes to a local agency. The agency searches for single operators (hotels, for instance), and queries them for the necessary information (e.g., prices and availability).

In this, the dynamics will have a high impact on the quality of the answer. We have network variance: the relevant databases are much more unstable in their being active and coordinated in the network, nodes come and go (for instance depending on the season), and so on. We have database variance: John travels around and queries different databases. The same query will get different results since each database will implement different degrees of coordination with the others, and so on. Thus, for instance, a query about hotels made to a hotel database will likely get an answer that is better than the answer obtained from a campsite database. We also have query variance: if you ask a query about campsites to a campsite database you will likely get a better quality answer than if you ask this database a query about hotels. Depending on the query, certain coordination mechanisms may or may not be activated. However, in this application, the agency doesn't need the best possible answer. It simply needs some answer. As long as, for instance, it gets a hotel John likes, this is good enough.

Compared to the previous medical example, in the tourism example much lower quality data coordination will suffice. The medical care and tourism domains are just examples. Things can get even more radical and complex when one thinks of applications where some of the nodes are mobile and where coordination happens on an even more occasional basis, for instance due to the physical proximity of two mobile peers. In these situations, and for certain kinds of applications, almost any answer will suffice. In terms of quality of answers, we can go from one extreme to the other. On one extreme, it may be usual to get poor quality answers. This may happen because the databases interact partially or do not interact at all or, even worse, they pass around data which are wrong (for instance because of unsolved problems of semantic heterogeneity). On the other extreme, there will be a tight coordination and it will be possible to achieve or, at least, approximate soundness and completeness. Between these two extremes there is a continuum of answers of different quality. This observation coincides with the ideas of the Semantic Web, where it is widely agreed that completeness and correctness in a logical sense can not be reached in many cases.

2. Ontology-Based Peer-to-peer Systems

Before we can present our approach to query processing in ontology-based peer-to-peer systems, we have to specify the systems we are talking about in more detail. We assume a system of independent peers that encapsulate the (possibly redundant) information of the whole system. Each peer uses one or more ontologies to model the information. These ontologies are used as a conceptual schema of the actual information that can be seen as an instantiation of the ontology. Peers exchange knowledge by formulating queries using the vocabulary defined in the ontologies they use and sending them to other peers in the network. The task of the receiving peer is to determine the answers to these queries relative to its own vocabulary and information. This leads to a situation where we are rather concerned with heterogeneous knowledge bases that plain data sources in the conventional sense.

In order to get a clearer notion of the problem of processing queries in such systems we make some simplifying assumptions. First of all we will only consider two peers that want to communicate. Then we assume that there are only two ontologies involved, a shared one and a private one of the peer trying to communicate. We further assume that both ontologies are encoded on the same language, preventing us from the problem of integrating the ontology languages.

This simplified communication problem can easily be extended to more realistic scenarios as communication is mostly bi-lateral even in complex systems.

There might be more than two ontologies involved in the communication, but they will all either be shared or private to one of the peers. The assumption that there are actually ontologies being shared by peers in the system is backed by the observation, that real-world ontologies are in most cases not build from scratch. It is rather common to at least start with an existing ontology (see for example `http://www.daml.org` for a library of ontologies about various domains. The existence of an internal mapping between the ontologies used by an individual peer is likely because if the peer wants to use more than one ontology as a basis for its information, it has to know about their relation. As a single peer is a rather static system compared to the overall network, we can use schema matching techniques that have been developed in the database community in order to find correspondences (see [14] for an overview). The only assumption that really is a simplification is the existence of a single ontology language. Investigating this problem, however, is out of the scope of this paper.

In the following we give formal definitions for the parts of an ontology-based peer-to-peer system that are concerned with query processing. These parts include the definition of ontologies and mappings as well as the notion of queries and answers in the setting of ontology-based information.

2.1. Ontological Knowledge

A number of languages for encoding ontologies on the Web have been proposed (see [6] for an overview). In order to get a general notion of ontological knowledge, we define the general structure of a terminological knowledge base (ontology) and its instantiation independent of a concrete language.

Terminological knowledge usually groups objects of the world that have certain properties in common. A description of the shared properties is called a class definition. Classes can be arranged into a subclass-superclass hierarchy. Classes can be defined in two ways, by enumeration of its members or by stating that it is a refinement of a complex logical expressions. The specific logical operators to express such logical definitions can vary between ontology languages; the general definitions we give here abstract from these specific operators. Further relations can be specified in order to establish structures between classes. Terminological knowledge considers binary relations that can either be defined by restricting their domain and range or by declaring them to be a sub-relation of an existing one. In order to capture the actual information content of a knowledge base we allow to specify single objects, also called instances. In our view on terminological knowledge, instances can be defined by stating their membership in a class. Further, we can define instances of binary relations by stating that two objects form such a pair.

Definition 1 (Terminological Knowledge Base). *A Terminological Knowledge Base* $\mathcal{T}$ *is a triple* $\mathcal{T} = \langle \mathcal{C}, \mathcal{R}, \mathcal{O} \rangle$ *where* $\mathcal{C}$ *is a set of class definitions of the form:*

- $c \equiv (o_1, \cdots, o_n)$ *where* c *is a class definition and* $o_1, \cdots, o_n$ *are object definitions.*
- $c_1 \sqsubseteq c_2$ *where* c_1 *and* c_2 *are class definitions.*

$\mathcal{R}$ *is a set of relation definitions of the form:*

- $r \sqsubseteq (c_1, c_2)$ *where* r *is a role definition and* c_1 *and* c_2 *are class definitions.*
- $r_1 \sqsubseteq r_2$ *where* r_1 *and* r_2 *are role definitions.*

and $\mathcal{O}$ *is a set of object definitions of the form:*

- $o : c$ *where* c *is a class definition and* o *is an individual.*
- $(o_1, o_2) : r$ *where* r *is a relation definition and* o_1, o_2 *are object definitions.*

In the following, we will consider terminological knowledge bases that consist of such axioms. Of course, any specific ontology language will have to further instantiate these definitions to specify logical operators between classes etc, but for the purposes of this paper, these general definitions are sufficient. Further, we define the signature of a terminological knowledge base $\langle \mathcal{C}, \mathcal{R}, \mathcal{O} \rangle$ to be a triple $\langle \mathcal{CN}, \mathcal{RN}, \mathcal{ON} \rangle$, where $\mathcal{CN}$ is the set of all names of classes defined in $\mathcal{C}$, $\mathcal{RN}$ the set of all relation names in $\mathcal{O}$ and $\mathcal{ON}$ the set of all object names occurring in $\mathcal{O}$.

We define a Tarski style semantics for the notion of terminological knowledge that is very much inspired by Description Logics (compare [3]). The formal definition of this semantics and the notion of logical consequence is omitted due to lack of space and can be found in an extended version of this paper [18].

2.2. Inter-Ontology Mappings

We assume that each peer has an integrated view on the ontologies it uses as a semantic foundation for its information. This integrated view is created by the mappings relates elements from different ontologies. The creation of these mappings is discussed in other work (see e.g. [14] for an overview) and is not further discussed in this paper. As our methods for query processing rely on these internal mappings of individual peers, we have to define the nature of the mappings. For this work, we adopted the mapping framework proposed in [11] summarized in the following.

Madhavan et.al. define mappings in terms of operations between expressions in two different domain models, in our case ontologies. They further demand that the resulting expression is consistent with the logical interpretation of the individual ontologies (we cover this point in the next section). As this framework is very generic, we instantiate it in the context of ontological knowledge as defined in the last section. In particular, we need to define the kinds of expressions, we consider and the operations used to relate them.

The expressions, we are considering here are the definitions of classes, relations and objects, respectively. Further, we define the following mappings between the different types of knowledge:

$$
\begin{aligned}
c_1 &\stackrel{m_C}{\longleftrightarrow} c_2, m_C \in \{\sqsubseteq, \sqsupseteq, \equiv\} \\
r_1 &\stackrel{m_R}{\longleftrightarrow} r_2, m_R \in \{\sqsubseteq, \sqsupseteq, \equiv\} \\
o_1 &\stackrel{\equiv}{\longleftrightarrow} o_2
\end{aligned} \tag{1}
$$

Intuitively the mappings marked with the operator $\equiv$ state that definitions in the different ontologies refer to the same class, relation or object. Mappings marked with $\sqsubseteq$ (and $\sqsupseteq$) state that the definition in the one ontology is a special (more general) case of the other definition. Further, Madhavan et.al. consider the use of a helper model individual models are mapped to. The helper model is then used to derive composed mappings between these models. In our view on ontology-based peer-to-peer systems, the shared ontologies can be seen as such helper models.

The formal semantics for terminological knowledge can easily be extended to cover mappings between different models. Here we assume a set of interpretation mappings into partially overlapping domains. Mappings impose constraints on these interpretations. A formal definition of the semantics of mappings can be found in [18].

2.3. Semantics and Logical Consequence

We can define semantics and logical consequence of a terminological knowledge base using an interpretation mapping $.^{\Im}$ into an abstract domain Δ such that:

- $c^{\Im} \subseteq \Delta$ for all class definitions c in the way defined above
- $r^{\Im} \subseteq \Delta \times \Delta$ for all relation definition r
- $o^{\Im} \in \Delta$ for all object definitions o

This type of denotational semantics is inspired by description logics [4], however, we are not specific about operators that can be used to build class definitions which are of central interest of these logics. Using the interpretation mapping, we can define the notion of a model in the following way:

Definition 2 (Model of a Terminological Knowledge Base). *An interpretation $\Im$ is a model for the knowledge base $\mathcal{T}$ if $\Im \models A$ for every axiom $A \in (\mathcal{C} \cup \mathcal{R} \cup \mathcal{O})$ where $\models$ is defined as follows.*

- $\Im \models c \equiv (o_1, \cdots, o_n)$, *iff* $c^{\Im} = \{o_1^{\Im}, \cdots, o_n^{\Im}\}$
- $\Im \models c_1 \sqsubseteq c_2$, *iff* $c_1^{\Im} \subseteq c_2^{\Im}$
- $\Im \models r \sqsubseteq (c_1, c_2)$, *iff* $r^{\Im} \subseteq c_1^{\Im} \times c_2^{\Im}$
- $\Im \models r_1 \sqsubseteq r_2$, *iff* $r_1^{\Im} \subseteq r_2^{\Im}$
- $\Im \models o : c$, *iff* $o^{\Im} \in c^{\Im}$
- $\Im \models (o_1, o_2) : r$, *iff* $(o_1^{\Im}, o_2^{\Im}) \in r^{\Im}$

In order to be able to handle multiple ontologies, we have to define the interpretation mapping over different models and mappings between them. In the following, we only consider an interpretation for two ontologies and mappings between them. The definitions, however, can easily be extended to more than two ontologies.

First of all, we divide the interpretation mapping $\Im$ into two sub-mappings $\Im^1$ and $\Im^2$ each defining the interpretation for one of the two ontologies in the way described above. Further, we define the interpretation of mappings between the ontologies in the following way:

$$\Im \models (c_1 \overset{m_C}{\longleftrightarrow} c_2) \text{ iff } \begin{cases} c_1^{\Im^1} = c_2^{\Im^2} \text{ for } m_C = \equiv \\ c_1^{\Im^1} \subseteq c_2^{\Im^2} \text{ for } m_C = \sqsubseteq \\ c_1^{\Im^1} \supseteq c_2^{\Im^2} \text{ for } m_C = \sqsupseteq \end{cases} \tag{2}$$

$$\Im \models (r_1 \overset{m_R}{\longleftrightarrow} r_2) \text{ iff } \begin{cases} r_1^{\Im^1} = r_2^{\Im^2} \text{ for } m_R = \equiv \\ r_1^{\Im^1} \subseteq r_2^{\Im^2} \text{ for } m_R = \sqsubseteq \\ r_1^{\Im^1} \supseteq r_2^{\Im^2} \text{ for } m_R = \sqsupseteq \end{cases} \tag{3}$$

$$\Im \models (c_1 \overset{\equiv}{\longleftrightarrow} c_2) \text{ iff } o_1^{\Im^1} = o_2^{\Im^2} \tag{4}$$

These definitions enable us to perform reasoning across different ontologies using the notion of logical consequence:

Definition 3 (Logical Consequence). *An axiom A logically follows from a set of axioms $\mathcal{S}$ if $\Im \models \mathcal{S}$ implies $\Im \models A$ for every model $\Im$. We denote this fact by $\mathcal{S} \models A$.*

In order to perform logical reasoning, we can use existing reasoning systems that have been build for reasoning about description logic knowledge bases. The system that has been used in the case study is the FaCT system [8].

2.4. Ontology-Based Queries

As mentioned in the beginning of this section, the peers in a system will exchange information by querying information from other peers in the network using terms from their own ontology. In the following we first define ontology based queries as well as the notion of answers to and relations between queries. We formalize queries in the following way: conjuncts of a query are predicates that correspond to classes and relations of the ontology. Further, variables in a query may only be instantiated by constants that correspond to objects in that ontology.

Definition 4 (Terminological Queries). *Let V be a set of variables disjoint from $\mathcal{ON}$ then an terminological query Q over a knowledge base $\mathcal{T} = \langle \mathcal{C}, \mathcal{R}, \mathcal{O} \rangle$ is an expressions of the form $Q(\bar{X}) \leftarrow q_{1_i} \wedge \cdots \wedge q_{m_i}$ where q_i are query terms of the form $x : c$ or $(x, y) : r$ such that $x, y \in V \cup \mathcal{ON}$, $c \in \mathcal{CN}$ and $r \in \mathcal{RN}$ or are of the form $x = o$ where $x \in V$ and $o \in \mathcal{ON}$*[1].

[1] Note that this may include data-type expressions as the type itself is can be considered to be a class, the actual value an instance of that class and the comparison operator a special relation.

The following expression in an example query based on an ontology used in the case study described later. It asks for hotels in castles that are located in towns in Mecklenburg and have less than 25 rooms:

$$\begin{aligned} Q(X) \quad \leftarrow \quad & X : Hotel \wedge (X,Z) : hat - Zimmer \wedge \; Z \leq 25 \wedge \\ & (X,W) : ist - in - Schloss \wedge W = ja \wedge (X,Y) : liegt - in - Ort \wedge \\ & (Y,V) : liegt - in - Land \wedge V = mecklenburg \end{aligned} \quad (5)$$

The fact that all conjuncts relate to elements of the ontology allows us to determine the answer to terminological queries in terms of instantiations of the query that are logical consequences of the knowledge base. The computation of query answers in the sense being defined above is the main inference task of peers within a system. In the next section we will discuss a logically well-founded approach for computing such answers.

3. Query Processing

After having introduced some basic notions related to ontology-based peer-to-peer systems we now turn our attention to the problem of query processing. The definition of query answers provides us with a deductive definition that describes correct answers with respect to a query over a single specific ontology. In the case of an ontology-based peer-to-peer system, however, we face a situation where we have to deal with more than one ontology. In many cases, the answering peer does not know all terms used in the query expression, because they are taken from the local ontology of the asking peer. In order to overcome this problem, we have to align the vocabularies the asking and the answering peer. In [16] we describe an approach for approximately translating classes from one ontology into another. We briefly summarize this approach in the next section and extend it to conjunctive queries. Further, we discuss the issue of the quality of approximations generated by our approach.

3.1. Approximating Class Descriptions

The notion of an interpretation given above is a very general one and does not restrict the nature of members of a concept. This is done by the use of operators for defining classes. These kinds of operators restrict the possible members of a class using an interpretation mapping to an abstract domain Δ. Figure 1 defines some operators we use in the following in order to define classes. These operators include the definition of a class by enumerating its members, the conjunction of two classes interpreted as the intersection of their members and existential restriction on a certain property defining that all members of that class have to be related to at least one object of a certain type C by the relation P. We use the the comparison of two numerical values as a special case of such a property (compare figure 1).

Operator	Extension $.^{\Im}$
$C_1 \sqcap C_2$	$C_1^{\Im} \cap \cdots \cap C_n^{\Im}$
$\{x_1, \cdots, x_n\}$	$\{x_1, \cdots, x_n\} \subset \Delta$
$(\exists P.C)$	$\{y \in \Delta \mid \exists x((y,x) \in P^{\Im}) \wedge x \in C^{\Im}\}$
$(\leq n)$	$\{x^{\Im} \in N \mid x^{\mathcal{E}} \leq n\}$

FIGURE 1. Some operators for Constraining Classes

These kinds of restriction are the basis for deciding whether a class definition is equivalent, more specialized or more general than another. Formally, we can decide whether one of the following relations between two classes can be deduced from the ontology:

subsumption:: $C_1 \sqsubseteq C_2 \iff C_1^{\Im} \subseteq C_2^{\Im}$
membership:: $x : C \iff x^{\Im} \in C^{\Im}$

The classes in an ontology form a hierarchy with respect to the subsumption relation. In the case of multiple ontologies connected by mappings such a hierarchy can also be computed for the united set of classes. Therefore, we will always have a set of direct super- and a set of direct subclasses of a class c_1 from the private ontology. We can use those direct sub- and super classes that belong to the shared ontology as upper and lower approximation for c_1 in the shared ontology:

Definition 5 (Lower Approximation). *Let $\mathcal{C}_1$ be the set of classes of a private ontology, $\mathcal{C}_2$ the set of classes of a shared ontology and $c \in \mathcal{C}_1$, then a class $c_{glb} \in \mathcal{C}_2$ is called a lower approximation of c in $\mathcal{C}_2$, if the following assertions hold:*

1. $c_{glb} \sqsubseteq c$
2. $(\exists c' \in \mathcal{C}_2 : c' \sqsubseteq c) \implies (c' \sqsubseteq c_{glb})$

The greatest lower bound $glb_{\mathcal{C}_2}(c)$ denotes the set of all lower approximations of c in $\mathcal{C}_2$.

Definition 6 (Upper Approximation). *Let $\mathcal{C}_1$ be the set of classes of a private ontology, $\mathcal{C}_2$ the set of classes of a shared ontology and $c \in \mathcal{C}_1$, then a class $c_{lub} \in \mathcal{C}_2$ is called an upper approximation of c in $\mathcal{C}_2$, if the following assertions hold:*

1. $c \sqsubseteq c_{lub}$
2. $(\exists c' \in \mathcal{C}_2 : c \sqsubseteq c') \implies (c_{lub} \sqsubseteq c')$

The least upper bound of $lub_{IS_2}(c)$ is the set of all upper approximations of c in $\mathcal{C}_2$.

The rational of using these approximations is that we can decide whether an entity x is a member of a class in the private ontology based on its membership in classes of the shared ontology. This decision in turn provides us with an approximate result on deciding whether x is the result of a query stated in terms of the private ontology, based on the following observation:

- If x is member of a lower bound of c_1 then it is also in c_1

- If x is not member of all upper bounds of c_1 then it is not in c_1

In [15] Selman and Kautz propose to use this observation about upper and lower boundaries for theory approximation. We adapt the proposal for defining an approximate classifier M' that assigns members of shared classes to private ones in the following way:

Definition 7 (Class Approximation). *Let C_1 be the set of classes of a private ontology, C_2 the set of classes of a shared ontology and x member of a class in C_2, then for every $c_1 \in C_1$ we define M' such that:*

- $M'(x, c_1) = 1$ *if* $x : \left(\bigvee_{c \in glb_{IS_2}(c_1)} c \right)$
- $M'(x, c_1) = 0$ *if* $x : \neg \left(\bigwedge_{c \in lub_{IS_2}(c_1)} c \right)$
- $M'(x, c_1) = ?$, *otherwise*

Where the semantics of disjunction and conjunction is defined in the obvious way using set union and intersection.

Based on the observation about the upper and lower bounds, we can make the following assertion about the correctness of the proposed approximate classification:

Proposition 1 (Correctness of Approximation). *The approximation from definition 7 is correct in the sense that:*

1. *If* $M'(x, c_1) = 1$ *then* $x^{\Im} \in c_1^{\Im}$
2. *If* $M'(x, c_1) = 0$ *then* $x^{\Im} \notin c_1^{\Im}$

Using the definition of upper and lower bounds the correctness of the classification can be established using the model-based semantics of ontologies and mappings (see [17] for a proof).

3.2. Queries as Classes

The result of the section 3.1 provides us with the possibility to compute a set of objects that are definitely members of a class expression and a set of objects that are possibly members of a class. This approach can directly be used to answer trivial queries that only ask for members of a particular class. We have shown that a slight variation of the mechanism can also be used to approximate Boolean queries over class names [16]. In order to compute (approximate) answers for ontology-based conjunctive queries, however, we also have to deal with binary relations in the query expression. In order to cope with relations as well, we use a method for translating conjunctive queries into class expressions that has been proposed by Horrocks and Tessaris [9]. The idea of the approach of Horrocks and Tessaris now to translate the query into an equivalent class expression, classify this new class and use standard inference methods to check whether an object is an instance of the query expression. This approach makes use of the fact that binary relations in a conjunctive query can be translated into an existential restriction in such a way that logical consequence is preserved after a minor modification of the object definition part of the ontology. Details are given in the following proposition.

Proposition 2 (Role Roll-Up [9]**).** *Let $\mathcal{T} = \langle \mathcal{C}, \mathcal{R}, \mathcal{O} \rangle$ be an ontology. Let further R be a role, C_I a set of class names in $\mathcal{CN}$ and $a, b \in \mathcal{ON}$ individual names. Given a new class name P_b not appearing in $\mathcal{CN}$, then $\langle \mathcal{C}, \mathcal{R}, \mathcal{O} \rangle \models (a, b) : R \wedge b : C_1 \wedge \cdots \wedge b : C_k$ if and only if $\langle \mathcal{C}, \mathcal{R}, \mathcal{O} \cup \{b : P_b\} \rangle \models a : \exists R(P_b \sqcap C_1 \sqcap \cdots \sqcap C_k)$*

The transformation of a complete query is more difficult due to the dependencies between the variables that occur in the query expression. In order to keep track of these dependencies during the transformation Horrocks and Tessaris introduce the notion of a query graph.

Definition 8 (Query Graph (Horrocks and Tessaris 2000)). *The graph induced by a query is a directed graph with a node for every variable and individual name in the query and an directed edge from node x to node y for every role term $(x, y) : R$ in the query.*

The correct transformation of a query into a class expression depends on the kinds of dependencies between the variables in the query which is reflected in the structure of the query graph. While the approach of Horrocks and Tessaris is more general, we restrict ourselves to queries where the query graph is a (directed) tree and its root node corresponds to the variable we are interested in. In especially, this requires that none of the roles used in the query is declared to be functional and that each constant only appears once in a query. While using this simplification, we would like to emphasize that the translation can be done for unions of conjunctive queries with an arbitrary number of result variables and a very expressive logical language for defining class expressions. Our simplifying assumptions lead to a simple method for transforming a query graph into a class expression. The result of applying this translation technique to our example query in equation 5 is the following expression:

$$\begin{aligned}(Hotel \ \sqcap \ & (\exists\, liegt - in - Ort.(\exists\, liegt - in - Land.\{mecklenburg\})) \sqcap \\ & (\exists\, hat - Zimmer.(\leq 25)) \sqcap \\ & (\exists\, ist - in - Schloss.\{ja\})) \end{aligned} \tag{6}$$

As this expression defines a new class in the overall ontology we can now apply the approximation techniques described in the last section in order to compute the sets of possible and the set of definite answers to the query. We will use this query as a running example in the following discussion on approximations.

3.3. Quality of Approximation

Unfortunately, proving the correctness of the approximation says nothing about the quality of the approximation. In the worst case, the upper and lower boundaries of concepts in the other hierarchy are always $\top$ and $\bot$ respectively. In this case the translated query always returns the empty set as result. We were not able to investigate the quality of approximations on theoretical level, however, we can provide some rules of thumb that can be used to predict the quality of an approximation:

Depths of hierarchies:: The first rule of thumb, we can state is that deeper class hierarchies lead to better approximations. For hierarchies of depth one it is easy to see that we will not be able to find good upper and lower bounds. We can also assume that deeper hierarchies provide finer grained distinctions between concepts that in turn often produce closer approximations.

Degree of overlap:: Our approach assumes a shared ontology, however, we cannot guarantee that different systems indeed use the same parts of this shared vocabulary. Therefore, the actual overlap of terms used in the existing definitions that are compared is important for predicting the quality of approximations. In general, we can assume that a high degree of overlap leads to better approximations.

Both criteria used in the rules of thumb above strongly depend on the application and on the creator of the corresponding models. At least for the degree of overlap, we can assume that hierarchies that are concerned with the same domain of interest will share a significant part of the vocabulary, thus enabling us to compute reasonable approximations.

In the course of a case study it turned out that in most cases the approximation of concept expressions returns good results, because people tend to share a reasonable number of concept names across different ontologies that provide a basis for creating mappings. These mappings can often be found using stemming and simple string matching. On the other hand, it turned out that it is much harder to come up with reasonable mapping between the relations used in different ontologies leading to a situation where we only have very sparse mappings between these relations. This in turn has a major impact on the quality of approximation applied to conjunctive queries. In fact the lack of mappings between relations often leads to a situation, where answers could not be found, because names of relations in the query were not known in the ontology in the answering peer. In the next section, we discuss an approach to overcome the problem of sparse mappings between relation names.

4. Query Relaxation

In the presence of sparse mappings, we face a situation where the descriptions of different peers referring to the same real-world object can be significantly different. In most cases, the descriptions are different in the sense that different relations are used to related same object to other objects in the domain. These relations may refer to the same properties of the object that cannot be matched due to a missing mapping or the set of properties itself used might be different. As a consequence, real-world objects that are meant to be an answer to a query are not returned because their description does not match the query that is formulated using terms form a different ontology. We address this problem by relaxing the query, i.e. by weakening those constraints from the query expression that are responsible for the failure. In order to be useful, this weakening process has to fulfill certain formal properties. In especially, we want to make sure that we do not loose any answers when modifying the query. We can guarantee this using the notion of query subsumption as described by Halevy:

Definition 9 (Query Containment and Equivalence (Halevy 2001)). *Let $\mathcal{T} = \langle \mathcal{C}, \mathcal{R}, \mathcal{O} \rangle$ and Q_1, Q_2 conjunctive queries over $\mathcal{T}$. Q_1 is said to be contained in another query Q_2 denoted by $Q_1 \sqsubseteq Q_2$ if for all possible sets of object definitions of a terminological knowledge base the answers for Q_1 is a subset of the answers for Q_2 : $(\forall \mathcal{O} : res(Q_1) \subseteq res(Q_2))$. The two queries are said to be equivalent, denoted as $Q_1 \equiv Q_2$ iff $Q_1 \sqsubseteq Q_2$ and $Q_2 \sqsubseteq Q_1$*

Based on these notions we compute a sequence of queries $Q_0, \cdots, Q_n$ such that the following properties hold:

1. $Q_0 \equiv Q$
2. $i < j \Longrightarrow Q_i \sqsubseteq Q_j$

The intuition behind this approach is to start with the original query and generate queries where each is more general than the one before, i.e. each query following in the sequence returns all results of the previous one, but might return more results. Our hope is that these new results contain the description of some real-world objects that should be answers, but were not found due to their description.

There are many different ways of making a query more general in order to increase the chance of matching a potential answer. In the following we discuss relaxation heuristics we consider useful for the purpose of query processing in a peer-to-peer setting.

4.1. Variable Elimination

The first heuristic is based on the fact that each variable in a conjunctive might fail to match a specific object if the object does not satisfy the constraints. Therefore, a way of increasing the chance of matching the target object in the head of the query is to successively eliminate non-answer variables from the query. In the example query in equation 5 for example, we have the variables V,W,X,Y and Z where X is the answer variable. Therefore we can weaken query by eliminating the variables V,W,Y and Z. This can be done by removing all conjuncts containing a specific variable from the query expression. It is easy to see that successively removing conjuncts from the query leads to a sequence of queries with the desired properties.

The main question that arises when adopting the variable elimination approach is the order in which the variables should be removed from the query.

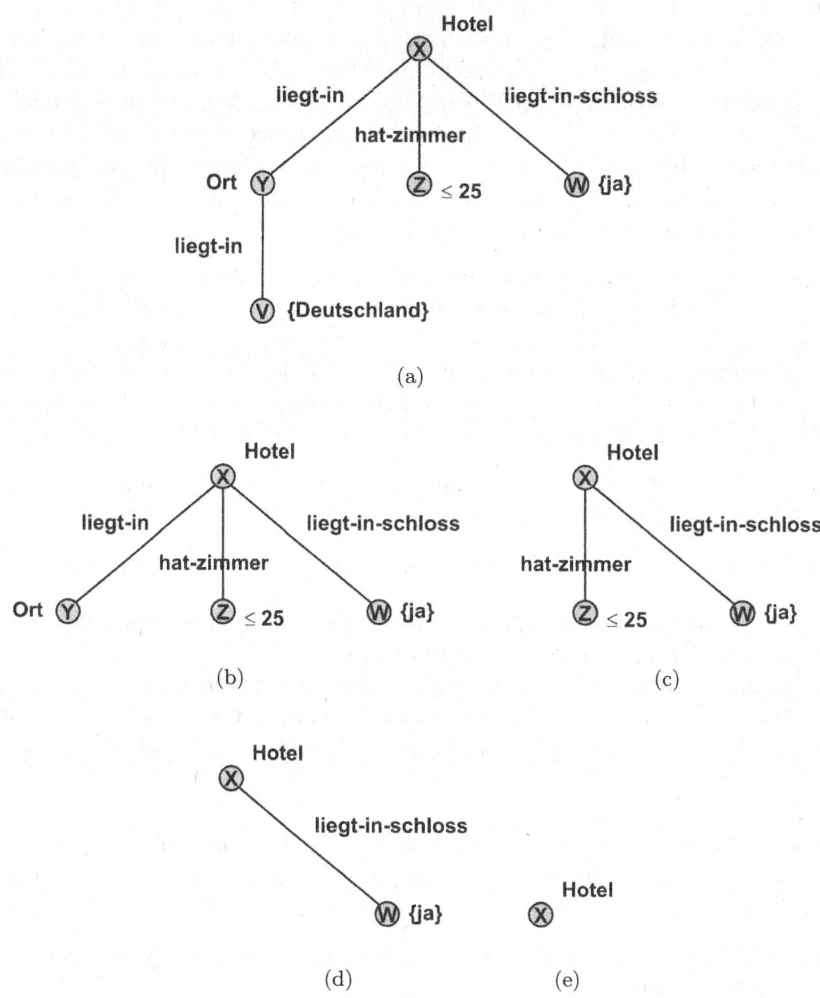

FIGURE 2. A possible sequence of query graphs

This order is partially constrained by the dependencies between the different variables. Removing the wrong variable first can break these dependencies and make remaining conjuncts useless. Looking at the example query this would happen if we first removed the variable Y. In this case the conjunct $V = Deutschland$ would be isolated, because the variable V only occurred in the removed conjuncts that connected it to the answer variable. In order to avoid breaking dependencies when removing conjuncts, we can use the query graph of the query to be relaxed (compare definition 8) as it explicates existing dependencies. In the query-graph dependencies between variables are represented by arcs between nodes. Therefore we have to ensure that the query graphs remains connected when removing the node that represents the variable we want to eliminate. Obviously, this is only the case if we eliminate variables that correspond to leaf nodes in the graph. Figure 2 illustrates the successive elimination of the variables V, Y, Z and W from the example query, showing the corresponding sequence of query graphs.

4.2. Guided Elimination

The major drawback of the variable elimination heuristic as explained so far is the high number of arbitrary choices that still exist in the order of elimination. More specifically, whenever the query tree has more than one leaf node, we have no strategy yet to decide which one to eliminate. In general, there are many possibilities for defining ordering heuristics, based on:

1. The nature of the domain
2. The preferences of the user
3. The task to be solved

As our approach does not aim at a specific domain, user or task, we will have to rely on rather general heuristics being aware that they will never be optimal. In our case, the only information we can use to decide on an elimination order is the existence of local mappings that relate the query vocabulary to the shared one that is actually used to compute the answer. The general idea is that we would rather drop conjuncts that represent concepts or relations without a suitable mapping into the shared ontology, because it can never be satisfied by any object classified according to that ontology. We have seen that for the case of concepts, we can often find a suitable approximation even if there is no direct counterpart in the shared ontology. Therefore, we focus on conjuncts representing relations and eliminate such variables first that are constrained by a relational conjunct that has no direct mapping to the shared ontology. The effect of this strategy is illustrated in the next section where we describe some experiments with approximating concepts and relaxing queries in a case study.

5. Examples from a case study

We performed a case study in order to validate the methods described above. The case study is based on three different ontologies in the domain of tourism. The ontologies are available in the DAML ontology library (`www.daml.org`) and have been created by independent groups of students at the University of Karlsruhe. All ontologies aim at describing the conceptualization of an Internet site that is advertising tourism in north-east Germany. All ontologies contain information about accommodation, tourist attractions and transportation facilities. While sharing these general topics, the different ontologies describe them in a very different way focusing on different parts of the overall domain. We chose these ontologies, because they very closely resemble the situation we expect in a peer-to-peer network, where peers model information about the same domain in different ways.

In the course of our case study, we imported the ontologies, each containing about 300 concepts and 50 to 70 relations, into an ontology editor using some syntactic transformations. We then analyzed the ontologies and created about 150 obvious mappings using simple string matching. In this way we created mappings mostly between concepts that have exactly the same name and between concepts where one name is the plural form of the other. Based on these mappings we computed two overlapping concept hierarchies consisting of about 600 concepts each. These hierarchies served as the basis for evaluating our concept approximation and query relaxation techniques. In the following, we describe examples of concept-approximation and of query-relaxation with respect to this hierarchy.

5.1. Concept approximations

As an example of concept approximation we use the concept "Ferien-Wohnung" (a flat used as accommodation during holidays). The relevant part of the overall hierarchy can be seen in Fig. 3. We can see that concepts from private and shared ontologies occur in this part of the hierarchy (The private concepts are shaded).

The approximations we are interested in are the direct sub- and superclasses of tourism example concept that are not from the same ontology. We can see in the figure that these are: "Bungalow" and "Appartment". If we look at the view of Peer B on the World we see also that the concept "Ferienhaus" (house used during holiday) would fall under this category. While this result is not completely true, because houses are not flats, it still serves the purpose very well, because all of the concepts describe accommodations that are reasonable replacements in the case that no flat is available.

If we determine the upper approximation of the example concept, we get the general concept "Unterkunft" (accommodation). Our method now determines all instances of this general concept to be potential members of the example concept. Besides the members of the already mentioned concepts, this also includes objects that are members of the concepts "Hotel" and "Campingplatz" (camp site) in the view of the answering peer B. We see, that these results are still closely related to the example concept, because they are all accommodations mainly used during holidays; however, hotels and camp sites are not really the kind of answer the user would assume to get when asking for a flat. Still, returning hotels and camp sites as answers to a query for a flat is still better than not returning any result, because the user might want to change her choice in favor of other preferences (e.g. the location).

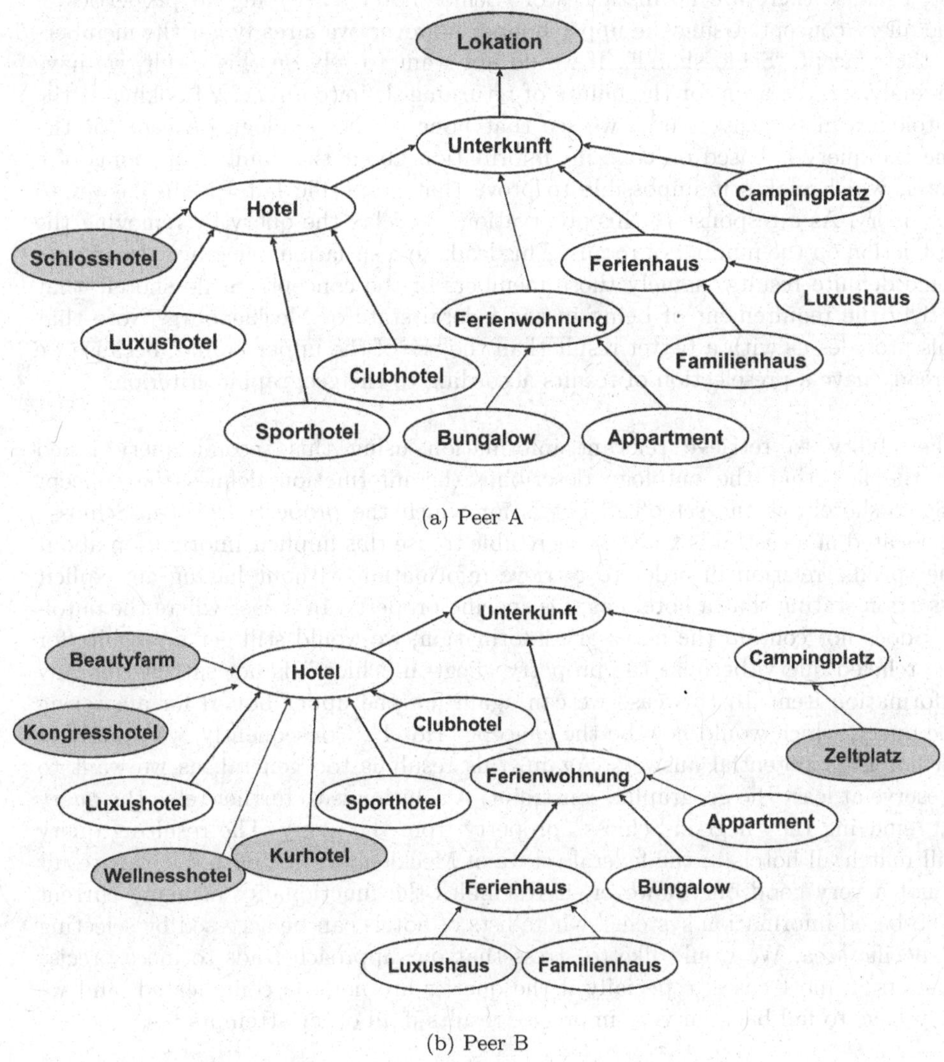

(a) Peer A

(b) Peer B

FIGURE 3. The views of two different peers of the same domain

5.2. Query relaxation

As an example for query relaxation, we take the example query. If we transform this query into a concept expression (Equation 6) and classify it into the overall concept hierarchy of the case study, it end up as a subconcept of "Schlosshotel" (castle acting as a hotel). Computing the answer to the query we get an empty set, because there are no instances of "Schlosshotel" satisfying all properties of the query concept. Using the upper bound, however, we already get the members of the concept "Schlosshotel". If we do not want to rely on this result, we have to analyze the reason for the failure of returning definite answers. Looking at the ontologies in the case study, we see that none of the ontologies except for the one the query is based on contains information about the number of rooms of a hotel, which makes it impossible to prove that a specific hotel is an answer to the query. As a response to this observation, we relax the query by removing the restriction on the number of rooms. This leads to a situation where we already get some definite results, namely those members of the concept "Schlosshotel" that satisfy the requirement of being in the federal state of Mecklenburg. Note that this provides us with a better result than the use of the upper bound, because we already have a preselection of results according to the geographic criterion.

The ability to retrieve relevant information using this second query relied on the fact that the ontology describing the information defines the concept "Schlosshotel" as the set of all hotels for which the property "liegt-in-Schloss" (is located in a castle) is true. We were able to use this implicit information about the specific relation in order to retrieve information without having an explicit assertion stating that a hotel has this specific property. In a case where the ontology does not contain the necessary information, we would still get no results for the relaxed query, because the property "liegt-in-Schloss" is not satisfied by any information item. In this case we can again use the upper bound for answering the query, which would now be the concept "Hotel". Consequently, we would get all hotels as potential answers. Again, this result is too general, as we want to preserve at least the geographic constraint. A solution is to further relax the query by removing the "liegt-in-Schloss" property from the query. The resulting query will match all hotels in the federal estate of Mecklenburg. Admittedly, this result is not a very good one; however, it resembles the functionality of many current Web-based information systems, where lists of hotels can be accessed by selecting a specific area. We would like to stress that our approach leads to more precise answers in most cases, especially if the queries are not too complicated, and we only have to fall back on very imprecise results if all other attempts fail.

6. Conclusions

The existing data integration technology is based on the assumption that it is possible to define a virtual global schema. A query is therefore posed to this schema and then suitably translated in local queries to the information bases being integrated. As hinted in this paper and more extensively argued elsewhere, this approach hardly scales to a highly dynamic P2P network.

In this paper we have proposed a novel approach based on the following key ideas:

1. We shouldn't think in terms of a global schema but, rather, in terms of independent autonomous nodes which, at run time, depending on the query, provide local answers which must then be integrated.
2. In most cases, the system will not be able to provide the best possible answer. It is more an issue of providing an answer which is good enough.

The proposed approach exploits ontologies as a conceptual "high level" schema which allows to hide local implementation details, and to exchange information using the vocabulary defined by the ontologies themselves. In this setting, good enough answers are obtained by posing queries to local ontologies, by allowing queries to be propagated by using inter- ontology mappings, and by using approximation techniques in order to avoid the problem of very sparse mappings.

We are only at the beginning and a lot of work is still to be done before integrating Semantic Web and P2P network technology. We list below some of the open problems we can foresee:

Foundations. Once we assume that we have no global schema we must also assume, among other things, that we no longer have a single domain of interpretation (a single set of models). To take this into account we must define a new semantics which allows for multiple interpretation domains, and for mappings which tell how ontology elements, and also domain elements, are mapped. In this framework, queries, query answers, and the mappings defined in this paper can be formally characterized and various (partial) completeness and correctness results can be provided (characterizing, for instance, to which extent, a query has been answered). Some preliminary ideas in this direction can be found in [2].

Semantic Routing. In a P2P network, in most if not all cases, a node has very little knowledge of its peers, and this knowledge becomes obsolete very quickly. Before worrying about how to answer a query (the problem we have mainly dealt with in this paper) a node has to worry about which nodes should be queried. This requires some mechanisms for peer discovery that, in general, will have again to deal with the problem of semantic heterogeneity (each node will advertise itself using some local vocabulary). A preliminary description of a possible solution has been provided in [5], which proposes "Interest Groups" as a way of collecting peers having knowledge about same or similar topics and a "locally centralized" mechanism for handling such groups.

Quality of Answers. We have already given up the hope for complete or, more simply, correct answers. But how do we judge when an answer is good answer? Whether an answer is good enough depends on many things: what the user wants, the status of the network, its connectivity, the topic of the query, and so on. If we want to make the approximation independent of human judgement, we have to provide formal quality measures that can be used to judge the quality of an approximation and provide a basis for deciding between alternative approximations. A promising proposal for such a quality measure is described in [13]. A particular question concerns the trade-off between the accuracy of an approximation and the complexity of computing it. One of the strengths of our approach is that determining the next approximation does not require logical reasoning itself due to the structure based relaxation criterion. It is very likely that we could further improve the accuracy of the approximation by using logical reasoning for finding alternatives for class and relation names rather than removing them from the query.

References

[1] S. Bergamaschi, S. Castano, and M. Vincini. Semantic integration of semi-structured and structured data sources. *SIGMOD Records*, 28(1):54–59, March 1999.

[2] P. Bernstein, F. Giunchiglia, A. Kementsietsidis, J. Mylopoulos, L. Serafini, and I. Zaihrayeu. Data management for peer-to-peer computing: A vision. Technical Report DIT-02-0013, Depertment of Information Technologies, University of Trento, 2002. Also appears in Proceedings of Web DB 2002.

[3] D. Calvanesea, G. De Giacomo, and M. Lenzerini. Description logics for information integration. In *Computational Logic: From Logic Programming into the Future*, Lecture Notes in Computer Science. Springer Verlag, 2001.

[4] F. M. Donini, M. Lenzerini, D. Nardi, , and A. Schaerf. Reasoning in description logics. In G. Brewka, editor, *Principles of Knowledge Representation*, Studies in Logic, Language and Information, pages 193–238. CSLI Publications, 1996.

[5] F. Giunchiglia and I. Zaihrayeu. Making peer databases interact - a vision for an architecture supporting data coordination. In *CIA 2002: Cooperative Information Agents*, Lecture Notes in AI. Springer, 2002.

[6] A. Gomez-Perez and O. Corcho. Ontology langauges for the semantic web. *IEEE Intelligent Systems*, January/February:54–60, 2002.

[7] A. Y. Halevy. Answering queries using views: A survey. *The VLDB Journal*, 10(4):270–294, 2001.

[8] I. Horrocks. The FaCT system. In H. de Swart, editor, *Automated Reasoning with Analytic Tableaux and Related Methods: International Conference Tableaux'98*, number 1397 in Lecture Notes in Artificial Intelligence, pages 307–312. Springer-Verlag, Berlin, May 1998.

[9] I. Horrocks and S. Tessaris. A conjunctive query language for description logic aboxes. In *AAAI/IAAI*, pages 399–404, 2000.

[10] M. Lenzerini. Data integration: A theoretical perspective. In *PODS*, pages 233–246, 2002.

[11] J. Madhavan, P. Bernstein, P. Domingos, and A. Halevy. Representing and reasoning about mappings between domain models. In *Eighteenth National Conference on Artificial Intelligence (AAAI'2002)*, Edmonton, Canada, 2002.

[12] M. Parameswaran, A. Sursala, and A. Winston. P2p networking: An information sharing alternative. *IEEE Computing*, 34(7), 2001.

[13] M. Peim, E. Franconi, and N. Paton. Estimating the quality of answers when querying description logic ontologies. *Data and Knowledge Engineering*, 2002. (submitted).

[14] E. Rahm and P. A. Bernstein. A survey of approaches to automatic schema matching. *The VLDB Journal*, 10(4):334–350, 2001.

[15] B. Selman and H. Kautz. Knowledge compilation and theory approximation. *Journal of the ACM*, 43(2):193–224, March 1996.

[16] H. Stuckenschmidt. Approximate information filtering with multiple classification hierarchies. *International Journal of Computational Intelligence and Applications*, 2002. to appear.

[17] H. Stuckenschmidt. *Ontology-Based Information Sharing in Weakly-Structured Environments.* PhD thesis, Faculty of Sciences, Vrije Universiteit Amsterdam, 2002.

[18] H. Stuckenschmidt, F. van Harmelen, and F. Giunchiglia. Query processing in ontology-based peer-to-peer systems. Technical report, Department of Department of Information and Communication Technology, University of Trento, November 2002.

[19] H. Wache, T. Voegele, U. Visser, H. Stuckenschmidt, G. Schuster, H. Neumann, and S.Huebner. Ontology-based integration of information - a survey of existing approaches. In *Ontologies and Information Sharing*, number 47, pages 108–117, Seattle, USA, August 2001.

Heiner Stuckenschmidt and Frank van Harmelen
Department of Mathematics and Computer Science
Vrije Universiteit Amsterdam
De Boelelaan 1081a, 1081 HV Amsterdam
The Netherlands
e-mail: {heiner,frankh}@cs.vu.nl

Fausto Giunchiglia
Department of Information and Communication Technology
University of Trento
38050 Povo di Trento,
Italia
e-mail: fausto@dit.unitn.it

Message Content Ontologies

Chris van Aart, Bob Wielinga and Guus Schreiber

Abstract. In this article we address the problem of how agents can handle message-based communication. Our approach is to look at ontology-based communication, in which the meaning and intention of messages is specified in message content ontologies. The idea is that agents can share semantics by committing to shared message content ontologies. We discuss a theoretical framework for message-based communication, in which we sketch an ideal world where an agent is capable of various ontological operations. A pragmatic approach is presented, which enables the creation and use of ontologies to support message-based communication between agents.

1. Introduction

In this article, we present a layered framework containing a Reference Model for ontology-based agent communication. Using ontologies in agent communication enables agents and agent engineers to add semantics to agent conversations.

A traditional distributed system interoperates with other systems by giving these other systems access to its information retrieval functions. One technique to interoperate, for instance to transfer information between distributed systems, is Remote Methods Invocation (RMI). Giving systems direct access to other systems' information retrieval functions leads to tightly coupled systems. However, multi-agent systems are loosely coupled distributed systems, where agents do not have direct access to each others functionalities (services). By exchanging messages, agents can access other agents' services. The messages are not only used to exchange information, but also to communicate on a higher level, such as negotiation about price, instructions and sharable knowledge [19, 23].

The case study on Legal services described is based on an Agentcities grant project (See www.acklin.nl/agentcities). The "Bean Generator" tool assists agent engineers in designing message content ontologies and export it to Java source code. The tool is designed by the author and is used by various institutions and companies that work with the JADE toolkit (See http://gaper.swi.psy.uva.nl/beangenerator).

Message-based communication can be described on several levels of detail: message transport, message encoding, communication languages, message interpretation and composition [24]. Message transport is involved with agent addressing and communication protocols. Whether a message is encoded in binary, string or other format is of concern at the message encoding level. Several agent communication languages exist, for example KQML or FIPA-ACL.

We focus on the ideas motivating the FIPA standardization, because it is supported in the agent community[1]. On top of the agent communication language, FIPA has adopted the idea of ontology-based communication from [28], where the meaning and intention of message contents is specified in message content ontologies. In order to share semantics, agents commit to shared message content ontologies. The agent engineer is free to design and implement the communication model of the agent around message content ontologies. The only requirement is that the content of messages exchanged commit to one or more message content ontologies. In this case, agents can interact without having to negotiate about message structure and message content. A similar approach can be found in Open-EDI [38].

The problem addressed in this chapter is defined by [9] as: *"Despite its crucial importance for guaranteeing the exchange of content information among agents, (...) a suitable "Reference Model" for ontologies needs to be established."* The assumption is that agents share a common Reference Model that provides the proper semantics in message-based communication. Specific message content ontologies will be based on this Reference Model. The question is, what such a Reference Model could look like and how agents can generate and interpret messages that commit to such a Reference Model.

In the remainder, we give a brief introduction on ontologies. Next, we discuss a layered framework containing a Reference Model for message content ontologies, in which we sketch an ideal world, where agents are capable of various ontological operations. Then, we discuss a pragmatic approach to the Reference Model based on the current state-of-the art in agent technology, which is applied in a case study on legal services. We conclude this chapter by a discussion on the two approaches and issues arising from this work.

2. Message Content Ontology Framework

In this section, we discuss a theoretical approach to establish a Reference Model (cf. [9]) for message content ontologies. The framework consists of a collection of ontologies, which we refer to as agent communication ontologies. The basis of these ontologies is the *speech acts* theory [24, 34, 4]. Messages exchanged between agents

[1] An alternative to FIPA is the Rosetta initiative(www.isi.edu/expect/projects/agents/rosetta.html) and available technology (See www.agentlink.org/software). In contrast to FIPA, the Rosetta architecture is based on middleware, which represents most of the agent's environment. This means that an agent should be equipped with an interface to the Rosetta architecture. The drawback of this approach is that the agents are not loosely coupled to the agent environment.

are annotated with speech acts, giving messages specific meanings. The theory originates from linguistics [33, 1], where it is used to analyze human speech and text. A speech act is composed of three components: *locutionary act*, *illocutionary act* and *perlocutionary act*. The *locutionary act* is concerned with the material generation of utterances. The *illocutionary act* is concerned with carrying out a speech act. An illocutionary act itself is composed of an *illocutionary force* and a *propositional content*. An *illocutionary force* can be seen as a performative, such as questioning, negotiating, ordering and asking to do something. The *propositional content* is the object of the illocutionary force, such as problem, price, product or activity. The *perlocutionary act* is concerned with the effect an illocutionary act has on the state of the receiver. We focus on the illocutionary force, which we refer to as *performative*.

Linguists have made a difference between explicit and implicit performatives [1]. Agent Communication languages such as KQML and FIPA-ACL make use of explicit performatives [24]. Here, every agent utterance (i.e. the sending of a message) is seen as a speech act, which is composed of a *propositional content* and a *performative*. The structure of a speech act is then of the form $E(I(A))$, where E is the explicit performative, I the implicit performative and A the arguments of the directive[2]. For example, a message containing an explicit performative is: promise(deliver(cd)), where promise is the performative (in this case a "commissive, because the speaker has committed him to a future course of action, c.f. [33]), deliver the intended transaction and cd the argument.

Most human communication does not explicitly express one of these types of speech acts. For example, one does not ask a question in the form of: "I direct you to the give me the price of a CD", or "I assert the price of a CD to 30 EURO". In order to come close to human communication, we will make use of implicit performatives. This means that we directly make use of a specific performative, without declaring the type of performatives. The form of an utterance is in the form of $I(A)$). For example, an utterance such as (Buy (CD :name "Mahler 1")) is to be read in a first-person present declarative form [24]. Hence, this message can be read as "hereby, I declare that I want to buy the CD with the name Mahler 1".

Concepts such as CD can be found in an existing ontology, cf. [6]. Therefore we can reuse existing concepts and relations of these ontologies into our agent communication ontology[3]. There are several methods to reuse and share ontologies, divided into syntactical and semantic methods [20, 31]. An example of a syntactical method (which operates on the symbol level) is the translation of an ontology into another ontology representation language. Semantic methods (which operate on the knowledge level), includes merging of one ontology with another and mapping of one concept to another.

[2] In more, detail $E(I(A))$ is the logical representation of a speech act. The actual representation of an utterance depends on the languages of agent communication (ACL). For example, in SL it is possible to express multiple performatives in one utterance.

[3] By reuse, we mean reusing one concept and related relations or the reuse of an entire branch of an ontology.

Another important communication theory is *conversational interaction* [18], which reasons on the use of performatives by conversation members. In every conversation there is at least one initiator and one other participant. Furthermore, there are rules that restrict the use of performatives. In the agent community, these rules are called *protocols*. Every participant in a conversation should follow these protocols. In our framework, we couple protocols to roles. In communication theory this is called *role-taking*[4] [25]. A protocol can dictate that for every question asked, an answer has to be given. For example in the IBROW architecture, if the broker asks a question to a librarian, both the broker and the librarian know what role to take and what performatives to use. So the broker as questioner sends ask(needed competences) to a librarian. The librarian as agent questioned, responds with reply(candidate PSMs).

2.1. Agent Communication Meta Ontology

The *Agent Communication Meta Ontology* defines generic concepts necessary for agent communication: *conversation domain concept*, *performative*, *protocol* and *agent role*. The elements of this ontology are not explicitly used in the messages exchanged between agents. Rather, these elements are used as reference by agents and agent engineers. Agents can use it to reason about interactions with other agents. For example, when an agent decides to consult another agent, it can select the appropriate vocabulary, performatives, protocol and role. When an agent engineer is designing an agent he can configure the functions of the communication model of the agent.

In order to bind the concepts together, a number of relations are defined: allowed concept, allowed performative and allowed protocol. The relation allowed concept means that every performative should contain one or more instances of domain concept. The relation allowed performative denotes that every protocol contains an ordered number of performatives. Finally, the relation allowed protocol tells that agent roles (part of the agent role ontology) should commit to one or more protocols.

Figure 1 shows shows the four subjects of agent communication: domain concept, performative, protocol and agent role. The relation between the performative and protocol metaclasses (from the Agent Communication Meta Ontology) and the Performative Ontology and Protocol Ontology (from the Reference Model) are of type `<<instance>>`. The elements of the Performative Ontology are discussed in Table 1. In Table 2, the elements of the Protocol Ontology are discussed

2.2. Reference Model

The four subjects of agent communication are defined into four agent communication ontologies: *conversation domain ontology*, *performative ontology*, *protocol ontology* and the *agent role ontology*. These four agent communication ontologies form the Reference Model. The relations between the ontologies are illustrated in Figure 2. The dependencies (i.e. the dashed arrowed lines, which are to be read as

[4]Other terms used are *feed forward* and *empathy*.

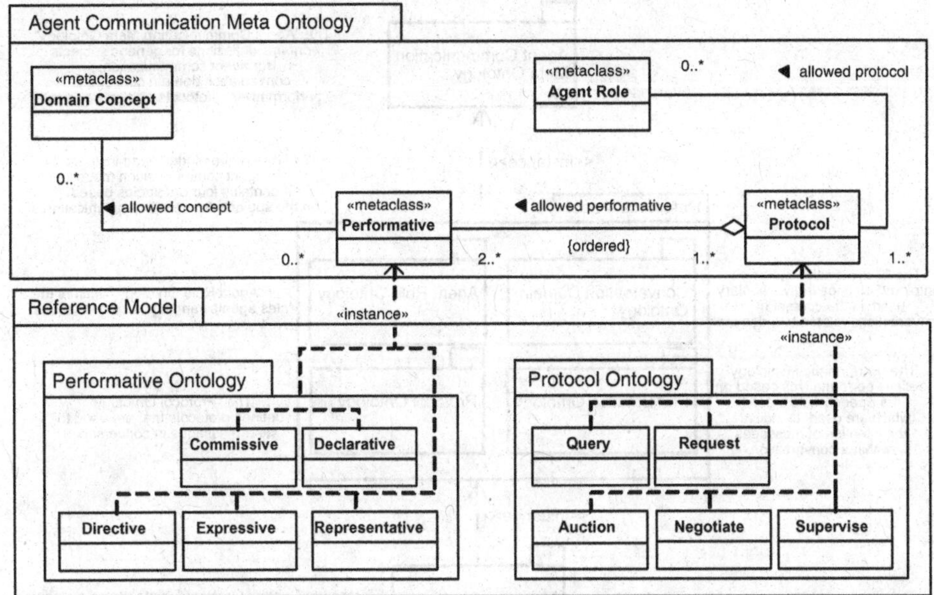

FIGURE 1. Agent Communication Meta Ontology and a part of the Reference Model.

"source depends on destination") show the relations between the ontologies. The Agent Communication Meta Ontology defines the subjects for agent communication ontologies: conversation domain concepts, performatives, protocols and agent roles. The Reference Model is an **instantiation** of the Agent Communication Meta Ontology. The Reference Model makes use of the four agent communication ontologies. Finally, the Message Content Ontology instantiates elements from the Reference Model

The relations between the Agent Communication Meta Ontology and the Reference Model are illustrated in Figure 1. Below, we discuss the agent communication ontologies in detail.

2.2.1. Conversation Domain Ontology. A *conversation domain ontology* defines the vocabulary used in the propositional content of conversations related to a domain. Examples are price, product, answer, question, proposal, offer, name, person and address. Furthermore, it defines the structure of a domain, for example a product has a price, a question has zero or more answers, an offer is related to one product, a person has a name and an address.

Several ontologies are available that can be used in the design of conversation domain ontologies. Elements of existing ontologies can be imported, adapted or translated into other ontologies. Several ontologies exists for identifying products in

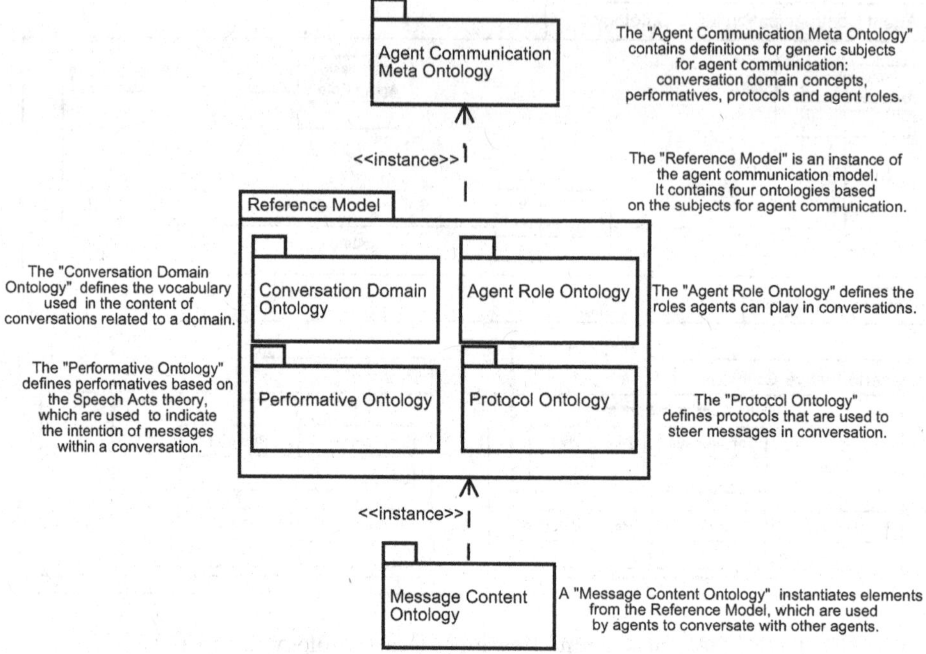

FIGURE 2. The agent communication ontologies represented by UML packages.

an electronic commerce applications through product descriptions, such as S95, the United Nations Standard Products and Services Codes, E-cl@ss, and RosettaNet[5].

2.2.2. Performative Ontology. The *performative ontology* defines performatives that are based on the Speech Acts theory. The Speech Acts theory is introduced into Agent Communication Languages to design agent communication as close to human communication as possible [24]. In traditional information exchange between systems, messages are only pieces of data [38]. In order to create a social effect, such as creating an obligation, performatives are added to messages. In a traditional setting one service would send a message (CD :name "Mahler 1") to a musicshop service, intending to *buy* a CD. Both services "know" that when one service sends a reference to a CD, that it wants to buy a CD. In agent systems, an agent would send the message (buy (CD :name "Mahler 1")), where the buy performative can be seen as a speech act (the message is an attempt to perform a transaction between a buyer and a seller).

The idea behind Speech Acts is that sentences can be categorized into particular types. We follow the classification as suggested by [33], see table 1. In this classification there are five basic categories of performatives (illocutionary forces):

[5]See www.s95.info, www.unspsc.org, www.eclass.de and www.rosettanet.org

Performative	*Description*	*Examples*
Representative	inform the addressee of some state of affairs	*asserting, concluding, describing* "The price of every CD is 30 EURO."
Commissives	commit the speaker to future course of action	*promising, threatening, offering and vowing* "If you buy 10 CDs, the price is 23 EURO."
Declaratives	"representatives" spoken by a recognized authority, such as a director or president	*marrying, naming, and firing from employment* "I allow this shop to sell CDs."
Directives	attempts by the speaker to get the addressee (or receiver) to do something	*requesting, questioning and commanding* "What is the price of a CD?" "Can I buy this CD?"
Expressives	express a psychological state	*greeting, thanking and congratulating* "Thank you for buying this CD!"

TABLE 1. Five basic categories of performatives (illocutionary forces), cf. [33].

Representatives, Commissives, Directives, Declaratives and Expressives. Representatives are speech acts that represent some state of affairs. For example, asserting facts about a domain, such as telling the price of a CD.

Commissives are speech acts that commit the speaker to some future course of action. In an economic setting, this can be used to have agents committing to a contract. For example, promising to perform a job in the future, such as: "at noon, I will buy a CD". Directives are speech acts whose intention is to get the addressee to carry out some action. For example, asking a question related to a domain, such as "what is the price of CD X?". Declaratives are speech acts that themselves bring about a state of affairs and which are spoken by a recognized authority. In order to give a Manager control over Operators, an Operator has to see a Manager as an authority. For example, an Manager instructs an Operator how to perform its activities. Expressives are speech acts that indicate the speaker's psychological state or mental attitude. For example, one agents "thanks" another agent for its services.

Several variations of the categorization of Searle exist, see [1, 35, 8]. Also in the Agent Field, specializations of Speech Acts have been reported. A number of explicit performatives are specified by Haddadi and FIPA, which can also be used as implicit performatives. Haddadi has defined a library of communication types [22]. A selection of these types is: Require, Order, Reject, Ask and Reply. FIPA has specified: Accept Proposal (which can be seen as an instance of a "representative"), Call for Proposal (directive), Confirm (commissive), Inform (representative), and request (directive) [11]. These performative or communicative types are either representatives, directives or commissives [35]. For example, the performative *inform* is supposed to give information and *request* corresponds to a demand for information. In order to allow authority, which is needed to construct organizational relations such as a Manager-Operator relation, "Declaratives" are needed. Furthermore, to allow learning based on feedback, the speech act "Expressive"

Protocol	*Description*	*Example utterance*	exchanged between two or more agents
FIPA-Query	asking for information	A to B (directive):	"What is the price of a CD?"
		B to A (commissive):	"Agree to answer the question."
		B to A (representative):	"The price of a CD is 30 EURO."
FIPA-Request	requesting to perform an action	A to B (directive):	"Can you order a CD?"
		B to A (commissive):	"Agree to perform the action."
		B to A (commissive):	"The CD will arrive next week."
FIPA-Auction	bid on object	A to B, C (directive):	"Who wants to buy this CD?"
		B to A (commissive):	"I bid 20 EURO."
		C to A (commissive):	"I bid 18 EURO."
		A to B, C (representative):	"Sold to A, for 20 EURO."
Negotiate	negotiate on object	A to B (directive):	"What is the price of a CD?"
		B to A (commissive):	"I offer the CD for 30 EURO."
		A to B (representative):	"I reject, price too high."
		B to A (commissive):	"I offer the CD for 25 EURO."
		A to B (representative):	"I accept."
Supervise	coordinate an agent or process	M to A (declarative):	"Follow my instructions."
		A to M (commissive):	"Agree."
		M to A (directive):	"Find a CD shop."
		A to M (representative):	"I found a CD shop."
		M to A (directive):	"Try to buy a CD for less then 28 EURO."
		A to M (representative):	"I bought a CD for 25 EURO."
		M to A (directive):	"Send CD to address X."
		M to A (expressive):	"You did a good job."

TABLE 2. A selection of types of communication protocols. In the example column, the letters "A", "B", "C" and "M" represent names of agents.

is needed. For example, a Manager can give positive or negative feedback on the activities performed by an Operator in order to learn the Operator coordination pattern.

2.2.3. Protocol Ontology. Next to individual message exchange, agents engage in conversations. Conversations can be seen as a shared sequence of messages that agents follow [24]. We have expressed the notion of sequencing between allowed type of messages by the `Ordered` relation in Figure 1. In order to guide conversations, (interaction) protocols can be used that restrict the allowed sequence of performatives. Examples of shared sequences are negotiations [5] and auctions [32]. The shared sequences of performatives are defined in the *protocol ontology*. For example, a directive, such as a question, should be followed by an representative to answer the question. The Protocol Ontology of the Reference Model, contains a number of generic protocols, which can be seen as a Reference Model for conversations, see Table 2. The *FIPA-Query*, *FIPA-Request* and *FIPA-Auction* protocols originate from the FIPA standards (cf. [15, 15, 12]) and are extended with speech act categories and examples related to the musicshop domain. The *Negotiate* and *Supervise* protocols are added to illustrate the variety of possible protocols.

FIPA has defined a number of interaction protocols. For example the FIPA-REQUEST protocol specifies that a request performative should be followed by a

Performatives/Protocols	*Representative*	*Commissives*	*Declaratives*	*Directives*	*Expressives*
Query	+	+		+	
Request	*	*		+	
Auction	+	+		+	
Negotiate	+	+	*	+	*
Supervise	+	*	*	+	*

TABLE 3. Examples of the Allowed Performative Relation relation, on the basis of the Performatives as given in Table 1 and protocols as given in Table 2. In this relation, performatives are required (+) or optional (*).

refuse, or an agree [15]. After the agree performative, the performative failure and inform are allowed.

Other interaction protocols deal with the Contract Net [12] and Auctions, such as the English auction [14] and the Dutch auction [13]. In addition, Haddadi has defined a library of message patterns [22]. Examples are, that an order performative has to be followed by a report performative, require has to be followed by agree or reject, and propose has to be followed by request, require or reject.

In Table 3 we have placed the performatives as given in Table 1 against the protocols as given in Table 2, in order to illustrate the AllowedPerformative relation. As shown, a number of performatives are required (+) or optional (*). The three existing protocols, *Query*, *Request* and *Auction*, allow the agree performative that confirms a directive. We see the agree performative as a commissive, which is optional. The idea is that agents "agree" on how to negotiate. Examples of agreements are the number of negotiation rounds, number of participants, object of negotiation and rule setting.

A negotiation protocol is also called the "rule of encounter", which enables agents to share allowed sequences of performatives in a negotiation [26]. In our negotiate protocol, directives are used to ask a participant of a negotiation for an offer, such as the price. In response, a commissive is used to offer a bid. Next, representatives are used to react positively or negatively on a bid.

In our supervision protocol, directives are used by an agent with a manager role to instruct its subordinates, such as an operator. The operator responds with representatives to report the result of the instructions. The use of the expressive performative can play a role in learning situations, because it enables a feedback, such as rewarding. Taking a situation where a manager supervises an operator, the manager could use feedback in the form of expressives, to teach the operator how to perform its activities. In the end, the operator could operate without direct supervision of the manager.

Ontologies that can be used as the basis of protocol ontologies are the Enterprise Ontology [37] and the Toronto Virtual Enterprise [21][6].

[6] See www.aiai.ed.ac.uk/enterprise/enterprise/ontology.html and www.eil.utoronto.ca/tove/toveont.html

2.2.4. Agent Role Ontology. The *agent role ontology* defines the roles that agents can play in conversations. An agent role defines the responsibility and allowed behavior of an agent. In the Reference Model, we modeled responsibility and allowed behavior of an agent as the protocols an agent is allowed to use. This is represented by the allowed protocol relation in Figure 1.

Typical roles in agent communication are: Operator, mediator, planner, coordinator, decision-maker, observer, executive, broker and Manager. Futhermore, FIPA has defined a number of agent roles: an agent platform's Directory Facilitator (DF) and Agent Manager Service (AMS). Furthermore, in an e-commerce setting there are roles, such as supplier, producer, partner, and consumer [38].

2.3. Message Content Ontology

Message content ontologies can be used by agents to discuss about facts, beliefs, hypotheses and predications related to specific domains. Hence, a message content ontology makes use of a conversation domain, performative, protocol and agent role ontologies. When agents want to communicate, the appropriate message content ontology is selected.

Based on the type of conversation, the required domain concepts and relations, performatives and protocols, and agent roles are referred to (i.e. instantiated). In our framework, a Message Content Ontology instantiates elements from the Reference Model (cf. Figure 2).

Several examples of message content ontologies can be found in the agent literature and agent programming manuals: *Agent Management Ontology*, *Currency ontology* and *Cinema Service Ontology*. We briefly discuss these ontologies and relate them to our agent communication ontologies.

The FIPA Agent Management Ontology is a message content ontology used for conversations between (visiting) agents and the agents on a FIPA compliant agent platform (cf. [10]): the AMS (agent management service) and the DF (directory facilitator). In order for a (visiting) agent to work on an agent platform, it has to behave according to an agent life cycle [10]. Every (visiting) agent that wants to join an agent platform should register itself with the AMS and the DF. The AMS maintains a register of physical agent addresses, and the DF maintains a register of agent service descriptions. If the agent decides to leave the agent platform, it should deregister itself.

This ontology is composed of a number of performatives: register, deregister, search and modify. Within our framework, the performatives register, deregister and modify are of type "directive", because visiting agents use them to *change* the DF's register. For example, the performative modify is used when an agent wants to change its address or service. In case the agent wants to locate other agents, it can use the performative search. This performative is of type directive, because it can be used to *question* the DF's register.

Examples of the relations between speech acts and domain concepts are: the performatives register *requires* the concept agent-description, which contains other properties such as name to identify the agent, address to locate the agent and services to describe the services the agent offers. Furthermore, the performative search *requires* the concept service, and the performative modify *requires* the domain concept agent-description. Allowed sequences of performatives are not specified in the ontology.

There is a notion of *visiting agent*, *DF* and *AMS*. The role of a visiting agent is to register itself on a platform and it can make use of the search, modify and deregister performative. However, these roles in relation to protocols are not specified.

The Cambia Currency Ontology is a message content ontology used by an agent that provides a service to make currency conversions between a number of currencies[7]. An agent should specify source and destination currency as well as the date, to determine the correct exchange rate, and the amount. The ontology contains the performative convert, which requires four domain concepts: from, to, rate and dateC. This performative is of type directive, because it is used to request the currency agent. The concept from is used to denote the source currency code (e.g. "USD") and the amount. To specify the target currency code (e.g. "EUR"), the concept to is used. The concept rate specifies the type of conversation, this can be "cash", "inter-bank" or "credit card". Finally, the concept dateC contains the date of conversion. There is no notion of role or protocol.

The Tilab Cinema Representation Service Ontology is a message content ontology used by the cinema broker agent that provides information concerning a selection of cinemas of the cities of Turin and Paris[8]. One of the specified performatives is: provide-cinema-info (of type directive) which can be used to question the cinema broker. The domain concepts are Show, Cinema and CinemaPreference. The concept Show contains attributes related to time of a show and price. The concept Cinema describes the address and contact details of a cinema. The preferences of a user, such as time and price are described in the concept CinemaPreference.

There is a notion of two roles: user agent and cinema broker. A user agent uses the performative provide-cinema-info combined with the concept CinemaPreference to ask the cinema broker, to acquire a list of available shows and cinemas. The relation between the user agent that can use the performative provide-cinema-info and the cinema broker agents, is not specified in the ontology.

In the three examples, we can identify the notion of performative and domain concepts, and the relation between the performatives and the allowed domain concepts. Roles, protocols and relations between roles, protocols and performatives are not specified. The reason for this is that these ontologies are applied in relative simple agent systems, with a limited number of agents, reasoning capabilities and possible interactions. Furthermore, these ontologies are designed "ad hoc".

[7] http://zurich.agentcities.whitestein.ch/Services/Cambia.html

[8] http://jade.cselt.it/AgentCities/CinemaRepresentativeServiceDescription.htm

2.4. Message Content Ontology Creation

In our approach, there are two steps for defining a message content ontology: *identification of conversation specific concepts* and *specification of conversation specific concepts.*

In the first step: Identification of Conversation Specific Concepts, the required conversation specific concepts for the Message Content Ontology are defined. This step takes as input the Agent Communication Meta Ontology and the ontologies of the Reference Model: the Conversation Domain, Agent Role, Performative and Protocol Ontology (see Figure 1). On the Agent Communication Meta Ontology level, the classes of the Reference Model are seen as instances[9]. The result of this step is (technically) an object diagram that shows the needed concepts for a conversation (see Figure 3). On the level of the Reference Model, the instances of the object diagram are seen as classes.

In the second step: Specification of Conversation Specific Concepts, the defined conversation specific concepts will be specified in detail. The step takes the object diagram and a selection of external ontologies as input. The attributes for the classes are defined in the Reference Model and linked to other, possibly already existing, classes. The result is a message content ontology represented as a class diagram(see e.g. Figure 4).

The idea is that the conversation specific concepts can make use of classes imported from other ontologies.

In the next two sections, we discuss *identification of conversation specific concepts* and *specification of conversation specific concepts* in detail.

2.4.1. Identification of Conversation Specific Concepts. Conversation specific concepts are defined based on generic classes of the Agent Communication Meta Ontology. In order to illustrate the process of creating the required classes of a message content ontology, we define an example in an electronic commerce domain, because it is a popular domain for agent systems [27]. Agents can represent parties that want to do business, such as buying and selling items. Both the buying agent and the selling agent will try to negotiate in order to get the best deal. An example of a negotiation is bargaining for the price of a CD in a musicshop.

In our example, we start with defining roles needed for CD bargaining: buyer and seller. The buyer role has as goal to buy a CD for a reasonable price. The role of seller is to sell as many CDs as possible. In order to have the two roles negotiate with each other, we defined two protocols: cdNegotiationBuy and cdNegotiation-Sell. The first protocol is coupled to the buyer and allows the performatives: ask, buy, reject and abort. The second protocol is coupled to the seller and allows the performatives: offer and abort. The performative ask is used by the buyer to start a negotiation by asking for the price of CD. The seller can offer a price, which the buyer can accept by using buy or continue the negotiation by using reject. Both roles can break off the negotiation by using the performative abort. The domain

[9]To define a class based on a metaclass, one has make an instantiation of a metaclass.

concepts involved are CD and price. The concept CD refers to the item subject of negotiation. The concept price refers to the argumentation used in the negotiation.

The instantiation of the required conversation specific concepts is illustrated in Figure 3. This object diagram shows the required conversation specific concepts for the musicshop example, as instances of the Agent Communication Meta Ontology (e.g. the object CD is an instance of the metaclass Concept). The name of an object is composed of the identification of an object, followed by the name of the metaclass (e.g. Concept, Directive, Negotiate and AgentRole). For example, the object Buy is an instance of the metaclass Representative. The relations between the objects are inherited from the Agent Communication Meta Ontology. As illustrated in Figure 1, the relation between AgentRole and Negotiation (which is of type Protocol) is allowed protocol. The relations between the Protocols and the directives, commissive and representative (which are of type Performative is allowed performative. The relation between the Performatives and the Concepts is of type allowed concept.

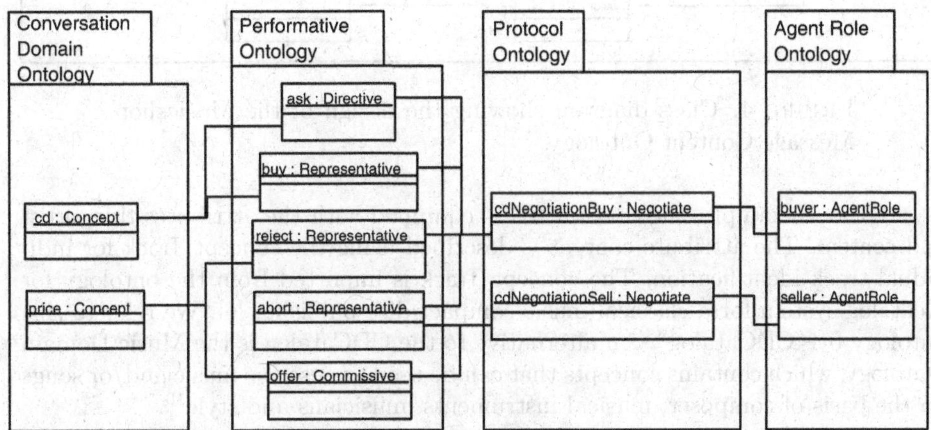

FIGURE 3. Object diagram showing the conversation-specific concepts as instances of the agent communication meta ontology.

2.4.2. Specification of Conversation Specific Concepts. In order to make the switch from the metalevel to the domain level, we map the defined instances of the Reference Model onto classes. For example, the instances defined in Figure 3 are mapped on the classes in Figure 4. The purpose of this step is to elaborate (i.e. make the generic classes specific) on the definition of the conversation specific concepts in terms of properties (or attributes) and relations. We refer to [30] for ways to define the properties of these classes. The resulting class diagram is illustrated in Figure 4.

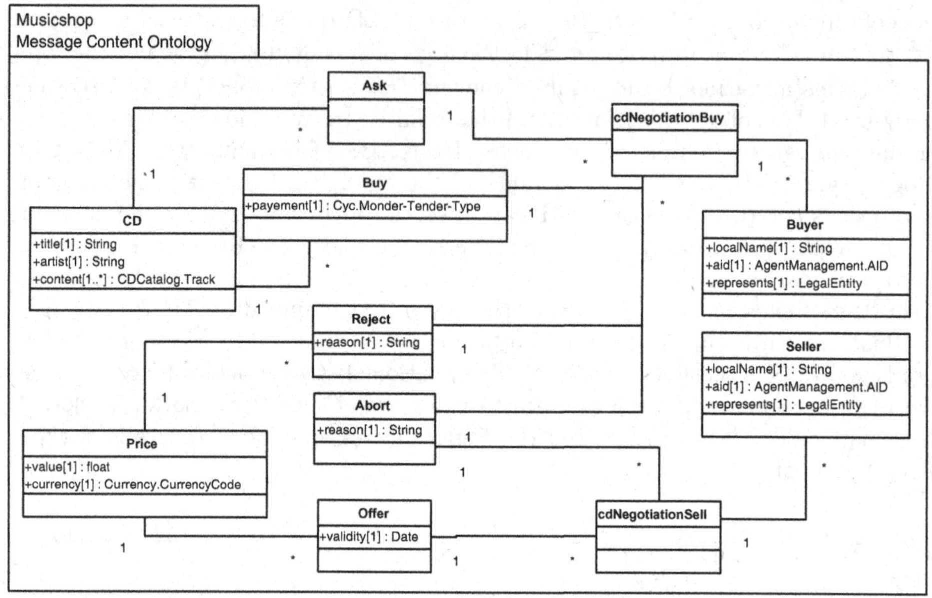

FIGURE 4. Class diagram showing the design of the Musicshop Message Content Ontology.

For our example, the concept CD is equipped with the attributes title, artist and content. The attribute content is described using the concept Track for individual track identification. The concept Track is imported from the ontology for a catalog system for a classical music compact disc publisher [6]. We refer to this ontology by "CDCatalog". An alternative to the CDCatalog is the Music Domain Ontology, which contains concepts that can be used to describe music and/or songs on the basis of composer, musical instruments, musicians and style[10].

The concept price contains the attributes value and currency. The currency attribute is of type CurrencyCode, which is imported from the currency ontology that specifies the "three letter currency codes" as defined by ISO 4217[11]. Given this attribute, the agents involved could use the above described currency conversation service.

The performative Buy makes use of the attribute payment of type Money-Tender-Type, which is imported from the Cyc upper level ontology[12]. This concept defines types of the payment form, such as credit card, cash and cyber coin. When the buyer wants to actually buy a CD, the buyer can also negotiate on the way of payment.

[10] See www.daml.org/ontologies/276

[11] See www.daml.ecs.soton.ac.uk/ont/currency.daml

[12] The Cyc upper ontology is reused in the HPKB-UPPER-LEVEL ontology. The Cyc ontology can be found at www.cyc.com.

In order to summarize the process from Agent Communication Meta Ontology to message content ontology, we have described a “trace” in Figure 5. As shown, the class buy is an instantiation of the class Representative from the Performative Ontology. The class Representative is an instance of the metaclass Performative from the Agent Communication Meta Ontology. The class Buy makes use of the class Money-Tender-Type of the external ontology Cyc, to describe the attribute payment.

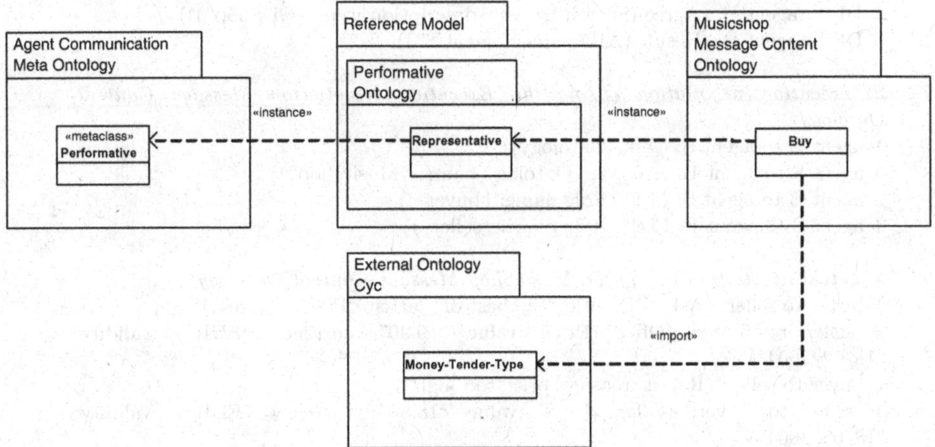

FIGURE 5. The process from Agent Communication Meta Ontology to Message Content Ontology.

2.5. Message Content Ontology Application

In order to discuss a message content ontology in action, we show how agents apply the musicshop ontology. In an ideal world, we can assume that all agents are capable of handling imported parts of message content ontologies. Problems related to ontology integration include mapping between different types of languages, versions of ontologies and levels of detail. For a discussion on the use of ontologies we refer to [36]. Furthermore, we assume that the agents are FIPA-Compliant, meaning that they have registered themselves at an agent platform and know how to consult a platform's DF (directory facilitator, i.e. an agent platform's yellow pages).

Below a part of a conversation is given, which is composed of four stages. The conversation in the third stage makes use of the Musicshop message content ontology. In the first stage, where agent B consults the DF to find an agent that represents a CDshop, the FIPA Agent Management Message Content Ontology is used. Then, agent B starts a negotiation with agent S (the agent suggested by the DF) on how to follow the message content ontology. This part of the conversation is based on the negotiation protocol and makes use of the *Execution Negotiation*

Message Content Ontology. Next, the agents start the actual negotiation by arguing on the price of a CD on basis of the Musicshop ontology and the negotiation protocol. Finally, the agents argue on the actual payment using the *Payment Negotiation Message Content Ontology.* We added the Execution Negotiation and Payment Negotiation Message Content Ontologies to illustrate how agents can switch between multiple message content ontologies.

1: service location (using the FIPA Agent Management Message Content Ontology)
① agent B to DF: (Search (service-description :type "CDShop"))
② DF to agent B: (Agree (Search (service-description :type "CDShop")))
③ DF to agent B: (Result (AID name: "agent S"))

2: execution negotiation (using the Execution Negotiation Message Content Ontology)
① agent B to agent S: (Ask (Ontology))
② agent S to agent B: (Answer (Ontology name: "Musicshop"))
③ agent B to agent S: (Tell (Role name: "buyer"))
④ agent S to agent B: (Tell (Role name: "seller"))

3: actual negotiation (using the MusicShop Message Content Ontology)
① buyer to seller: (Ask (CD :title "the best of" :artist "Paolo Conte"))
② seller to buyer: (Offer (Price :value "19.90" :currency "EUR") :validity "18/02/2004")
③ buyer to seller: (Reject :reason "price too high")
④ seller to buyer: (Offer (Price :value "18.50" :currency "EUR") :validity "18/02/2004")
⑤ buyer to seller: (Reject :reason "price too high")
⑥ seller to buyer: (Offer (Price :value "18.00" :currency "EUR") :validity "18/02/2004")
⑦ buyer to seller: (Buy (CD :title "the best of" :artist "Paolo Conte") :payment "credit-card")

4: payment negotiation (using the Payment Negotiation Message Content Ontology)
① seller to buyer: (Ask (CreditCard))
② buyer to seller: (Offer (CreditCard :number "1111 2222 3333 4444" :validity "1203"))
③ seller to buyer: (Reject :reason "credit card not valid")
④ buyer to seller: (Offer (CreditCard :number "2222 3333 4444 5555" :validity "0105"))
⑤ seller to buyer: (Accept :comment "CD will be delivered within 1 week")
...

In the first stage, agent B sends message ① to the agent platform's DF to search for an agent that offers services belonging to the "CDshop" domain. After a lookup in the DF's repository, the DF suggests to contact agent S with message ②. The conversation between the DF and agent S, are based on the Agent Management Ontology, see Section 2.3 and [10]. The applied protocol in this conversation is the Request-Protocol.

In the second stage, agent B and agent S start a discussion on how to perform the negotiation. Two decisions are made: one on the message content ontology (see messages ① and ②) to apply and on the division of roles (see messages ③ and ④). From here on agent B plays the role of "buyer" and agent S plays the role of "seller". More work on ontology negotiation can be found in [2]. Here we assume that the imported ontologies used in the musicshop ontology are available (e.g. via an online ontology repository). If not, the agents should be capable of finding a substitute ontology or can decide to stop the negotiation. In addition, version problems have to be solved. For example, agent A and agent S make use of different versions of the musicshop ontology or one or more of the imported ontologies. We assume that the agents are capable of detecting version problems and are capable of resolving it, by upgrading to a common version. There can also be problems related to the level of detail of the imported ontologies. For example, one attribute can be of a type in an upper ontology and another in an application ontology. In this case, we assume that the agents are capable of building mappings or bridges between levels of detail. The applied protocol in this conversation is the negotiation-protocol.

In the third stage, the buyer begins the actual negotiation, based on the Musicshop ontology and the negotiation-protocol. The negotiation starts with message ① using the action Ask combined with the concept CD to ask for an offer of the seller. The seller responds with message ②, which has the action Offer including a validity attribute and the object Price. The validity attribute is used to refer to the validity of the offer for this particular CD. Next, the buyer sends message ③ containing the action Reject and a reason, in order to reject the offer. The seller responds with message ④ containing a new Offer, which is rejected by message ⑤. The offer in and ⑥ is accepted by the buyer, and sends message ⑦ to the seller, which contains the action Buy.

Finally, in the fourth stage, the seller and buyer try to settle the payment, which is based on the negotiation-protocol. As shown, the seller asks the buyer for details on the selected payment form, i.e. "credit card". The first answer of the buyer is rejected due to an invalid credit card. The second answer of the buyer is accepted and a delivery date is offered.

3. Operationalization of Ontology-based Communication

In the previous section we presented a framework containing a Reference Model. In this section, we argue that not all parts of the Reference Model are always required for agent communication. For example, the agent role ontology is meant to model more elaborate roles, such as Manager and Operator. One of the reasons to distribute the task of a system is to separate responsibilities, which are connected to roles. Given, the current state of the art in agent technology, agent designers often choose to have agents commit to one role, e.g. Broker, Librarian, Manager or Operator. Therefore, given the current state of the art, the use of agent roles can be seen as superfluous. Consequently, the relation between protocols and agent roles can become redundant. For example, in the case of the FIPA Agent Management

Ontology, visiting agents already know the existence of the AMS and the DF. Even registration procedures (with the AMS and the DF) are hardwired in agent tool kits as two separate agents [3].

Most agents at this moment are relatively simple, in terms of reasoning power. One reason for that is that implementing agents with traditional AI languages is problematic [24][13]. A lot of existing tools such as JADE are designed in Java, because of its popularity and of the availability of reusable components. Furthermore, more low level standardization has to be realized [27].

The role of a Reference Model is to provide means for agents and agent engineers to reason about ontology-based agent communication. Therefore, we propose to use a *Minimal Ontology*, which only defines conversation specific concepts. The *Minimal Ontology* is discussed in detail in Section 3.1. When designing relative simple agents using the current state of the art, the Minimal Ontology can be applied.

In the remainder of this section, we answer the following two questions: *How can ontologies for message content be designed?* and *How can messages be generated and interpreted, both on the basis of a* Minimal Ontology*?* The first question is related to ontology modeling. Typical issues related to ontology modeling are, domain of interest, knowledge to be stored in the ontology and the maintenance of the ontology [30]. The second question is related to the application of the ontology. In this case, ontologies are used to support relatively simple conversations between relative simple agents. These conversations are built up out of multiple messages, which can contain questions, answers, offers and so forth.

3.1. Minimal Agent communication ontology

The minimal agent communication ontology[14], presented, is preliminary and contains only basic concepts and relations based on the Agent Communication Meta Ontology. The idea is, that when we gained enough experience with this Minimal Ontology, and possible conversations, extensions in the direction of the Reference Model can be made. The trade-off is between expressive power and usability. A Minimal Ontology that is very expressive may not be easy to use. For example, a Minimal Ontology could demand that the state of an agent and the overall goals of the system have to be specified. The idea could be that the sending agent, specifies its internal state and denotes for what goal a message is sent. This could lead to an overload of information, where the agents spend more time on processing information than on its actual task.

As mentioned above, FIPA has specified ontology-based communication, in which the semantics of message contents is specified in message content ontologies. The JADE toolkit has implemented the FIPA specifications[15]. The ontology handling functionalities within this toolkit are extended to explicit ontology handling.

[13] Although this claim originates from 1999, little is known on agents with considerable reasoning power, such as learning and reasoning on different types of ontologies and knowledge

[14] In the remainder we refer to "minimal agent communication ontology" by "Minimal Ontology".

[15] It has successfully passed so called interoperability tests held by FIPA, see http://jade.cselt.it.

JADE is Java oriented, therefore ontology specifications have to be expressed in Java code. This code will be part of the agent.

Every concept in an ontology has to be defined as a *Java Bean*. A Java Bean is a special type of a Java class, which adheres to a specific design. A Java Bean has members (i.e. attributes) that can be written with a `set` operation and be read with a `get` operation or an `is` operation[16].

One of the content languages FIPA has described and for which tools are available is FIPA-SL0[17] [16]. The SL0 representation of this class is (CD :name "the best of" :artist "Paolo Conte"). We focus on the creation of the ontologies and use the SL0 format to describe examples of the content of messages.

For every sent message, a translation from the internal Java instances to SL0, has to be made. For every received message, a translation from SL0 representation to internal Java instances has to be made. A more elegant alternative functionality is to manipulate ontologies as external resources expressed in SL0. However, no concrete implementation of a SL0 knowledge base is available.

The JADE toolkit offers limited ontology manipulation, we follow its (limited) view on ontologies. The reason for this is that a lot of agent engineers use the toolkit to develop agents in. Within the JADE toolkit, there are a limited number of basic ontological classes[18] with corresponding concepts that can form the basis of a Minimal Ontology. The candidate elements of the Minimal Ontology are *Concept* and *Action*, because they correspond with the *domain concept* and *performative* from our Reference Model. We neglect the notion of role and protocol in order to keep the ontology minimal.

A *Concept* is a superclass of the domain concepts that are subject of discussion, such as good, price, person, and address. This element refers to the conversation domain ontology. A Concept has *properties* that can have values. For example, a CD can have the properties *title* and *artist* instantiated with the values "the best of" and "Paolo Conte".

An *Action* is a superclass of the intentions (or performatives) that can change the world. This element refers to the performatives of the performative ontology. Examples of actions are sell, offer, ask, tell, propose and buy.

Every Action contains at least one *Concept*. This means that every action is coupled to one or more objects in the world. For example, Buy is connected to a CD and offer is connected to a price. Therefore, we include the relation AllowedConcept in the Minimal Ontology, to relate Concepts to the Action class.

An example message content ontology related to a musicshop is illustrated in Figure 6. As illustrated the conversation specific concepts are defined as abstract classes (i.e. the classes printed in italic letters) and not as meta classes. The reason for this is to keep the creation of message content ontologies less complicated compared to the Agent Communication Meta Ontology. We can already see a

[16]The `is` operation is used to check the value of boolean typed members.

[17]SL0 is a subset of FIPA-SL. The syntax of SL is based on *s-expressions* used in LISP, which are balanced parenthesis lists [24].

[18]These elements (i.e. Java classes) can be found in the jade.content package.

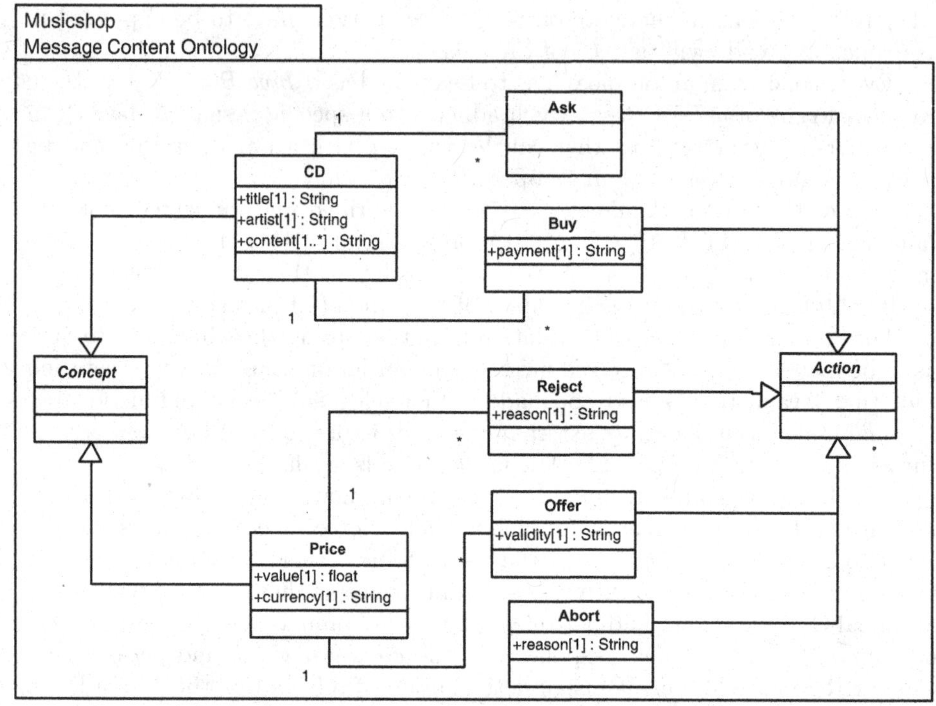

FIGURE 6. Musicshop Message Content Ontology for a conversation in a CD shop (see also Figure 4), based on the Minimal Ontology.

drawback of the Minimal Ontology, because it does not include the possibility to define axioms and rules. For example, the rule that the seller has to respond with the action Offer after receiving an action Ask, cannot easily be modeled in the ontology.

In the remainder of this section, we discuss a tool that is a first attempt to automate agent coding. With the use of Protégé message content ontologies can be defined based on the Minimal Ontology. The ontologies defined within Protégé can be translated to Java code, which can be used for buildings agents with the JADE toolkit.

3.2. Defining Message Content Ontologies

Defining a message content ontology means specializing the elements of the Minimal Ontology. In order to be able to use the current ontology editors to design our Minimal Ontology we decided to comply with the OKBC knowledge model, used in Protégé 2000, Protégé 2000 is a commonly used ontology editor, which enables engineers to graphically model ontologies. Furthermore, additional functionality and storage formats can be "plugged in" into the system. An ontology within Protégé

Facet	*Description*	*Examples*
cardinality of a slot	the number of values the slot can have, i.e. 0,1,N.	class *person* can only have one father ($c = 1$), class *father* can have multiple children ($c = N$).
allowed values	restriction of the value type of a slot.	Integer, String, Instance of a class.
numeric boundaries	the minimum and maximum value for a numeric slot	the slot *age* is between 0 and 150.
required or optional	whether a slot is required or not	the slot *name* is required for the class *person*.

TABLE 4. Facets of the slots part of ontologies within Protégé including description and examples.

is based on a frame-based (OKBC) knowledge model [29]. Therefore, ontologies modeled with this tool, can be mapped onto Java structures.

The ontology model of Protégé consists of classes, slots and slot facets [29]. Classes are concepts in the domain of discourse, with which a taxonomic hierarchy can be constructed. Slots describe properties or attributes of these classes. A slot in itself is a frame that has a type. This can be a primitive class, like String, Integer and Float, or an instance of another class. Furthermore, a slot has a value. Slot facets (see Table 4) describe properties (or constraints) of slots.

The design of the musicshop ontology is given in Figure 7 and Figure 6. As shown the concept CD has three slots: title, artist and tracks. The slots title and artist are modeled as String, are required and the cardinality is single. This means that every instance of CD, such as the Paolo Conte's CD, needs exactly one title and artist. We also added the slot tracks, to define the content of a CD. The slot is defined as multiple instances, which means that the slot refers to a collection (sequence) of instances of the type Track. Each class Track has the slots title and duration.

The concept Price has two slots: value and currency. The slot value denotes the amount of the price and currency the corresponding currency. In order to comply with the currency slot with international standards, the values of this slot could be restricted to an ontology that has defined internal currency codes. The International Organization for Standardization (ISO), a worldwide federation of national standards bodies, has specified the *ISO 4217 standard*, which contains global currencies and the three-character currency codes that are generally used to represent them[19]. In order to keep the ontology simple, this step is omitted by only considering EUROs, which is represented by "EUR".

In order to have the agents discuss on CDs in a musicshop setting, four Action types were modeled: Buy, Ask, Reject and Offer. These actions can be used to negotiate on the price of CDs. The actions correspond with the implicit performatives defined in Section 2.4.

[19] See www.xe.com/iso4217.htm

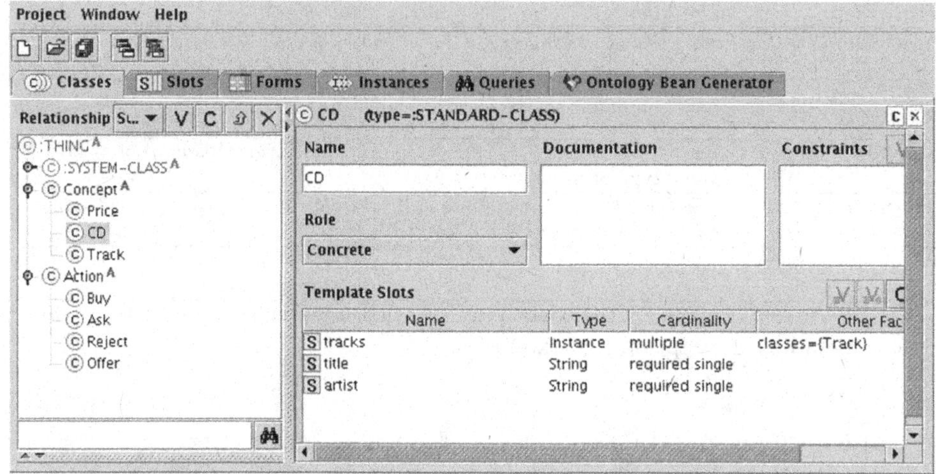

FIGURE 7. Screenshot from Protégé containing the Musicshop Message Content Ontology based on the Minimal Ontology.

One of the advantages of the Protégé tool is that other ontologies can be imported. Repositories of existing ontologies ranging from Biological domains to market place product and service descriptions, can be found at the Protégé community page and at the DAML site[20]. The languages used to represent these ontologies can range from XML, RDF, DAML-OIL, XMI, SQL to UML.

3.3. Mapping from Ontology Design to Java Beans

To support the agent engineer in creating and using message content ontologies, we developed a plug-in for the Protégé 2000 environment called the *Bean Generator.*With this plug-in, a domain ontology within Protégé can be developed and exported to Java beans.

Every class in the Minimal Ontology, i.e. `Concept` and `Action` is the basis for the generation of a Java class. The taxonomic structure (i.e. inheritance relations) of the domain model is mapped on the inheritance capabilities of Java.

3.4. Message Content Ontology Application

Agents can generate and interpret the content of messages, using *content encoding* and *content decoding* processes. An encoder is used by an agent when sending messages. There are two basic reasons for an agent to send a message. First, to start a conversation, such as asking for the price of a CD. Secondly to participate in a conversation, such as responding to a question. In both cases, the agents have to make translations from their internal state (i.e. collection of java instances) to an ACL language, such as SL0.

---

[20]See http://protege.stanford.edu/ontologies.html and www.daml.org/data

When an agent receives a message, the content has to be translated into the internal model of the agent, using a decoder. For example, when receiving a message filled with the content: (Offer :id 1 (Price :value "19.90" :currency "EUR")) the appropriate instances have to be generated. In this case, instances of the class Offer and Price are generated.

4. Legal Advisor

In this section we show the application of the message content ontologies and the above described approach in the domain of European Competition Law. We choose another domain then the Musicshop in order to show the variety of message content ontologies.

European Competition Law focuses on determining what law system(s) and rules are applicable in case of international business. Law systems include for instance national competition law and European competition law. Whereas rules include acts, statutes, regulations, directives, treaties, etc. For example, a company from country A wants to take over a company situated in country B. The question then is, which laws and rules are applicable when doing business on an international level?

There are several methods to enable companies to determine which laws and/or rules are applicable. One way is to look at the transaction amount of a take-over. This can determine whether European Law or national law is applicable. Another way is to look at the impact of the take-over with regard to the (European) competition. This can determine whether this take-over can be granted. Finally, does a take-over result in a dominant position of power with regard to the European Competition. If so, the take-over might not be granted.

4.1. Architecture

The system is composed of different types of agents: the *law expert agent*, the *law services broker* and the *personal law assistant*. The multi-agent architecture is drawn in Figure 8, showing the agents involved: the *law expert agent*, the *law services broker* and the *personal law assistant*, and their interactions. The *law expert agent* is drawn as a prototype for the the *web expert*, the *article expert* and the *rules expert*. The "consultation" between the *law expert agent* and *personal law assistant* are based on a sequence of Tell (of type directive) and Answer (of type representative) performatives, based on the FIPA-Request protocol.

4.1.1. Law Expert Agent. The *law expert agents* have the necessary knowledge about parts of European competition law. It means that they can reason about a part of a legal domain and exchange their finding with other agents. The *law expert agents* are able to agree on certain legal practices applicable to the question posed to them by the *personal law assistant*. In order to offer their services the agents register their competences at the *law services broker*.

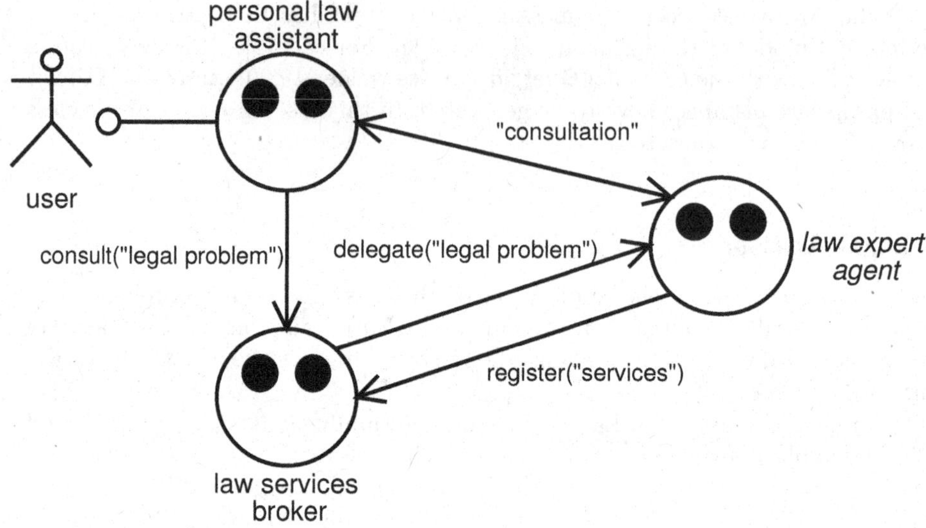

FIGURE 8. The Legal Advisor multi-agent architecture.

The first task of a *law expert agent*, i.e. register itself at the *law services broker*, is handled by the environment model. The *law services broker* uses the registrations of the *law expert agents* in order to select the proper *law expert agent* that can solve the issues submitted by the *personal law assistant*. The second task is to provide answers to questions posed by the *personal law assistant*.

Three types of *law expert agents* are defined: the *web expert*, the *article expert* and the *rules expert*. The *web expert agent* is able to translate a question from the *personal law assistant* to a query for a search engine (e.g. Google). To make sure that the results are within the required domain, certain keywords, such as "law" are added to the search query. The article expert is able to match a question from the *personal law assistant* to an XML annotated set of laws. We used an "ad hoc" article annotation. A formalized schema for annotation is METAlex[21], which is used in markup of legal sources, such as the Rome Statute, Belgian Income Tax Law, Dutch Corporate Tax Law and Dutch Penal Code.

The rules expert consults a SWI-Prolog-driven knowledge base, which is able to reason with a set of production rules. If the reasoner has insufficient information about the legal situation, it sends a message back, asking for more specific information. To be able to query the Prolog KB from within the agent, the JPL[22] library is used.

After interviews with legal experts, it appeared that there are no knowledge bases available that cover European Law. The decision was made to use an available

[21] www.metalex.nl

[22] http://sourceforge.net/projects/jpl/

knowledge base, describing a set of law articles about the "opium laws" in the Netherlands, provided by the Department of Computer Science and Law of the University of Amsterdam[23].

4.1.2. Law Services Broker. The *law services broker* functions as a central hub in the system, it has a notion of existing *law expert agents* and is able to delegate questions to the *law expert agents* that are posed by the *personal law assistant.* Every *law expert agent* has to register at the *law services broker.* The "location" of the *law expert agents* is maintained by the environment model. The "services" of the *law expert agents* is maintained by the competence model.

On the basis of a matching strategy (such as pattern matching) and a question of a *personal law assistant*, the *law services broker* selects a *law expert agent.* The *law services broker* will delegate a consul to the selected *law expert agent.*

4.1.3. Personal Law Assistant. The *personal law assistant* is the agent with whom the end-user of the system interacts. The agent maintains a user profile of the user and processes interaction with the user. Furthermore, the agent interacts with the *law services broker* and *law expert agents* selected by the *law services broker* on the basis of the Legaladvisor message content ontology.

Based on answers a user has given to queries, the *personal law assistant* can provide domain knowledge to *law services broker* and *law expert agents.* The answers of the *law expert agents* agents are presented as results to the user. This is operationalized by a web service which enables the user to provide its input. Furthermore, results of consults can be displayed.

4.2. Message Content Ontology Design

By combining the ontology design of the Protégé tool with the Bean Generator, it was possible to create a Java object hierarchy which is used by the agents in the system. We will now look at the design of the *LegalAdvisorOntology.* A part of the ontology as designed in Protégé is given in Figure 9.

The LegalAdvisorOntology ontology contains a limited set of classes on the basis of the Minimal Ontology, in order to balance the expressive power of the ontology and the competences of the agents, which are in this case limited. Reason for this is that the agents have access to services with limited functionalities.

Conforming to the Minimal Ontology, we first defined subclasses of type *Action.* These subclasses are *Ask*, *AskYesNo*, *AskOption*, *Register*, *Consult*, *Delegate*, *Tell*, *TellYesNo* and *TellOption.* The action *Ask* is applied by the expert agents to inquire information. This action is specialized into *AskYesNo*, to inquire boolean questions and *AskOption*, to inquire for one or more options. *Register*, which is used to register agents at the broker. *Consult* is used by the UserAgent to consult the broker agent. *Delegate* is used by the BrokerAgent to delegate a legal problem to one or more expert agents. *Tell* is used to answer an *Ask* action. Similar to the *Ask* action. *Tell* is specialized into *TellYesNo* and *TellOption.*

[23] www.lri.jur.uva.nl

Next we defined the subclasses of type *Concept*: *Option*, *LegalService* and *LegalProblem*. The concept *Option* defines the possible options used in the action *AskOption*. *LegalService* is a description of a service offered by an ExpertAgent. *LegalProblem* is a simplification of the problem owned by a UserAgent.

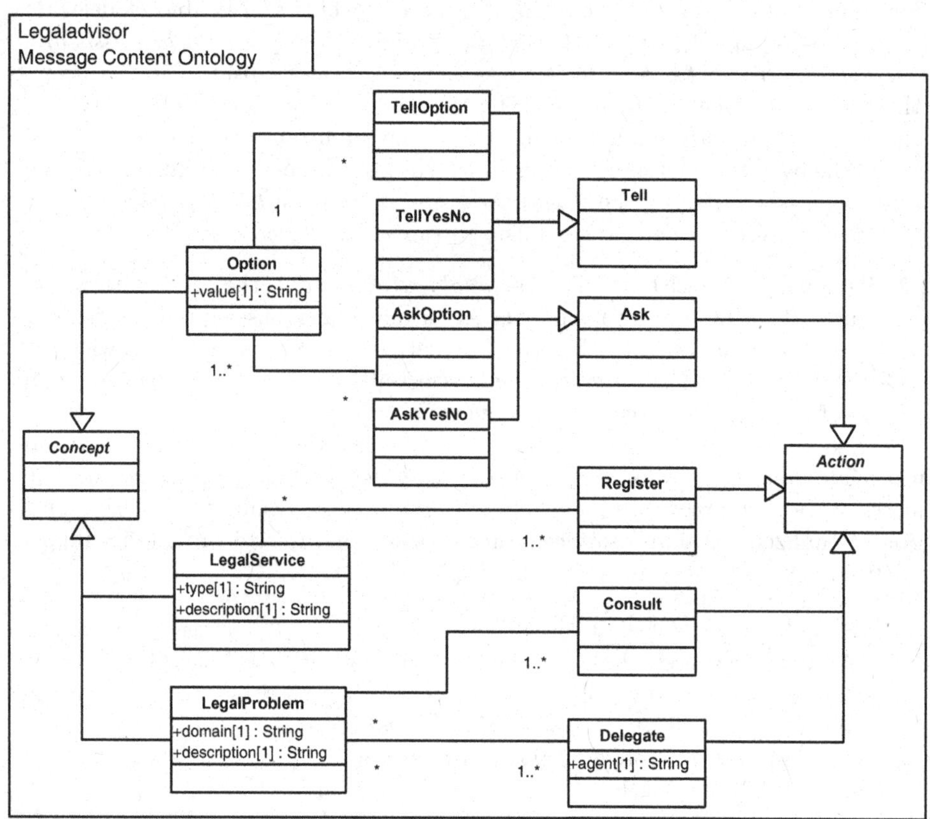

FIGURE 9. The Legaladvisor Message Content Ontology design for the Legal Advisor system, based on the Minimal Ontology.

4.3. Simple Scenario

This section describes a simple example scenario to show how the agents within the system interact with each other, using the LegalAdvisorOntology. The scenario starts when the agent platform has been launched and the agents have been created. Each agents has to register its services at the *law services broker*. An example message sent from the webagent to the broker is:

web expert to law services broker: (Register :legalservice (LegalService :type "keywordsearch" :description "Googlesearch"))

The message shows a description of the service that the agent can offer. As mentioned above, we did not use a full-fleshed ontology. Therefore, the service description is a very basic one.

The next step in the scenario is when a user enters information into a web form and submits this to the *personal law assistant.* Unknowing what the (semantic) content of the user's information is, it starts asking the *law services broker* for a suitable expert agent. The agent does this by forwarding the user's question to the broker:

personal law assistant to law services broker: (Consult (LegalProblem :domain "competition law" :description (sequence "European" " competition" "law" "regulations"))"

The broker analyzes the content of the message, and tries to find an appropriate agent. This is done by applying a basic lookup mechanism in the broker's register. In this case, the broker decides to delegate the legal problem to the *web expert agent.* Therefore, the webagent is selected, since it can ask any question to Google. Whether the answer of Google is usable is to be decided by the end user.

This decision is then sent to the *web agent* by the message:

law services broker to web expert: (Delegate (Consult (LegalProblem :domain "competition law" :description (sequence "European" "competition" "law" "regulations")) :agent "personal law assistant")

This message tells the *web expert* that it should find an answer to the specified LegalProblem and give the answer back to the agent "useragent". To find an answer to the LegalProblem, the *web expert* consults Google. The answer of Google, i.e. a list of URLs is translated into a sequence of the object Option and embedded into a TellOption action:

web expert to personal law assistant: (TellOption :options (sequence (Option value: "http://europa.eu.int")(Option value: "http://www.ellispub.com")(Option value: "http://www.etsi.org") ...))

From there, the user agent presents the received answer to the end-user.

4.4. Evaluation

Although there have been a few concessions to the original design, we succeeded in building a stable and fully functional law assistance agent system. The system makes use of the relative simple message content ontology in order to show the generation and application of message content ontologies on a general level. The agents' functionality is limited, due to the unavailability of usable legal knowledge bases. We did not model an ontology that fully represents a legal domain. For example, in the musicshop example, the notion of a CD is relatively well-defined. However, the notion of a legal problem in the Legal Advisor System needs to be further elaborated. Furthermore, we only paid attention to the type of conversations, i.e. Tell-Answers combinations.

The legal services and legal problems are expressed as keywords. Real life conceptualization of legal services and legal problems need more elaborate constructs. For this, existing ontologies and knowledge bases could be included, such as the CIA world fact-book that contains basic information related to countries, CYC containing common sense knowledge and various (in DAML represented) information sources[24]. The problem with this, however, is that conceptualization conflicts need to be resolved.

A drawback of the presented approach is that it does not consider complex constraints between concepts[25]. It is not (yet) possible to define what an allowed sequence of messages is. For example, a message containing the action class of type Ask, should be followed by a message containing an action class of type Tell. If we want to do so, we need to enhance the ontology mapping mechanism, in such a way that constraints can be stored in the ontology-mapping file.

5. Discussion

In this chapter, we addressed the problem of how agents can handle message-based communication. We have defined a framework for message content ontologies containing a Reference Model in order to provide semantics in message-based communication. The framework is built up out of a generic part and a specific part. The generic part is represented by an Agent Communication Meta Ontology that defines types of performatives and protocols based on (human) communication theory: speech acts and conversational interaction. The specific part is composed of a collection of domain dependent ontologies that describe the domain of the conversation, performatives, protocols and agent roles. We described and extended an existing categorization of speech acts for the definition of performatives. Furthermore, in order to show the variety of conversation protocols, we adjusted three existing protocols (i.e. Query, Request and Auction) and added two new ones (Negotiation and Supervision).

The Agent Communication Meta Ontology defines the subjects of agent communication: concepts, performatives, protocols and agent roles. We showed that a *message content ontology* is an instantiation of the Agent Communication Meta Ontology, which can be mapped onto a class diagram and specified in detail. From a theoretical point of view, it is appealing to define as much information as possible into a "full fledged" Reference Model. However, when designing an agent that is capable of handling this information, a lot of overhead emerges (due to the need for ontology operations and pre-negotiation activities). When making use of a full fledged Reference Model, the question is if all its concepts and relations are needed.

Based on our framework, we defined a "Minimal Ontology", which can be used in more pragmatic agent solutions. The ontology contains the classes Concept and Action, and the relation AllowedConcept. We explained that agents without an inference engine need a representation of an ontology in terms of their internal representation (such as Java beans) and means (such as an ontology mapping

---

[24] www.cia.gov/cia/publications/factbook, www.opencyc.org and www.daml.org.

[25] Constraints on slots can be made, with facets as described in Table. 4.

file) to map instances of an ontology into their internal representation. On the basis of the presented tool, encoders and decoders can respectively be used for translating an agent's internal model to agent communication utterances and vice versa. However, in this approach, the ontology and ontology translation is hard coded. This means that if an ontology changes, the java code for the agent needs to be regenerated and the agent needs to be deployed again.

Both the construction of the Message Content Ontology Framework and the Minimal Ontology can be seen as a first step towards the standardization of ontologies in agent communication and conversation. A possible method to define message content ontologies starts with choosing an Agent Communication Meta Ontology as a Reference Model, such as defined in Section 2.1. Next, based on generic classes of the Agent Communication Meta Ontology, conversation specific concepts of a message content ontology need to be defined (see Section 2.4.1). Then, these concepts can be specified in more detail by defining their properties (or attributes) and relations (see Section 2.4.2). Finally, ontology operations (such as encoding and decoding) have to be defined and added into an agent model.

Future research on message content ontologies includes elaboration on means to represent both syntax and semantics of message content ontologies, handling issues related to accessibility, i.e. how to store ontologies and how to retrieve them. From a methodological point of view, future research should address problems related to redefinition of ontologies.

For the case study, we designed a system with an information-driven character (cf. [17]) using notions of information processing actions (i.e. ask and tell). In the future, dedicated minimal ontologies suited for specific processes or specific domains can be defined. Other interesting domain are when agents with a knowledge-driven character communicate at the knowledge level. For this, content ontologies could be defined that can handle concepts like competences, knowledge, methods and protocols. A starting point can be UPML [7].

An alternative approach to ontology handling is having agents to manipulate existing ontologies and even to learn new ones. For example, agents could negotiate on the meaning of concepts and relations. Another alternative approach to ontology handling is that the agent sends serialized Java code[26] that represents (parts of) an ontology. The receiving agent can process this code into its own ontology model. Next to automatic generation of Java beans, semi-automatic generation of Java classes that define the behavior of agents can be considered. For example, *encoders* and *decoders* could take care of all aspects of conversation management. Tasks of conversation management are to keep track of state of conversations, follow interaction protocols and negotiate meaning. Probably the method of generating static code can be useful in well defined situations. However, when agents operate in dynamic environments and need to change their strategy and models at runtime,

---

[26] Within Java it is possible to translate (i.e. serialize) the structure and state of objects into a transportable format.

other techniques such as maintaining an explicit message content ontology and behavior patterns are to be considered.

References

[1] J.L Austin. *How to Do Things with Words.* Oxford University Press, 1976.

[2] S.C. Bailin and W. Truszkowski. Ontology Negotiation between Scientific Archives. In *Thirteenth International Conference on Scientific and Statistical Database Management*, 2001.

[3] F. Bellifemine, Caire G., T. Trucco, and G. Rimassa. *JADE Programmer's Guide.* 2003.

[4] A. Bond and L. Gasser. *Readings in Distributed Artificial Intelligence.* Morgan Kaufmann publishers Inc.: San Mateo, CA, USA, 1988.

[5] A. Chavez and P. Maes. Kasbah: An agent marketplace for buying and selling goods. In *Proceedings of the First International Conference on the practical Application of Intelligent Agents and Multi-agent systems*, 1996.

[6] S. Cranefield and M. Purvis. Uml as an ontology modelling language. In *Workshop on Intelligent Information Integration, 16th International Joint Conference on Artificial Intelligence (IJCAI-99)*, 1999.

[7] D. Fensel, V.R. Benjamins, E. Motta, and B.J. Wielinga. UPML: A framework for knowledge system reuse. In *Proceedings of IJCAI-99, Stockholm, Sweden*, 1999.

[8] J. Ferber. *Multi-Agent Systems.* Addison-Wesley, Reading, MA, 1999.

[9] FIPA. FIPA Ontology Service Specification. Technical Report XF000086, Foundation for Intelligent Physical Agents, http://www.fipa.org/specs/fipa00086/, 2001.

[10] FIPA. FIPA Agent Management Specification. Technical Report SC00023, Foundation for Intelligent Physical Agents, http://www.fipa.org/specs/fipa00023/, 2002.

[11] FIPA. FIPA Communicative Act Library Specification. Technical Report SC00037J, Foundation for Intelligent Physical Agents, http://www.fipa.org/specs/fipa00037, 2002.

[12] FIPA. FIPA Contract Net Interaction Protocol Specification. Technical Report SC00029, Foundation for Intelligent Physical Agents, http://www.fipa.org/specs/fipa00029/, 2002.

[13] FIPA. FIPA Dutch Auction Interaction Protocol Specification. Technical Report XC00032, Foundation for Intelligent Physical Agents, http://www.fipa.org/specs/fipa00032/, 2002.

[14] FIPA. FIPA English Auction Interaction Protocol Specification. Technical Report XC00031, Foundation for Intelligent Physical Agents, http://www.fipa.org/specs/fipa00031/, 2002.

[15] FIPA. FIPA Request Interaction Protocol Specification. Technical Report SC00026H, Foundation for Intelligent Physical Agents, http://www.fipa.org/specs/fipa00026, 2002.

[16] FIPA. FIPA SL Content Language Specification. Technical Report SC00008, Foundation for Intelligent Physical Agents, http://www.fipa.org/specs/fipa00008/, 2002.

[17] J. Galbraith. *Designing complex Organizations.* Addison-Wesley, 1973.

[18] M.L. Geis. *Speech Acts and Conversational Interaction.* Cambridge University Press, 1995.

[19] M. Genesereth and S. Ketchpel. Software agents. *Communications of the ACM*, 37(7):48–53, 1994.

[20] A. Gomez-Perez. Ontological engineering: A state of the art. *Expert Update*, 2(3):33–43, 1999.

[21] M. Gruninger and M. Fox. The Role of Competency Questions in Enterprise Engineering. In *Workshop on Benchmarking - Theory and Practice*, 1994.

[22] A. Haddadi. *Communication and Cooperation in Agent Systems.* Berlin, Springer-Verlag, 1995.

[23] M.N. Huhns and L.M. Stephens. Multiagent systems and societies of agents. In G. Weiss, editor, *Multiagent Systems: A Modern Approach to Distributed Artificial Intelligence*, pages 79–120. The MIT Press, Cambridge, MA, USA, 1999.

[24] Y. Labrou, T. Finin, and Y. Peng. The current landscape of agent communication languages, 1999.

[25] S.C. Levinson. *Pragmatics.* Cambridge University Press, Cambridge, 1991.

[26] A. R. Lomuscio, M. Wooldridge, and N. Jennings. A classification scheme for negotiation in electronic commerce. *International Journal of Group Decision and Negotiation*, 12(1):31–56, 2003.

[27] M. Luck, P. McBurney, and C. Preist. *Agent Technology: Enabling Next Generation Computing: A Roadmap for Agent Based Computing.* AgentLink II, 2003.

[28] R. Neches, R. Fikes, T. Finin, Gruber T., R. Patil, T. Senatir, and W. Swarout. Enabling technology for knowledge sharing. *AI Magazine*, 12(3):36–56, 1991.

[29] N. Noy, R. Fergerson, and M. Musen. The knowledge model of Protege-2000: Combining interoperability and flexibility. In *2th International Conference on Knowledge Engineering and Knowledge Management (EKAW'2000), Juan-les-Pins, France*, 2000.

[30] N. Noy and D. L. McGuinness. Ontology Development 101: A Guide to Creating Your First Ontology. 2001. Technical report, Stanford Medical Informatics, 2001.

[31] H.S. Pinto and J.P Martins. Reusing Ontologies. In *AAAI 2000 Spring Symposium Series, Workshop on Bringing Knowledge to Business Processes*, 2000.

[32] J.A. Rodríguez-Aguilar, F.J. Martin, P. Noriega, P. Garcia, and C. Sierra. Towards a test-bed for trading agents in electronic auction markets. *AI Communications*, 11(1):5–19, 1998.

[33] J.R. Searle. *Seech Acts.* Cambridge University Press, 1969.

[34] . Shoham, Y. Agent oriented programming. *Artificial Intelligence*, 60(1):51–92, 1993.

[35] M.P. Singh. Agent Communication Languages: Rethinking the Principles. *IEEE Computer*, 31(12):40–47, 1998.

[36] M. Uschold and M. Grüninger. Ontologies: principles, methods, and applications. *Knowledge Engineering Review*, 11(2):93–155, 1996.

[37] M. Uschold, M. King, S. Moralee, and Y. Zorgios. The Enterprise Ontology. *The Knowledge Engineering Review*, 1998.

[38] H. Weigand and W. Hasselbring. An Extensible Business Communication Language. *International Journal of Cooperative Information System*, 10(4):423–411, 2001.

Chris van Aart
Molenstraat 229
5342 CB
Oss
The Netherlands
e-mail: chris@vanaart.com

Bob Wielinga
University of Amsterdam
Human-Computer Studies Laboratory
Kruislaan 419
1098 VA Amsterdam
The Netherlands
e-mail: wielinga@science.uva.nl

Guus Schreiber
Free University Amsterdam
Department of Computer Science
De Boelelaan 1081a
1081 HV Amsterdam
The Netherlands
e-mail: schreiber@cs.vu.nl

Incorporating Complex Mathematical Relations in Web-Portable Domain Ontologies

Muthukkaruppan Annamalai and Leon Sterling

Abstract. The growing use of agent systems and the widespread penetration of the Internet have opened up new avenues for scientific collaboration. We have been investigating the possibility for agent systems to aid with collaboration among Experimental High-Energy Physics (EHEP) physicists. An apparent necessary component is an agreed scientific domain ontology, which must include concepts that rely on mathematical formulae involving other domain concepts such as the energy and momentum, for their meaning. We claim that the current web ontology specification languages are not sufficiently equipped to be useful for explicit representation of mathematical expressions. We adapt some previous work on representing mathematical expressions to produce a set of representational primitives and supporting definitions to incorporate complex mathematical relations among existing domain concepts in web ontologies, illustrated with examples arising from our interactions with the EHEP physicists.

1. Introduction

The growing use of agent systems and the widespread penetration of the Internet has opened up new avenues and created new challenges for scientific collaboration. On one hand, it is possible to make large amounts of scientific analyses of Experimental High-Energy Physics (EHEP) experiments available to scientists around the world [3, 4, 7]. On the other hand different scientific groups, even within a single collaboration, utilise different calculation methods, and it is sometimes difficult to know how to interpret particular analyses. It is assumed that practitioners in the EHEP domain possess the necessary background knowledge to interpret the intended meaning of the intuitive concepts and appropriated jargon in the domain of discourse. Unfortunately, application developers, newcomers to this field, and software agents lacking in relevant expertise are not capable of making a similar kind of interpretation. Knowledge models, or ontologies built to express specific facts about a domain can serve as the basis for understanding the discourse in that domain [5].

The notion of ontology as specification of a partial account of shared conceptualisation [14, 17] is adopted in this paper, that is an ontology defines a set of representational vocabulary for specific classes of objects and the describable relationships that exist among them in the modelled world of a shared domain.

In 2002, we were involved in a project [1, 8] supported by the Victorian Partnership for Advanced Computing [25] to investigate whether ontologies would be useful for EHEP collaboration, in particular in the Belle [4] collaboration. The research is founded on the idea that suitable web ontologies be developed and reused to facilitate this scientific community to produce and share information effectively on the semantic web. While the final verdict has not been reached, it is clear that our project extends existing capabilities of web ontology specification languages and tools.

One concerning issue is as to how to define mathematical concepts in the EHEP domain ontology. Mathematical concepts are equated with mathematical formulae involving other domain concepts such as the energy and momentum. A mathematical concept is a manifestation of an n-ary mathematical relation binding a set of concepts that co-exist in the ontology. The current web ontology specification languages, such as DAML [18] and OIL [10] (which has since evolved into OWL [23]) are founded on Description Logic [2] and can only express unary and binary relations. They offer no representational features for expressing both mathematical semantics and n-ary relations involving terms in the ontology. We ask, "How do we facilitate the semantic recognition of mathematical concepts in web ontology?" The answer to this question led us to cognise the extensions required for additional expressivity in web ontology. This paper shows the approach we have taken in order to ensure that we could describe complex mathematical relations linked to mathematical concepts and appropriately structure them in the web-portable domain ontology.

This paper is organised as follows. In Section 2, we provide a glimpse of the event selection variable in the EHEP domain ontology, which will be augmented with mathematical qualities to facilitate a coherent description of EHEP experimental analysis. In Section 3, we describe the principles of dealing with mathematical relations in domain ontology, and our approach to the problem is elaborated in Section 4. Section 5 proposes to adopt a related XML standard so that the augmented domain ontology remains XML-compliant. The future work is mentioned in Section 6, and finally Section 7 concludes the contribution of this paper.

2. The EHEP Experimental Analysis

The foundation for the Belle experimental data analysis is the knowledge about certain B particle decay channels and unbiased analysis of huge event data.[1] A particular data analysis attempts to recognise interesting B decay events by systematically discarding the background events in the data set.

A key information appreciated by the physicists is the event selection criteria, which prescribes a set of 'cuts' to determine the acceptance or rejection of an event. *Cuts* are constraints specified on event selection variables, whose values are either measured directly or mathematically derived from values of other variables. Loosely restricted cuts (or skimming), followed by more decisive topological, kinematic and geometric cuts is aimed to produce a set of desired event data for justified analysis of the empirical findings.

One use of the EHEP domain ontology being developed is to help clarify the *cuts* specified in the event selection criteria in definite terms – an essential requirement for the rudiments of the analysis to be interpreted and processed by supporting tools and agents.

2.1. Event Selection Variables in the EHEP Domain Ontology

The primary concept in the EHEP experimental analysis is event selection variable. A category of event selection variables is defined in the EHEP domain ontology. Figure 1 illustrates a partial hierarchy of event track variable concepts in the model. These terms are identified based on their need to specify the event selection cuts.[2] A set of competency questions [16] drawn-up while the ontology being built guides the conceptualisation of these required event-variables. The competency questions outline the competence of the EHEP ontologies. A typical competency question is: "What is the kinematic selection criteria applied in a specified analysis?" The ensuing answer would list the selection criteria enforced, such as: "Beam constrained mass $M_{bc} > 5.2\ GeV/c^2$, Track transverse momentum $P_T > 100\ MeV/c$, Energy difference $\Delta E < 0.2\ GeV$, Likelihood of electron over kaon $L_{e/K} > 0.95$". The EHEP ontology must define the necessary vocabulary to represent the competency questions that arose and the answers that were generated.

Following the web ontology modelling approach, we defined the hierarchically organised concepts and their distinguishing properties using frames. We used Protege [13], a frame-based modelling tool to construct the domain model. Consequently, the concepts are conceived using notations as class, subclass, property (slot), property type, cardinality and facets. Figures 2, 3 and 4 exemplify the internal structure for concepts *Energy*, *Momentum* and *InvariantMass*, respectively.

[1]The B subatomic particles in the meson family, has mass 10,331 times that of an electron and average lifetimes of 1.6×10^{-12} seconds. The unstable B particle naturally decays into a range of simpler particles. Physicists are particularly interested to study B decay channels that violate the Charge-Parity symmetry prescribed by the standard physics model, which the physicists believe may explain the dominance of matter over anti-matter in the universe.

[2]The subscripted-A at the end of a track variable name denotes that it is regarded as an abstract concept. Individuals cannot be instantiated from such general concepts.

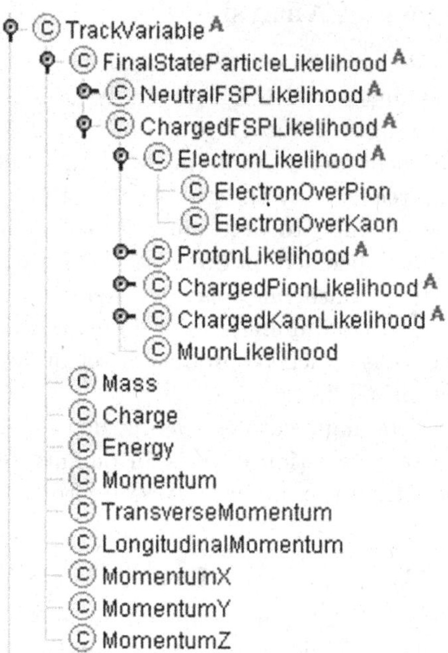

FIGURE 1. Partial Hierarchy of Event Track Variables

The *Energy* class has been defined as a subclass of *TrackVariable* with properties like *value* and *unit*. The energy quantity of a track particle is described as a real number together with its unit of measurement. The property *unit* denotes a symbolic unit of measurement symbol. In the case of energy, a set of allowed values for *unit* is represented by a facet, restricting the allowed symbol to eV, KeV, MeV, and so on. The definitions of *Momentum* and *InvariantMass* are similar, except for a different set of symbols utilised to denote their respective units of measurement.

The *Track* class describes a group of characteristics such as its charge, energy, invariant mass and momentum, which helps to distinguish a candidate track particle. A partial definition of *Track* is given in Figure 5. Notice that there are four types of momentum properties defined in this class. The property *momentum* relates to the magnitude of a track particle's momentum, whose fundamental momentums along the X-, Y- and Z-axes in the laboratory frame are described as *momentumX*, *momentumY* and *momentumZ*, respectively.

The definitions of these concepts in the model are rather simple. Also, notice that the track variables have been defined somewhat independent of one another, apart from indicating they are all subclasses of *TrackVariable*. In reality, these concepts are mathematically related to one another. The restricted features offered

class Energy		
subClassOf TrackVariable		
Property	**Property Type**	**Cardinality**
value	Real	=1
unit	Symbol	=1

FIGURE 2. Partial Definition of Class Energy

class Momentum		
subClassOf TrackVariable		
Property	**Property Type**	**Cardinality**
value	Real	=1
unit	Symbol	=1

FIGURE 3. Partial Definition of Class Momentum

class InvariantMass		
subClassOf TrackVariable		
Property	**Property Type**	**Cardinality**
value	Real	=1
unit	Symbol	=1

FIGURE 4. Partial Definition of Class InvariantMass

by web ontology modelling tools and languages do not allow us to define these relationships explicitly.

We are also not able to represent vectors such as 3-momentum and flight direction of a track particle. We circumvented this situation by defining three properties to describe the individual components of a vector, like the way the three fundamental momentums of a track particle are defined in *Track*. Again, the close affinity between these fundamental momentums is not describable in the current model, which can potentially lead to inconsistency in the knowledge base.

On the other hand, the calculation oriented event analysis to which we propose to apply this ontology, compels related domain terms to exhibit considerable numeric-ability. The domain ontology must explicitly represent the mathematical relationships among peer concepts so as to limit their possible interpretation and relations in the ontology. More usefully, a mathematical relationship helps to trace the derivability of a 'function' event selection variable from related constants and 'constant' event selection variables. In the ensuing discussion, we elucidate such relationships that exist in the EHEP domain.

2.2. Constant and Function EHEP Event Selection Variables

The EHEP event variables provide a 'handle' for specifying the event selection *cuts*. We sometimes refer to 'event selection variables' simply as 'event variables' for

class Track subClassOf EHEPEntity		
Property	**Property Type**	**Cardinality**
signalTrack	Boolean	
candidateParticle	Particle	=1
charge	Charge	=1
energy	Energy	=1
mass	InvariantMass	=1
momentum	Momentum	=1
momentumX	MomentumX	=1
momentumY	MomentumY	=1
momentumZ	MomentumZ	=1

class Charge subClassOf TrackVariable
class Energy subClassOf TrackVariable
class InvariantMass subClassOf TrackVariable
class MomentumX subClassOf TrackVariable
class MomentumY subClassOf TrackVariable
class MomentumZ subClassOf TrackVariable

FIGURE 5. Partial Definition of Class Track

short. There are two classes of event variables in the EHEP domain depending on how the quantity associated with these variables is determined. The quantities of 'constant' event variables are directly measured in a particular event; whereas the quantities of 'function' event variables are derived from the quantities of constant event variables.

In the illustrative example given in the first paragraph of the previous section, $L_{e/K}$ is a constant event variable; whereas, M_{bc} is a function event variable. $M_{bc} = \sqrt{E_{beam}^2 - P_B^2}$, where E_{beam} is an experiment constant that represents the energy of beam, while P_B is the momentum of a B-candidate particle.[3] P denotes the norm of a 3-dimensional momentum vector. It is a function event variable derived from the 3-Momentum vector as follows, $P = \|P_3\|$. P_3 is a constant event variable.

[3]While constants such as energy of beam, E_{beam} remains invariable for the whole experimental analysis, the quantities assigned to event selection variables, either measured or calculated, remain fixed in a single event analysis. The numerical quantity, such as 5.2 GeV/c^2 that appears on the right-hand side of a cut specification is user-defined constant.

A function event variable is expressed mathematically in terms of its related constants and constant event variables. A first order function event variable accepts only constants or constant event variables as parameters. Examples are momentum of particle, P and transverse momentum of particle, P_T. The function event variable P is given above, while $P_T = \sqrt{P_x^2 + P_y^2}$. Both variables are derived from 3-Momentum, P_3. In the latter, the momentums along the X- and Y-axes, denoted respectively as P_x and P_y must be first extracted from P_3 in order to derive P_T. Notice that function event variables are always grounded in constant event variables.

Other examples of first order function event variables are the Fox-Wolfram Moment-0, H_0 and Fox-Wolfram Moment-1, H_1 that utilise Fisher Discriminant technique to combine a set of correlated event variables [11]. $H_0 = \sum_j \sum_k (P_j \times P_k)$ and $H_1 = \sum_j \sum_k (P_j \times P_k \times \cos\theta_{jk})$. Both function variables are derived from a set of 3-Momentums. H_0 summatively combines the product of all pairs of momentums belonging to a set of track particles in an event, while H_1 summatively combines their scalar product. The indices j and k enumerate the tracks in an event and θ_{jk} is the polar angle between them in the laboratory frame of reference.

A higher-order function event variable admits other function event variables as parameters. The beam constrained mass, M_{bc}, which relies on function event variable momentum, P as parameter is an example of higher-order function event variable. In fact, invariant mass of a particle, $M = \sqrt{E^2 - P^2}$ is derived from its energy, E and momentum, P. Another example of higher-order function event variable is the normalised Fox-Wolfram Moment-1, $R_1 = \frac{H_1}{H_0}$. Note that both parameters of R_1 are function event variables. Anyhow, higher-order function event variables are eventually grounded in constant event variables.

3. The Principles of Our Approach

We are focusing on the meaningful representation of relations that mathematically bind a set of the domain concepts in web ontology. Our development is quite different from the work being pursued by the mathematical-knowledge representation community that is concerned about content theories of mathematics and experiment with different formalisms for representing theories, definitions, axioms, proofs, etc. in the field of mathematics. In contrast, our effort to incorporate mathematical relations in domain ontologies is closer in spirit to that of EngMath [15], with the qualification that our scope is aligned to knowledge sharing on the web.

EngMath ontology is an extensive past attempt to capture the semantics associated with mathematical expressions in engineering models. This declarative first order KIF [12] axiomatisation for mathematical modelling in engineering is built on abstract algebra and supported by sets of theories for describing mathematical objects such as scalar, vector and tensor.

To a lesser degree, general-purpose ontologies like CYC [9] and SUMO [24] also attempt to declaratively capture the semantics of mathematical function.

However, such function is categorised as unary, binary, ternary and quaternary; thereby placing a limit on the number of its argument. Perhaps, this restraint is imposed in order to refer to a function's argument based on its order in the 'argument list'. On the contrary, we do not wish to limit the number of arguments of a function. In addition, a function argument must be able to denote a collection of class instances (both extensional and intensional sets), which CYC and SUMO do not allow.

Although, the EngMath approach of providing rigorous descriptions appears to faithfully represent mathematical expressions in instantiated models, it is difficult to understand and apply to working systems.[4] More importantly, the EngMath ontology that is constituted from declaratively specified n-ary relations, functions and axioms is not amenable on the web.

Since we aim to build an ontology that can be ported on the web, we have bypassed the declarative style of EngMath, but still need to ground the expression describing a mathematical relation in the formal language of mathematics. As such, we will have to regard the generic mathematical notations as primitives in our model. The idea is to utilise these mathematical primitives together with a set of epistemological primitives as the basis for incorporating mathematical relations among existing domain terms in the web ontology. We list below the principles of our approach.

I. Web ontologies are frame-based. In light of this fact, we built on the original domain model that was constructed using Protege to incorporate mathematical relations among the relevant domain terms. The augmented concept definition is represented using notions as metaclass, class, subclass, property (*template-slot* and *own-slot*), property type, cardinality and facets, which feature in Protege's knowledge model [21].

II. Mathematics deal with numeric quantities. Therefore, the domain concepts united by mathematical relations ought to be treated as quantities. Physically significant quantities usually have dimension and units of measurement associated with them.

III. We have introduced the notion of *Simple* and *Compound* quantities. The values of simple quantities are directly assigned to them. The values of compound quantities are derived from the values of its dependent quantities.

IV. The mathematical relation described by a mathematical concept is grounded in a compound quantity.

V. The quantities are modelled upon mathematical data types. Simple quantity is modelled upon scalar and vector. Compound quantity is modelled upon function. Collection of homogeneous quantities is modelled as set. Aggregate of heterogeneous quantities are treated as tuple (record). The data types

[4]The theories specified formally as KIF axioms, not only entails high specification effort, but are also hard to read and understand. It is difficult to envisage how practitioners in the domain could be influenced to use it.

define the semantics of its associated data values and the operations that can be applied on them.

VI. The algebra of scalars and vectors need to be extended to simple quantities allied with units of measurement, so that it is possible to reason effectively about the mathematical relations involving these quantities.

4. Explicating the Mathematical Relations In the EHEP Domain Ontology

The constant and function event variables mentioned in Section 2.2 are physical quantities. We need to first define suitable concepts for representing these quantities in the ontology. Then, we will propound a scheme for providing an abstract description of mathematical relations involving these quantities.

4.1. Representing Quantity

The need to deal with physical quantities in scientific ontologies is obvious. Physical quantity reflects the property of things that can be measured in the ontology. The conceptualisation of physical quantity is based upon our viewpoint on how quantities, dimension and units are treated in the EHEP domain.

A species of physical quantities is broadly organised in a tree as shown in Figure 6. *Physical Quantity* is divided into *Simple Quantity* and *Compound Quantity*. A *Simple Quantity* holds a constant value of measurement. We represent simple quantities as *Scalar Quantity* and *Vector Quantity*, the two significant types of quantities that govern physical modelling in science. Their respective mnemonic names indicate the type of values held. A *Compound Quantity* is categorised as *Static Compound Quantity* or *Dynamic Compound Quantity* in our model. Both static and dynamic compound quantities are further sub classified as scalar and vector quantities, depending on the type of their derived output.[5]

The physical quantities are defined as a hierarchy of metaclasses. The subclass relation between the defined classes reflects the organisation of quantity-concepts outlined in Figure 6. The root and intermediate classes in the hierarchy are 'abstract' classes, while the leaves are 'concrete' classes. Only the concrete subclasses of *PhysicalQuantity* can be instantiated. Our rationales for defining physical quantities as metaclasses rather than classes are as follows:

I. Domain concepts (represented as classes in the domain ontology) that will be related mathematically are physical quantities. Therefore, we want to be able to describe the event variables and related classes in the EHEP domain ontology as specific types of physical quantities. For example, *Energy* should be represented as scalar quantity, *3-Momentum* as vector quantity and *InvariantMass* as a form of compound quantity. The properties required to describe a type of physical quantity must be representationally attached to an event

[5]The constant event variables mentioned in Section 2.2 are simple quantities; the function event variables are compound quantities.

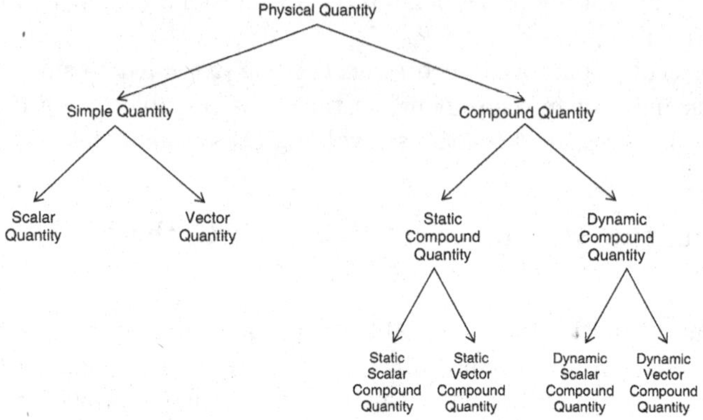

FIGURE 6. Physical Quantities

variable class to describe the class itself. In frame terminology, these kind of properties are called *own-slots* of the class. A practical way for a class to acquire *own-slots* is by being instance of metaclass that has those properties as *template-slots* [21].[6]

II. We are mindful of the fact that an existing domain ontology that was constructed to suit some tasks requirement in the domain is being extended to incorporate mathematical relations among domain concepts. Any modification to these domain concepts should be kept minimal so that prospective users who have adopted the original version can continue to rely upon the augmented ontology, and not be overwhelmed with mathematical extensions unrelated to their need. The approach we have taken is to model metaclasses of physical quantities as a framework overarching the classes in the domain ontology. They physical quantities are integrated with the classes in the domain ontology through *instanceOf* relationships (not by additional *subClassOf* relationships, which will introduce the unwieldy multiple inheritance in the domain ontology). The properties of the domain classes instantiated as physical quantities has acquired additional properties (*own-slots* from metaclass and modeller-defined *template-slots*), without overly compromising the existing properties and relations of the classes.

The root concept, *PhysicalQuantity* is defined as a metaclass having properties *magnitude* and *dimension* as *template-slots.* This first-level conceptualisation identifies these properties to describe all instances of physical quantities. The

[6]The *own-slots* of a class describe the properties of a class rather than the properties of instances of the class. In contrast, the properties ordinarily attached to a class are known as *template-slots*, which describe the properties that instances of a class shall have. A *template-slot* of a class becomes *own-slot* on the instances of the class.

metaclass PhysicalQuantity		
Property	**Property Type**	**Cardinality**
magnitude$^{\mathbf{T}}$	Scalar, Vector	$=1$
dimension$^{\mathbf{T}}$	DimensionUnit	$=1$

FIGURE 7. Definition of Metaclass PhysicalQuantity

concept-oriented definition shown in Figure 7 is an abstract idea of a physical quantity described in a Protege-like representation.

We use the term 'reify' to mean instantiating a class from a specific metaclass as a way to make the class more concrete by specifying its intrinsic properties using *own-slots*.

The superscripted symbol $^{\mathbf{T}}$ at the end of a property name denotes that the signified relation in the reified physical quantity relates to the type (class) identifying a set of individuals and not to a particular individual in the set, as often implied in web ontology specification languages. In other words, the *magnitude* of an instantiated subclass of *PhysicalQuantity* is identified as either a scalar or vector data type, rather than an individual instantiated from either of these types. More specifically, the *ScalarQuantity* and *VectorQuantity* are defined as concrete subclasses of *SimpleQuantity* whose *magnitude* are directly related to scalar and vector types, respectively. Similarly, the *dimension* in the instantiated class is related to a dimension type, indicated by the choice dimension-unit category name (such as MassUnit or MomentumUnit), rather than a specific unit instance associated with this dimension.

Relating *magnitude* and *dimension* properties in an instantiated physical quantity to the type of individual rather than a specific individual is an important distinction. For example, the *Energy* event variable defined in Figure 8 is a reified class of *ScalarQuantity*. Its *magnitude* is characterised as `Real` and *dimension* as `EnergyUnit`, representing their respective classes of values. Note however that the *magnitude* and *dimension* properties acquired from *ScalarQuantity* metaclass are structured as *own-slots* of *Energy*. This is denoted by the superscripted symbol $^{\mathbf{O}}$ at the end of the property name of the signified relation. These properties acquired from the metaclass are not visible to individuals extended from *Energy*.

The properties attached to *Energy* class, namely *value* and *unit* relate to instances of real number and units of energy dimension, respectively. They are referred to as its *template-slots*. An individual extended from *Energy* will inherit these properties. For instance, the energy of a track particle object can be featured as *value* $= 700.0$ and *unit* $= MeV$. The former is congruent with the magnitude of the scalar quantity, while the latter is an instance of a unit of measurement according to the specified dimension of the scalar quantity. Therefore, an extension of *Energy* has a representation that respects the expected property of scalar class.

class Energy : ScalarQuantity subClassOf TrackVariable		
Property	**Property Type**	**Cardinality**
value	Real	=1
unit	EnergyUnit	=1
Property	**Property Value**	
magnitude^{O}	`Real`	
dimension^{O}	`EnergyUnit`	

FIGURE 8. Partial Definition of the Augmented Class Energy

The main role of the *own-slots*: *magnitude* and *dimension* in simple quantities is to help to enforce and/or validate the conformity of the instantiated *template-slots*: *value* and *unit* of objects extended from these simple quantities. This is necessary in order for the object to be seen as semantically and syntactically well-formed.[7]

Scalar quantities such as mass, energy and charge are represented by a single magnitude. In contrast, quantities such as velocity and momentum are described by both magnitude and direction. They are called vectors. Position or direction vectors that are the basis for kinematic and geometric analysis in physical science are mapped to 3-dimensional space. This type of vector is defined by its relationship to a Cartesian coordinate system for a particular reference frame.

A position vector $\vec{R}$ can be formally represented as a linear combination of three orthogonal unit vectors: $\vec{R} = R_x\hat{\imath} + R_y\hat{\jmath} + R_z\hat{k}$ or implicitly by a triple of real numbers $< R_x, R_y, R_z >$. Here, R_x, R_y, R_z are the X-, Y-, Z-components of the vector and $\hat{\imath}$, $\hat{\jmath}$ and $\hat{k}$ are the unit vectors along the three axes. The frame of reference establishes the context of the vector. For instance, in the Belle [4] EHEP laboratory frame, the interaction point on the beam axis is regarded as the origin of the coordinate system, the beam axis is the Z-axis, and the XY-plane is transverse to the beam axis.

A *VectorQuantity* is defined as a physical quantity whose magnitude description is supplemented with direction or orientation in a reference frame. The *magnitude* of a *VectorQuantity* is a vector data type. The *dimension* of a *VectorQuantity* is related to an appropriate dimension-unit type. As an illustration, the track momentum, *3-Momentum* event variable is defined in Figure 9 as a reified class of *VectorQuantity*, whose *magnitude* is a vector type and its dimension refers to class of momentum units.

Subsequently, an individual can be extended from *3-Momentum* with *value* equals $< 100.0, 225.0, 350.0 >$ and *unit* equals KeV/c to denote a track particle's momentum vector in laboratory frame, whose individualised momentum along the X-, Y- and Z-axes are $100KeV/c$, $225KeV/c$ and $350KeV/c$, respectively. Note

[7]We will see later in the paper that *own-slot* properties have a more significant role in the conceptualisation of compound quantity.

class 3-Momentum: VectorQuantity subClassOf TrackVariable		
Property	**Property Type**	**Cardinality**
value	Vector	=1
unit	MomentumUnit	=1
Property	**Property Value**	
magnitude^{O}	`Vector`	
dimension^{O}	`MomentumUnit`	

FIGURE 9. Partial Definition of Class 3-Momentum

the dependence of vector components on X-, Y- and Z-axes is only implied by the order of elements in the triple.

A *CompoundQuantity* defines the functionality of a mathematical concept, abstracting from how the function is computed and its output can be derived. A compound quantity is distinguished from simple quantity by the fact that the value measured by a compound quantity object is derived from other simple quantities. Therefore, a compound quantity can be viewed as a function that maps one or more simple quantities (input parameters) to a simple quantity (output). Consequently, a compound quantity can be casted into simple quantity by anchoring it in the domain ontology.

We distinguish between static and dynamic compound quantities in our model. A static compound quantity statically binds one or more predetermined quantifiable terms in the ontology. An example of static compound quantity is the function describing the track event variable *TransverseMomentum*, which is always derived from *3-Momentum*. In other words, the parameter classes of static compound quantity are fixed. On the other hand, a dynamic compound quantity closely models a generic function that dynamically binds a specified number of parameter instances according to need and purpose.

An example of dynamic compound quantity is the function representing the geometric event variable *PolarAngle* that describes the angle between any two unit vectors in a common frame of reference. In one instance, it could be the angle between the flight directions of two daughter particles in a decay. In another instance, it could be the angle between a track particle flight direction and the beam axis.[8] We elaborate on compound quantities in Section 4.4.

4.2. Representing Units of Measurement

A unit is a measure of quantity in some dimension. Each physical quantity belongs to exactly one dimension, while pure scalars and vectors are quantities with no dimension. There is a range of units associated with each dimension in the EHEP

[8] *FlightDirection* and *BeamAxis* are vector quantities in the augmented domain ontology.

domain. For example, the units for Energy dimension are eV, KeV, MeV, GeV and TeV.[9]

The EHEP physicists mainly discuss their work in terms of kinematic, geometric and topological analysis. The kinematic quantities are specified in natural units, in which the fundamental constants such as **c** (that denotes the speed of light), $\hbar$ (Planck's constant) and k_B (Boltzmann's constant) are equal to unity. The geometric and topological quantities are mostly without dimension, since the calculation makes use of dimensionless unit vectors derived from momentum vectors of tracks and vertices.

The predominant quantities in kinematic analysis are related to mass, momentum and energy dimensions. Relativistic physics asserts that $Energy = Momentum \times SpeedOfLight$. Accordingly, the Momentum units such as eV/c, KeV/c, MeV/c etceteras are always derived from Energy units in this domain. Likewise, $Momentum = Mass \times SpeedOfLight$. So, Mass units such as eV/c^2, KeV/c^2, MeV/c^2 etceteras are always derived from Momentum units.[10]

Note that in this system of units, the constant **c** is an integrated part of dimension of a quantity and the symbol **c** is featured as part of its unit. This rather unconventional way of specifying a quantity of measurement in natural units not only allows the physicists to omit this constants from mathematical equation, but also work with a limited set of dimension unit symbols. It conveniently facilitates the dimensional analysis of algebraic expressions involving related quantities.

The EHEP physicists are parsimonious in the use of derived units of measurement to avoid indeterminate situations that arise when unit of measurement of a particular quantity can be derived in more than one way from fundamental dimension units, as mentioned in the previous footnote. As a result, the unit of measurement of a derived compound quantity in the ontology will not be composed from a set of fundamental dimensions as prescribed in EngMath and SUMO sub-model on 'Unit of Measure'. On the contrary, a physical quantity is directly related to a unit instance from a predefined set of dimensions in the ontology (See Figure 10. Naturally, we have restricted our attention to dimension types that we have found of particular interest to us. The onus of dimensional consistency in algebra over the quantities and the subsequent assignment of an appropriate unit to a derived quantity rest with the modeller. However, the ontology is needed to support the unit analysis involving those quantities.

Based on the above standpoint, we have assigned a set of canonical units of measurement to each of the dimensions that appear in the EHEP ontology. In order to facilitate unit analysis over a dimension, a base unit is selected for each dimension. The conversion factor between units of measurement to the base unit within the same dimension scales on the metric system of numbers, which is based on powers of 10. For example, the base unit for Energy dimension is eV. Its

[9] eV stands for electronvolt, is a non-standard unit for energy. The standard international (SI) unit for energy is J (joule). $1eV \approx 1.60218 \times 10^{-19} J$.

[10] The SI unit for mass is kg (kilogram) and momentum is Ns (newton second) or $kg.m/s$, depending on the dimensions that are employed in its derivation.

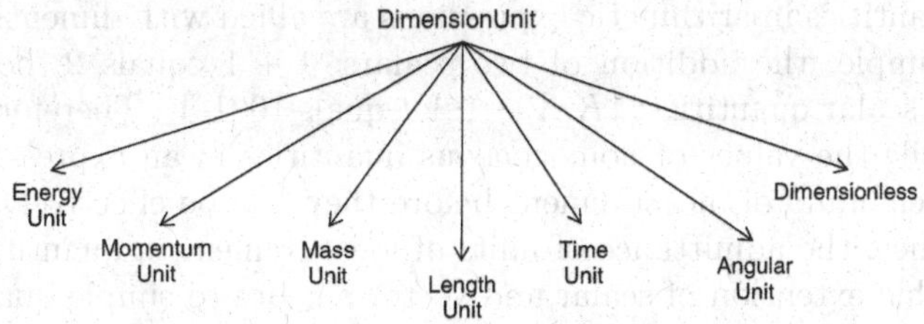

FIGURE 10. Dimensions of Units of Measurement in EHEP Ontology

class EnergyUnit subClassOf DimensionUnit		
Property	**Property Type**	**Cardinality**
multiplier	Real	=1
baseUnit	EnergyUnit	=1
baseUnitOf	EnergyUnit	≥ 1
Property	**Inverse Property**	
baseUnitOf	baseUnit	

FIGURE 11. Definition of Class EnergyUnit

succeeding units, *KeV*, *MeV*, *GeV* and *TeV* are 10^3, 10^6, 10^9 and 10^{12} multiples of the base unit, respectively. The class *EnergyUnit* is defined as the subclass of *DimensionUnit* in Figure 11. The properties *multiplier* is a real number that specifies the conversion factor between an energy unit of measurement and its *baseUnit.*

All physical quantity objects have *value* and *unit* assigned to them. Homogeneous quantities must be of same dimension, but may have different units of measurement. For example, one quantity may be specified in *eV*, while the other in *KeV*. In this case, the difference in their conversion factor can be used to reconcile the homogeneous quantities before they are operated upon.

Note also that *baseUnitOf* is defined as the inverse property of *baseUnit.* As a result, we are able to assert that *eV* is the *baseUnitOf KeV*, *MeV* and so on, enabling the representation of a calculated quantity of measurement in units of higher order.

4.3. Quantity and Data Type

Data type defines the type of values that can be assumed by physical quantities and also expressions involving them. More importantly a data type specifies a set of operations that are allowed on its individuals. We will make use of mathematical data types [6] to model the data types of quantities in our ontology.

Simple quantities in arithmetic expressions are allied with dimensional units. As a quick example, the addition of two scalars: $1 + 1$ equals 2, however, the addition of two scalar quantities: $1KeV + 1eV$ equals $1001eV$. Therefore, it is requisite to reconcile the values of homogeneous quantities in an expression by first harmonising their units of measurement before they can be effectively utilised in calculation. Hence, the admittance of units of measurement in quantities necessitates polymorphic extension of scalar and vector algebra to simple quantities.

4.3.1. Basic Data Type. The basic data types are scalar and boolean types. The data values of scalar quantities in our ontology are Real, Integer and Rational, directly related to real numbers, integers and rational numbers. Other scalar types such as complex numbers would be included, when the need arises.

For instance, the properties of subatomic particles in the EHEP ontology are scalar quantities. The quantity value of *Charge* is specified as type integer[11], *InvariantMass* as type real and the half-integral *Spin*(specified as factor of Planck's constant, $\hbar$) as type rational.[12]

The scalar operators in Figure 12 are required to construct arithmetic expression involving scalar quantities. The operator names are mnemonic algebraic terms. Binary operators such as *plus*, *minus* and *times* have signature: $ScalarQuantity \times ScalarQuantity \rightarrow ScalarQuantity$, while a unary operators like *unaryminus*, *abs* and *log* have signature: $ScalarQuantity \rightarrow ScalarQuantity$.

plus	minus	times	divide	power	mod
abs	log	ln	exp	cos	unaryminus
cos	sin	tan	arccos	arcsin	arctan

FIGURE 12. Scalar Operators

A boolean is a mathematical data type associated with two-valued logic values, namely *false* or *true*. The boolean operators required to support this type are *and*, *or* and *not*. The *and* and *or* operators have signature: $Boolean \times Boolean \rightarrow Boolean$. The *not* operator's signature is: $Boolean \rightarrow Boolean$.

We also need the relational operators *lt*, *gt* and *eq* that maps a pair of scalar quantities to boolean. Logical expressions constructed using the boolean and relational operators listed in Figure 13 will be used to specify conditions and constraints on quantities in an arithmetic expression. Together, the arithmetic and logical sub-expressions constitute an arithmetic-logical expression.

[11]Electric charge is specified in atomic unit based on the electric charge carried by a proton particle, which is equals to +1. Charges of all particles except quarks are indivisible units.
[12]Although no calculation is currently performed on rational numbers, their values may still be compared and discriminated from one another.

and	or	not

lt	gt	eq

FIGURE 13. Boolean and Relational Operators

4.3.2. Composite Data Type. The basic data types mentioned in the previous section are defined without reference to other data types. The composite data types, on the other hand are built upon other data types. They are specified and partly defined in terms of primitive and other composite data types. We have identified five kinds of composite data types in the ontology, namely tuple, vector, record, set and matrix, but only the first four data types are covered in this paper.
Tuple. A tuple is useful to aggregate several heterogeneous data types and consider it as a single entity. The components of tuples can be accessed randomly based on their position in the tuple. Tuples are commonly used to refer to elements of Cartesian product.
Vector. A vector is commonly defined as a point in the generalised Euclidean N-space, R^N, given by N-coordinates [20, *keyword: Vector*]. In R^N, the vector $\vec{A}$ is specified by N-tuple $< A_1, A_2, ..., A_N >$, where A_i is a component of vector $\vec{A}$. A vector derives its meaning from its components; the category of value assigned to a component of vector denotes its magnitude and the component's position signifies the orientation of the magnitude in the coordinate system. For instance, we have confined our attention to a subtype of vector by restricting the number of its components to 3 real-scalar quantities in order to represent the ordinary Euclidean 3-space in our ontology.

The vector operators in Figure 14 are required to express the algebra on vectors. Operations on vector quantities have an additional 'twist' due to the introduction of units of measurement in quantities. Recall that a vector quantity is comprised of a scalar-vector and a unit of measurement. The scalar-vector represents the magnitude and orientation of the described vector object in a spatial coordinate system, and the unit of measurement is common to all the scalar-vector components. As in the case of scalar operators, we have to augment the traditional operations on vector with function useful for operating vector quantities.

vector	vectorselector	dotproduct	crossproduct	norm
vectoradd	vectordiff	multiply	unitvector	

FIGURE 14. Vector Operators

The n-ary operator *vector* constructs a vector quantity from a homogeneous scalar quantities (of the same dimension-unit category). It is the onus of the modeller to pass the appropriate set of arguments to this operator, so that the resulting vector is semantically well-formed. For example, it makes no sense to pass three mass quantities to *vector* since mass is not a vector quantity.

Operator *vectorselector* has signature: $VectorQuantity \times integer \rightarrow Scalar\text{-}Quantity$ and denotes the function that selects a particular component of the vector quantity, whose ordinal number is specified by an integer. The unit of measurement of the scalar quantity returned by this function is same as the unit of the vector quantity. Suppose *3-Momentum* vector quantity, $\vec{P_3}$ has *value* equals $< 100.0, 225.0, 350.0 >$ and *unit* equals KeV/c. The operation $vectorselector(\vec{P_3}, 2)$ will return a scalar quantity whose *value* equals 225.0 and *unit* equals KeV/c. This happens to be the particle's momentum along the Y-axis in a Cartesian coordinate system.

Operator *dotproduct* performs the scalar product of a pair of vector quantities and returns a scalar quantity. Operator *crossproduct* performs vector product of a pair of 3-dimensional vector quantities and will return a 3-dimensional scalar-vector. Note that vector product can only be performed on 3-dimensional vectors.

Operator *vectoradd* and *vectordiff* are functions that perform vector addition and vector subtraction of a pair of vectors, respectively. Operator *multiply* has signature: $VectorQuantity \times real \rightarrow VectorQuantity$. It does a scalar multiplication on a vector quantity and returns a vector quantity. Note that *real* is indeed a dimensionless real-valued scalar quantity.

The unary operator *norm* generates the length of a vector represented by the vector quantity and returns a scalar quantity. Operator *unitvector* is also a unary operator that generates the unit vector of the vector represented by a vector quantity. The normalised unit vector indicates the direction of the original vector and has a norm equals 1. Therefore, the resulting vector quantity has no unit of measurement.

Record. A record is composed of a fixed number of heterogeneous data types, similar to tuple. However, unlike tuple whose components are accessed by their position, the fields of record are accessed by using a name. Therefore, record can be regarded as classified tuple of labelled components. A record is analogous to class construct in ontology specification language. The property name conveniently serves as the identifier of a record field.

We utilise record data type to model a set of disparate quantities such as *Track* (Figure 15). The track information is feasibly denoted by a tuple of distinct quantities, partially described as $< charge, energy, momentum, transverseMomentum, mass >$. However, unlike the case of *3-Momentum*, where we can rely upon the generally accepted ordinal of the components in the 'classified tuple', $< momentum - X, momentum - Y, momentum - Z >$, the organisation of quantities that are part of track information is an arbitrary decision. Such is the case, it is only appropriate to represent these kind of grouped quantities as record because we are able to provide explicit identifiers for the individual quantities in the aggregate.

Note that the augmented track class ably distinguishes the attributes of a track particle by their typical quantity types. It is now possible to represent the mathematical relation involving these track attributes. Note also that the *3momentum* property relates to the *3-Momentum* vector quantity, in place of three disparate fundamental momentums (see earlier definition in Figure 5 on page 206).

class Track : Record subClassOf EHEPEntity		
Property	**Property Type**	**Cardinality**
signalTrack	Boolean	
candidateParticle	Particle	=1
charge	Charge	=1
energy	Energy	=1
3momentum	3-Momentum	=1
mass	InvariantMass	=1

class Charge : ScalarQuantity subClassOf TrackVariable

class Energy : ScalarQuantity subClassOf TrackVariable

class 3-Momentum : VectorQuantity subClassOf TrackVariable

class InvariantMass : StaticScalarCompoundQuantity subClassOf TrackVariable

FIGURE 15. Partial Definition of the Augmented Class Track

An access operator called *recordselector* is required to select individual fields of a record. For example, *recordselector(T, momentum)* accesses the *momentum* field in track information *T*.

Set. A set is a mathematical abstraction of a collection of things. The elements of set are not ordered. Multiplicity of elements is disregarded in set. Nonetheless, arithmetic function over a set of quantities can return two or more similar quantities. The resulting set will ignore repeated elements and this can be problematic. For this reason alone, we need to deal with multisets, in which multiplicity is explicitly significant. Having said that, we will continue to use the term 'set' to also refer to multiset.

In the context of our work, we depended on a restricted subtype of set by limiting the bounds of elements in its value space to homogeneous individuals, that is, class instances of same type. A mathematical operation on a set is valid only if all the individuals in the set are quantities. The operators listed in Figure 16 are required to support set operations. All the operators in the top row and *cartesianproduct* in the bottom row are conventional set operators, while the rest of the operators in the bottom row are specially defined to facilitate mathematical operations involving set of simple quantities.

set	setof	union	intersect	setdiff	size	in
max	min	summation	cartesianproduct	map	filter	

FIGURE 16. Set Operators

An extensional set entity is fully determined by the enumerated individuals in its collection. The n-ary operator *set* is used for exhaustively enumerating a set of individuals. A supplementary set constructor *setof* is required to describe a set constructed using expression over elements involving collection of finite entities, such as *setof(recordselector(Event,tracks))*, where *Event* is an instance of *EHEPEvent* record, whose *tracks* field refer to a set of *Track* individuals in the EHEP domain ontology.[13]

The binary operators *union*, *intersect*, *setdiff* and *cartesianproduct* are functions that construct the union, intersection, set difference and the cartesian product of two sets, respectively. The unary operator *size* is a function for determining the cardinality of a set, and *in* is a binary operator for checking set membership.

Unary operators *max* and *min* have signature: *Set* $\rightarrow$ *ScalarQuantity* and represent functions that select the element with maximum and minimum value in a set of scalar quantities, respectively. The unary operator *summation* has a similar signature and is used to represent the function that calculates the sum of values held by the entire quantities in a set. This operator repeatedly applies the plus operation on all the individuals in the set of scalar quantities.

The binary operator *map* has signature: *Function* $\times$ *Set* $\rightarrow$ *Set*. It maps a mathematical function involving elements of a first set, on the first set to generate a second set. In other words, the mapped function describes the relation between two sets in which one element of the generated set is assigned to each element of the first set.

The binary operator *filter* applies a predicate (logical function) to a set to filter a subset of desired elements. The predicate assumes the value *true* on the elements of the filtered set. The operator has signature: *Set* $\times$ *Predicate* $\rightarrow$ *Set*.

Intensional set elements are formally specified with the help of mathematical and logical functions in operators as *map* and *filter*. We demonstrate *map* and *filter* operation in Section 4.4.3. The *map* operator is used in the definition of *Fox-Wolfram Moment-0* event shape variable. Both *map* and *filter* operators are used to partly define the *Sphericity* event shape variable.

4.4. Structuring Mathematical Concept as Compound Quantity

The mathematical relation underlying mathematical concept is represented by compound quantity in our ontology. Compound quantity typifies a physical quantity that is mathematically derived from other quantities. It is invoked with a set of parameters, representing simple quantities, which always map to a simple quantity. The compound quantity clarifies the dependencies between the resulting quantity and its parameters, with the aid of an arithmetic-logical expression. This expression is an intensional description of the relation involving the parameters, portraying what the modeller intends to resolve by use of this compound quantity.

---

[13]The *EHEPEvent* record describes the entities that make up an EHEP event, via fields as *tracks*, *clusters* and *vertices*. All these record fields have cardinality greater than 1 to indicate that they relate to a collection of individuals.

metaclass CompoundQuantity		
subClassOf PhysicalQuantity		
Property	**Property Type**	**Cardinality**
parameter	Parameter	≥ 1
intension	ArithmeticLogicalExpression	
magnitude$^{\mathbf{T}}$	Scalar, Vector	$= 1$
dimension$^{\mathbf{T}}$	DimensionUnit	$= 1$

FIGURE 17. Definition of Metaclass CompoundQuantity

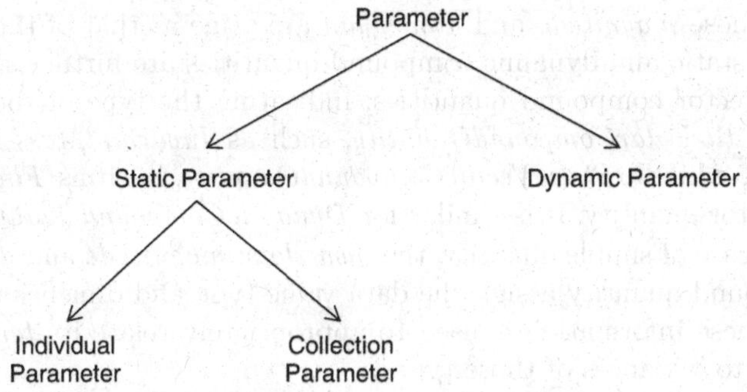

FIGURE 18. Parameters of Compound Quantities

We give the definition of the metaclass *CompoundQuantity* in Figure 17. It is conceptualised as an abstract subclass of *PhysicalQuantity* with a set of properties, namely *parameter*, *intension*, *magnitude* and *dimension*. The property *parameter* describes the cardinality and sort of parameter objects, and is related to one or more instances of *Parameter* class. The property *intension* is an arithmetic-logic expression that binds the parameter objects and the resulting quantity. A compound quantity inherits the *magnitude* and *dimension* properties from *PhysicalQuantity*, which together denote the characteristics of the resulting simple quantity.

We have categorised *CompoundQuantity* as *StaticCompoundQuantity* and *DynamicCompoundQuantity* for representing static and dynamic relations in the ontology (see Figure 6 on page 210).

Static relation depicts a permanent relationship that exists between domain concepts in the ontology. Example of static relations in the EHEP event analysis are the relations describing the derivation of function event variables, such as *InvariantMass*, which is composed from its *Energy* and *3-Momentum*; *FlightDirection* and *TransverseMomentum*, which are generated from *3-Momentum*. A static compound quantity is statically bound to its parameter objects.

On the other hand, dynamic relation among terms does not readily exist in the ontology. They are construed as dynamic compound quantities to serve as convenient 'handle' for expressing relations over individuals extended from reified quantities. They may be regarded as peripheral data type operators that are not included in the set of core operators described in Section 4.3. Examples of dynamically derived quantities in the EHEP domain are *QuantitySquaredDifference*, which represents the function that calculates the absolute difference between a pair of squared- scalar quantities, and *PolarAngle*, which represents the function that generates the angle between two vector quantities.

4.4.1. Result of Compound Quantity. The result of a compound quantity is a simple quantity, whose *magnitude* and *dimension* are same as that of the compound quantity. Both static and dynamic compound quantities are further sub classified as scalar and vector compound quantities, indicating the type of their resulting quantity. A *StaticScalarCompoundQuantity*, such as *InvariantMass* results in a scalar quantity, while a *StaticVectorCompoundQuantity*, such as *FlightDirection* results in a vector quantity. It is similar for *DynamicCompoundQuantity*.

As in the case of simple quantity, the *own-slots*: *magnitude* and *dimension* of a reified compound quantity assign the data value type and dimension-unit type, respectively. These information is used to appropriately relate its *template-slots*, *value* and *unit* to instances of those types.

4.4.2. Intension of Compound Quantity. The intension of a compound quantity is conveyed by an arithmetic-logical expression. The semantics in this constrained sequence of symbols is determined largely by the data type of the 'object' symbols linked to parameters of compound quantity, and the operations applied on them.

4.4.3. Parameter of Compound Quantity. Parameters identify the types of objects that are involved in a mathematical relation described by compound quantity. In Figure 18 we show a category of parameter classes that outlines the different parameters of compound quantity. The significant difference between *StaticCompoundQuantity* and *DynamicCompoundQuantity* is in the manner the parameters of these two quantities are specified. The parameters of *StaticCompoundQuantity* and *DynamicCompoundQuatity* are related to *StaticParameter* and *DynamicParameter*, respectively.

Each parameter of a static compound quantity either denotes an individual quantity or a collection of quantities. The distinguishability of collection from individual is necessary to allow for different treatment on these types of arguments. Consequently, we have defined two concrete subclasses of *StaticParameter*, namely *IndividualParameter* and *CollectionParameter*. The parameter objects of *StaticCompoundQuantity* is instantiated from one of these concrete classes. *DynamicParameter* is a concrete class of *Parameter* and is analogous to *IndividualParameter* of static compound quantity. We cannot foresee a dynamic compound quantity needing collection parameter at this stage.

class IndividualParameter subClassOf StaticParameter		
Property	**Property Type**	**Cardinality**
argument	SimpleQuantity, StaticCompoundQuantity	= 1

FIGURE 19. Definition of Class IndividualParameter

class InvariantMass : StaticScalarCompoundQuantity subClassOf TrackVariable		
Property	**Property Type**	**Cardinality**
value	Real	=1
unit	MassUnit	=1
Property	**Property Value**	
parameter^{O}	E, P_3	
intension^{O}	*abs(power(minus(power(E,2), power(norm(P₃), 2)), 0.5))*	
magnitude^{O}	`Real`	
dimension^{O}	`MassUnit`	

class E : IndividualParameter	
Property	**Property Value**
argument	Energy

class P_3 : IndividualParameter	
Property	**Property Value**
argument	3-Momentum

FIGURE 20. Partial Definition of the Augmented Class InvariantMass

Individual Parameter of Static Compound Quantity. The definition of *IndividualParameter* is shown in Figure 19. The property *argument* relates to a specific instance of *SimpleQuantity* or *StaticCompoundQuantity*. The latter is necessary to define 'higher-order' compound quantities, which admits other compound quantities as parameters.[14]

Figure 20 illustrates the definition of *InvariantMass* compound quantity and its two parameters. Each parameter denotes a specific simple quantity argument, namely *Energy* scalar quantity, and *3-Momentum* vector quantity. This definition establishes the static binding of *Energy* and *3-Momentum* to *InvariantMass*, according to the specified intension. The bound quantities coherently describe a common target object, a track particle in our case. This static compound quantity results in a scalar quantity.

[14]Care must be exercised in here so as not to introduce circular definition in static compound quantities.

Collection Parameter of Static Compound Quantity. The parameters of *StaticCompoundQuantity* can also denote a collection of individuals composed from simple and static compound quantities, such as a collection of 3-Momentum quantities or a collection of event tracks. For practical purpose, we have restricted the individuals in the collection to be of same kind and are typically applied to set operators as a whole.

There are three ways of defining and referring to a collection of individuals in the ontology: (1) Define a collection by exhaustively enumerating its individuals and refer to it by its given name; (2) Construct a collection using *union*, *intersect*, *map* and *filter* set operators; and (3) Relate to a named collection of individuals referred to by a field of an instantiated record. Consequently, the property *argument* of *CollectionParameter* is associated with an instance of *Collection* or *Record.* Both types are constituted of simple and/ or static compound quantities in our ontology.

Collection parameter is typically used to represent a collection of event tracks. We give two example usage of collection parameter in the definition of static compound quantities *Fox-Wolfram Moment-0* and *Sphericity.*

The *Fox-Wolfram Moment-0* event shape variable summatively combines the product of all pairs of particle momentum belonging to a set of event tracks, $H_0 = \sum_j \sum_k (P_j \times P_k)$. The intension of the compound quantity that represents this event variable is expressed as follows:

```
summation( map( lambda(j, lambda(k,
  times( norm(recordselector(j,momentum)), norm(recordselector(k,momentum))))),
   cartesianproduct( setof(recordselector(Event,tracks)),
     setof(recordselector(Event,tracks))))
```

Note the use of lambda abstraction to represent an unnamed mathematical function in the above. The function constructor *lambda* binds the variable to a mathematical expression to form the function, which is the lambda extraction of the expression. In this example, the lambda function represents the product of two vector norms.[15] Subsequently, this function is applied to the set of all ordered-pairs in the constructed cartesian product of two sets of event tracks. The *map* operation in turn creates a set of scalar quantities, and the *summation* operator adds up these quantities.

The definition of *Sphericity* event shape variable requires to sum up the transverse momentum of event tracks that makes a polar angle of more than 45° with the event thrust axis ($\hat{T}$). This can be represented by the arithmetic-logic expression as follows:

```
summation( map( lambda(j, recordselector(j,transverseMomentum)),
```

[15]Recall that *norm* is a vector operator to find the length of a vector and returns a scalar quantity as result.

class DynamicParameter		
subClassOf Parameter		
Property	**Property Type**	**Cardinality**
argumentType^{T}	PhysicalQuantity	≥ 1

FIGURE 21. Definition of Class DynamicParameter

filter(setof(recordselector(Event,tracks)),
lambda(k, gt(PolarAngle(recordselector(k,flightDirection), $\hat{T}$*),* $\pi/4$*)))))*

In this example, the 'predicate' associated with the *filter* function is a lambda extraction that expresses the logical constraint on the polar angle between a track particle's flight direction and the Thrust axis in an event. Subsequently, a *map* function is applied to the filtered set of event tracks in order to extract the transverse momentum quantities from the individual *Track* record in the set. Finally, these scalar quantities are summed up by the *summation* operator. Recall that *PolarAngle* is a geometric event variable that represents the angle between any two vectors in a common frame of reference. The terms *transverseMomentum* and *flightDirection* are fields of *Track* record.

Dynamic Parameter of Dynamic Compound Quantity. Unlike in the case of static compound quantity, we cannot be certain about the arguments of a dynamic compound quantity. Nonetheless, we can still provide a partial definition of this quantity based on what is known, such as the number of parameters and their types, what it intends to resolve and the type of resulting quantity. These general information can be used to ground the dynamic compound quantity dynamically at the time of their invocation.

The dynamic parameters are associated with dynamic compound quantities. We can only specify the argument generically, belonging to one or more *PhysicalQuantity* types, that is unlike the arguments of individual and collection parameters, which are related to specific instance of those types. The definition of *DynamicParameter* is shown in Figure 21. The superscripted symbol $^{\mathbf{T}}$ at the end of a *argumentType* denotes that this property is associated with type (not instance) of physical quantity.[16] Note the unusual property name 'argumentType', in the place of 'argument' in the parameter class definition.[17]

In retrospect, a static compound quantity describes the mathematical relationship among classes of reified quantities. This static relationship can be imposed on the class instances associated with a common target object. On the other

[16]This denotation is consistent with the manner the properties *magnitude* and *dimension* are specified in the *PhysicalQuantity* metaclass.

[17]We could have used the same property name 'argument' to describe the arguments of both static and dynamic parameters, by locally restricting their property types, but thought it will be best to keep these two relations separate to avoid confusion in their interpretation. The argument of a static parameter is a physical quantity instance, whereas, the argument of a dynamic parameter relates to one or more physical quantity class.

class PolarAngle : DynamicScalarCompoundQuantity subClassOf GeometricVariable		
Property	**Property Type**	**Cardinality**
actualArgument	EHEPAttribute	=2
value	Real	=1
unit	AngularUnit	=1
Property	**Property Value**	
parameter^{O}	V_1, V_2	
intension^{O}	*arccos(divide(dotproduct(V_1,V_2), times(norm(V_1),norm(V_2))))*	
magnitude^{O}	`Real`	
dimension^{O}	`AngularUnit`	

class V_1 : DynamicParameter	
Property	**Property Value**
argumentType	`VectorQuantity`, `StaticVectorCompoundQuantity`

class V_2 : DynamicParameter	
Property	**Property Value**
argumentType	`VectorQuantity`, `StaticVectorCompoundQuantity`

FIGURE 22. Partial Definition of Class PolarAngle

hand, a dynamic compound quantity describes the dynamically bound mathematical relationship among instances of reified quantities. A reified dynamic compound quantity must be invoked with explicit arguments. For the invocation to be seen as syntactically well-formed, the classes from which its actual argument is instantiated must matched with an instance of the class denoted by *argumentType*.

For illustration, we give the definition of *PolarAngle* compound quantity in Figure 22. It has two parameters, V_1 and V_2. The type of argument of each of the parameters can be a reified class of vector quantity or static vector compound quantity. This means the *actualArgument* objects must be an instance of these types. In this example, the actual arguments are instantiated from *EHEPAttribute* class, whose subclasses are EHEP event variables and constants. The pair of argument objects is dynamically bound according to the specified intension at the time of usage. This dynamic compound quantity results in a scalar quantity.

Allowing dynamic compound quantities in knowledge model raises some problem. Firstly, the semantic well-formedness of the dynamically bound relation cannot be verified. Secondly, the verification of syntactic well-formedness of the relation is also not conclusive. In addition, the values of *actualArgument* must be treated as a list since it is important to maintain the order of the values in some cases. In spite of all these drawbacks, dynamic compound quantities are essential to represent unconventional (peripheral) data type operators in certain domain and task. Consequently, the onus is on the modeller to instantiate and use dynamic compound quantities correctly.

5. Encoding the Arithmetic-Logic Expression of Compound Quantities

Web ontologies are founded on XML [26], a mark up language intended to encode metadata concerning web document. The mathematically augmented concepts in the domain ontology must be XML-compliant to be consistent with the syntax of web ontologies. This includes the specification of the arithmetic-logic expression that conveys the intension of compound quantity, which also needs to be encoded using XML format.

A candidate that can be leveraged on is XML-based OpenMath [22], a W3C standard for exchanging mathematical objects on the web.[18] Figure 23 shows a possible way to encode the arithmetic-logical expression that describes the intension of *InvariantMass* in OpenMath. (The class definition of *InvariantMass* is given in page 223).

Expressions encoded in OpenMath are constrained by XML-syntax with implied semantics. An OpenMath object (OMOBJ) is a sequence of one or more application objects (OMA). OpenMath maintains reportative definitions of the mathematical-oriented metadata in a set of content dictionaries. In this example, the content dictionary (cd) named *arith1* holds the definition of the following symbols (OMS): *abs*, *power* and *minus*. These symbols coincide with the scalar operators identified in Section 4.3. The parameter or variable (OMV) is associated with simple quantity, in our case.

While targeting a subset of the concepts in the evolving OpenMath standard as the basis for representing the arithmetic-logic expression, it is important to stress that we ought to be more explicit than that is allowed in OpenMath expression as concerns the ontological mark of quantities which we have to deal with. OpenMath only recognises scalar values such as integer (OMI) and real (OMF). The design decision will also have to consider on how to extend the scalar and vector algebra to cover the simple quantities in the ontology.

6. Future Work

We have two compelling issues to tackle. The first one has to do with the treatment of vectors in the ontology. For sake of convenience, we have fixed the orthogonal basis of vector quantities in the laboratory frame of reference. In reality, the data represented by vector quantity is dynamic. If the frame of reference changes, the vector is displaced in the 3-dimensional space. For example, the re-orientation of vector needs to be considered to purposefully describe the following event selection *cut*: "*The angle between the flight direction of candidate B particle and the flight direction of ρ daughter particle in the ρ rest frame*". The frame of reference in the *cut* is aligned with the momentum of ρ particle (no longer the laboratory frame of

[18] Another independent XML data exchange standard is MathML [19]. While OpenMath focuses on the semantics in mathematical expression, MathML gives importance to the presentation (rendering) of the mathematical expression.

```
<OMOBJ>
  <OMA>
    <OMS cd="arith1" name="abs"/>
    <OMA>
      <OMS cd="arith1" name="power"/>
      <OMA>
        <OMS cd="arith1" name="minus"/>
        <OMA>
          <OMS cd="arith1" name="power"/>
          <OMV name="E"/>
          <OMI> 2 </OMI>
        < /OMA>
        <OMA>
          <OMS cd="arith1" name="power"/>
          <OMA>
            <OMS cd="linealg?" name="norm"/>
            <OMA>
              <OMS cd="linealg2" name="vector"/>
              <OMV name="P3"/>
            <OMA>
          <OMA>
          <OMI> 2 </OMI>
        < /OMA>
        < /OMF dec="0.5"/>
      < /OMA>
    < /OMA>
  < /OMA>
< /OMOBJ>
```

FIGURE 23. A Possible Encoding of the Intension of Invariant-Mass in OpenMath

reference). We ask, "What pertinent knowledge should be captured in the ontology to support this kind of vector re-orientation?", and "How do we represent the choice of reference frame in the vector quantity?" An orthogonal matrix is needed to represent and work with orthogonal transformation. This raises the question, "How do we instantiate an orthogonal matrix from the knowledge about a particle's momentum?"

The second issue concerns with 'unified' event selection variable constructed ad hoc using mathematical methods. An example is the use of Fisher Discriminant method to combine a set of correlated event variables. Different experimental analysis entails different sets of correlated event variables. Similarly, the Likelihood Ratio analysis method is utilised to combine a set of uncorrelated event variables. First, we need to know which event selection variables can be effectively combined. Additionally, these methods generate and refer to statistical resources such as probability density functions associated with the variables being combined. Clearly knowledge about mathematical methods does not belong in domain ontology. We ask, "Should we develop a method ontology for describing specialised procedures such as above, or could we simply treat these variable unification tasks as computational services?"

7. Conclusion

Scientific domain ontology such as the EHEP ontology should provide the necessary representational vocabulary to facilitate the scientific community to collaborate effectively on the web. These ontologies must include concepts that are related mathematically to restrict their possible interpretation and implication. One concern however is due to the limitations of web ontology languages, which disallow the direct representation of mathematical relations in ontologies. The existing web ontology languages falter when the need to specify n-ary relations and functions arises. They also lack the necessary epistemological and mathematical primitives to explicitly represent mathematical relations involving domain concepts.

This paper highlights the additional vocabulary and language features required to incorporate complex mathematical relations in web-portable domain ontologies. Future web ontology languages may offer a richer set of primitives to express this sort of relationships among entities. Until such time, our approach recommends the use of supplementary epistemological concepts (categories of physical quantities, parameters, and dimension-oriented units of measurement) and mathematical primitives (data types and operators), modelled using classes and metaclasses to describe the meaning of the mathematical relations in the domain ontology.

References

[1] M. Annamalai, L. Sterling, and G. Moloney. A collaborative framework for distributed scientific groups. In S. Cranefield, S. Willmott, and T. Finin, editors, *Proceedings of AAMAS'02 Workshop on Ontologies in Agent Systems*, volume 66 of *CEUR-WS*, Bologna, Italy, 2002.

[2] F. Baadar and W. Nutt. Basic description logics. In F. Baadar, D. McGuiness, D. Nardi, and P. Patel-Schneider, editors, *Description Logic Handbook: Theory, Implementation and Applications.* Cambridge University Press, 2002.

[3] The Babar Physics Collaboration. http://www.slac.stanford.edu/BFROOT/.

[4] The Belle Physics Collaboration. http://belle.kek.jp/belle.

[5] B. Chandrasekaran and J. Josephson. What are ontologies, and why do we need them? *IEEE Intelligent Systems*, pages 20–26, January/February 1999.

[6] J. Cleaveland. *An Introduction to Data Types.* Addison-Wesley, 1986.

[7] The Cleo Physics Collaboration. http://www.lns.cornell.edu/public/CLEO.

[8] L. Cruz, M. Annamalai, and L. Sterling. Analysing high-energy physics experiments. In B. Burg, J. Dale, T. Finin, H. Nakashima, L. Padgham, C. Sierra, and S. Willmott, editors, *Proceedings of AAMAS'02 Workshop on AgentCities*, LNCS, Bologna, Italy, 2002. Springer-Verlag.

[9] CYCorp. http://www.cyc.com.

[10] D. Fensel, I. Horrocks, F. van Harmelen, D. McGuiness, and P. Patel-Schneider. OIL: Ontology infrastructure to enable the Semantic Web. *IEEE Intelligent Systems*, pages 38–45, March/April 2001.

[11] G. Fox and S. Wolfram. Observables for the analysis of event shapes in $e+e-$ annihilation and other processes. *Physical Review Letters*, 41(23):1581–1585, December 1978.

[12] M. Genesereth and R. Fikes. Knowledge Interchange Format. Technical Report Logic-92-1, Computer Science Department, Stanford University, 1992.

[13] W. Grosso, H. Eriksson, R. Fergerson, J. Gennari, S. Tu, and M. Musen. Knowledge modeling at the millennium (the design and evolution of Protege-2000). In *Proceedings of KAW'99 Workshop on Knowledge Acquisition, Modelling and Management*, Banff, Alberta, 1999.

[14] T. Gruber. A translation approach to portable ontologies. *Knowledge Acquisition*, 5(2):199–220, 1993.

[15] T. Gruber and G. Olsen. An ontology for engineering mathematics. In J. Doyle, P. Torasso, and E. Sandewall, editors, *Proceedings of KR'94 Conference on Principles of Knowledge Representation and Reasoning*. Morgan Kaufmann, 1994.

[16] M. Gruninger and M. Fox. Methodology for the design and evaluation of ontologies. In *Proceedings of IJCAI'95 Workshop on Basic Ontological Issues in Knowledge Sharing*. Montreal, Canada, 1995.

[17] N. Guarino. Ontologies and knowledge base: Towards a terminological clarification. In N. Mars, editor, *Towards Very Large Knowledge: Knowledge Building and Knowledge Sharing*, pages 25–32. IOS Press, Amsterdam, 1995.

[18] J. Hendler and D. McGuiness. The Darpa Agent MarkUp Language. *IEEE Intelligent Systems*, pages 67–73, November/December 2000.

[19] Mathematics MarkUp Language. http://www.w3.org/TR/MathML2.

[20] Mathworld Mathematical Encyclopedia. http://mathworld.wolfram.com.

[21] N. Noy, R. Fergerson, and M. Musen. The knowledge model of Protege-2000: Combining interoperability and flexibility. In *Proceedings of EKAW'2000 Conference on Knowledge Engineering and Knowledge Management*, Juan-Les-Pins, France, 2000.

[22] Openmath MarkUp Language. http://monet.nag.co.uk/cocoon/openmath/index.html.

[23] The OWL Web Ontology Language. http://www.w3.org/TR/owl-features.

[24] Suggested Upper Merged Ontology. http://ontology.teknowledge.com.

[25] Victorian Partnership for Advanced Computing. http://www.vpac.org.

[26] EXtensible MarkUp Language. http://www.w3.org/XML.

Acknowledgment

We are grateful to Glenn Moloney and Lyle Winton of the Physics department in The University of Melbourne for providing insights into EHEP experimental analysis.

Muthukkaruppan Annamalai and Leon Sterling
Department of Computer Science & Software Engineering
The University of Melbourne
Victoria 3010
Australia
e-mail: mkppan@cs.mu.oz.au
leon@cs.mu.oz.au

The SOUPA Ontology for Pervasive Computing

Harry Chen, Tim Finin and Anupam Joshi

Abstract. This paper describes SOUPA (Standard Ontology for Ubiquitous and Pervasive Applications) and the use of this ontology in building the Context Broker Architecture (CoBrA). CoBrA is a new agent architecture for supporting pervasive context-aware systems in a smart space environment. The SOUPA ontology is expressed using the Web Ontology Language OWL and includes modular component vocabularies to represent intelligent agents with associated beliefs, desire, and intentions, time, space, events, user profiles, actions, and policies for security and privacy. Central to CoBrA is an intelligent broker agent that exploits ontologies to support knowledge sharing, context reasoning, and user privacy protection. We also describe two prototype systems that we have developed to demonstrate the feasibility and the use of CoBrA.

Keywords. Semantic web ontology, pervasive computing, smart spaces, agents.

1. Introduction

Pervasive computing is a natural extension of the existing computing paradigm. In the pervasive computing vision, software agents, services, and devices are all expected to seamlessly integrate and cooperate in support of human objectives – anticipating needs, negotiating for service, acting on our behalf, and delivering services in an anywhere, any-time fashion [17]. An important next step for pervasive computing is the integration of intelligent agents that employ knowledge and reasoning to understand the local context and share this information in support of intelligent applications and interfaces. We describe a new architecture called the Context Broker Architecture (CoBrA) for supporting context-aware systems in smart spaces (e.g., intelligent meeting rooms, smart homes, and smart vehicles).

A key difference between CoBrA and the existing pervasive computing systems [15, 11, 37, 39, 26, 23] is in the use of ontology [7]. Computing entities in

This work was partially supported by DARPA contract F30602-97-1-0215, NSF award 9875433, NSF award 0209001, and Hewlett Packard.

CoBrA can share context knowledge using the CoBrA ontology, which extends the SOUPA ontology (Standard Ontology for Ubiquitous and Pervasive Applications) [10]. These ontologies are expressed in the Web Ontology Language OWL [29]. Central to CoBrA is an intelligent broker agent called *Context Broker*. Using the CoBrA ontology and the associated logic inference engines, the Context Broker can reason about the local context of a smart space, and detect and resolve inconsistent context knowledge acquired from disparate sensors and agents. Human users in the CoBrA system can use an OWL representation of the Rei policy language [22] to define privacy policies to control the sharing of their private information in a pervasive context-aware environment.

Context-aware systems are computer systems that can provide relevant services and information to users by exploiting context [6]. By context, we mean information about a location, its environmental attributes (e.g., noise level, light intensity, temperature, and motion) and the people, devices, objects and software agents that it contains. Context may also include system capabilities, services offered and sought, the activities and tasks in which people and computing entities are engaged, and their situational roles, beliefs, and intentions [7].

The design of CoBrA addresses the following research issues in building pervasive context-aware systems: (i) *context modeling* (i.e., how to represent and store contextual information), (ii) *context reasoning* (i.e., how to interpret context based on the information acquired from the physical environment; how to detect and resolve inconsistent context knowledge due to inaccurate sensing), (iii) *knowledge sharing* (i.e., how to help independently developed computing entities to share context knowledge and interoperate), and (iv) *user privacy protection* (i.e., how to protect the privacy of users by restricting the sharing of contextual information acquired by the hidden sensors or agents).

The rest of this paper is organized as follows: In the next section, we describe the problems in existing pervasive computing systems and our motivation to use ontologies in CoBrA. In Section 3, we describe the SOUPA ontology and how it can be used to represent various types of contextual information. In Section 4, we present the design of CoBrA. In Section 5, we describe two different prototype systems that implement CoBrA. One is a prototype for supporting context-aware services in a smart meeting room system called EasyMeeting, and the other is a toolkit for building stand-alone demonstrations of the Context Broker. Future work and conclusions are given in Section 6 and Section 7, respectively.

2. Problems in the Existing Pervasive Computing Systems

A number of pervasive computing prototype systems have been designed and implemented. Contributions to the field have been made in various aspects of pervasive computing. Dey [15] developed a middle-aware framework to facilitate context acquisition, Coen et al. [11] defined new extensible programming libraries for building intelligent room agents, and several groups [37, 39] have created badge-size tracking devices for determining people's location in an indoor environment.

Major shortcomings of these systems are that they are weak in supporting knowledge sharing and reasoning and lack adequate mechanisms to control how information about individuals is used and shared with others. In Dey's Context Toolkit framework [15], Schilit's context-aware architecture [37], and the Active Badge system [39], context knowledge is embedded in programming objects (e.g., Java classes) that are often inadequate for supporting knowledge sharing and data fusion operations. The designs of these systems also make strong assumptions about the accuracy of the information acquired from the hardware sensors. In an open and dynamic environment, such assumptions can lead to system implementations that cannot cope with the frequently occurred inconsistent context knowledge. In the Intelligent Room system [12] and the Cooltown architecture [26], information about a user can be freely shared by all computing entities in the environment. As physical environments are populated with ambient sensors, users may be unaware of the use and the sharing of their private information, which can create great concerns for privacy.

The design of CoBrA is aimed to address these issues using ontologies. We believe ontologies are key requirements for building context-aware systems for the following reasons: (i) a common ontology enables knowledge sharing in an open and dynamic distributed system [33], (ii) ontologies with well defined declarative semantics provide a means for intelligent agents to reason about contextual information, and (iii) explicitly represented ontologies allow devices and agents not expressly designed to work together to interoperate, achieving "serendipitous interoperability" [19].

3. The SOUPA Ontology

The SOUPA project began in November 2003 and is part of an ongoing effort of the Semantic Web in UbiComp Special Interest Group[1], an international group of researchers from academia and industry that is using the OWL language for pervasive computing applications and defining ontology-driven use cases demonstrating aspects of the ubiquitous computing vision. The SOUPA ontology is expressed using the OWL language and includes modular component vocabularies to represent intelligent agents with associated beliefs, desires, and intentions, time, space, events, user profiles, actions, and policies for security and privacy.

The goal of the project is to define ontologies for supporting pervasive computing applications. The design of SOUPA is driven by a set of use cases. While the SOUPA vocabularies overlap with the vocabularies of some existing ontologies, the merits of SOUPA is in providing pervasive computing developers a shared

[1]`http://pervasive.semanticweb.org`

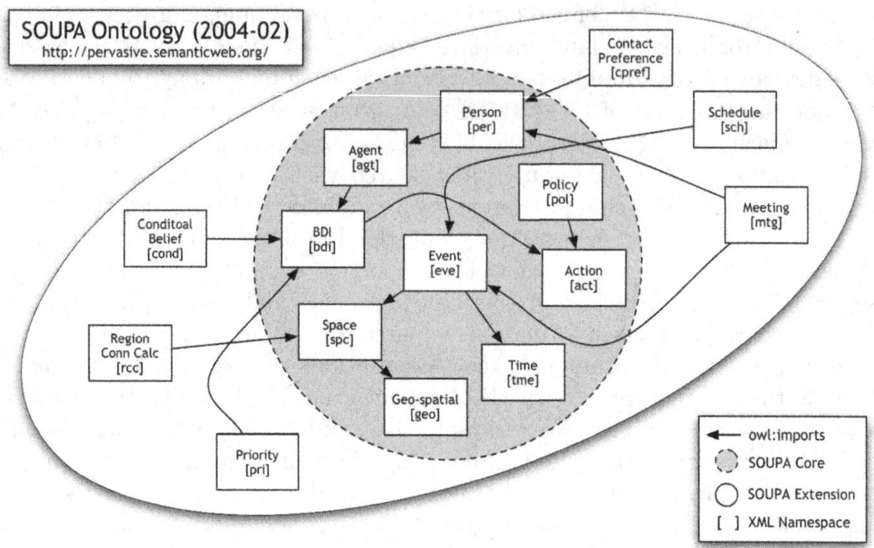

FIGURE 1. SOUPA consists of two sets of ontology documents: SOUPA Core and SOUPA Extension. The OWL `owl:imports` construct is used to enable a modular design of the ontology. Different domain vocabularies are grouped under different XML namespaces.

ontology that combines many useful vocabularies from different consensus ontologies. By providing a shared ontology, SOUPA can help developers inexperienced in knowledge representation to quickly begin building ontology-driven applications without needing to define ontologies from scratch and to be more focused on the functionalities of actual system implementations.

SOUPA consists of two distinctive but related set of ontologies: *SOUPA Core* and *SOUPA Extension*. The set of the SOUPA Core ontologies attempts to define generic vocabularies that are universal for building pervasive computing applications. The set of SOUPA Extension ontologies, extended from the core ontologies, define additional vocabularies for supporting specific types of applications and provide examples for defining new ontology extensions.

Note that the structure of the ontology merely suggests certain vocabularies are more general than the others in supporting pervasive computing applications, and there is no inherent computational complexity difference in adopting either set of the ontologies. The complete set of SOUPA ontologies is available at `http://pervasive.semanticweb.org`.

3.1. The Web Ontology Language OWL

The OWL language is a Semantic Web language for use by computer applications that need to process the content of information instead of just presenting information to humans [29]. This language is developed in part of the Semantic Web initiatives sponsored by the World Wide Web Consortium (W3C).

The current human-centered web is largely encoded in HTML, which focuses largely on how text and images would be rendered for human viewing. Over the past few years we have seen a rapid increase in the use of XML as an alternative encoding, one that is intended primarily for machine processing. The machine which process XML documents can be the end consumers of the information, or they can be used to transform the information into a form appropriate for humans to understand (e.g., as HTML, graphics, and synthesized speech). As a representation language, XML provides essentially a mechanism to declare and use simple data structures, and thus it leaves much to be desired as a language for expressing complex knowledge. Enhancements to the basic XML, such as XML Schemas, address some of the shortcomings, but still do not result in an adequate language for representing and reasoning about the kind of knowledge essential to realizing the Semantic Web vision.

OWL is a knowledge representation language for defining and instantiating ontologies. An ontology is a formal explicit description of concepts in a domain of discourse (or classes), properties of each class describing various features and attributes of the class, and restrictions on properties [30].

The normative OWL exchange syntax is RDF/XML. Ontologies expressed in OWL are usually placed on web servers as web documents, which can be referenced by other ontologies and downloaded by applications that use ontologies. In this paper, we refer to these web documents as *ontology documents.*

3.2. Related Ontologies

Part of the SOUPA vocabularies are adopted from a number of different consensus ontologies. The strategy for developing SOUPA is to borrow terms from these ontologies but not to import them directly. Although the semantics for importing ontologies is well defined [1], by choosing not to use this approach we can effectively limit the overhead in requiring reasoning engines to import ontologies that may be irrelevant to pervasive computing applications. However, in order to allow better interoperability between the SOUPA applications and other ontology applications, many borrowed terms in SOUPA are mapped to the foreign ontology terms using the standard OWL ontology mapping constructs (e.g., `owl:equivalentClass` and `owl:equivalentProperty`).

The ontologies that are referenced by SOUPA include the Friend-Of-A-Friend ontology (FOAF) [3, 35], DAML-Time and the entry sub-ontology of time [20, 31], the spatial ontologies in OpenCyc [27], Regional Connection Calculus (RCC) [36], COBRA-ONT [7], MoGATU BDI ontology [32], and the Rei policy ontology [21]. In the rest of this section, we describe the key features of these related ontologies and point out their relevance to pervasive computing applications.

FOAF. This ontology allows the expression of personal information and relationships, and is a useful building block for creating information systems that support online communities [16]. Pervasive computing applications can use FOAF ontologies to express and reason about a person's contact profile and social connections to other people in their close vicinity.

DAML-Time & the Entry Sub-ontology of Time. The vocabularies of these ontologies are designed for expressing temporal concepts and properties common to any formalization of time. Pervasive computing applications can use these ontologies to share a common representation of time and to reason about the temporal orders of different events.

OpenCyc Spatial Ontologies & RCC. The OpenCyc spatial ontologies define a comprehensive set of vocabularies for symbolic representation of space. The ontology of RCC consists of vocabularies for expressing spatial relations for qualitative spatial reasoning. In pervasive computing applications, these ontologies can be exploited for describing and reasoning about location and location context [7].

COBRA-ONT & MoGATU BDI Ontology. Both COBRA-ONT and MoGATU BDI ontology are aimed for supporting knowledge representation and ontology reasoning in pervasive computing environment. While the design of COBRA-ONT focuses on modeling contexts in smart meeting rooms [7], the design of MoGATU BDI ontology focuses on modeling the belief, desire, and intention of human users and software agents [32].

Rei Policy Ontology. The Rei policy language defines a set of deontic concepts (i.e., rights, prohibitions, obligations, and dispensations) for specifying and reasoning about security access control rules. In a pervasive computing environment, users can use this policy ontology to specify high-level rules for granting and revoking the access rights to and from different services [24].

3.3. SOUPA Core

The SOUPA core ontology consists of nine ontology documents. Together these ontology documents define vocabularies for describing person contact information, beliefs, desires, and intentions of an agent, actions, policies, time, space, and events.

Person. This ontology defines typical vocabularies for describing the contact information and the profile of a person. The OWL class `per:Person` is defined to represent a set of all people in the SOUPA domain, and is equivalent to the `foaf:Person` class in the FOAF ontology (i.e., the `owl:equivalentClass` property holds between the `per:Person` and `foaf:Person` class). An individual of the class can be described by a set of properties, which include basic profile information (name, gender, age, birth date, etc.), the contact information (email, mailing address, homepage, phone numbers, instant messaging chat ID, etc.), and social and professional profile (people that a person is friend of, organizations that a person belongs to). In addition, all property vocabularies that are applicable to describe a person in the FOAF ontology can also be used to describe an individual of the `per:Person` class. This is because all individuals of the `per:Person` class are also individuals of the `foaf:Person` class. Figure 2 shows a partial ontology description of the person Harry Chen.

Agent, Action & BDI. Sometimes when building intelligent pervasive computing systems, it is useful to model computing entities as *agents* [40]. In SOUPA, agents are defined with a strong notion of agency [40], which is characterized by a set of *mentalistic* notions such as knowledge, belief, intention, and obligation. In this ontology, both computational entities and human users can be modeled as agents.

When the goals, plans, desires, and beliefs of different agents are explicitly represented in the ontologies, this information can help independently developed agents to share a common understanding of their "mental" states, helping them to cooperate and collaborate. The explicitly represented human user's mental states can help computing agents to reason about the specific needs of the users in a pervasive environment.

Three ontology documents are related to this ontology: `agent`, `bdi`, and `action`. The `agt:Agent` class represents a set of all agents in the SOUPA domain and is associated with three properties that can be used to characterize an agent's "mental" state: `agt:believes`, `agt:desires`, and `agt:intends`. The respective range values of these properties are the `bdi:Fact`, `bdi:Desire`, and `bdi:Intention` classes. The goals of an agent are considered to be a special type of desire, which is expressed by defining the `agt:hasGoal` property as a sub-property of the `agt:desires` property.

The `bdi:Fact` class is a subclass of the `rdf:Statement` class, which represents a set of reified RDF statements [2]. A reified RDF statement consists of the `rdf:subject`, `rdf:object`, and `rdf:predicate` properties.

The `bdi:Desire` class defines a set of world states that agents desire to bring about. Every instance of this class can be characterized by the property `bdi:endState`. The range restriction of this property is unspecified in the `bdi` ontology document. Application developers are responsible for defining the representation of different world states. Some suggested representations are (i) symbolic names, e.g., a set of pre-defined RDF resource URI and (ii) meta-representation, e.g., each world state description is a set of reified RDF statements.

The `bdi:Intention` class represents a set of plans that agents intend to execute. Plans are defined in terms of actions, pre-conditions, and effects. The `action` ontology document defines the `act:Action` class with associated properties `act:preCondition` and `act:effect`. The representation of pre-conditions and effects are unspecified in this ontology, and it is left to be defined by the application ontologies.

Sometimes it may be useful to describe whether or not different desires of an agent are in conflict of each other, and whether or not certain desires are achievable. The cause of desire conflicts may be due to inconsistent beliefs in the knowledge base or conflicting user preferences or systems policies. The cause

```
<!DOCTYPE rdf:RDF [
   ...
   <!ENTITY foaf    "http://xmlns.com/foaf/0.1/#">
   <!ENTITY per     "http://pervasive.semanticweb.org/dev/person#">
   ]>

<rdf:RDF ... >

<per:Person>
  <per:firstName rdf:datatype="&xsd;string>Harry</per:firstName>
  <per:lastName rdf:datatype="&xsd;string>Chen</per:lastName>

  <per:gender rdf:resource="&per;Male"/>

  <per:birthDate rdf:datatype="&xsd;date">1976-12-26</per:birthDate>

  <per:homepage rdf:resource="http://umbc.edu/people/hchen4"/>

  <foaf:weblog rdf:resource="http://umbc.edu/people/hchen4"/>

  <per:hasSchoolContact rdf:resource="#SchoolContact"/>
  <per:hasHomeContact rdf:resource="#HomeContact"/>

  <foaf:workplaceHomepage rdf:resource="http://ebiquity.umbc.edu"/>
  <foaf:workplaceHomepage rdf:resource="http://www.umbc.edu"/>
  <foaf:workplaceHomepage rdf:resource="http://www.cs.umbc.edu"/>
</per:Person>

<per:ContactProfile rdf:ID="SchoolContact">
  <per:address rdf:datatype="&xsd;string">
    Dept. of CSEE, UMBC, 1000 Hilltop Circle, Baltimore, MD 21250, USA
   </per:address>
   <per:phone rdf:datatype="&xsd;string>+1-410-455-8648</per:phone>
   <per:email rdf:resource="harry.chen@umbc.edu"/>
   <per:im rdf:resource="aim:goim?screenname=hc1379"/>
</per:ContactProfile>

<per:Email rdf:about="harry.chen@umbc.edu"/>

<per:Homepage rdf:about="http://www.aim.com"/>

<per:ChatID rdf:about="aim:goim?screenname=hc1379">
  <per:providedBy rdf:resource="http://www.aim.com"/>
</per:ChatID>

<per:ContactProfile rdf:ID="HomeContact">
  ...
</per:ContactProfile>

<foaf:knows>
  <foaf:Person>
    <foaf:name>Tim Finin</foaf:name>
    <foaf:mbox_sha1sum>49953f47b9c33484a753eaf14102af56c0148d37</foaf:mbox_sha1sum>
  </foaf:Person>
</foaf:knows>
</rdf:RDF>
```

FIGURE 2. A partial ontology description of the person Harry Chen. Vocabularies from both the SOUPA ontology and the FOAF ontology can be used to describe a person.

```
<!DOCTYPE rdf:RDF [
   ...
   <!ENTITY jade    "http://pervasive.semanticweb.org/dev/fipa-jade#>
   <!ENTITY pol     "http://pervasive.semanticweb.org/dev/policy#">
   ]>
<rdf:RDF>
<pol:Policy>

  <pol:creator>
    <per:Person>
      <foaf:name>Tim Finin</foaf:name>
    </per:Person>
  </pol:creator>
  <pol:enforcer>
    <agt:Agent>
      <jade:name rdf:datatype="&xsd;string">Context Broker in ITE328</jade:name>
      <jade:agentID rdf:datatype="&xsd;string">ctb@cobra1.cs.umbc.edu:1099/JADE</jade:agentID>
    </agt:Agent>
  </pol:enforcer>

  <pol:rule rdf:resource="#r1"/>
  <pol:rule rdf:resource="#r2"/>
</pol:Policy>

<pol:Prohibition rdf:ID="r1">
  ...
</pol:Prohibition>

<pol:Right rdf:ID="r2">
  ...
</pol:Right>

</rdf:RDF>
```

FIGURE 3. An instance of the `pol:Policy` class is the entry point to a SOUPA policy definition. In this example, the policy is created by a person with `foaf:name` "Tim Finin", and is enforced by the Context Broker in the Room ITE328. The definition of the two associated policy rules (i.e., `r1` and `r2`) is shown in the next figure.

of unachievable desires may be due to the change of situational conditions. In the `bdi` ontology document, different subclasses of the `bdi:Desire` class, namely `bdi:ConflictingDesire`, `bdi:NonConflictingDesire`, `bdi:AchievableDesire`, and `bdi:UnachievableDesire`, are defined for classifying different types of agent desires.

Policy. Security and privacy are two growing concerns in developing and deploying pervasive computing systems [4, 25, 18]. Policy is an emerging technique for controlling and adjusting the low-level system behaviors by specifying high-level rules [14].

Part of the SOUPA policy ontology adopts the vocabularies of the Rei policy language [21]. In SOUPA, a policy is a set of rules. Rules are defined by a *policy creator* (e.g., a user or an agent), and the rules are to be enforced by one or more *policy enforcer* (e.g., a security authority or a privacy protection agent). The

```
<pol:Prohibition rdf:ID="r1">
  <!-- Any owl:Thing that is an audience of the defined Ebiquity Group meeting
       is prohibited from changing presentation slides. -->
  <pol:actor>
    <!-- a special class for expressing "For all X"-->
    <pol:Variable/>
  </pol:actor>

  <pol:action rdf:resource="ChangePresentationSlides"/>

  <pol:constraintMemebershipClass>
    <owl:Class>
      <rdf:subClassOf rdf:resource="&mtg;Audience"/>
      <rdfs:subClassOf>
        <owl:Restriction>
          <owl:onProperty rdf:resource="&mtg;ofMeeting"/>
          <owl:hasValue rdf:resource="http://ebiquity.umbc.edu/v2.1/event/html/id/15/"/>
        </owl:Restriction>
      </rdfs:subClassOf>
    </owl:Class>
  </pol:constraintMemebershipClass>
</pol:Prohibition>

<pol:Right rdf:ID="r2">
  <!-- Person Harry Chen has the right to adjust room lighting if he is
       a speaker of the defined Ebiquity Group meeting -->

  <pol:actor>
    <per:Person>
      <foaf:name>Harry Chen</foaf:name>
    </per:Person>
  </pol:actor>

  <pol:action rdf:resource="#AdjustRoomLighting"/>

  <pol:constraintMemebershipClass>
    <owl:Class>
      <rdf:subClassOf rdf:resource="&mtg;Speaker"/>
      <rdfs:subClassOf>
        <owl:Restriction>
          <owl:onProperty rdf:resource="&mtg;ofMeeting"/>
          <owl:hasValue rdf:resource="http://ebiquity.umbc.edu/v2.1/event/html/id/15/"/>
        </owl:Restriction>
      </rdfs:subClassOf>
    </owl:Class>
  </pol:constraintMemebershipClass>
</pol:Right>
```

FIGURE 4. The `pol:Prohibition` and `pol:Right` are subclasses of the `pol:DenoticObject` class. Instances of these classes represent individual SOUPA policy rules.

definition of each rule gives specific enforcement instructions to the policy enforcer over a set of actions. For example, an action may be adjusting the lighting in a room, changing presentation slides on a projector device, or printing documents to a nearby printer.

Every enforcement instruction given to the policy enforcer falls under one of the following four categories: (i) the enforcer should permit the agents of certain class to perform the specified action, (ii) the enforcer should prohibit the agents of certain class to perform the specified action, (iii) the enforcer should assign the agents of certain class to be responsible for performing the specified action, and (iv) the enforcer should waive the agents of certain class to be responsible for performing the specified action.

The entry point to the SOUPA policy ontology is the `pol:Policy` class. An individual of this class represents a policy document. The property `pol:rule` relates a policy rule instance to a policy document. Each policy document can have zero or more defined policy rules. Figure 3 shows a partial description of a SOUPA policy.

Policy rules are typically defined as individuals of one of the four rule classes: (i) `pol:Right`, (ii) `pol:Prohibition`, (iii) `pol:Obligation`, and (iv) `pol:Dispensation`. The semantics of these four class definitions correspond to the four enforcement instructions that are described above. These four classes are subclasses of the `pol:DenoticObject` class, and the set of individual members of each class disjoints with each other.

The `pol:DeonticObject` class has three defined properties: `pol:action`, `pol:actor`, and `pol:constraintMemebershipClass`. The `pol:action` property relates a policy rule to a specific action that it applies to, which must be type of `act:Action`. The `pol:actor` property defines a named agent who may be the actor of the defined action. By default, an actor does not have the right to perform an action unless it also satisfies the membership class constraint defined by the `pol:constraintMembershipClass` property.

The range of the `pol:constraintMemebershipClass` property is `owl:Class`. The purpose for this construct is to define a template class to match the class membership types of a given actor. An actor belongs to the constraint membership class if it is `rdf:type` of the defined class. In which case, the enforcement instruction given by the rule applies to the actor. Figure 4 shows examples of two SOUPA policy rules.

Time. SOUPA defines a set of ontologies for expressing time and temporal relations. They can be used to describe the temporal properties of different events that occur in the physical world.

Part of the SOUPA ontology adopts the vocabularies of the DAML-time ontologies and the entry sub-ontology of time. The basic representation of time consists of the `tme:TimeInstant` and `tme:TimeInterval` classes. All individual members of these two classes are also members of the `tme:TemporalEntity` class, which is an OWL class that is defined by taking the union of the `tme:TimeInstant` and `tme:TimeInterval` classes. The set of all temporal things that are divided into two disjoint classes: `tme:InstantThing`, things with temporal descriptions that are type of time instant, and `tme:IntervalThing`, things with temporal descriptions that are type of time interval. The union of these two classes forms the `tme:TemporalThing` class.

In order to associate temporal things with date/time values (i.e., their temporal descriptions), the `tme:at` property is defined to associate an instance of the

```
<tme:TimeInterval>
  <tme:from>
    <tme:TimeInstant>
      <tme:at rdf:datatype="xsd;dateTime">2004-02-01T12:01:01</tme:at>
    </tme:TimeInstant>
  </tme:from>
  <tme:to>
    <tme:TimeInstant>
      <tme:at rdf:datatype="xsd;dateTime">2004-02-11T13:41:21</tme:at>
    </tme:TimeInstant>
  </tme:to>
</tme:TimeInterval>
```

FIGURE 5. A representation of a time interval using the SOUPA time ontology. The beginning and the ending of a time interval are defined by the `tme:from` and `tme:to` properties, respectively.

`tme:InstantThing` with an XML `xsd:dateTime` datatype value (e.g., 2004-12-25T12:32:12), and the `tme:from` and `tme:to` properties are defined to associate an instance of the `IntervalThing` with two different `tme:TimeInstant` individuals. Figure 5 shows the representation of a time interval with the associated temporal description.

For describing the order relations between two different time instants, the ontology defines the following properties: `tme:before`, `tme:after`, `tme:beforeOrAt`, `tme:afterOrAt`, and `tme:sameTimeAs`. Both `tme:before` and `tme:after` properties are defined of type `owl:TransitiveProperty`. The `tme:sameTimeAs` property expresses that two different time instants are associated with equivalent date/time values and is defined of type `owl:SymmetricProperty`.

For describing the order relations between two different temporal things (i.e., time instants and time intervals), the ontology defines the following properties: `tme:startsSoonerThan`, `tme:startsLaterThan`, `tme:startsSameTimeAs`, `tme:endsSoonerThan`, `tme:endsLaterThan`, `tme:endsSameTimeAs`, `tme:startsAfterEndOf`, and `tme:endsBeforeStartOf`. The first three properties respectively express that for any two given temporal things A and B, the starting time of A is before the starting time of B, the starting time of A is after the starting time of B, and the starting time of A is the same as the starting time of B. The next three properties respectively express that for any two given temporal things A and B, the ending time of A is before the ending time of B, the ending time of A is after the ending time of B, and the ending time of A is the same as the ending time of B. The `tme:startsAfterEndOf` property expresses that the beginning of one temporal thing is after the ending of another temporal thing, and the `tme:endsBeforeStartOf` property expresses the inverse of this property.

Space. This ontology is designed to support reasoning about the spatial relations between various types of geographical regions, mapping from the geo-spatial coordinates to the symbolic representation of space and *vice versa*, and the representation of geographical measurements of space. Part of this ontology vocabularies are adopted from the spatial ontology in OpenCyc and the OpenGIS vocabularies [13]. Two ontology documents are related to this ontology: `space` and `geo-measurement`. The first ontology document defines a symbolic representation of space and spatial relations, and the second document defines typical geo-spatial vocabularies (e.g., longitude, latitude, altitude, distance, and surface area).

In the symbolic representation model, the `spc:SpatialThing` class represents a set of all things that have spatial extensions in the SOUPA domain. All spatial things that are typically found in maps or construction blueprints are called `spc:GeographicalSpace`. This class is defined as the union of the `spc:GeographicalRegion`, `spc:FixedStructure`, and `spc:SpaceInAFixed-Structure` classes.

An individual member of the `spc:GeographicalRegion` class typically represents a geographical region that is controlled by some political body (e.g., the country USA is controlled by the US government). This relation is expressed by the `spc:controls` property, the domain of which is `spc:GeopoliticalEntity` and the range of which is `spc:GeographicalRegion`. Knowing which political entity controls a particular geographical region, a pervasive computing system can choose to apply the appropriate policies defined by the political entity to guide its behavior. For example, a system may apply different sets of privacy protection schemes based on the policies defined by the local political entities.

To support spatial containment reasoning, individual members of the `spc:GeographicalSpace` class can relate to each other through the `spc:spatiallySubsumes` and `spc:spatiallySubsumedBy` properties. For example, a country region may spatially subsume a state region, a state region may spatially subsume a building, and a building may spatially subsume a room. Knowing the room in which a device is located, we can infer the building, the state and the country that spatially subsumes the room.

In the geo-spatial representation model, the individual members of the `spc:-SpatialThing` class are described by location coordinates (i.e., longitude, latitude, and altitude). This relation is expressed by the `spc:hasCoordinates` property, the range of which is the `geo:LocationCoordinates` class. In this model, multiple location coordinates can be mapped to a single geographical region (e.g., a university campus typically covers multiple location coordinates.). This relation is useful for defining spatial mapping between different geographical locations and GPS coordinates. This information can enable a GPS-enabled device to query the symbolic representation of its present location for a given set of longitude, latitude, and altitude.

Event. Events are event activities that have both spatial and temporal extensions. An event ontology can be used to describe the occurrence of different activities,

```
<owl:Class rdf:ID="DetectedBluetoothDev">
  <rdfs:subClassOf rdf:resource="&eve;TemporalSpatialEvent"/>
</owl:Class>

<owl:ObjectProperty rdf:ID="foundDevice">
  <rdfs:domain rdf:resource="#DetectedBluetoothDev"/>
</owl:ObjectProperty>

<DetectedBluetoothDev>
  <spc:hasCoordinates>
    <geo:LocationCoordinates>
      <geo:longitude rdf:datatype...>-76.7113</geo:longitude>
      <geom:latitude rdf:datatype...>39.2524</geom:latitude>
    </geo:LocationCoordinates>
  </spc:hasCoordinates>

  <foundDevice rdf:resource="url-x-some-device"/>
  <tme:at>
    <tme:TimeInstant>
      <tme:at rdf:datatype="xsd;dateTime">2004-02-01T12:01:01</tme:at>
    </tme:TimeInstant>
  </tme:at>
<DetectedBluetoothDev>
```

FIGURE 6. An example shows the representation of a sensing event using the SOUPA space, time and event ontology. In this example, the Bluetooth network interface of a device has been detected at the time instant `2004-02-01T12:01:01` at a location with the GPS coordinates (-76.7113/39.2524).

schedules, and sensing events. In the `event` ontology document, the `eve:Event` class represents a set of all events in the domain. However, the definition of this class is silent about its temporal and spatial properties.

The `eve:SpatialTemporalThing` class represents a set of things that have both spatial and temporal extensions, and it is defined as the intersection of the `tme:TemporalThing` and `spc:SpatialThing` classes. To specifically describe events that have both temporal and spatial extensions, `eve:SpatialTemporal-Event` class is defined as the intersection of the `eve:SpatialTemporalThing` and `eve:Event` classes.

Figure 6 shows how the ontology can be used to describe an event in which a Bluetooth device has been detected on 2004-02-01 at 12:01:01 UTC, and the event occurs at a location that is described by longitude -76.7113 and latitude 39.2524.

3.4. SOUPA Extension

The SOUPA Extension ontologies are defined with two purposes: (i) to define an extended set of vocabularies for supporting specific types of pervasive application domains, and (ii) to demonstrate how to define new ontologies by extending the SOUPA Core ontologies. At present, the SOUPA Extension consists of experimental ontologies for supporting pervasive context-aware applications in smart spaces and peer-to-peer data management in a pervasive computing environment.

Priority. By default the BDI ontology is silent about the priority relation among the set of desires and intentions of an agent. The priority ontology defines additional vocabularies for assigning priority values to an agent's desires and intended actions. At times when there are conflicts between different desires or actions, priority values can be used to set the precedence.

Conditional & Unconditional Belief. This ontology defines the vocabularies for describing conditional beliefs. A conditional belief statement can be attributed by temporal values, accuracy values, or locally defined conditions. Statements defined with conditional attributes will be believed to be true if the associated time stamp is valid, the accuracy value is above a pre-defined threshold, and all the locally defined conditions are satisfied. Otherwise, the statements will be believed to be false.

Contact Preference. This ontology defines the vocabularies for describing a user's contact preference, which is a set of rules that specify how the user likes to be contacted by the system under different situational conditions (i.e., in meeting, out of town, on the weekends). For example, a user may specify the system to contact her on a cellphone when she is out of town, and to contact her using only SMS when she is in a meeting.

Meeting & Schedule. These two ontologies define the vocabularies for describing a meeting event, schedules, and the associated attendees. They can help smart meeting systems to represent and reason about the context of a meeting (e.g., are all scheduled attendees located in the meeting room? What is the end time of this meeting?)

4. The Context Broker Architecture

CoBrA is a broker-centric agent architecture for supporting context-aware systems in smart spaces [8]. Central to the architecture is the presence of a Context Broker, an intelligent agent that runs on a resource-rich stationary computer in the space. The responsibility of the Context Broker is to (i) provide a centralized model of context that can be shared by all devices, services, and agents in the space, (ii) acquire contextual information from sources that are unreachable by the resource-limited devices, (iii) reason about contextual information that cannot be directly acquired from the sensors (e.g., intentions, roles, temporal and spatial relations), (iv) detect and resolve inconsistent knowledge that is stored in the shared model of context, and (v) protect user privacy by enforcing policies that the users have defined to control the sharing and the use of their contextual information.

Our centralized design of the context broker is motivated by the need to support small devices that have relatively limited resources available for context acquisition and reasoning. With the presence of a broker, small devices such as cellphones, PDA and watches can offload their burdens of managing context knowledge onto a resource rich context broker, including reasoning with context, detecting

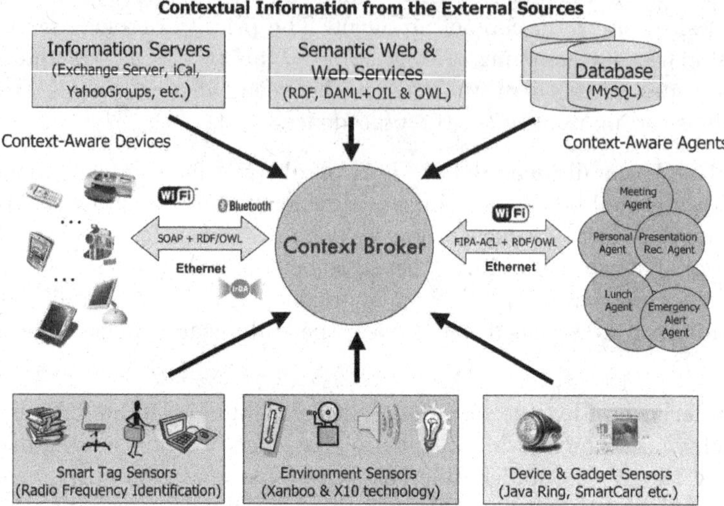

FIGURE 7. A Context Broker acquires contextual information from heterogeneous sources and fuses into a coherent model that is then shared with computing entities in the space.

and resolving inconsistent context knowledge. Furthermore, in an open and dynamic environment, users may desire that their personal contextual information be kept private. A centralized management of context knowledge makes it easy to implement privacy protection and information security.

The design of a Context Broker consists of the following four parts:

1. **CoBrA Ontology (COBRA-ONT):** A set of ontology documents that define the vocabularies for representing contextual information and for supporting the context reasoning. This ontology extends the SOUPA ontology and introduces additional domain specific vocabularies. COBRA-ONT v0.5[2] is the latest version of this ontology, which defines an ontology of the UMBC eBiquity Research Group meetings and a spatial ontology that describes the geographical location of UMBC.
2. **Context Knowledge Base:** This knowledge base stores the contextual information that is acquired from the physical environment and knowledge that is inferred by the Context Reasoning Engine. In our prototype implementation [9], this knowledge base is stored in a relational database[3] using the Persistent Ontology Model API of the Jena 2 semantic web framework [5]. All knowledge in this knowledge base is expressed as RDF triples.

[2]COBRA-ONT is available at `http://cobra.umbc.edu`.

[3]The current implementation uses the MySQL system.

3. **Context Reasoning Engine:** It is a rule-based component that provides logic inference support for interpreting context and for detecting knowledge inconsistency. This engine has a two-tier design: Tier-1 and Tier-2. A key difference between the reasoners in Tier-1 and Tier-2 is in the type of inferences that they support. While Tier-1 only supports ontology inferences using either the built-in or the customized ontology axioms, Tier-2 supports domain heuristics inferences using an external logic inference engine. We have prototyped two reasoners – one in Prolog [8] and the other one in Jess [9].
4. **Privacy Protection Module:** This module is responsible for analyzing user defined policy rules and helps the Context Broker to decide whether context knowledge about a user can be shared with a particular agent in the system. In our prototype design, this module reads in user privacy policies that are expressed in the SOUPA policy ontology. Before the Context Broker shares the context knowledge about a user, the Context Broker calls this module to check whether the receiving agent is permitted to acquire this information.

5. CoBrA Applications

To demonstrate the use and the feasibility of CoBrA for supporting pervasive context-aware systems, we have developed two prototype systems. Both prototypes exploit the SOUPA and COBRA-ONT ontology to support context modeling, context reasoning, and knowledge sharing. The first prototype system, called EasyMeeting, is a smart meeting room system that is aimed to facilitate typical user activities in an everyday meeting. The second prototype system is a toolkit for building demonstrations of the CoBrA system without needing to set up a complete pervasive computing infrastructure.

5.1. The EasyMeeting System

EasyMeeting is an extension to Vigil [38], a third generation pervasive computing infrastructure developed at UMBC. The goal of developing EasyMeeting is to create a smart meeting room that can facilitate typical user activities in an everyday meeting. This includes setting up presentations, allowing users to control services via speech, and adjusting lighting and background music in a room based the state of the meeting.

In EasyMeeting, the role of a Context Broker is to provide a shared model of context for all agents and services. In particular, it is responsible for acquiring and maintaining consistent knowledge about (i) the location of meeting participants, (ii) the event schedule of a meeting, (iii) the presentations that are scheduled for the meeting, (iv) the profiles of the speakers, and (v) the state of a meeting. To acquire this knowledge, the Context Broker explores different sources of information that is published on the Semantic Web and provided by the sensor agents (e.g., the Bluetooth Sensing Agent in Figure 8).

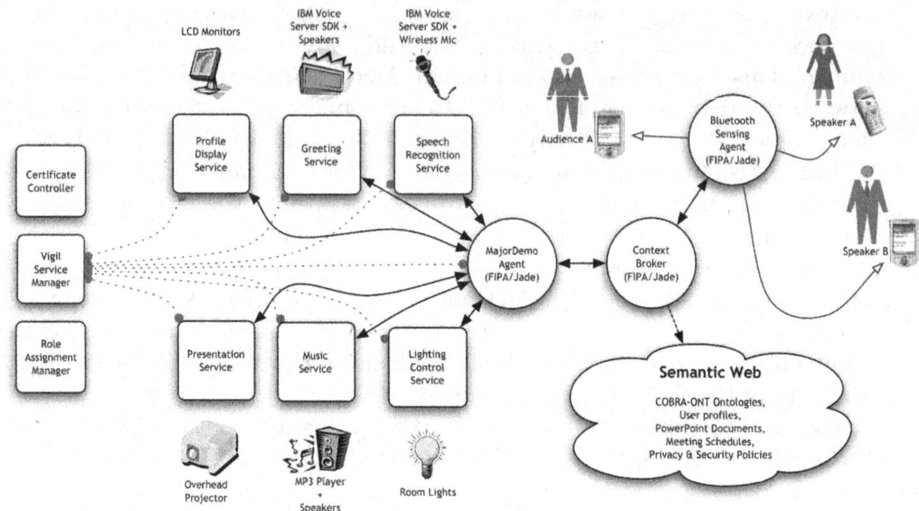

FIGURE 8. In EasyMeeting the Context Broker shares its contextual knowledge with the MajorDemo agent. Using this knowledge, MajorDemo selects and then invokes appropriate Vigil services to provide relevant services and information to the speakers and audiences.

The following is a typical EasyMeeting use case: Room 338 is a smart meeting room. On January 8th, 2004, a presentation is scheduled to take place from 1:00-2:30 PM in this room. Moments before the event starts, the room's Context Broker acquires the meeting's schedule from the Semantic Web and concludes the meeting is about to take place in the Room 338. As the meeting participants begin to arrive, the room's Bluetooth Sensing Agent detects the presences of different Bluetooth enabled devices (e.g., cellphones, PDA's). Because each device has a unique device profile that is described by standard Semantic Web ontologies, the sensing agent can share this information with the Context Broker.

Based on the user profile ontologies that are stored in the Context Broker's knowledge base (e.g., who owns what devices), without knowing any evidence to the contrary, the Context Broker concludes the owners of the detected devices are also located in the Room 338. Among the arrived participants, there are Harry (the speaker) and President Hrabowski (the distinguished audience). The Context Broker shares the location information of these participants with the subscribed MajorDemo agent.

Knowing that President Hrabowski has a distinguished audience role, the MajorDemo agent invokes the Greeting Service to greet him. At 1:00 PM, the Context Broker informs the MajorDemo agent that all listed *key* participants have arrived and that the presentation can be started. Knowing all the lights in the meeting are currently switched on and the background music is also playing, the agent invokes the Dim Light Method on the the Light Control Service and the Stop Music Method on the Music Service.

As Harry walks to the front of the meeting room, he speaks to the system using a wireless microphone, "load Harry's presentation". The voice command is received by the Voice Recognition Service and a corresponding CCML command is generated. The MajorDemo agent sends this text string command to the Presentation Service along with the URL at which Harry's presentation can be downloaded (this information is provided by the Context Broker). As the Presentation Service loads Harry's PowerPoint slides, the MajorDemo agent invokes the Profile Display Service to show Harry's home page. Few seconds later, all LCD displays sitting on the conference table start showing Harry's biosketch and his profile. Using the same wireless microphone, Harry speaks to the system to control his presentation.

5.2. CoBrA Demo Toolkit

This toolkit a set of software applications for demonstrating the key features of CoBrA. It is aimed to provide a proof-of-concept demonstration and stimulate future system design and development. This toolkit has three key components: (i) a stand-alone Context Broker implementation in JADE, (ii) a customizable JADE agent called *ScriptPlay* for facilitating demo scripts, and (iii) an Eclipse Plug-in called CoBrA Eclipse Viewer (CEV) for monitoring the knowledge base changes in the Context Broker.

Using this toolkit, we can develop customized demonstrations to show how the knowledge base of a Context Broker changes when new contextual information is acquired or when the logic inference for context reasoning is triggered. Through a graphical user interface, users can (i) inspect the ontology schemas and data instances that form the Context Broker's belief about the present context, (ii) view privacy policies that the individual users have defined to protected their private information, and (iii) monitor the communication messages that are sent between the Context Broker and other agents.

CEV is a tool for browsing the context model in the knowledge base of the Context Broker and to monitor its changes while the Context Broker acquires new information from other agents or infers new context knowledge. Figure 9 shows a screenshot of the CEV plug-in that displays partial knowledge of the Context Broker.

One of our demonstration scenario is to show the Context Broker's ability to detect knowledge inconsistency when maintaining the location information of a person. In this demonstration, the ScriptPlay agent is configured to simulate a group of location tracking agents that individually send sensed people location information to the Context Broker. To simulate a real world scenario, some of the reported location information are intentionally made to be inconsistent with each other. For example, one report may express that a person is located in the Room ITE 325, which is part of the ITE building on the UMBC campus, and the other report may express the same person is located in some place in the state

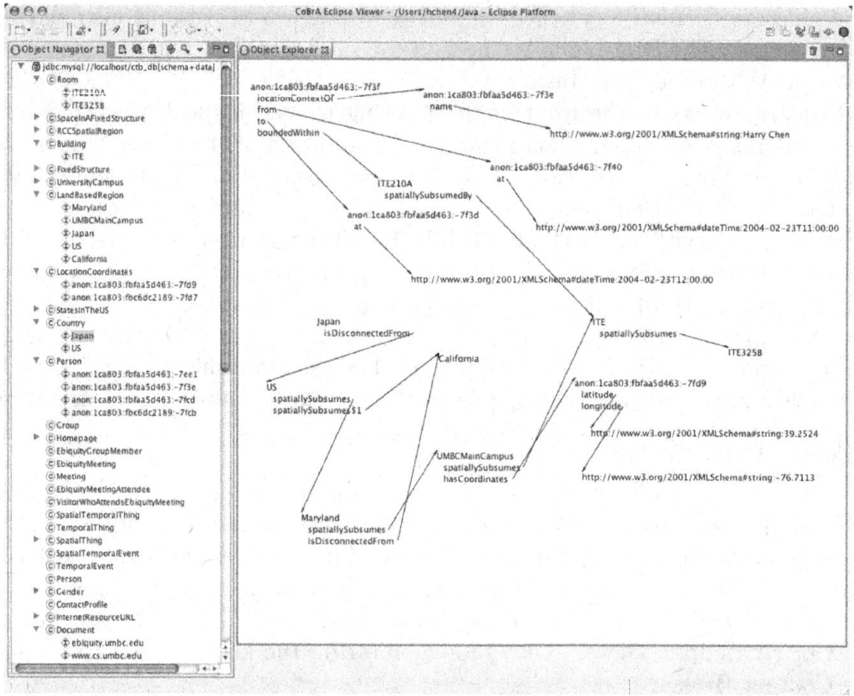

FIGURE 9. A screenshot of the CoBrA Eclipse Viewer (CEV). On the left, CEV lists the ontology classes and instances that are part the Context Broker's knowledge base. On the right, CEV users can explore the properties of individual class instances.

of California during the same time interval. Because the UMBC campus in in the state of Maryland, which is a geographical region that is disconnected from the state of California, the previous two reports of the same person's location context are inferred to be inconsistent.

In this demonstration, the Context Broker continuously waits to receive incoming reports about people's location context and notifies the senders when the reported information is inconsistent with its stored knowledge. If the incoming report is consistent with the stored knowledge, the Context Broker replies with a confirmation message and adds the new information to its knowledge base. Figure 10 shows a UML sequence diagram of a complete run of this demonstration[4]. At present, our implementation only handles the *detection* of inconsistent knowledge and does not handle the *resolution* of inconsistent knowledge. We are investigating different strategies for resolving inconsistent knowledge after it has been detected.

[4]A QuickTime video of this demonstration is available at `http://cobra.umbc.edu`

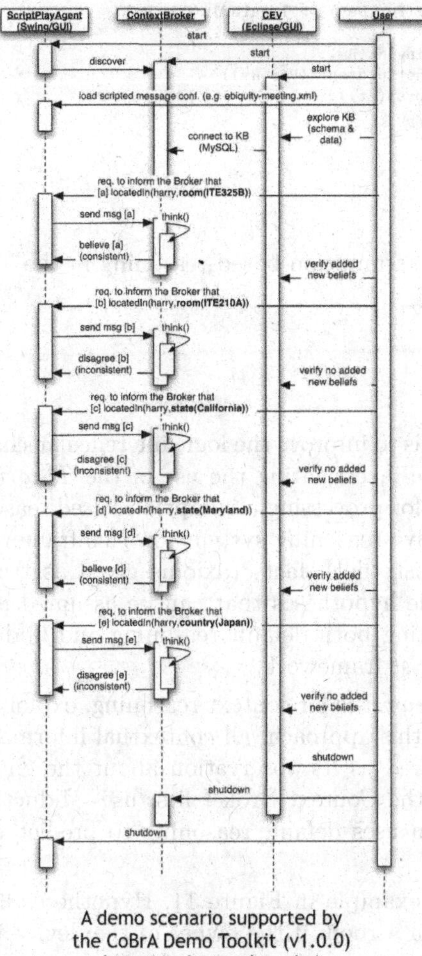

FIGURE 10. Using the CoBrA Demo Toolkit, users can monitor the underlying behavior and the knowledge base of the Context Broker and inspect the communication messages between the Context Broker and other agents. This demo shows the Broker's ability to detect inconsistent location information about a person when there are inaccurate sensing reports. Upon receiving information that is inconsistent with its existing belief, the Broker notifies the sender of the information and refuses to add this information to its knowledge base.

```
H1: locatedIn(Per,Rm), owner(Per,Dev) => locatedIn(Dev,Rm).

H2: locatedIn(Per,Rm), meeting(Mt,Rm),
    speakerOf(Per,Mt), not(notLocatedIn(Per,Rm))
      => intends(Per,give_prst(Mt)).

F1: locatedIn(t68i,rm338).
F2: owner(harry,t68i).
F3: meeting(m1203,rm338).
F4: speakerOf(harry,m1203).
```

FIGURE 11. Rules for assumption-based reasoning in the Theorist framework.

6. Future Work

Our near term objective is to improve the logic inference mechanism in the Context Knowledge Base. We are investigating the use of the *Theorist* framework [34], a Prolog meta-interpreter for processing assumption-based reasoning. Different from the conventional deductive reasoning systems, in this framework, the premises of the logic inference consists both facts (axioms given as true) and assumptions (instances of the possible hypotheses that can be assumed if they are consistent with the facts). Supporting both default reasoning and abductive reasoning is a key feature of the *Theorist* framework.

One way to use *Theorist* is for context reasoning, exploiting both default and abductive reasoning. In this approach, all contextual information acquired by the Context Broker are viewed as its observation about the environment. When an observation is received, the Context Broker first uses abduction to determine the possible causes and then uses default reasoning to predict what else will follow from the causes [28].

Let's consider the example in Figure 11. Hypotheses `H1` states that a personal device is located in a room if the owner of the device is also in that room. Hypotheses `H2` states that if a person is in a room where a meeting is scheduled to take place, the same person is the speaker of the meeting, and no evidence showing the person is not in that room, then the person intends to give a presentation at the meeting. Fact `F1` states that Cellphone T68i is located in the room RM338. Fact `F2`, `F3`, and `F4` state that Harry is the owner of the Cellphone T68i, Meeting m1203 is scheduled to take place in the room RM338, and Harry is the speaker of the Meeting m1203, respectively. We expect `F1` to be knowledge acquired from the sensors, and `F2`, `F3`, and `F4` to be knowledge acquired from the Semantic Web.

Our first objective is to infer the cause for the observation that the Cellphone T68i is located in the room RM338 (i.e., `F1`). We use abduction. Based on the given knowledge, {`locatedIn(harry,rm338)`, `owner(harry,t68i)`} is a plausible explanation for `locatedIn(t68i,rm338)`. Knowing Harry is in room RM338, our second objective is to predict his intention in that room. We use default reasoning. Using `H2`, we can infer Harry intends to give a presentation in the Meeting m1203.

7. Conclusions

The Semantic Web languages and ontologies defined using these languages are of great importance to future pervasive context-aware systems. Using the OWL language we can define ontologies for modeling context and for supporting context reasoning. Shared ontologies can also help agents, services, and devices to share context knowledge and to interoperate in an open and dynamic environment. As the Semantic Web tools and ontologies emerge, they will bring new research opportunities in developing pervasive context-aware systems.

We have described the SOUPA ontology, an emerging standard ontology for supporting ubiquitous and pervasive computing applications. Based on our experience in prototyping CoBrA, the SOUPA ontologies have shown great promises in supporting context modeling, context reasoning, and knowledge sharing. The results of EasyMeeting and the CoBrA Demo Toolkit have successfully demonstrated aspects of the CoBrA system. In the EasyMeeting system, the Context Broker helped the smart meeting room services to provide relevant services and information to the meeting participants based on their context. In the demonstration supported by the CoBrA Demo Toolkit, we have shown the ability of the Context Broker to detect inconsistent information about people's location by reasoning with a set of geographical spatial ontologies. In the future, we will expand the demonstration to show the Context Broker's ability to resolve knowledge inconsistency and to protect the privacy of users.

References

[1] Sean Bechhofer, Frank van Harmelen, Jim Hendler, Ian Horrocks, Deborah L. McGuinness, Peter F. Patel-Schneider, and Lynn Andrea Stein. *OWL Web Ontology Language Reference*, w3c recommendation 10 february 2004 edition, February 2004.

[2] Dan Brickley and R.V. Guha. Rdf vocabulary description language 1.0: Rdf schema. In *W3C Recommendation*. RDF Core Working Group, 2004.

[3] Dan Brickley and Libby Miller. *FOAF Vocabulary Specification*, revision 1.47 edition, Sept 2003.

[4] Roy Campbell, Jalal Al-Muhtadi, Prasad Naldurg, Geetanjali Sampemane1, and M. Dennis Mickunas. Towards security and privacy for pervasive computing. In *Proceedings of International Symposium on Software Security*, Tokyo, Japan, 2002.

[5] Jeremy Carroll, Ian Dickinson, Chris Dollin, Dave Reynolds, Andy Seaborne, and Kevin Wilkinson. Jena: Implementing the semantic web recommendations. Technical Report HPL-2003-146, Hewlett Packard Laboratories, 2003.

[6] Guanling Chen and David Kotz. A survey of context-aware mobile computing research. Technical Report TR2000-381, Dartmouth College, Computer Science, Hanover, NH, Nov 2000.

[7] Harry Chen, Tim Finin, and Anupam Joshi. An ontology for context-aware pervasive computing environments. *Special Issue on Ontologies for Distributed Systems, Knowledge Engineering Review*, 2003.

[8] Harry Chen, Tim Finin, and Anupam Joshi. A context broker for building smart meeting rooms. In *Proceedings of the Knowledge Representation and Ontology for Autonomous Systems Symposium, 2004 AAAI Spring Symposium.* AAAI, AAAI Press, March 2004.

[9] Harry Chen, Filip Perich, Dipanjan Chakraborty, Tim Finin, and Anupam Joshi. Intelligent agents meet semantic web in a smart meeting room. In *Proceedings of the Thrid International Joint Conference on Autonomous Agents & Multi-Agent Systems*, July 2004.

[10] Harry Chen, Filip Perich, Tim Finin, and Anupam Joshi. SOUPA: Standard ontology for ubiquitous and pervasive applications. Technical report, University of Maryland, Baltimore County, 2004. Submitted to The First Annual International Conference on Mobile and Ubiquitous Systems: Networking and Services (MobiQuitous 2004).

[11] Michael Coen, Brenton Phillips, Nimrod Warshawsky, Luke Weisman, Stephen Peters, and Peter Finin. Meeting the computational needs of intelligent environments: The metaglue system. In *Proceedings of In 1st International Workshop on Managing Interactions in Smart Environments (MANSE'99)*, Dublin, Ireland, 1999.

[12] Michael H. Coen. Design principles for intelligent environments. In *Proceedings of AAAI/IAAI 1998*, pages 547–554, 1998.

[13] Simon Cox, Paul Daisey, Ron Lake, Clemens Portele, and Arliss Whiteside. Geography markup language (gml 3.0). In *OpenGIS Documents.* OpenGIS Consortium, 2003.

[14] Nicodemos Damianou, Naranker Dulay, Emil Lupu, and Morris Sloman. The ponder policy specification language. *Lecture Notes in Computer Science*, 1995:18–??, 2001.

[15] Anind K. Dey. *Providing Architectural Support for Building Context-Aware Applications.* PhD thesis, Georgia Institute of Technology, 2000.

[16] Edd Dumbill. Finding friends with xml and rdf. In *IBM developerWorks, XML Watch.* xmlhack.com, June 2002.

[17] Tim Finin, Anupam Joshi, Lalana Kagal, Olga Ratsimore, Vlad Korolev, and Harry Chen. Information agents for mobile and embedded devices. *Lecture Notes in Computer Science*, 2182:264–??, 2001.

[18] Fabien L. Gandon and Norman M. Sadeh. Semantic web technologies to reconcile privacy and context awareness. *Web Semantics Journal*, 1(3), 2004.

[19] Jeff Heflin. *Web Ontology Language (OWL) Use Cases and Requirements*, w3c candidate recommendation 18 august 2003 edition, 2003.

[20] Jerry R. Hobbs. A daml ontology of time. `http://www.cs.rochester.edu/~ferguson/daml/daml-time-20020830.txt`, 2002.

[21] Lalana Kagal, Tim Finin, and Anupam Joshi. A Policy Based Approach to Security for the Semantic Web. In *2nd International Semantic Web Conference (ISWC2003)*, September 2003.

[22] Lalana Kagal, Tim Finin, and Anupam Joshi. A policy language for a pervasive computing environment. In *IEEE 4th International Workshop on Policies for Distributed Systems and Networks*, 2003.

[23] Lalana Kagal, Vlad Korolev, Harry Chen, Anupam Joshi, and Timothy Finin. Centaurus : A framework for intelligent services in a mobile environment. In *Proceedings*

of the International Workshop on Smart Appliances and Wearable Computing (IW-SAWC), 2001.

[24] Lalana Kagal, Massimo Paolucci, Naveen Srinivasan, Grit Denker, Tim Finin, and Katia Sycara. Authorization and privacy for semantic web services. *AAAI 2004 Spring Symposium on Semantic Web Services*, March 2004.

[25] Lalana Kagal, James Parker, Harry Chen, Anupam Joshi, and Tim Finin. *Handbook of Mobile Computing*, chapter Security, Trust and Privacy in Mobile Computing Environments, pages ??–?? CRC Press, 2004.

[26] Tim Kindberg and John Barton. A web-based nomadic computing system. *Computer Networks*, 35(4):443–456, 2001.

[27] Douglas B. Lenat and R. V. Guha. *Building Large Knowledge-Based Systems: Representation and Inference in the Cyc Project.* Addison-Wesley, February 1990.

[28] Alan K. MacKworth, Randy G. Goebel, and David I. Poole. *Computational Intelligence: A Logical Approach*, chapter 9, pages 319–342. Oxford University Press, 1998.

[29] Deborah L. McGuinness and Frank van Harmelen. Owl web ontology language overview. `http://www.w3.org/TR/owl-features/`, 2003.

[30] Natalya Fridman Noy and Deborah L. McGuinness. Ontology development 101: A guide to creating your first ontology. Technical Report KSL-01-05, Stanford Knowledge Systems Laboratory, 2001.

[31] Feng Pan and Jerry R. Hobbs. Time in owl-s. In *Proceedings of AAAI-04 Spring Symposium on Semantic Web Services*, Stanford University, California, 2004.

[32] Filip Perich. *MoGATU BDI Ontology*, 2004.

[33] Stephen Peters and Howie Shrobe. Using semantic networks for knowledge representation in an intelligent environment. In *1st Annual IEEE International Conference on Pervasive Computing and Proceedings of the 1st Annual IEEE International Conference on Pervasive Computing and Communications (PerCom'03)*, March 2003.

[34] David Poole. Compiling a default reasoning system into prolog. *New Generation Computing*, 9(1):3–38, 1991.

[35] Shelley Powers. *Practical RDF.* O'Reilly & Associates, 2003.

[36] David A. Randell, Zhan Cui, and Anthony G. Cohn. A spatial logic based on regions and connection. In *Proceedings of the 3rd International Conference on Knowledge Representation and Reasoning*, 1992.

[37] William Noah Schilit. *A System Architecture for Context-Aware Mobile Computing.* PhD thesis, Columbia University, 1995.

[38] Jeffrey Undercoffer, Filip Perich, Andrej Cedilnik, Lalana Kagal, Anupam Joshi, and Tim Finin. A secure infrastructure for service discovery and management in pervasive computing. *The Journal of Special Issues on Mobility of Systems, Users, Data and Computing*, 2003.

[39] Roy Want, Andy Hopper, Veronica Falcao, and Jon Gibbons. The active badge location system. Technical Report 92.1, Olivetti Research Ltd., ORL, 24a Trumpington Street, Cambridge CB2 1QA, 1992.

[40] Michael J. Wooldridge and Nicholas R. Jennings. Intelligent agents: Theory and practice. *Knowledge Engineering Review*, 10(2):115–152, June 1995.

Harry Chen, Tim Finin and Anupam Joshi
Dept. of CSEE
University of Maryland, Baltimore County
USA
e-mail: hchen4@cs.umbc.edu
finin@cs.umbc.edu
joshi@cs.umbc.edu

A UML Ontology and Derived Content Language for a Travel Booking Scenario

Stephen Cranefield, Jin Pan and Martin Purvis

Abstract. This paper illustrates an approach to combining the benefits of a multi-agent system architecture with the use of industry-standard modelling techniques using the Unified Modeling Language (UML). Using a UML profile for ontology modelling, an ontology for travel booking services is presented and the automatic derivation of an object-oriented content language for this domain is described. This content language is then used to encode example messages for a simple travel booking scenario, and it is shown how this approach to agent messaging allows messages to be created and analysed using a convenient object-oriented application-specific application programmer interface.

1. Introduction

This paper is a response to the challenge problem for the AAMAS 2003 Workshop on Ontologies in Agent Systems. The challenge problem [1] was based on the description of a travel agent domain previously developed for an ontology tool assessment exercise organised by the Special Interest Group on Enterprise-Standard Ontology Environments within the European Union's OntoWeb research network [2]. The OAS'03 challenge was to "describe the design and (preferably) an implementation of a multi-agent system in that domain" with emphasis on "the ways in which ontological information is referenced, accessed and used by agents".

In this paper we illustrate the application of our previous work on the use of the Unified Modeling Language (UML) for ontology and content language modelling [3] and the automatic generation of Java classes from these models [4]. This work rests on four observations:

- The Unified Modeling Language is a widely known and standardised modelling language with a compact graphical notation, an XML-based serialisation format, and a lot of existing tool support. We believe that the use of

UML for ontology modelling has great benefits in terms of industry acceptance of agent technology [5]. Its principal weakness is the lack of (official) formal semantics, but we believe that ongoing efforts in this direction will remove this shortcoming [6].

- Much current software development is done using the Java programming language, and the majority of widely used agent development tools are based on Java. Programmers using these tools are most familiar with the use of object-oriented representations and application programmer interfaces (APIs).
- The use of object-oriented structures to refer to domain objects within messages is convenient, but must be restricted to precise well-understood usages in order to avoid semantic problems. [7].
- Multi-agent systems must coexist and interact with other distributed systems (both technological and human). These other systems have existing techniques for referring to domain objects using reference schemes such as World Wide Web Uniform Resource Identifiers (URIs). This style of reference goes beyond the notion of "standard names" (logical constants that denote each domain object) that lie behind the semantics of FIPA ACL's `query-ref` communicative act, and it is desirable to allow agents to use a more general notion of object reference when answering queries.

These observations have led us to develop our UML-based model-driven approach to implementing multi-agent systems. In Section 2 we give a brief overview of this approach, before presenting a simple UML travel booking ontology in Section 3, a discussion of the automatically generated ontology-specific content language in Section 4 and an illustration of its use in an agent application in Section 5. A comparison between our approach and the JADE agent platform's support for ontology-specific content language classes is presented in Section 6. The paper closes with some comments on the applicability of this techique and some areas for future work.

2. Overview of our approach

Figure 1 presents a schematic overview of our approach to designing and implementing the message-handling component of agent systems.

The designer of an agent must have a mental model of the conceptual structure of the domain (the ontology) as well as an understanding of the structure of information describing instances of these concepts and their relationships. We believe the graphical nature of UML makes it a powerful tool for visualising these models: an ontology can be represented by a UML class diagram and instance information can be conveyed as a UML object diagram that shows the values of object attributes and the links (instances of associations) that exist between objects.

When creating the agent application, the programmer must translate these mental models into structures that can be manipulated within a programming

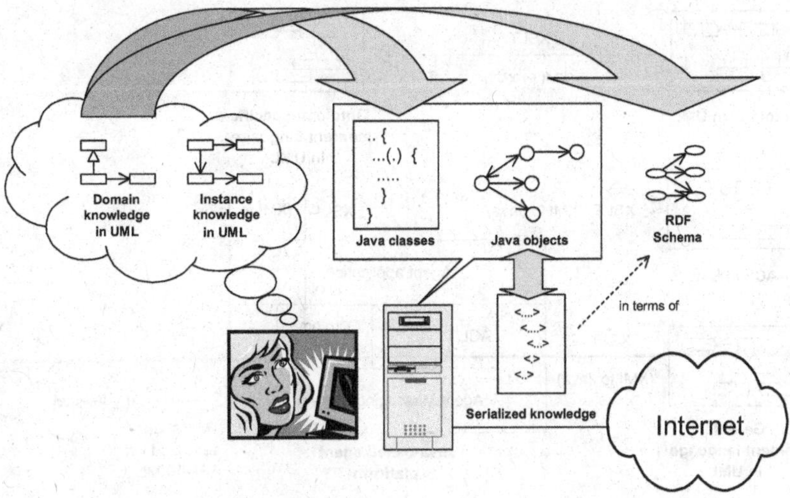

FIGURE 1. Overview of our approach

language. When using Java, the natural counterpart to a concept in an ontology is a Java class. Although other representations can be used, such as string-based encodings of languages defined by grammars, the most convenient representation for a Java programmer is to have Java classes corresponding directly to the concepts that the agent will need to refer to when manipulating information about the world. To make this possible, we have defined XSLT [8] stylesheets that produce Java class definitions from an XMI [9] serialisation of a UML model (currently we support XMI 1.0 for UML 1.3) [4].

As agents need to communicate information about the world, it is beneficial to provide a straightforward mapping from the progammer's model of the domain (inter-related Java objects in our case) and the content language used to encode information within messages. However, standard agent content languages such as FIPA SL and KIF use a string-based logical representation. These are generic and weakly typed languages in which domain concepts can only be referred to by name, rather than by more stongly typed mechanisms such as instantiation, and thus messages that do not conform to the agent's known ontologies can only be detected by run-time analysis. As an alternative to this approach, our Java classes generated from the ontology have a built-in serialisation mechanism that allows networks of inter-related objects describing domain objects to be included within messages. The serialisation uses the XML encoding of the Resource Description Framework (RDF) [10], which makes reference to concepts defined in an RDF schema that is also generated automatically from the ontology in UML [11].

This mechanism can also be used to serialise entire messages, including the outer agent communication language (ACL) layer. By defining the ACL in UML as

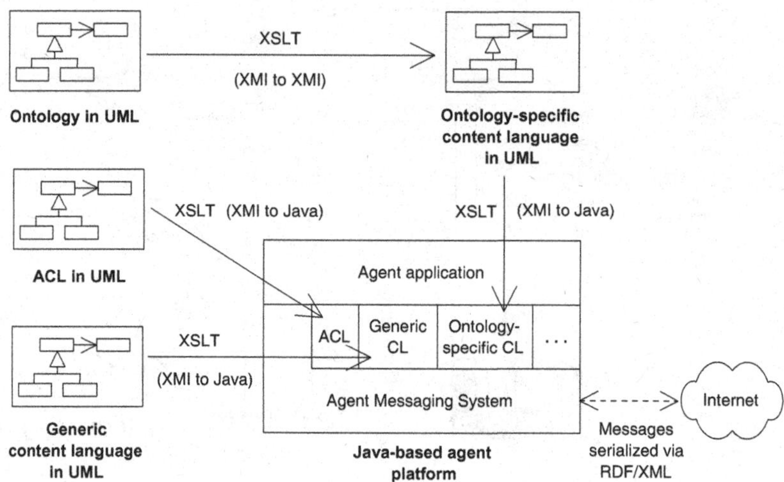

FIGURE 2. Integration with an agent platform

well, and defining a set of UML 'marker' interfaces representing the concepts (such as *predicate* and *action description*) that comprise the required argument types for the ACL's various communicative acts, it is possible to conceptualise messages with arbitrary content languages (if modelled in UML) as object diagrams (see Figures 5 and 6 later in the paper).

Figure 2 illustrates how this technology can be integrated with a Java-based agent platform, and highlights a crucial aspect that addresses the third observation from the introduction: the need for careful use of object-oriented representations within messages. The figure shows a number of UML models: an ontology (top left), definitions of an ACL and a generic (i.e. SL-like) content language, and the definition of an ontology-specific content language (top right). The ACL and the content languages are given as input to the XMI-to-Java transformation, and this results in Java classes that provide an object-oriented application programming interface that sits on top of the platform's built-in messaging system classes. However, the ontology is not directly translated to Java classes. We regard an ontology as a model of the problem domain, not as a model of the language used to encode *information* about the domain. In other words, an instance of an ontological class `Dog` would be an actual dog, not a description of a dog. When a structured expression corresponding to the structure of the `Dog` class appears within a message, this cannot be taken to be playing the role of a logical *term* (which always has a unique denotation), but instead might (depending on the context) play the role of a *proposition* (stating that an object with the specified properties exists) or an *identifying reference expression* (a reference to a possibly non-existent or non-unique object by describing its attribute values) [7, 3].

To avoid any confusion between the notions of ontology and content language, we provide the facility to use domain-specific object-oriented expressions within messages by generating from the ontology a UML model representing a specialised ontology-specific content language. From this, Java classes can be generated as for the ACL and generic content languages models. The generated ontology-specific content language for the travel booking domain is described in Section 4 and its use to create messages is illustrated in Section 5.

3. A travel booking ontology in UML

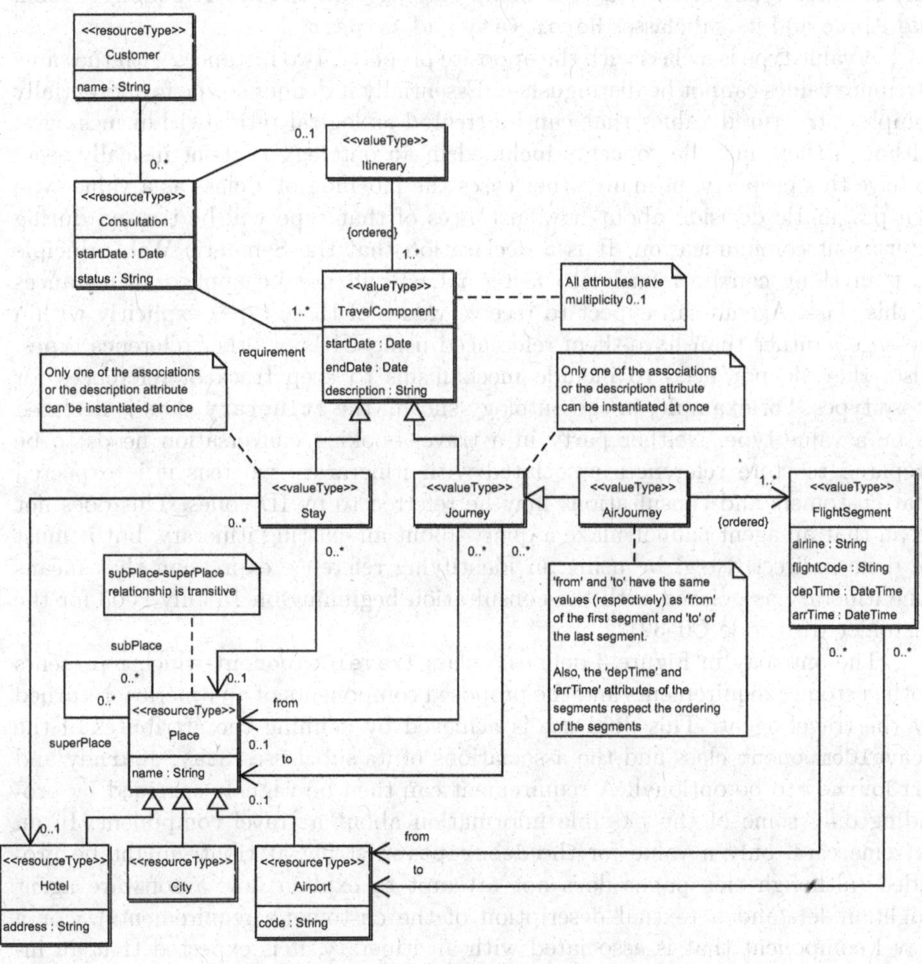

FIGURE 3. A travel booking ontology

Figure 3 shows a simple ontology in UML for the travel booking scenario. This uses two stereotypes, «resourceType» and «valueType», from a UML profile for ontology modelling that has been presented previously [3]. A resource type is a type of class for which the instances have an intrinsic identity, i.e. two instances with the same attribute values can be distinguished from each other. There is a possibility that an object of that class might be referred to using an identifier such as a unique name in some naming system, a UUID, or a World Wide Web Uniform Resource Identifier (URI). The semantics of the stereotype declare that the class has an additional optional association with a class representing some type of reference (e.g. the concept of a URI). This type is declared using a tagged value in the resource type class declaration, but this feature will not be used in this paper. The resource types in the travel booking ontology are `Customer`, `Consultation`, and `Place` and its subclasses `Hotel`, `City` and `Airport`.

A value type is a class with the opposite property: two instances with the same attribute values cannot be distingushed. Essentially it defines a type for potentially complex structured values that can be treated as logical terms within messages. Although there may be concepts included in an ontology that intrinsically seem to have this property, in many other cases the labelling of a class as a value type is a pragmatic decision about how instances of that type will be treated during inter-agent communication. It is a declaration that the Semantic Web principle that anything can be referred to using a URI will *not* be applied to instances of this class. Agents can expect to receive values of these types explicitly within messages, rather than have them referenced using URIs or other reference types. Also, they do not need to include mechanisms to keep track of references for those types. For example, in the ontology shown, the `Itinerary` class is declared to be a value type. Neither party in a travel booking conversation needs to be prepared to store references associated with itineraries, whereas it is expected that customers and consultations may be referred to by ID codes. This does not mean that an agent cannot make a query about an existing itinerary, but it must be done indirectly, e.g. by using an identifying reference expression that means "the itinerary associated with the consultation beginning on 15 July 2003 for the customer with code C05321".

The ontology in Figure 3 defines a class `TravelComponent` which represents both customer requirements and the proposed components of an itinerary returned by the travel agent. This dual use is achieved by defining the attributes of the `TravelComponent` class and the associations of its subclasses `Stay`, `Journey` and `AirJourney` to be optional. A requirement can then be vaguely specified by providing only some of the possible information about a travel component. In an extreme case, only a value for the `description` string attribute might be provided (although this paper does not attempt to explain how a software agent might understand a textual description of the customer's requirements). For a travel component that is associated with an itinerary, it is expected that all information is provided, with the possible exception of the `description` attribute (this constraint could be included in the ontology, but is not modelled at present).

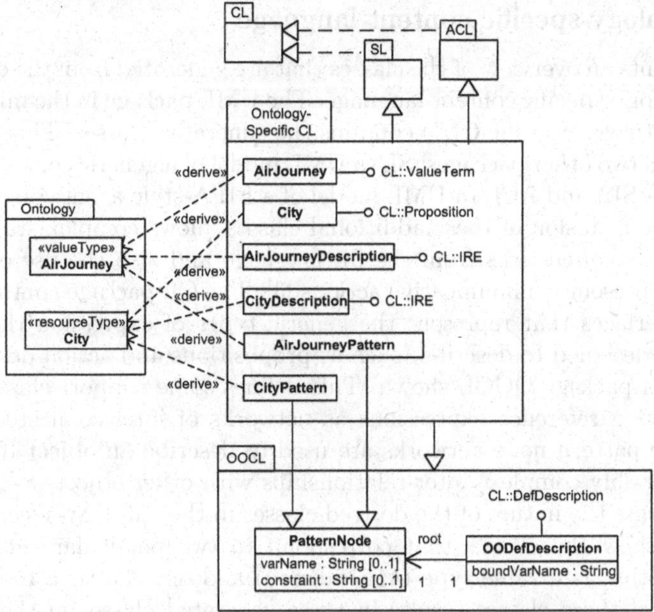

FIGURE 4. Derived classes in an ontology-specific content language

Note that a consultation object may be linked directly with travel components representing the customer requirements as well as indirectly with other, different, travel component objects via an itinerary. The latter represent the final bookings.

The ontology includes a number of constraints, presented as notes in dog-eared rectangles. These could be defined in more detail using the UML's Object Constraint Language, but are shown here in English for clarity. It is not intended that these constraints be used for inference in the current design—rather they serve as part of the specification for the correct implementation of agents using this ontology.

The ontology is not intended to be a complete model of the travel booking domain. It does not include many concepts needed for a realistic account (including the cost for a given itinerary). Also, to keep the model simple it does not use more advanced features of UML, such as the ability to define enumerated types (which could be used to define the possible values for the `Consulation` class's `status` attribute). For simplicity we regard the types `String`, `Date` and `DateTime` as being 'built in' primitive types in our UML profile that are handled specially during the generation of Java classes.

4. The ontology-specific content language

Figure 4 presents an overview of the classes that are generated from the ontology to form the ontology-specific content language. The UML package in the middle of the diagram ("Ontology-Specific CL") contains the generated classes. This also inherits classes from two other packages: SL (a UML model of a generic content language based on FIPA SL) and ACL (a UML model of a FIPA-style agent communication language). The inclusion of these additional classes allows complex statements to be formed using connectives from the SL language and also the use of ACL expressions to represent communicative actions [3]. The CL package contains the set of marker interfaces that represent the generic types of expression that content languages are designed to describe (such as propositions and action descriptions). There is also a package OOCL shown. This defines some support classes used to create identifying reference expressions as networks of inter-connected "pattern nodes". These pattern node networks are used to describe an object by its properties and (possibly complex) inter-relationships with other objects.

To illustrate the nature of the derived classes in the ontology-specific content language we show the classes that correspond to two particular classes in the ontology: one that is a value type (`AirJourney`) and one that is a resource type (`City`). Each of these classes results in three generated classes in the ontology-specific content language[1]. (Note that the dashed arrows labelled «derive» are UML dependencies, so they are directed from each derived class back to the one it depends on.)

As discussed in Section 3, an instance of a valuetype can be treated as a logical term within a content language, and so a corresponding class with the same name and structure (e.g. `AirJourney`) is generated and declared to implement the `CL::ValueTerm` interface. Some associations between `AirJourney` and other classes may need to be modified when translated to the new content language, e.g. a reference to a resource type must be replaced by a reference to a derived ...`Description` class for that resource type (this type of class is discussed below).

An agent might also want to refer to a value type instance using an identifying reference expression. Therefore, for each value type class there are two corresponding generated classes that can be used for this purpose: a simple ...`Description` class and a more complex ...`Pattern` class. The description class (e.g. `AirJourney Description`) implements the interface `CL::IRE` to show that that this can be used as an identifying reference expression (in particular, as a definite description—the only type of IRE currently supported). Under the mapping, all attributes and associations become optional because (for example) although an air journey in real life must necessarily have at least one flight segment, it is possible to refer to an air journey simply by specifying its date or departure and arrival cities.

The ...`Pattern` class is the same as the ...`Description` class, except it also extends the class `OOCL::PatternNode` and any association with another class must

[1]The details of the rules for deriving content language classes from value types and resource types are beyond the scope of this paper but can be found elsewhere [3].

be changed to be an association with the appropriate ...`Pattern` class. The use of this type of class is illustrated in Figure 5 (which is discussed later in the paper).

For resource type classes, there can be no derived class that implements the `CL::ValueTerm` interface as it is not semantically meaningful to embed instances of that type within a message[2]. Instead, corresponding ...`Description` and ...`Pattern` classes are generated, as for value types. In addition, a class implementing `CL::Proposition` is generated in order to allow a convenient object-oriented form of proposition about objects to be used within messages. For this generated class, all attributes and associations become optional.

Further details of this approach to generating ontology-specific content languages can be found elsewhere [3], although the presentation here takes account of some subsequent minor updates to that previous work.

5. Using the generated content language

In this section we illustrate the use of an ontology-specific content language generated from the travel booking ontology. Figures 5 and 6 show UML object diagrams representing (respectively) query and response messages in a conversation between a customer and a travel booking agent. The query is an instance of the class `QueryRef` (predefined in the ACL package). This corresponds to the FIPA `query-ref` message type which represents a question asking another agent to identify an entity that satisfies particular properties. The content part of the message (represented by a link from the `QueryRef` object in Figure 5) is an instance of the class `OODefDescription` shown at the bottom of Figure 4. This class represents an object-oriented version of the `iota` binding operator from FIPA SL. It has an attribute `boundVarName` representing a variable name to be used to refer to the subject of the `query-ref`. This object is then linked to a network of typed pattern nodes, each of which describes some object in terms of its attributes and relationships with other objects. One of these pattern nodes is expected to have a `varName` attribute value matching the `boundVarName` value of the `OODefDescription` object. The other nodes may also have variable names specified, and these may be referred to within Object Constraint Language expressions appearing as the values of the optional `constraint` attribute of other nodes (this feature is not used in Figure 4). The message in the figure represents the following query:

Given a customer named Stephen Cranefield having a consultation with the requirements of flying from Dunedin to Melbourne on 14 July 2003 and needing accommodation there from the 14th until the 19th, what is the associated itinerary? (For simplicity, we assume that the customer wishes to remain uncommitted after the 19th).

---

[2]We would argue that even electronic entities such as instances of electronic currency are best regarded as external objects that agents refer to using references.

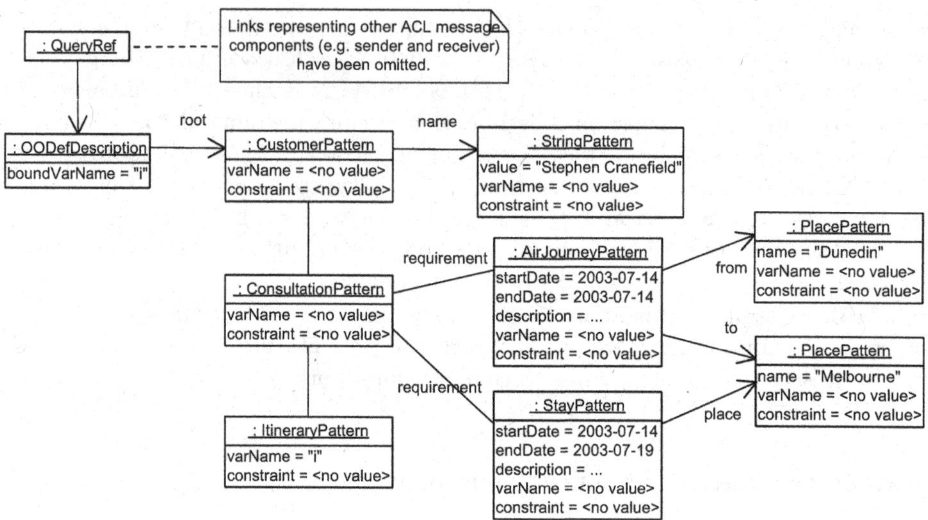

FIGURE 5. A travel booking request message

Figure 6 shows a UML object diagram representing a possible reply to this request. The message is an instance of the `InformRef` class from the ACL package. This is a structured version of FIPA ACL's `inform-ref` message type with two content expressions: a definite description (generally this will be the one that was included in the preceding `query-ref`) and an expression that identifies the entity that satisfies the query—this may be a value of a primitive type or a value type, a reference to an object (e.g. a URI), or another, hopefully more detailed, definite description. In the case of Figure 6, the definite description (not depicted in full) is the same as the one contained in the query message, with two additional links that provide references for the customer and the consultation objects.

The bottom part of Figure 6 represents the answer to the query and contains an instance of the `Itinerary` value type that comprises fully detailed value type instances for the air journey and the stay. The details about the hotel, airports and cities are encoded by links to ...`Description` objects, which describe those external instances of resource types in terms of their attribute values and some required relationships between the objects.

Note that these diagrams conceptualise the messages as UML object diagrams. As shown in Figure 1, the messages are physically realised as Java objects within the agent at run time and as RDF documents when being transported between agents. The Java classes are generated using an XSLT stylesheet [4] and they include code that handles the marshalling and unmarshalling of messages between the in-memory Java representation and the RDF serialisation format [11].

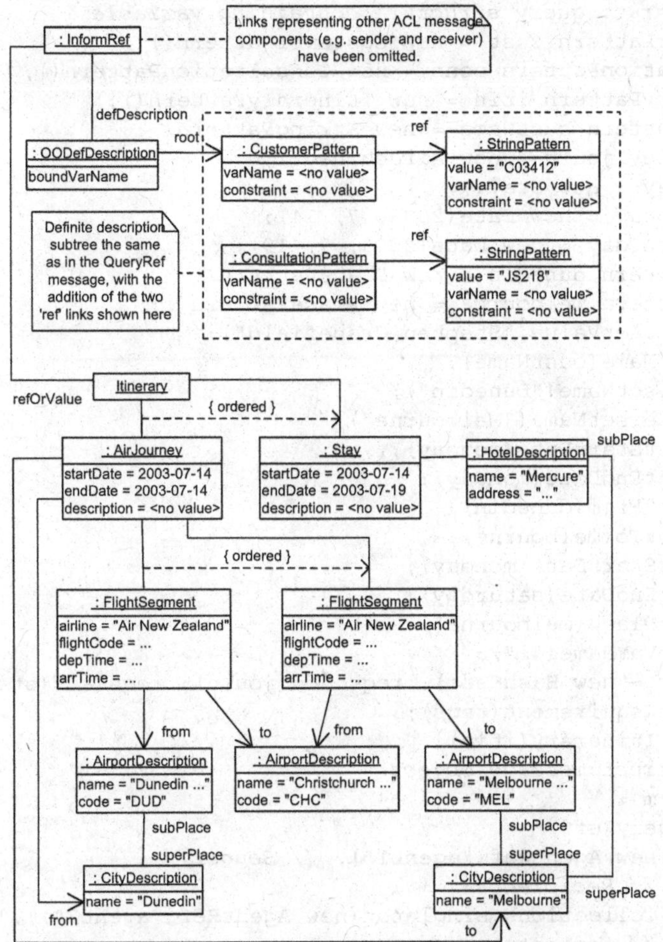

FIGURE 6. A reponse message from the travel booking agent

Figure 7 shows an example of how the query message can be created and sent from Java code, using the generated classes for the ACL and the content language (this is based on a simplication of the ACL model presented previously [3]).

There is no doubt that using this object-oriented API to construct messages as shown is more cumbersome for the programmer than writing a string expression in FIPA SL. However, it is likely that most messages will be constructed dynamically within code rather than by a static sequence of Java statements as shown in the figure. This approach also has the benefits of being strongly typed and model-driven: support for new ACLs and content languages can quickly be provided once they have been defined using UML. Furthermore, any disadvantages

```
// Construct query structure containing variable i
CustomerPattern cust = new CustomerPattern();
ConsultationPattern cons = new ConsultationPattern();
ItineraryPattern itin = new ItineraryPattern();
StringPattern custName = new StringPattern();
AirJourney journ = new AirJourney();
Stay stay = new Stay();
Date monday = new Date(2003, 7, 14);
Date saturday = new Date(2003, 7, 19);
PlacePattern dunedin = new PlacePattern();
PlacePattern melbourne = new PlacePattern();
custName.setValue("Stephen Cranefield");
cust.setName(custName);
dunedin.setName("Dunedin");
melbourne.setName("Melbourne");
journ.setStartDate(monday);
journ.setEndDate(monday);
journ.setFrom(dunedin);
journ.setTo(melbourne);
stay.setStartDate(monday);
stay.setEndDate(saturday);
stay.setPlace(melbourne);
itin.setVarName("i");
Set reqs = new HashSet(); reqs.add(journ); reqs.add(stay)
cons.setRequirement(reqs);
cons.setItinerary(itin);
// Construct message object
Message m =
  new QueryRef(
        new AgentRef("agent1"), // Sender
        // Recipients:
        Collections.singleton(new AgentRef("agent2")),
        // Content:
        new OODefDescription("i", patternNetwork));
// Send message
m.send();
```

FIGURE 7. Using the generated Java code to create and serialise a message

for the creation of messages are balanced by advantages in the analysis of incoming messages: it is much easier to examine a message using its object structure than by performing string-matching operations.

6. Comparison with JADE

A technique for allowing ontology-specific Java classes to be used when creating and analysing agent messages has also been developed as part of the JADE agent

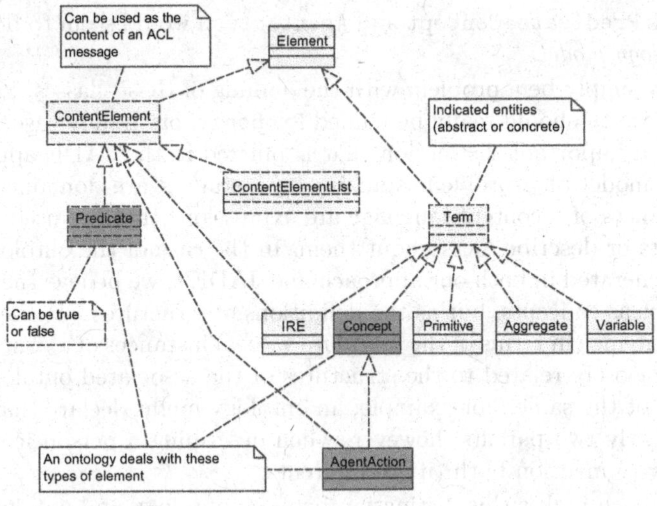

FIGURE 8. The JADE content reference model (reproduced from [13])

platform [12]. JADE allows ontologies to be defined using a frame-based language. An ontology is constructed at run time by application code that creates an empty ontology object and calls methods to add "schema" objects to it that represent the ontology's concepts, predicates and agent actions [13]. Methods can then be invoked on the schema objects to add slot definitions to them by specifying each slot's name, type and properties (e.g. the cardinality). The recommended practice is to encapsulate this ontology definition code within the constructor of a singleton class that represents the ontology.

Each schema object is also associated with a Java class provided by the agent developer. This class must implement one of JADE's `Concept`, `Predicate` or `AgentAction` interfaces as appropriate, and the method signatures must correspond to the slots defined in the schema object according to a specific set of rules. Instances of these classes can be used by the agent application code to create a message content, and a content language codec takes care of translating between Java objects and the appropiate content language syntax. A third-party plug-in for the Protégé ontology editor has been developed to generate these Java classes from an ontology defined using Protégé [14].

6.1. Ontologies vs. content languages

The `Concept`, `Predicate` and `AgentAction` interfaces mentioned above are part of JADE's "content reference model" (CRM) [13], which is shown in Figure 8. This is JADE's equivalent of our "generic content language concepts model" [3, Fig. 3]. However, the JADE CRM contains classes from two distinct types of model within a single inheritance hierarchy. Most of the classes are part of an abstract *content language model* (e.g. `ContentElement`, `Term`, `Variable`, etc.), but the classes `Predicate`, `Concept` and `AgentAction` would seem to belong in an abstract *ontology model*.

This may simply be a problem with the naming of these classes, e.g. perhaps the class `Predicate` should really be named `Proposition`. In any case, we believe that there is an important distinction that is blurred in the JADE approach. An ontology is a model of a problem domain. Its instances are domain objects. In contrast, instances of a content language are expressions that are used to identify domain objects or describe facts about them. In the case of the ontology-specific Java classes generated in both our approach and JADE's, we believe these are best understood not as concepts, but as the definitions of structures for asserting facts about or identifying (in terms of the attribute values) instances of a concept. These structures are closely related to the structures of the associated ontology classes, but they are not the same. For example, an ontology might declare that a Person must have exactly two parents; however, when describing a person it should not be compulsory to mention both (if any) parents.

Our approach makes this distinction between ontology and ontology-specific content language clear (see the top part of Figure 2). Furthermore, once this distinction is made, it becomes clear that ontology-specific object-oriented content language expressions may play several *different* roles: as identifying reference expressions *describing* objects in terms of their properties (with the assumption that objects with these properties exist), as terms *denoting* structured values (for ontology classes that model data types rather than concepts with a notion of individual identity), or even as propositions asserting that particular objects have the specified attributes and relationships to each other. In our approach, a class `Person` in an ontology maps to two classes: a `PersonDescriptor` class and a `PersonProposition` class, while a `Vector` class would map to a `VectorTerm` class and a `VectorProposition` class.

6.2. Concept names vs. function symbols

The JADE content reference model has the class `Concept` as a subclass of `Term`. This (together with the examples that illustrate its use [13]) suggests that ontology class names can be regarded as functional symbols, so that a particular person might be *denoted* by a Java `Person` object with its name attribute set to "John" and its age attribute set to 33. This approach follows the approach used in the FIPA SL content language, but we have argued [7] that this use of class names to form functional terms is semantically flawed. In logic, functional terms *always* denote an element of the domain of discourse, whereas a 'term' formed using a class symbol and some attribute-value bindings may not denote any object (e.g. there is no guarantee that any car is described by the term `(car :registration "lemon")`.

Our solution to this problem is to treat object-oriented content expressions that are intended to identify objects as identifying referring expressions (IREs) rather than terms (except for the subset of ontology classes where each constructor expression really does describe a unique object).

6.3. Terms vs. IREs

The JADE CRM has `IRE` as a subclass of `Term`. We believe this is inappropriate as the semantics of IREs and terms are completely different (a term always has a denotation and has compositional semantics, whereas an IRE may not have any denotation and its semantics is not independent of its enclosing sentence, being defined in terms of a rewriting of the sentence [15]). In our model, these concepts have no common parent.

6.4. Strongly vs. weakly typed descriptor classes

The JADE model uses "abstract descriptor classes" to encode IREs that involve variables (these are not shown in Figure 8). These classes are weakly typed: the same descriptor classes are used for queries involving all classes. In contrast, in our approach a concept-specific (and therefore strongly typed) descriptor class is generated for each ontology class [3]. These classes can be used to encode complex queries as networks of objects, with variable bindings and matchings, and constraints included if desired.

6.5. Content language codecs

JADE allows different content language codecs to be registered for serialising messages. It appears that these must be implemented manually for each content language encoding. At present, when using ontology-specific content languages, we only support a serialisation using RDF/XML. However, the serialisation code is generated automatically as part of the ontology-specific content language classes.

6.6. Generating action description classes

To date we have not investigated the generation of Java classes that correspond to action types defined in an ontology. These could be instantiated by an agent developer and used as a strongly typed way of generating action descriptions within messages. Providing this facility would be a straightforward extension of our approach. JADE includes support for the use of Java schema classes corresponding to strongly typed actions (i.e. those having specific arguments declared).

7. Conclusion

This paper has addressed the OAS'03 workshop challenge problem by illustrating the application of our UML-based model-driven approach to defining ontologies and then automatically generating related ontology-specific content languages along with corresponding Java classes and an RDF-based serialisation mechanism. We believe this approach has strong benefits for the software engineering task of designing and implementing agents to peform particular tasks in a given domain. Our work does not currently provide support for the construction of agents that are expected to have more general abilities, where inference may be required in order to determine how to respond to messages. However, the Object Management Group (OMG) is currently developing the Ontology Definition Metamodel (ODM)

[16], currently proposed to be a set of metamodels for common ontology languages, UML 2.0 profiles specifying how to represent ontologies in these languages using UML notation, and some mappings between the metamodels. The ODM will allow UML-based model-driven techniques, including the approach described in this paper, to be applied to a variety of ontology modelling languages, including the World Wide Web Consortium's Web Ontology Language (OWL).

An important avenue for future work is the enhancement of the API offered to programmers for constructing messages by providing a larger range of constructors in the generated classes. It would also be highly desirable to develop a technique for annotating the UML definition of ACLs and content languages with information that describes a concrete string-based syntax in such a way that parsers for this language can be generated automatically. This will allow interoperation with traditional FIPA agent platforms and will also give programmers the option of using the string-based syntax for creating messages within agent application code.

One question raised by this work is the suitability of XSLT for defining transformations on models serialised as XMI files. As a declarative language, XSLT was favoured over the procedural approach of writing transformation code using an API for model inspection, e.g. the Java Metadata Interface (JMI) [17]. However, an XSLT stylesheet must work with the physical rather than the logical structure of an XMI file, i.e. it must view the model as a tree with a complex mechanism used to encode relationships between its nodes. This mechanism makes use of proxy elements: XML elements standing for another node in the tree and linked to it using one of three different types of linking attributes. Proxy elements can be chained. Furthermore, in generating the XMI file, the exporting software has some freedom in whether certain types of information are encoded as XML elements or attributes, and newer versions of XMI have offered increasing flexibility in the encoding. This means that in order to write a fully general XMI-processing XSLT stylesheet, all possible encoding options must be catered for. This leads to complexity and duplicated logic that is due to the XML structure of the document rather than the logical structure of the model it encodes, making development and maintenance of the stylesheet difficult. As an alternative approach we are working on a JMI-based tool to produce RDF encodings of UML models and plan to investigate approaches for transforming these RDF models using RDF transformation tools. We will also consider the use of the OMG's MOF Query/View/Transformation language [18] once work on this is complete.

References

[1] OAS 2003 Committee. OAS'03 challenge problem. http://oas.otago.ac.nz/OAS2003/Challenge/challenge.html, 2003.

[2] OntoWeb project. Project Web pages. http://www.ontoweb.org, 2003.

[3] S. Cranefield and M. Purvis. A UML profile and mapping for the generation of ontology-specific content languages. *Knowledge Engineering Review*, 17(1):21–39, 2002.

[4] S. Cranefield, M. Nowostawski, and M. Purvis. Implementing agent communication languages directly from UML specifications. In *Proceedings of the 1st International Joint Conference on Autonomous Agents and Multi-Agent Systems (AAMAS 2002)*, volume 2, pages 553–554. ACM Press, 2002.

[5] S. Cranefield and M. Purvis. UML as an ontology modelling language. In *Proceedings of the Workshop on Intelligent Information Integration, 16th International Joint Conference on Artificial Intelligence (IJCAI-99)*, 1999. http://CEUR-WS.org/Vol-23/cranefield-ijcai99-iii.pdf.

[6] Precise UML Group. The Precise UML Group home page. http://www.puml.org, 2004.

[7] S. Cranefield and M. Purvis. Referencing objects in FIPA SL: An analysis and proposal. In *Proceedings of the Workshop on Agentcities: Challenges in open agent environments, 2nd International Joint Conference on Autonomous Agents and Multi-Agent Systems (AAMAS 2003)*, 2003. http://www.agentcities.org/Challenge03/Proc/Papers/ch03_cranefield.pdf.

[8] XSL transformations (XSLT) version 1.0. World Wide Web Consortium Web page, 2003. http://www.w3.org/TR/xslt.

[9] XML metadata interchange specifications. Object Management Group, 2004. http://www.omg.org/technology/documents/modeling_spec_catalog.htm#XMI.

[10] Resource Description Framework. World Wide Web Consortium Web page, 2004. http://www.w3.org/RDF/.

[11] S. Cranefield. UML and the Semantic Web. In I. Cruz, S. Decker, J. Euzenat, and D. McGuiness, editors, *The emerging Semantic Web*, pages 3–20. IOS Press, Amsterdam, 2002.

[12] Telecom Italia Lab. JADE: Java agent development framework. http://jade.tilab.com/, 2004.

[13] G. Caire. *JADE tutorial: application-defined content languages and ontologies.* Telecom Italia Laboratory, JADE 2.6 edition, 2002. http://jade.tilab.com/doc/CLOntoSupport.pdf.

[14] C.J. van Aart, R.F. Pels, G. Caire, and F. Bergenti. Creating and using ontologies in agent communication. In *Proceedings of the Workshop on Ontologies in Agent Systems, 1st International Joint Conference on Autonomous Agents and Multi-Agent Systems*, 2002. http://CEUR-WS.org/Vol-66/oas02-17.pdf.

[15] B. Russell. On denoting. In R. C. Marsh, editor, *Logic and Knowledge: Essays, 1901-1950.* Allen and Unwin, 1956. http://www.santafe.edu/~shalizi/Russell/denoting/.

[16] DSTC, IBM, and Sandpiper Software. Ontology definition metamodel: Revised submission to OMG/RFP ad/2003-03-40. http://www.omg.org/docs/ad/05-01-01.pdf, 2005.

[17] Sun Microsystems. Java Metadata Specification. http://java.sun.com/products/jmi/, 2002.

[18] T. Gardner, C. Griffin, J. Koehler, and R. Hauser. A review of OMG MOF 2.0 Query / Views / Transformations submissions and recommendations towards the final standard. http://www.omg.org/docs/ad/03-08-02.pdf, 2003.

Stephen Cranefield, Jin Pan and Martin Purvis
Department of Information Science
University of Otago
PO Box 56
Dunedin
New Zealand
e-mail: scranefield@infoscience.otago.ac.nz

Some Experiences with the Use of Ontologies in Deliberative Agents

Ian Dickinson and Michael Wooldridge

Abstract. We present our initial response to the OAS '03 Challenge Problem. The Challenge Problem proposes an agent-assisted travel scenario, and asks what the role of ontologies would be to support the agent's activity. We discuss a belief-desire-intention (BDI) approach to the problem using our Nuin agent platform, and illustrate various ways in which ontology reasoning supports BDI-oriented problem solving and communications by the agents in the system.

Keywords. Agent applications, BDI agents, ontology, semantic web.

1. Introduction

The call for papers for the AAMAS '03 workshop on Ontologies and Agent Systems (OAS'03) includes a challenge problem, adapted from an exercise by the OntoWeb project to assess different ontology environments. The challenge problem outlines a set of objectives for an agent-assisted travel planning system, in which an agent-based travel agent must co-operate with other agents to book a trip for a human client.

We have been investigating the design and development of belief-desire-intention (BDI) [19] agents for use in the Semantic Web [6]. One outcome of this research is a BDI agent platform, *Nuin*, which has been designed *ab initio* to work with Semantic Web information sources. At the time of writing, Nuin is still a work in progress. Nevertheless, we have investigated how key parts of the OAS challenge problem would be addressed by our platform.

This paper reviews the salient features of the Challenge Problem, in the context of a BDI agent. We briefly review some of the characteristics of the Nuin platform, before presenting a series of vignettes that show how we address some

Thanks to Dave Reynolds of HP Labs for his comments and suggestions, and to the anonymous reviewers of a previous version of this paper.

of the challenges in the Challenge Problem. As it represents a rich and plausible scenario, we are continuing development of a complete solution to the Challenge Problem using the Nuin platform.

2. Outline Problem

The scenario for the Challenge Problem is based on a travel agent in New York, for which we are asked to develop an agent-based application. The travel agency's clients come to make bookings for trips they wish to take, and the agency is responsible for making reservations with various travel service providers (airlines, hotels, train companies, etc) to satisfy the client's needs. The Challenge Problem outline gives a rich description of the kinds of knowledge possessed by various actors in the scenario, from which we distil the following principal objectives and assumptions:

1. Clients come to the travel agency with more-or-less specific objectives for their trip, for example a departure date and destination, a tourist attraction to visit or an academic conference to attend.
2. Clients have individual preferences about many aspects of the travel services that may be booked, including dietary choice, smoking/non-smoking, cost, comfort level, choice of provider, etc.
3. The travel agency does not possess the data to arrange trips or trip segments, but must request this information from other agents. For simplicity in building the model, we have assumed that the travel agency does know the identities of the supplier agents (a more realistic interpretation would be to require that the agency contacts suppliers through a brokerage or advertising service).
4. Requests from the travel agency to the suppliers may be made at varying levels of specificity (for example "a flight from Washington to London" vs. "a seat on BA1234 from Washington to London").
5. Interaction with the suppliers will produce multiple potential solutions to the client's initial request. Priority should be given to solutions that match the clients' preferences, noting that the preferences may not be unambiguously consistent.
6. Solutions may specify constraints that are not relevant to the client ("no dogs in the hotel"), or may be of unknown relevance.

The vocabularies used by different suppliers and the travel agency may vary - for example, one may use kilometres while another uses miles.

2.1. Issues from the challenge problem

From the distilled problem statement, we highlight the following challenges for agents to address in this scenario. Note that this is not intended to be an exhaustive list.

- modelling the motivations and attitudes of the actors - there are a number of actors in the scenario, and we assume each to be predominantly self-interested. The BDI model accounts for the mental attitudes of a given agent, but to correctly represent the scenario, the travel agency agent, for example, must also account for at least the goals and preferences of the user. In particular, we do anticipate that it will be difficult, in practice, for users to specify their preferences as utility functions [20], pp 589ff), an encoding sometimes used to express user's desired outcomes. Utility functions are highly amenable to formal analysis using game theory or micro-economics approaches [7], but it is hard to imagine how a user could express a valuation for members of a, perhaps very long, list of possible world states, even were some interface available that could present such a list.
- ownership and responsibility - arguably, the motivations of the travel agency itself should be accounted for. For example, should the agent recommend suppliers that have high commission rates for agency, even if the utility to the client is neutral or reduced? Should the agent explicitly model its contract to the client and the travel agency?
- reconciling vocabularies -different agents or services will use different vocabularies, for the same or overlapping concepts. A simple example is the use of miles and kilometres for distance, but other examples will be more subtle or complex.
- varying degrees of detail in queries - at different stages in the trip design process, queries will have differing degrees of specificity. For example, "is it possible to take a train from London to Paris", compared to "when would a train departing Waterloo at around 10:00 on the 27th arrive in Paris?"
- checking solutions for acceptability - testing for basic feasibility, including such constraints as not being in two separate vehicles at the same time
- ranking and critiquing candidate solutions - given that more than one possible solution exists, the user's preferences should be used to rank the solutions. This is likely to be needed incrementally, to control the growth of the search space.
- choosing which constraints to relax during negotiation - even if a good solution is not available with the current constraints, it may be that relaxing some of them will yield an acceptable solution. For example, a three star hotel might have to be used to keep the cost within the client's budget.
- choosing when to ask the client to resolve choices or provide more preference constraints - this involves managing the dialogue with the client to neither require them to 'brain-dump' their entire preference set at the beginning, nor to be barraged with low-level questions.

Not all of these issues are addressed by the use of ontologies, though it would seem that the use of an ontology representation has some impact on the solutions to most of them.

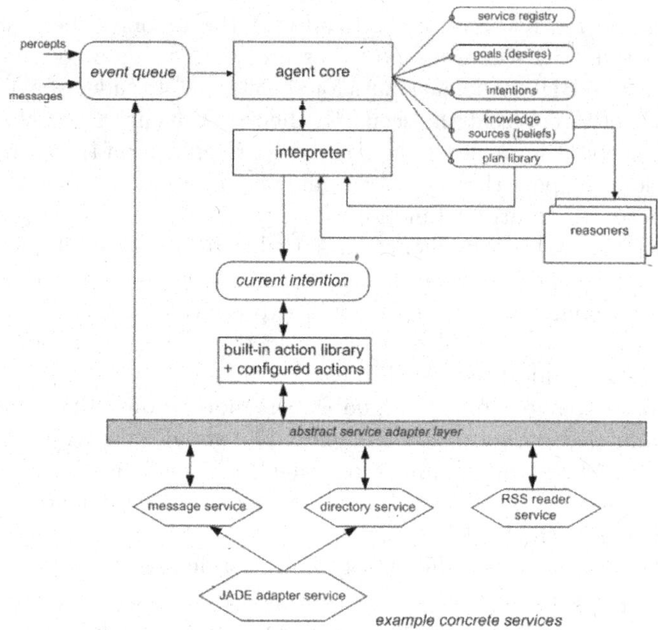

FIGURE 1. Schematic view of Nuin

3. Overview of the Nuin Platform

Nuin ([10], see also http://www.nuin.org) is an agent platform we have created to assist agent designers to program deliberative agents, with a particular emphasis on BDI [19] agents. Nuin is inspired by Rao's AgentSpeak(L) [18], and extended to make a practical, Java-based programming tool. In this section, we briefly introduce some of the key features of Nuin, in order to provide some background for the solution vignettes in section four, below.

A key objective in developing Nuin was to create a flexible platform for building practical agents from high-level abstractions, such as beliefs, desires, intentions and plans. The emphasis has not been on building agent infrastructure services: we assume the existence of an underlying services architecture. Nuin provides a *services abstraction layer* that allows agents to bind to a particular infrastructure service fabric, for example the Jade agent platform [4]. Nuin's architecture is influenced by the FIPA abstract architecture [13], in order to better utilise existing agent infrastructure projects. We do not, however, assume that Nuin will operate only in an FIPA environment.

As Figure 1 shows, each Nuin agent has an interpreter, which runs one or more *scripts* to control the agent's behaviour. An agent has a set of beliefs, as first-order sentences, and any number of other knowledge sources, each of which is labelled by a distinct symbol. A *knowledge store* provides the means of storing logical sentences, whereas a *knowledge source* provides an additional layer of inferencing or query capabilities. Backwards-chaining reasoners attempt to solve queries that they are given. Forwards-chaining reasoners opportunistically assert additional entailments when formulae are asserted or removed into the underlying knowledge store.

The key abstraction from the script language that defines an agent's behaviour is the *plan*. Following AgentSpeak(L), a plan has one or both of: a triggering event condition or a logical postcondition. Internal control flow within the interpreter is managed by a queue of events, which can be exogenous or endogenous, and include messages from other agents as a sub-type. A triggering condition is a Boolean expression formed from two predicates over events: `on( E )` is true when E unifies with the current event at the head of the event queue, whereas **`after( E )`** is true when E unifies with an event from the agent's memory of past events. The body of a plan is a set of individual actions, composed with either a sequence operator (;) or a non-deterministic choice (|). Plans may invoke other sub-plans directly or by post-condition, and may recurse. Currently, a *plan library* is supplied to the agent as part of its configuration. However, there is no a *priori* reason why the plans could not be dynamically generated by an online planner, and this is a capability we would like to explore in the future.

All of the abstractions shown in figure 1 are specified using Java interfaces, and created using the Factory design pattern. This makes it very easy for a programmer to provide a customised variant of a particular part of the system. This flexibility and extensibility was a key design goal for the Nuin platform.

Given that we want to develop agents for the Semantic Web, we allow RDF [24] stores as knowledge sources, using Jena [16]. Jena's ontology reasoners are used to extend the entailments in the RDF stores, where OWL or DAML+OIL sources are available.

3.1. Nuinscript scripting knowledge representation language

Internally, actions, plans and other control objects are represented using Java objects. The interpreter executes actions using the Command design pattern [14]. While these objects could be generated in a variety of different ways, including online planning and machine learning, the principal means today of generating action and plan objects for agents is by parsing agent scripts. The Nuinscript language provides a syntax for expressing high-level agent behaviours, and relating them to the agent's beliefs, desires and intentions.

Nuinscript includes a knowledge representation language, since much of the behaviour of a deliberative agent is taken up with manipulating symbolic knowledge. It is not our intention to provide a single reasoning toolkit that is capable of all or even most reasoning tasks and algorithms. Rather, our aim is to define a notation that covers a broad range of logical formalisms, so that Nuin agents can receive knowledge as logical sentences, and then invoke the appropriate reasoning services according to their configuration.

The Nuinscript KR language has as its base a language of concrete values. These include scalar values, such as integers, strings and real numbers, symbols, functional terms (consisting of a symbol functor and zero or more arguments), lists and single-assignment variables. Following standard Semantic Web practice, all symbolic constants are URI's [5]. A functional term expresses a relationship over some fixed set of positional parameters:

```
ex:person( ex:ian, ex:dickinson, <mailto:ian.dickinson@hp.com> ).
```

FIGURE 2. Term with fixed parameters

Such positional arguments are often useful, but, equally, they can be limiting. Nuin also allows terms to have named parameters as well as fixed parameters:

```
ex:person() { ex:firstName = ex:ian,
              ex:lastName = ex:dickinson,
              ex:email = <mailto:ian.dickinson@hp.com> }
```

FIGURE 3. Term with named parameters

These structures are particularly suited to agent messages, where the terms in any given message may vary from interaction to interaction, even with the same interlocutor. Unification is extended in the obvious way to cover named parameter terms.

The logical sentence language contains predicates, whose arguments are taken from the language of concrete values. Other sentence constructors are: conjunction, disjunction, negation, universal and existential quantifiers, material implication and modal operators. In addition, a class of *reference expressions* are introduced to encode the corresponding terms `FIPA SL: iota`, `some` and `all`. Iota, for example, denotes "the unique x such that some given predicate is true of x".

Finally, note that sometimes the strict layering of sentences and values is too rigid. Specifically, an incoming message from some other agent is a value (e.g. a string or other concrete datatype). However, the *content* of the message is typically a logical sentence. We introduce the operator `sentence` which *reifies* a given sentence as a value. Thus `sentence( p(x) )` is the value whose interpretation is the predicate `sentence p(x)`. This reified sentence can then be used as a component of some other composite value, such as a message term.

3.2. Nuinscript plan language

Space does not permit a detailed exposition of the Nuinscript plan language here. Suffice to say that the principal unit of behaviour abstraction in Nuinscript is the *plan*. When a plan becomes active, for example by being triggered by some pattern of events, it forms an *intention-to* perform the plan. The intentions are controlled and scheduled by the interpreter. A plan may be simultaneously active in multiple intentions. For example, the `go_to` plan may be active with the parameter Milan, forming an intention to go to Milan, and also with the parameter Paris forming a separate intention to go to that city. The agent would then have to schedule resources so that both intentions can be discharged without conflict. Suppose the agent is a dedicated follower of new fashions, and will travel to any city that has a fashion show. We can express this as follows:

```
plan
   on event fashion:newFashionShow( ?location )
  do
   intend go_to( ?location )
end.
```

FIGURE 4. illustrative plan

In general, the *plan body*, which follows the do keyword, consists of an action expression in which individual actions (such as adopting another named plan as an intention) are composed with binary operators seq (expressed in Nuinscript syntax as the semi-colon, ;) and `alt` (the pipe symbol, |).

4. Solution Examples using Nuin

4.1. Preamble: use of ontologies

In the challenge problem description, a sample ontology for this domain is provided by Corcho et al [8]. We decided to create our own ontology, although it shares some characteristics with that of Corcho and colleagues. Our ontology is written in OWL [9], which allows us to use richer constructs than that in the sample ontology. For example, figure 8 shows a 5-star hotel in our formulation:

Compare this with the definition from the sample ontology (slightly abbreviated):

RDFS is not expressive enough to declare that quality ratings may have exactly one of one, two, three, four or five as values. Nor is it possible to infer in RDFS that having a five-star rating and being a hotel *entails* being in the class FiveStarHotel. In the sample RDFS ontology, membership of this class must be stated explicitly. Finally, we note that the RDFS ontology requires class hotel5star to be treated as an instance, since the class itself is the subject of the statement `'numberOfStars 5'`. Were this pattern to be retained in the OWL ontology, the use of classes as instances necessarily places the ontology in the OWL Full variant

```
<owl:Class rdf:ID="QualityRating">
 <owl:oneOf rdf:parseType="daml:collection">
  <travel1:QualityRating rdf:about="#OneStar"/>
  <travel1:QualityRating rdf:about="#TwoStars"/>
  <travel1:QualityRating rdf:about="#ThreeStars"/>
  <travel1:QualityRating rdf:about="#FourStars"/>
  <travel1:QualityRating rdf:about="#FiveStars"/>
 </owl:oneOf>
</owl:Class>

<owl:Class rdf:ID="FiveStarHotel">
 <rdfs:subClassOf rdf:resource="#Hotel"/>
 <rdfs:subClassOf>
  <owl:Restriction>
   <owl:onProperty rdf:resource="#rating"/>
   <owl:hasValue rdf:resource="#FiveStars"/>
  </owl:Restriction>
 </rdfs:subClassOf>
</owl:Class>
```

FIGURE 5. OWL ontology fragment

```
<rdfs:Class rdf:ID="hotel5star">
 <rdfs:comment>First class hotel</rdfs:comment>
 <rdfs:subClassOf rdf:ID="#hotel" />
 <NSO:numberOfStars>5</NSO:numberOfStars>
</rdfs:Class>
```

FIGURE 6. RDFS fragment from OAS'03 call for papers

of OWL[1] , for which it is known that inferencing is expensive and incomplete. Note that we have chosen not to use cardinality restrictions to define hotel star-classes. Consider the following definition:

Figure 7 suggests that the Quite-Nice hotel is a four star hotel, but we cannot know this for certain. At issue is the *open world assumption* of the semantic web:

[1]The Web Ontology Language (OWL) [9] has three distinct language profiles: Lite, DL, and Full. OWL DL has compromises and constraints on the expressiveness of the language to ensure that the drawing entailments is known to be complete and decidable. OWL Lite is designed to be even less expressive than OWL DL, and correspondingly easier to process. There is no known complete, tractable reasoning procedure for the whole of OWL Full.

```
<owl:Class rdf:ID="FourStarHotel">
 <rdfs:subClassOf rdf:resource="#Hotel" />
 <rdfs:subClassOf>
  <owl:Restriction>
   <owl:onProperty rdf:resource="#hasStar" />
   <owl:cardinality rdf:value="4" rdf:datatype="&xsd;integer"/>
  </owl:Restriction>
 </rdfs:subClassOf>
</owl:Class>

<Hotel rdf:about="http://quite-nice.com">
 <hasStar rdf:value="*" />
 <hasStar rdf:value="*" />
 <hasStar rdf:value="*" />
 <hasStar rdf:value="*" />
</Hotel>
```

FIGURE 7. Using cardinality restrictions to define hotel classes

we cannot assume that we have yet collected all of the relevant information about a resource[2] . We may yet discover an additional hasStar statement, making the hotel a five star hotel. Given the information in Figure 7, we are strictly only entitled to infer that the Quite-Nice hotel is not three stars or less. In general, the open-world basis of the semantic web is a departure from traditional ontology applications, and may bring a number of subtle problems to agents processing semantic web information sources.

Space does not permit a full explanation of our experimental OAS ontology in this paper. Elements of the ontology will be introduced below as needed. Figure 8 shows a fragment of our ontology class hierarchy (displayed in SWOOP [17]):

4.2. Initial client to agent communication

At the beginning of the travel booking process, the client's basic goal to take a trip must be communicated to the agent. We leave aside the machinery of the human-computer interface (important though it is), to consider the overall process. The agent must have access to two kinds of knowledge:

- the primary goal that initiated the travel request, and
- the client's travel preferences

We assume that a message is delivered to the agent with the first of these, and that the second can be queried from a general database of known preferences. Since

[2]Resource is the general term denoting a subject about which statements may be made in the semantic web.

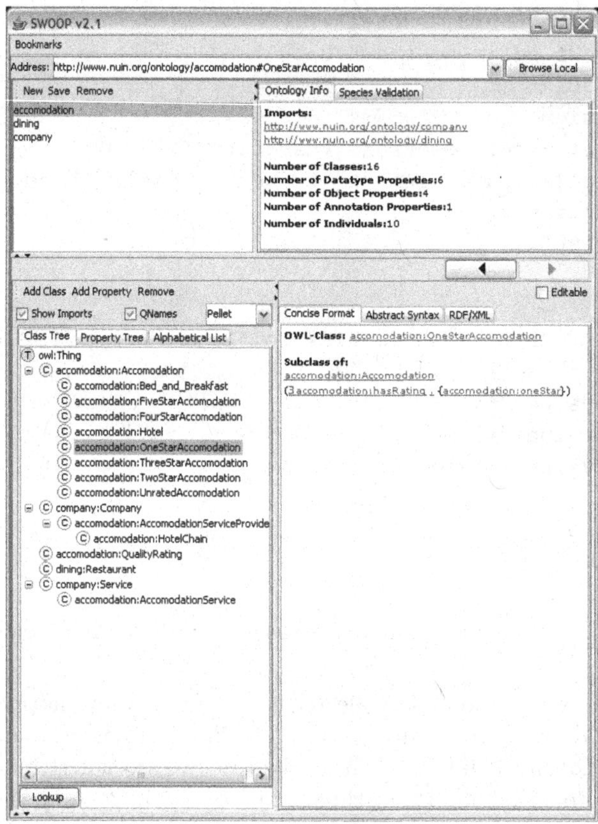

FIGURE 8. Fragment of class hierarchy displayed in SWOOP

we are interested in Semantic Web agents, we assume that the client preference information is available in at least RDF (if not OWL).

What should the initial message contain? An important choice is whether the agent is seen as a collaborative partner, or a subordinate. In the second case, the message might be a FIPA request message, which takes an action as parameter. The action is essentially an encoding of "book a trip respecting these constraints". The agent would directly adopt an intention to carry out the action. The first case would correspond to sending a FIPA `inform` message[3] saying "the client has a goal to go on a trip, with these constraints". We would then rely on the agent being programmed with social or behavioural rules that would translate this recognition of the user's goal into an intent of its own to assist with the development of the travel plan. For the scenario of a single client arriving at the

[3]Note that the FIPA ACL specification [12] does not include a performative that directly delegates a goal to another agent.

travel agency's office seeking to make a booking, the difference between the *inform* and *request* approaches (which we label *collaborative* and *directive* respectively) is slim. Indeed, the collaborative approach adds extra complexity that the directive approach avoids. However, consider the frequently mooted desire for *proactive* agents (such as the agents in [6]). The recognition of the user's goal may arise by many means, not only by a directive from the user. If the agent is able to infer that the user has a goal to make a trip (e.g. by having a paper accepted at a conference), it can proactively instigate the travel planning process in a collaborative style. Note there are two distinct sets of goals being discussed: the user's goal to travel, and the agent's goal to assist the user to make booking. These are not same.

We would argue that only the collaborative approach really makes use of the agent-nature of the travel-agency. The directive approach could be straightforwardly implemented with *web services* [25], an increasingly popular architecture. Unless an application architecture is intended to exploit the unique features of software agents, it is unclear why software designers should pick agents, with their additional complexity and relative immaturity, as the implementation method.

Both the collaborative and directive approaches can be modelled by Nuin. Figure 9 shows a plan fragment that reacts to an incoming message that the user has a goal to make a booking, and creates a suitable intent.

```
plan
 on message()
    {acl:performative = acl:inform,
     acl:content = D (?user) bookTrip( ?tripID ),
     acl:sender = ?user
    }
 do
   holds cooperateWith( ?user ) ;
   achieve satisfactory( trip( ?t ), ?tripID, ?user )
end.
```

FIGURE 9. plan to adopt user goal as agent intention

Thus: if a message is received informing the agent that the user has a goal to make a given trip, and the agent believes it should be cooperative with that user (it may, of course, be predisposed to be generally cooperative), then adopt an intention to achieve a satisfactory proposal for a `trip ?t`, respecting the constraints the user has attached to the trip (identified by trip ID).

Figure 9 introduces a subtle question about the representation of the user's goal. Since this is quite a central issue, we consider it in detail below.

4.2.1. Representation of user goals. In the example above, we expressed the user's goal with the sentence $\mathtt{D}_{user}$ `bookTrip(?t)`, making use of the modal operator D expressing an actor's desire. The predicate `bookTrip` is assumed to be drawn from a shared ontology, so that the basic meaning is shared. It corresponds to an utterance by the user, upon arriving in the travel agency, that "I would like to make a booking". However, the user may just as well have said "I would like to book a trip to Paris", or "I would like to book a trip to Paris and then Milan", or even "I would like to go somewhere sunny for a holiday in July". Two things are clear: an effective solution will allow significant flexibility in the representation of the initial user goal, and the initial goal is only partially expressed. All of the given goals are under-constrained, and thus have many potential solutions. The agent must collaborate with the user to refine the constraints until a satisfactory solution is determined.

One way to refine the goal would be to add additional conjuncts to the goal itself. So, after giving some additional information, the goal might be refined to:

$$D_{user} bookTrip(?t) \wedge destintation(?t, Paris) \wedge departure(?t, ?tDep) \wedge during(?tDep, July)$$

Thus: the user has a goal to take a trip whose destination is Paris and which departs in July. This formulation would work, although it would quickly become unwieldy for complex trip planning. It could also be argued that the user's actual goal remains to book a trip, and that the additional clauses are simply additional information that is known about the trip. This suggests an alternative formulation, in which the top level goal sentence remains $\mathtt{D}_{user}$ `bookTrip(?t)`, but the agent's knowledge base is augmented with assertions about the object identified by the symbol (i.e. URI) `?t`. In particular, a convenient way to express this additional knowledge is to `treat ?t` as an OWL class definition, expressing the condition that `?t` denotes the class of all possible trips that satisfy the user's goals and preferences. For example:

```
Duser bookTrip(?t).
rdfs:subClassOf( ?t, travel:trip ).
rdfs:subClassOf ( ?t, owl:restriction( travel:destination, owl:hasValue(
Paris ) ) ).
```

In this formulation, additional class axioms are added to the KB as more is learned about the user's detailed requirements. A description logic reasoner can then be used to test whether a given proposal matches the user's needs. The reasoner can also be used to detect unsatisfiable goals, as the class expression will be equivalent to $\perp$. A further advantage from using an ontological approach to encoding the user's goals is that it may allow certain useful kinds of generalisation, for example that a destination of the Sheraton Hotel (location Paris) entails that Paris itself is a destination. One technique we would like to apply would be to test the goal description against the current solution, and identify constraints that need to be satisfied. This is not straightforward, however, thanks to the open world assumption (see above). Suppose, for example, that a proposed solution S does not contain statements about the itinerary of the trip, and that the goal G states that the destination is Paris. We would like to test whether G subsumes S, and if not, what needs to be added or removed from S. But in an open world, S plus some as-yet undiscovered information is subsumed by G, so no inconsistency is detected.

We are still evaluating this approach. Some problems are apparent: OWL does not have a means of expressing temporal constraints (e.g. the user departs sometime during July), and the combination of the different representation styles mandates the use of a relatively complex set of specialised reasoning services by the agent.

4.3. Interactions with suppliers

The travel agency's agent does not handle provisioning of the various elements of the trip itself. It will therefore need to communicate with the various suppliers in order to decide on flights, rail journeys, hotels and so on. It could be the case that the interface to each supplier is a web service, and the agent's job would then be to invoke the web service by fashioning a suitable SOAP [23] call, or whatever the appropriate mechanism is for that service. This can be accommodated in Nuin by either designing a custom web-service action that gets invoked from the script, or by registering a Java object binding that gets invoked by the built-in invoke service action. However, for the purpose of this exercise, we assume that the suppliers are also agent-based, and that collaboration becomes a problem of inter-agent communication. First we note that a similar problem arises between agents as between the client and the travel agency agent. Should the agents invoke actions on the other agents, or delegate an intention or goal? One determining factor may be the need to build a coherent and optimal solution according to the client's preferences. The travel agency agent could determine which of the customer's preferences were relevant to a given subgoal, and pass these to the supplier agent. Indeed, if the client's preferences are available as a Semantic Web source, then (ignoring the important details of security and privacy) the supplier agents could access the client's preferences directly. The potential difficulty here, though, is building a globally optimal solution. Having each supplier agent construct an optimal segment of the journey does not guarantee that the overall solution is optimal. It may well be possible to use inter-agent negotiations among the whole community of stakeholder agents to build a globally optimal solution, but that is not the focus of our current research. Therefore we assume that the travel agency agent sends queries to the supplier agents, and assembles the solution pieces into an overall trip proposal. All negotiations are then pair-wise, with one of the parties always being the travel agency agent. The travel agency agent is solely responsible for optimising the solution.

The FIPA `query-ref` performative seems appropriate for the task of seeking solution elements from the suppliers. But what should the content of the message be? At the beginning of the process, we may know that John wants to travel from Madrid to Washington. We could query all known transportation services providers for routes that originate in Madrid. This, however, would generate many air-routes from Madrid, including those taking John away from the USA, plus road and train journeys to France and Portugal. We could ask for routes starting in Madrid and terminating in Washington DC, which would allow airlines to report their suggested routes (via Paris Charles de Gaulle, for example). Another tactic would be to use the geographic elements of the ontology to test whether a supplier is able to provide a single journey to a given region (e.g. Madrid to the Eastern USA) and use this to prune the search space by querying in more detail only those agents that can provide suitable routes in principle. This tactic may be invoked directly from the agent's script; it may also be invoked by the agent monitoring the responses to queries, noticing a high branching factor in the search space, and adopting an improved strategy. The current version of Nuin does not support this meta-monitoring directly. We will investigate convenient mechanisms for doing so in future versions.

The FIPA communication primitives are not always suitable to our purposes. For example, if an agent was known to be able to process Semantic Web queries, it would be natural to query for certain kinds of data using an RDQL query [21]. Such a query, however, does not strictly fit the given semantics for FIPA's `query-if` or `query-ref` performatives.

We make the distinction in our ontology between journeys, routes and bookings. Initially, we query the supplier agent for information on routes. A route has a start and end location, distance and vehicle. A given instance of a route may start at Madrid airport and end in Paris Charles de Gaulle, and use an Airbus A320. We can infer that an A320 is an `AirbusPlane` which is an `Airplane`, thus this trip is also in the class AirTravel because `AirTravel` is defined as the class that has `vehicleType` of class Airplane.

This distinction highlights a specific difficulty with ontology development: when to uses classes vs. instances. We can define A320 as an instance of the class `AirbusPlane`, and for many applications it is sufficient to know that a given route uses an (i.e. some unknown) A320. But for other applications, such as aircraft maintenance or scheduling, we need to be able to identify individual instances of the aircraft, which implies that A320 should be a class, and instances of it would be named by the individual aircraft identifiers. However for defining a route, naming the individual plane is incorrect, since different actual planes will fly the route on different days. Using OWL, we can define an auxiliary Route subclass using a restriction:

For any A320Route, it is easy to see that the transporting vehicle is an Airbus A320, even if we don't know which individual plane. However, this may make it difficult to answer the question "how many upper-deck seats are there on that route?". It remains an open question, therefore, whether the extra complexity introduced by this style of definition is worthwhile, or whether we should have multiple ontologies (e.g. one for travel and one for maintenance) and a process that would translate between them when necessary.

```
<owl:Class rdf:ID="A320Route">
 <rdfs:subClassOf rdf:resource="#Route" />
 <rdfs:subClassOf>
  <owl:Restriction>
   <owl:onProperty rdf:resource="#vehicleType"/>
   <owl:allValuesFrom rdf:resource="#AirbusA320" />
  </owl:Restriction>
 </owl:subClassOf>
</owl:Class>
```

FIGURE 10. class description for routes that fly A320's

In Nuin, we implement the process of sending the `query-ref` as a `message send` action, followed by a `suspend` until the reply is received. This works for a single communication with another agent. If, however, there are multiple agents involved, a better alternative would be to send a series of messages out, and have plans that trigger on the incoming reply messages. There are two difficulties with the second approach: firstly, enough state has to be asserted into the agent's beliefs (or other KS) to allow the agent to continue developing the plan from that point, and secondly it is harder for the agent to monitor a lack of response from the remote agents and adapt accordingly. We solve the first by assigning each partial trip its own unique identifier, and use the `reply-with` field to relate incoming answers to the results of previous planning. This then generates a set of new, extended partial plans that get new identifiers. For the second problem we do not have a convenient solution.

A possible future extension to the Nuin platform will be to include first-class support for the FIPA interaction protocols [2]. We hope that a clear and practical solution to the meta-monitoring problem will emerge, either directly as a result of supporting interaction protocols, or as a result of implementing the necessary supporting code. Note that, in our opinion, it remains an open question as to whether the ability of PRS-based agent architectures to recurse to meta-level planning is a viable solution to this problem (without creating enough complexity in the agent plan to make it difficult to perform software design and maintenance).

4.4. Reconciling vocabularies

In general, determining the correspondences between two (or more) ontologies is a very difficult task, requiring extensive human intervention [?]. Once the mapping between two ontologies is defined, it is possible that translations between a value expressed in one ontology and a value expressed in another can be automated. Some transformations are fairly straightforward, such as the units conversion (e.g. from km to miles and vice versa).

In a multi-agent system, it is unclear whose responsibility it is to do ontology conversion. One possibility is for each agent to have a normal form that it uses for its own knowledge representation. Each received sentence would then normalised, using the information from ontology mappings where necessary. This would cope well with allowing communications from agents that used different measurement units, for example, providing that the units themselves are explicit in the ontology. An alternative is that the ontology used by the receiving agent is advertised in a public directory, and it is the originating agent's responsibility to do any necessary translations before sending a sentence as part of a message. A further alternative is an intermediate position between these two, where the agent community includes translator agents that can handle two-way translations between agents using different ontologies. A version of the intermediary architecture may be needed when providing large semantic web or other legacy information sources into the agent community. It is often impractical to translate the entire information source to a different ontology, but it may well be possible to wrap the information source with a mediating agent that dynamically performs the necessary ontology-based transformations on queries and results. We used this strategy effectively in a project that used DMOZ [1] information in a distributed knowledge-sharing application [3]. Rather than convert the very large DMOZ data set to RDF, it was stored in a custom database layout and queries and query results were dynamically translated to RDF as needed.

Using Nuin, we can define a plan that triggers when incoming messages are received, and use this to check that the message content is in a suitable ontology. If not, it may be a simple action to do the translation locally if the agent is capable of doing so, or the agent may adopt an intention to translate the message content to a suitable ontology. This intention may then be discharged in different ways, for example by sending a request to the translator agent. Once the message is expressed in a known ontology, an event is raised to trigger further processing on the message content. Note that, in the FIPA ACL message specification, the :ontology parameter is not particularly helpful in solving this problem. In practice, once a Semantic Web agent starts processing information from multiple sources, it is highly likely that a given message will contain terms drawn from many different ontologies. To some extent the original need for the :ontology parameter - which essentially introduces a dictionary to disambiguate identical symbols that are intended to have different meanings - is obviated by the use of URI symbols as constants. Each URI is already declared within its own namespace.

Our current experiments with the Challenge Problem make the simplifying assumption that the global ontology is shared. This assumption is only valid for such a self-contained exercise. Any realistic scale of application, especially one that uses open semantic web information sources, will be exposed to the ontology reconciliation problem.

4.5. Critiquing and ranking solutions

As the travel agency agent begins to assemble solutions to the client's requested travel goal, it will be faced with a rapidly expanding search space. In order to improve its chances of success, it should choose to pursue only those partial solutions that are promising. If the agent waits until solutions (i.e. travel plans) are complete to critique them, it is likely still to be processing long after the client's patience has run out and they have left the store. The agent must be able to critique partial solutions to the problem, and select which ones will be further expanded. We note that planning algorithms have been studied extensively for many years in AI, and it is not our intent in this short paper to revisit the many choices that a planning system can adopt to be able to plan effectively [22]. Pending deeper investigation of this topic, our current design uses a simple forward-chaining means-end search algorithm. As mentioned above, we assign each partial solution a unique identifier. A solution is a series of segments, each of which is either a journey segment or an accommodation segment. The journey segment identifies the route, and may be composed of a series of individual journeys. A segment has an associated cost.

Reviewing the Challenge Problem text, we hypothesise that the following represent typical preferences a client may have over journey segments:

- type vehicle (e.g. Airbus A370)
- cost
- quality rating (first class, business class, economy, five star, etc)
- existence of facilities (TV, Internet connection, smoking rooms, pool)
- preference of mode of transport (fly vs. drive) - which may be conditional on other factors, such as accessibility of airport
- distance to local amenities (sightseeing, ski, beach, etc)

Some of these preferences will be fixed, some context dependent. On a business trip, customers might be less cost-sensitive than on a personal vacation (or vice versa!). In summer, proximity to ski resorts is probably less important than proximity to the beach.

We would like to explore making this preference information as widely available as possible, so encoding it as a semantic web resource seems plausible (we ignore for the time being important requirements to do with security and privacy).

One natural approach is to consider the various categories of alternatives that the client might prefer as ontological classes. Thus, a customer who prefers non-smoking hotel rooms has a preference for a room in the class NonSmoking over class Smoking. A simple way to encode this in the client's profile is shown in fig 9:

```
<user:Preference>
  <user:prefer rdf:resource="#NonSmoking" />
  <user:over rdf:resource="#Smoking" />
</user:Preference>
```

FIGURE 11. First attempt at encoding user preferences

```
<user:Preference>
  <user:prefer>
    <NonSmoking />
  </user:prefer>
  <user:over>
    <Smoking />
  </user:over>
</user:Preference>
```

FIGURE 12. Alternative encoding for user preferences

This example uses classes as individuals, so again, exceeds the limitations of OWL DL and OWL Lite. An alternative approach would be to treat the preference arguments as expressions, using RDF blank nodes (bNodes) as existential variables (an interpretation sanctioned by RDF theory [15]). This transforms the preference from Figure 11 into Figure 12.

The difference between these approaches may be subtle to readers unfamiliar with RDF. In the first encoding (Figure 4.5), the arguments to the preference relation are the classes themselves. In the second encoding, the term `<NonSmoking />` is RDF shorthand for:

```
<rdf:Description>
  <rdf:type rdf:ID="NonSmoking" />
</rdf:Description>
```

that is, an anonymous node of type `NonSmoking`. To use this second encoding, the agent must match the existential query implicit in the graph to the data at hand. This exploits a feature of RDF that meta-level information can be encoded in the same formalism as the object-level information. The preference query can be seen as expressing a predicate over the proposed solution classes, but is encoded in the same graph structure as the data itself.

By using pair-wise preferences of this kind, whichever approach is adopted, we obtain a partial ordering over sets of solutions. The reified `user:Preference` relationship is transitive, so a data source aware of this fact could pre-compute the transitive closure of preferences. Thus, if the client stated their preference was for 5-star hotels over 4-star, and 4-star over 3-star, the transitive closure would allow two proposed segments, one for a 5-star hotel and one for a 3-star hotel to be ranked correctly. Since the ordering would be partial, however, not all solutions could be ranked, so the solution evaluator would need to allow for sets of equally preferred candidates at any one time.

The client should be able to order their preferences, so that the preference for a certain cost band is allowed to dominate over the preference for smoking rooms, or vice versa. This could be achieved by adding a weight to the each `Preference` instance, or allowing preferences that ranked other preferences recursively. It is not clear which, if either, of these choices would work better in practice, and more experimentation is needed.

Again, speculating about the design (we have not yet implemented the solution ranking mechanism), we could encode context-dependent preferences by adding a condition clause to the `user:Preference` instance. The problem we here is that there is, at the time of writing[4] , no standard mechanism for encoding general predicates in RDF. Thus any mechanism that allowed the encoding of "if summer-time" on a preference of `NearBeach` over `NearSkiRun` would be dependent on a processor being aware of the encoding scheme used. The choices presented above, assuming that the existence of `Preference` is recognised, stay closer to standard RDF interpretations.

Given that we can achieve a satisfactory encoding of user preferences, we must then incorporate them into the strategy for prioritising the search space. We envisage a plan that is triggered by the asserting of a partial solution into the agent's beliefs KS, and which would rank the new solution against the current unexpanded partial solutions. Thus each partial solution is in one of two states: either it has been selected for expansion, or it has not been expanded yet, but is sorted according to the partial order defined by the user's preferences. It would only be necessary to find the highest ranked plan that has not yet been expanded that is preferred over the new solution, so searching from the front of the candidates list will be effective.

A more general question, and one that we have not yet addressed, is to be able to critique full and partial solutions, rather than just rank them. For example, if the agent was able to determine that a client could save a substantial amount of money by accepting a certain hotel that meets all criteria except having in-room Internet connections, it may be able to propose this to the user. Alternatively, such deductions might form the basis for negotiation strategies that suggest which factors to yield on, and which to stand firm on. This seems to be a fruitful area for future investigation.

5. Evaluation and conclusions

We have presented some vignettes of parts of the solution to the OAS'03 Challenge Problem using our BDI agent platform, Nuin. The key goal in the Challenge call for papers is to explore how agents would actually use ontological information. Much of the foregoing discussion represents our design explorations, since we have not yet built the complete solution.

Our agents are strongly knowledge-based, and use logical sentences and mental attitudes for their internal modelling. Ontological information is clearly useful

[4]However, there are various proposals for rule-languages to extend the extant semantic web languages. It is possible that, once mature, these rule languages will suffice for the preference ordering problem.

for compactly describing the domain of discourse (especially if the ontologies are shared with other agents), and allows the agent to use class and property hierarchies to generalise and specialise queries and results.
Given our interest in building agents for the semantic web, we have restricted ourselves to the common semantic web ontology languages, particularly OWL. These languages' designs are based on description logic (DL) reasoning. The use of description logic reasoners in practical agent applications is not a widely explored topic, due in part to a limited availability of DL reasoners. More such reasoners are now becoming available[5], and we can expect more research into this area in future. A key component of the description logic approach is *class description*, and we have shown above some instances of using class descriptions in the agent's reasoning. Using class descriptions and a meta-level prefers predicate to encapsulate the client's preferences appears to be a useful way to make those preferences available to a wider range of semantic web services. The limitations of description logic sentences, however, suggest that richer representations will need to be developed to encode a broadly useful sub-set of the client's general preferences.

While we have shown the use of ontology information by BDI agents, both as additional open knowledge sources for the agent to access, and as additional entailments that the agent reasoners can draw upon, we nevertheless feel that this is only a preliminary account of the integration of these two areas. Further practical experiences will help to resolve this, and we continue to develop a complete implementation of the Challenge Problem in the Nuin framework. We also look forward to the development of theoretical treatments of the interactions between the principles of deliberative agents and the principles of description logics.

References

[1] *ODP - The Open Directory Project.* http://www.dmoz.org

[2] *FIPA Interaction Protocol Specifications.* 2003. http://www.fipa.org/repository/ips.php3

[3] Dave Banks, Steve Cayzer, Ian Dickinson, and Dave Reynolds. *The ePerson Snippet Manager: a Semantic Web Application.* (HPL-2002-328) HP Labs Technical Report. 2002. http://www.hpl.hp.com/techreports/2002/HPL-2002-328.html

[4] F. Bellifemine, A. Poggi and G. Rimassa . Developing Multi Agent Systems With a FIPA-Compliant Agent Framework. *Software Practice and Experience.* Vol. 31:2. 2001. pp. 103-128.

[5] T. Berners-Lee, R. Fielding and L. Masinter. *Uniform Resource Identifiers (URI): Generic Syntax.* (RFC2396) Internet Draft Standard. 1998.

[6] Tim Berners-Lee, James Hendler and Ora Lassila *The Semantic Web.* Scientific American. 2001.

[5] At the time of writing, an extension to Jena to allow it to interact with description logic reasoners via a DIG interface has just been released. We will be incorporating access to DIG reasoners into Nuin shortly.

[7] K. Binmore, A. Kirman and P. Tani. (eds).*Frontiers of Game Theory.*MIT Press, 1994.

[8] O. Corcho, M. Fernandez-Lopez and A. Gómez-Pérez *An RDF Schema for the OAS Challenge Problem.* 2003. http://oas.otago.ac.nz/OAS2003/Challenge/MadridTravelOntology.rdfs

[9] M. Dean, G. Schreiber, F. van Harmelen, J. Hendler, I. Horrocks, D. McGuinness, L. Patel-Schneider, F. Peter and S. Lynn Andrea. *OWL Web Ontology Language Reference.* 2003. http://www.w3.org/TR/owl-ref

[10] I. Dickinson and M. Wooldridge. Towards Practical Reasoning Agents for the Semantic Web. In *Conf. on Automomous Agents and Multi-Agent Systems (AAMAS'03).* 2003.

[11] DMQ) D. Dou, D. McDermott, P. Qi. Ontology Translation by Ontology Merging and Automated Reasoning. In *Proc. EKAW Workshop on Ontologies for Agent Systems.* 2002. pp. 3-18. http://cs-www.cs.yale.edu/homes/dvm/papers/DouMcDermottQi02.ps

[12] FIPA. *FIPA ACL Message Structure Specification.* (XC00061) 2000.

[13] FIPA. *Abstract Architecture Specifiation.* 2002. http://www.fipa.org/specs/fipa00001

[14] E. Gamma, R. Helm, R. Johnson and J. Vlissides. *Design Patterns.* Addison Wesley Longhttp://www.fipa.org/specs/fipa00061 man, 1994.

[15] P. Hayes. *RDF Semantics.* 2004. http://www.w3.org/TR/rdf-mt

[16] HP Labs. *The Jena Semantic Web Toolkit.* 2004. http://jena.sourceforge.net

[17] A. Kalyanpur. *SWOOP (Semantic Web Ontology Overview and Perusal).* 2004. http://www.mindswap.org/2004/SWOOP

[18] A. Rao AgentSpeak(L): BDI Agents Speak Out in a Logical Computable Language. In *Proc. 7th European Workshop on Modelling Autonomous Agents in a Multi-Agent World (MAAMAW '96).* Springer-Verlag, 1996. pp. 42-55.

[19] A. Rao and M. Georgeff. BDI Agents: From Theory to Practice. In *Proc. First Int. Conf on Multi-Agent Systems (ICMAS-95).* 1995.

[20] SJ. Russell, P. Norvig. *Artificial Intelligence: a Modern Approach.* (second edition) ed. Prentice Hall, 2003.

[21] A. Seaborne. *RDQL - a query language for RDF.* 2004. http://www.w3.org/Submission/2004/SUBM-RDQL-20040109

[22] P. Traverso. *Automated Planning : Theory & Practice.* Morgan-Kaufmann, 2004.

[23] W3C. *Simple Object Access Protocol (SOAP). 1.1.* 2000. http://www.w3.org/TR/SOAP

[24] World Wide Web Consortium (W3C). *The Resource Description Framework (RDF).* 2004. http://www.w3.org/RDF

[25] World Wide Web Consortium (W3C). *Web Services Activity.* 2004. http://www.w3.org/2002/ws

Ian Dickinson
Hewlett-Packard Laboratories
Filton Road, Stoke Gifford Bristol
BS34 8QZ U.K.
Tel: +44 (117) 312 8796
Fax: +44 (117) 312 8924
e-mail: ian.dickinson@hp.com

Michael Wooldridge
Department of Computer Science
University of Liverpool
Liverpool L69 7ZF
U.K.
e-mail: m.j.wooldridge@csc.liv.ac.uk

Location-Mediated Agent Coordination in Ubiquitous Computing

Akio Sashima, Noriaki Izumi and Koichi Kurumatani

Abstract. A fundamental issue of Ubiquitous computing concerns the coordination gaps separating devices, services, and humans. Numerous heterogeneous devices, various information services, and users have different intentions and are physically located in environments, how can we coordinate the services and devices to assist a particular user in receiving a particular service so as to maximize the user's satisfaction? We propose an agent-based coordination framework for ubiquitous computing to solve this human-centered service coordination issue. It is called location-mediated coordination. This paper explains some coordination gaps in ubiquitous computing. It describes a conceptual framework of the location-mediated agent coordination and its implementation, context-aware information assistant systems in museums.

Mathematics Subject Classification (2000). Primary 68T35; Secondary 68U35.
Keywords. Web agents, semantic web, ubiquitous computing, service coordination.

1. Introduction

Recently, computing frameworks that specialize in handling real world information and physical objects, such as Ubiquitous computing [1], have received much interest in both research and application.

Although ubiquitous computing is a promising framework for intelligent services like context-aware information assistance, many research issues remain. A fundamental issue is coordination of devices, services, and users. Numerous heterogeneous devices (e.g., terminals, RF-IDs, cameras, information appliances, etc.), various information services that use those devices (e.g., navigation aids, guides, information retrievals, controlling devices, etc.), and users who have different intentions are physically located in a ubiquitous computing environment. In such a situation, how can we coordinate services and devices to assist a particular user in receiving a particular service and thereby maximize the user's satisfaction? In other words, how can we dynamically coordinate the physically distributed heterogeneous services and devices and integrate them into a consistent human-centered service according to a user's intention?

This study specifically addresses the Semantic Web[2] to solve this human-centered coordination issue in ubiquitous computing. The research goal of the Semantic Web is to establish a methodology to manage that rich diversity of web content that have proliferated on the Internet by adding "meta-data" of web content. Those meta-data are Resource Description Framework (RDF) [3] and RDF Schema (RDFS) [4]. Meta-data have well-defined meanings based on the ontology. For that reason, "Semantic Web Agents", which are autonomous computer programs that read the meta-data, can use meta-data to understand logical meanings of web content. Semantic web agents choose proper content out of myriad contents on the Internet on behalf of users. They also coordinate the contents for users and assist them in accessing the content.

Inspired by this semantic web agent capability, we have developed an agent-based service coordination framework in ubiquitous computing, called location-mediated agent coordination. In such coordination, agents coordinate services, users and devices in a ubiquitous computing environment based on their locations and meta-information, which are described by RDF. This framework is an attempt to realize semantic web agents that choose proper resources from numerous resources, coordinate those resources on behalf of users, and assist users in accessing resources of ubiquitous computing environments.

This paper describes some research issues realizing the human-centered service coordination in ubiquitous computing, namely intention gaps and representation gaps. We describe the idea of location-mediated agent coordination to solve these issues.

2. Coordination Gaps in Ubiquitous Computing

2.1. Intention Gaps between Services, Devices and Humans

Services should be selected and composed according not only to the service provider's assumption, but also the user's intention. Thereby, we can realize human-centered service coordination on behalf of users.

Service selection is easy if the provided services are few and the users clearly recognize their own intentions. However, user selection of a service that matches an intention from among myriad information services (e.g., navigation, guide, information retrieval, controlling device, etc.) becomes difficult when those services are physically co-located.

In addition, an isolated service cannot satisfy the intention. In such a case, combining two isolated services might fit a user's intention. For example, combination with a schedule service of a theater and car navigation systems can satisfy the user's request, as in: Take me – *I'd like to go to see "Kill Bill" tonight.* Such combinatory processes may require device functionality and services beyond the designer's assumption because they are designed to perform a certain task presumed by the designer.

Such gaps are "*Intention gaps*" for the purposes of this study.

2.2. Representation Gaps between Services, Devices and Humans

Recently, many localization-devices, such as GPS, RF-ID, Infrared sensors, etc., have been adopted. Each device has a certain communication speed, memory capacity and sensing accuracy. Therefore, their output data formats are usually ad hoc raw information about the locations. For example, while GPS device output shows latitudes and longitudes, output of infrared sensors shows the presence of a user near the devices.

Similarly, many context-aware services that use location-information have been proposed. The services are designed to engage for some tasks, such as navigation. The task usually requires its own spatial representation representing a certain task-oriented view of the environments. For example, to provide some information based on the user's location, the agents should understand the user's location as "*the user is in a museum now*", rather than as "*the user is at Longitude: 140.38.54 E, Latitude: 35.77.44 N at Mon., Jan 13 12:47:06 2003 JST*". In other words, information gaps occur between device-oriented information like "*Longitude*" and service-oriented information like "*in museum.*h

In addition, each user has their own spatial representation about surrounding environments. Users have a personalized, embodied view of environments, sometimes called a "*personal space*" in Social Psychology. Such perceptions of space differ idiosyncratically based on body size, social background, etc.

Most context-aware services that use location-information ignore this difference in spatial representations. They are designed for a specific device and are tightly bound to device-oriented spatial representation. For that reason, it is difficult to place a presupposed device into a different context. For example, a location service that has presupposed RF-ID-sensor-data cannot be applied to a location service that has presupposed infrared sensor or GPS data.

This study refers to these gaps in spatial representation for ubiquitous computing environments as "*representation gaps.*"

3. Location-Mediated Agent Coordination

We introduce a multi-agent based coordination framework to bridge the intention gaps and representation gaps in ubiquitous computing. It is called "*Location-Mediated Agent Coordination*". Although each agent manages a specific type of information resource, their coordination enables users to access heterogeneous service resources as a seamless service. The coordination framework is an extension of middle agent framework [5][6][7]. it is a framework that provides the service that matches service provider agents to service requester agents, initiates their communication, and sometimes mediates the flow of information among them.

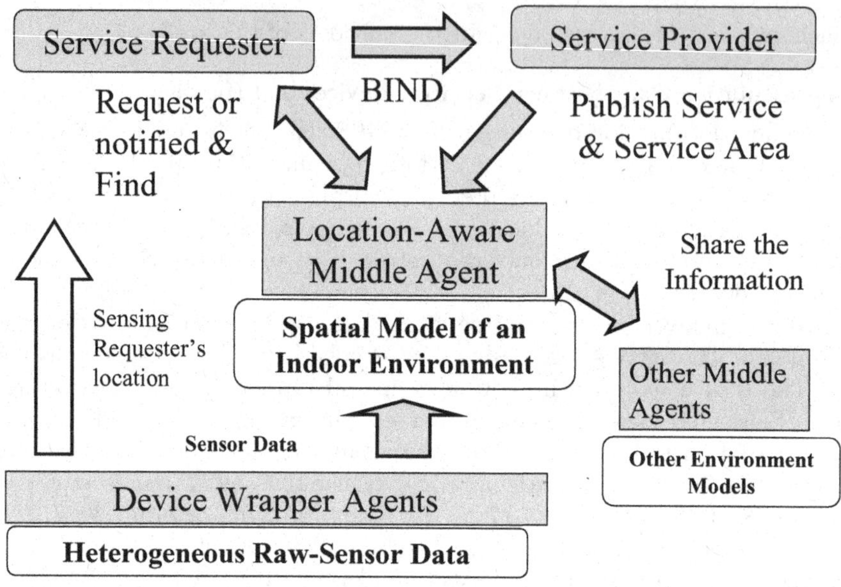

FIGURE 1. Location-Mediated Agent Coordination

The location-mediated agent coordination framework consists of the following types of agents.

Service Provider (Service Agent): the agent wraps a Web service, asks a middle agent to register their capabilities and physical service areas, and provides other agents to the service.

Service Requester (Personal Agent): the agent asks a middle agent to register their physical appearance, such as sensor signal ID, and requires service provider agents to perform some service (e.g. Web Services) on behalf of a human user.

Location-aware Middle Agent: the agent plays matchmaker between Service Providers and Service Requesters by considering their locations, capabilities and requirements; it then initiates their communication. They manage the spatial model of environments and reasoning about spatial relations of objects in the environments.

Device Wrapper Agent: the agent wraps a sensor device having Web service interfaces; it also provides sensor information to the middle agent.

3.1. Bridging Intention Gaps between Services, Devices and Humans

Figure 1 shows an outline of location-mediated coordination. The middle agent plays matchmaker between service providers (e.g. wrapper agents of Web Services) and service requesters (e.g. personal agent on behalf of a user) by considering their locations, capabilities and requirements. It then initiates their communication. Thereby, it bridges the intention gaps that separate services and humans. The coordination process is as follows:

1. Service agents (e.g. wrapper agents of Web Services) advertise their capabilities and service rules that includes location information, such as service areas, to middle agents;
2. Personal agents request the middle agents to store their public properties that includes sensor-based appearance (e.g. RF-IDs);
3. Device wrapper agents (e.g. wrapper agents of location sensor devices) request the middle agents to store their sensor specifications and physical settings (e.g. locations of the devices));
4. The middle agents have a world model of the environments. They integrate the received information into the model. They also monitor the sensor data received from sensor wrapper agents, map the sensor data on the world model. They check the personal agents that match the stored service rules. If they detect such a personal agents, they request the personal agent to access the service;
5. If the personal agent accepts an offer, it asks the service agents to provide the requested services.

3.2. Bridging Representation Gaps between Services, Devices and Humans

To solve this representation-gap issue, the location-aware middle agent coordinates various formats of spatial information using meta information from devices and services. Figure 2 shows an outline of the location-aware middle agent and other agents. All information in Figure 2 is described by RDF and RDFS [1]; all agent communication messages are described by FIPA messages [8] (See Table 1).

Table 1: An example of the observation data embedded in a FIPA message

```
(REQUEST
    :sender     RoomADeviceWrapper@tokyo.agentcities.net
    :receiver   RoomAReasoner@tokyo.agentcities.net
    :content   "<rdf:RDF
       xmlns:rdf=\"http://www.w3.org/1999/02/22-rdf-syntax-ns#\"
```

Continued on next page

[1]http://www.carc.aist.go.jp/consorts/2004/ubicomp-schema

```
        xmlns:fipa=\"http://localhost/2004/fipa-rdf0#\"
        xmlns:ubis=\"http://localhost/2004/ubicomp-schema#\">
        <ubis:Fact
            rdf:about=\"http://localhost/2004/cyber-
                  museum#observed-id2543521311080288113959\"
            ubis:timestamp=\"1080288197468\">
        <ubis:observer
            rdf:resource=\"http://localhost/2004/cyber-
                  museum#rfid-receiver-id2543521311080288113454\"
            rdf:type=\"http://localhost/2004/ubicomp-
                  schema#DeviceWrapperAgent\"/>
        <ubis:observable>
            <ubis:RFSignal
              rdf:about=\"http://localhost/2004/cyber-
                  museum#signal-id2543521311080288113463\">
            <ubis:detectAt
              rdf:resource=\"http://localhost/2004/cyber-
                  museum#output-id2543521311080288113958\"
              rdf:type=\"http://localhost/2004/ubicomp-
                  schema#Point2D\"
              ubis:x=\"13\"
              ubis:y=\"6\"/>
            </ubis:RFSignal>
        </ubis:observable>
        </ubis:Fact>
        <fipa:Action
           rdf:about=\"http://localhost/2004/cyber-
                  museum#register\"
           fipa:actor=\"RoomAReasoner\">
        <fipa:argument
           rdf:resource=\"http://localhost/2004/cyber-
                  museum#observed-id2543521311080288113959\"/>
        </fipa:Action>
        </rdf:RDF>"
     :language  JenaRDFCodec
     :ontology  http://localhost/2004/ubicomp-schema
)
```

The location-aware middle agent manages spatial information based on a world model, a spatial reasoner, a spatial information repository, and an interpreter of meta-information. The repository stores a history of sensor data, which we call *observation data*, received from device wrapper agents (See Table 1). The

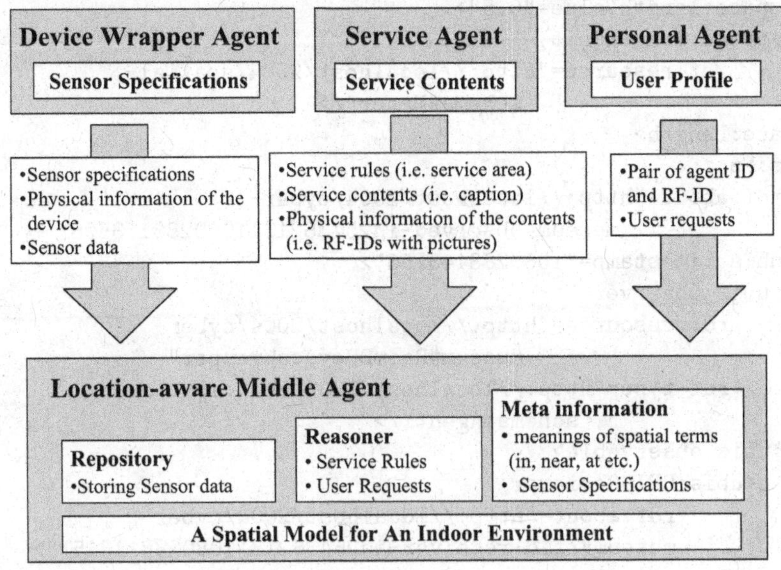

FIGURE 2. Outline of Location-Aware Middle Agent

observation data consist of an observer name, an observed-object name, an object location, and a timestamp. Data are described by RDF/RDFS-based device-oriented raw representation. The middle agents use the meta information of the raw representation data, such as data formats, sensor type, etc. to integrate information of observation data into a world model (See Figure 3 and Table 2).

Table 2: An example of sensor data meta information

```
<rdf:RDF
   xmlns:rdf="http://www.w3.org/1999/02/22-rdf-syntax-ns#"
   xmlns:fipa="http://localhost/2004/fipa-rdf0#"
   xmlns:space="http://localhost/2004/spatial-schema#"
   xmlns:ubis="http://localhost/2004/ubicomp-schema#">
  <space:Length
     rdf:about="http://localhost/2004/cyber-
                 museum#length-id254352131108028811352 5"
```

Continued on next page

```
    space:lengthValue="0.5">
    <space:lengthUnit
        rdf:resource="http://localhost/2004/spatial-
                        schema#Meter"/>
</space:Length>
<ubis:Fact
    rdf:about="http://localhost/2004/cyber-
                museum#observed-id25435213110802881l3528"
    ubis:timestamp="1080288145156">
    <ubis:observer
        rdf:resource="http://localhost/2004/cyber-
                        museum#RoomDDeviceWrapper"
        rdf:type="http://localhost/2004/ubicomp-
                    schema#Agent"/>
    <ubis:observable>
      <ubis:RFIDReciever
            rdf:about="http://localhost/2004/cyber-
            museum#rfid-receiver-id2543521311080288113457">
      <ubis:range>
        <space:CircleRegion
            rdf:about="http://localhost/2004/cyber-
                museum#range-id2543521311080288113519">
          <space:radius>
            <space:Length
                rdf:about="http://localhost/2004/cyber-
                    museum#length-id2543521311080288113515"
                space:lengthValue="2">
                <space:lengthUnit
                    rdf:resource="http://localhost/2004
                            /spatial-schema#Meter"/>
            </space:Length>
          </space:radius>
        </space:CircleRegion>
      </ubis:range>
      <ubis:dataType
          rdf:resource="http://localhost/2004/ubicomp-
                        schema#Point2D"/>
      <ubis:dataUnit
          rdf:resource="http://localhost/2004/cyber-
                    museum#length-id2543521311080288113525"/>
```

Continued on next page

```
      <ubis:atSegment>
        <ubis:OriginOfSensorData
            rdf:about="http://localhost/2004/cyber-
                    museum#origin-id25435213110802881135l4">
          <ubis:atSegment
            rdf:resource="http://localhost/2004/spatial-
                          schema#GroundFloorSegment_10_18"/>
          <ubis:y_orientation
            rdf:resource="http://localhost/2004/spatial-
                          schema#North"/>
        </ubis:OriginOfSensorData>
      </ubis:atSegment>
    </ubis:RFIDReciever>
  </ubis:observable>
</ubis:Fact>
<fipa:Action
    rdf:about="http://localhost/2004/cyber-
            museum#register"
    fipa:actor="RoomDReasoner">
  <fipa:argument
      rdf:resource="http://localhost/2004/cyber-
                  museum#observed-id2543521311080288113528"/>
</fipa:Action>
</rdf:RDF>
```

The middle agents also require mapping information between sensor signals (e.g. RF-IDs) and users to integrate users' locations into a world model. For that reason, personal agents request the middle agents to store the mapping information of them (See Table 3).

Table 3: An example of a mapping information between a sensor-ID and a personal agent

```
<rdf:RDF
  xmlns:rdf="http://www.w3.org/1999/02/22-rdf-syntax-ns#"
  xmlns:fipa="http://localhost/2004/fipa-rdf0#"
  xmlns:ubis="http://localhost/2004/ubicomp-schema#">
  <fipa:Action
```

Continued on next page

```
     rdf:about="http://localhost/2004/cyber-
                museum#register"
     fipa:actor="RoomAReasoner">
    <fipa:argument>
      <ubis:Fact
        rdf:about="http://localhost/2004/cyber-
                   museum#observed-id25435213110802881134 85"
         ubis:timestamp="1080288123968">
        <ubis:observer>
          <ubis:Guest
              rdf:about="http://localhost/2004/cyber-
                         museum#DummyAgent4"
              rdf:type="http://localhost/2004/ubicomp-
                         schema#PersonalAgent">
            <ubis:with>
              <ubis:RFID
                 rdf:about="http://localhost/2004/cyber-
                         museum#rfid-id2543521311080288113466">
                 <ubis:emit
                   rdf:resource="http://localhost/2004/cyber-
                     museum#signal-id2543521311080288113466"
                   rdf:type="http://localhost/2004/ubicomp-
                     schema#RFSignal"/>
              </ubis:RFID>
            </ubis:with>
          </ubis:Guest>
        </ubis:observer>
        <ubis:observable
            rdf:resource="http://localhost/2004/cyber-
                             museum#DummyAgent4"/>
      </ubis:Fact>
    </fipa:argument>
  </fipa:Action>
</rdf:RDF>
```

Similarly,mapping information between sensor signals and embedded services are used to integrate the "service zones", where the services are available, into a world model. For that reason, service agents request the middle agents to store the mapping information of them (See Table 4).

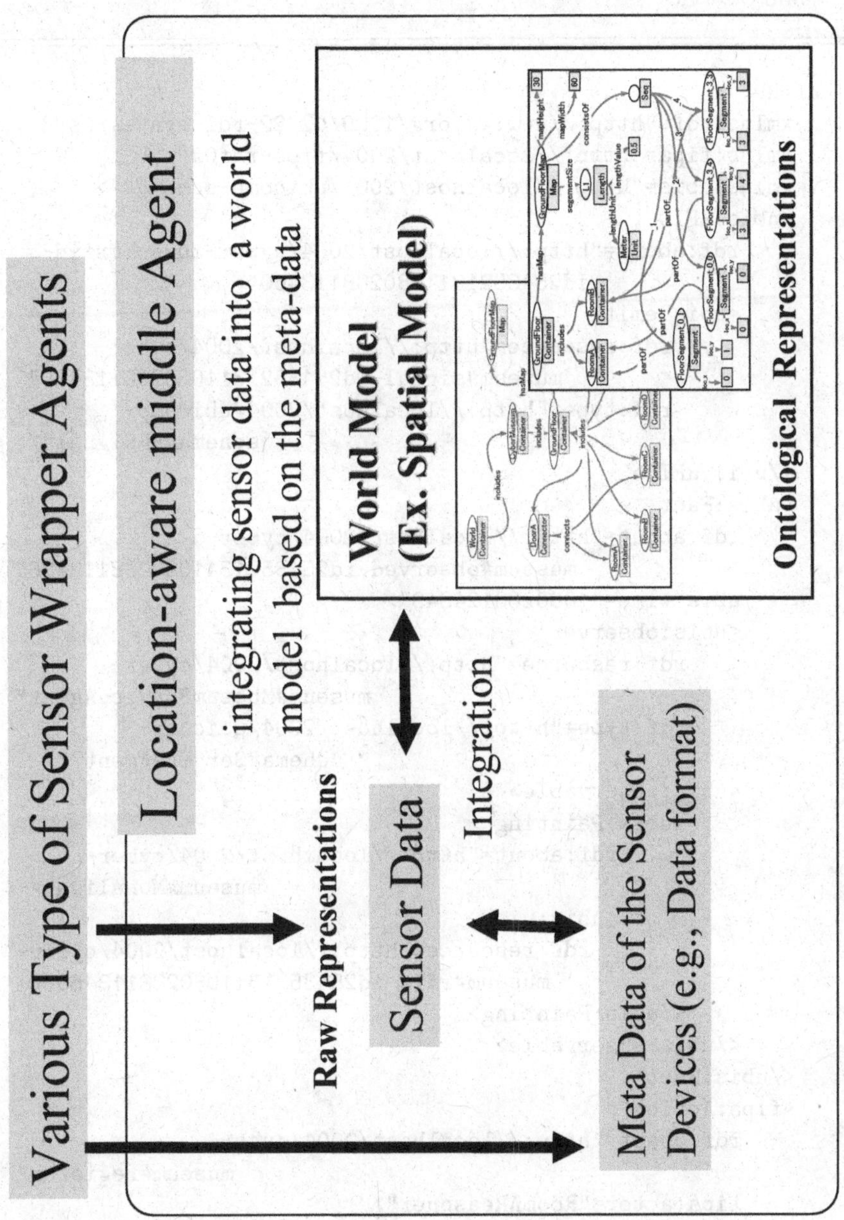

FIGURE 3. Integration of ovservation data into a world model

Table 4: An example of a mapping information between a sensor-ID and a service

```
<rdf:RDF
    xmlns:rdf="http://www.w3.org/1999/02/22-rdf-syntax-ns#"
    xmlns:fipa="http://localhost/2004/fipa-rdf0#"
    xmlns:ubis="http://localhost/2004/ubicomp-schema#">
    <ubis:RFID
        rdf:about="http://localhost/2004/cyber-museum#rfid-
                   id25435213110802881l3460">
        <ubis:emit
            rdf:resource="http://localhost/2004/cyber-
                  museum#signal-id25435213110802881l3460"
            rdf:type="http://localhost/2004/ubicomp-
                                        schema#RFSignal"/>
    </ubis:RFID>
    <ubis:Fact
        rdf:about="http://localhost/2004/cyber-
                  museum#observed-id25435213110802881l3486"
        ubis:time="1080288124343">
        <ubis:observer
            rdf:resource="http://localhost/2004/cyber-
                                museum#MuseumServiceAgent"
            rdf:type="http://localhost/2004/ubicomp-
                                    schema#ServiceAgent"/>
        <ubis:observable>
            <ubis:Painting
                rdf:about="http://localhost/2004/cyber-
                                        museum#Monalisa">
                <ubis:with
                  rdf:resource="http://localhost/2004/cyber-
                    museum#rfid-id25435213110802881l3460"/>
            </ubis:Painting>
        </ubis:observable>
    </ubis:Fact>
    <fipa:Action
        rdf:about="http://localhost/2004/cyber-
                                        museum#register"
        fipa:actor="RoomAReasoner">
        <fipa:argument
```

Continued on next page

```
            rdf:resource="http://localhost/2004/cyber-
                    museum#observed-id25435213110802881l3486"/>
    </fipa:Action>
</rdf:RDF>
```

Although some standardized spatial ontologies exist, such as SUMO [9] and OpenCyc [10], we adopt a newly created spatial ontology on top of RDF/RDFS as a basic representation in spatial repository because SUMO and OpenCyc are not suitable for describing an indoor space, but an outdoor space.

On the other hand, the reasoner stores service rules received from service agents. The rule consists of a precondition and an effect, like DAML-S [11]. The rules are described by RDF/RDFS based service-oriented qualitative representation, such as "near the painting" (See Table 5). The middle agent translates spatial constraints in precondition into the spatial areas on the world model. It periodically checks the applicability of the rules into the observation data.

Table 5: An example of the service rule

```
<rdf:RDF
   xmlns:rdf="http://www.w3.org/1999/02/22-rdf-syntax-ns#"
   xmlns:fipa="http://localhost/2004/fipa-rdf0#"
   xmlns:ubis="http://localhost/2004/ubicomp-schema#">
  <ubis:ServiceAgent
      rdf:about="http://localhost/2004/cyber-
              museum#MuseumServiceAgent"/>
  <ubis:Precondition
      rdf:about="http://localhost/2004/cyber-
            museum#spConstraint-id25435213110802881l3495">
   <ubis:spatialConstraint>
     <ubis:VariableObject
      rdf:about="http://localhost/2004/cyber-museum#x">
       <ubis:near
         rdf:resource="http://localhost/2004/cyber-
                museum#Monalisa"
         rdf:type="http://localhost/2004/ubicomp-
              schema#Exhibition"/>
     </ubis:VariableObject>
   </ubis:spatialConstraint>
```

Continued on next page

```
    <ubis:temporalConstraint
        rdf:resource="http://localhost/2004/ubicomp-
                       schema#Anytime"/>
  </ubis:Precondition>
  <fipa:Action rdf:about="http://localhost/2004/cyber-
                          museum#register"
    fipa:actor="RoomAReasoner">
    <fipa:argument>
      <ubis:Rule
            rdf:about="http://localhost/2004/cyber-
                       museum#rule-id25435213110802881 13494">
        <ubis:effect>
          <ubis:Service
            rdf:about="http://localhost/2004/cyber-
                       museum#information-Monalisa">
            <ubis:provider
               rdf:resource="http://localhost/2004/cyber-
                             museum#MuseumServiceAgent"/>
          </ubis:Service>
        </ubis:effect>
        <ubis:precondition
             rdf:resource="http://localhost/2004/cyber-
               museum#spConstraint-id25435213110802881 13495"/>
      </ubis:Rule>
    </fipa:argument>
  </fipa:Action>
</rdf:RDF>
```

The world model, a basic spatial representation to describe observation data and service rules, consists of the relation of spatial regions, and their properties. The model is described by a spatial ontology[2] that we have developed to describe an indoor space using a tree representation and a grid representation (See Figure 4 and Figure 5).In these figures, rectangular boxes represent RDF resources; oval boxes represent class of the resources; arrows represent RDF properties.

The tree representation is based on the human understanding of a spatial concept generally called mereological thinking[12], or reasoning about "part-of" relations. The representation consists of part-of relations among 2-dimensional spatial regions in the real world. We formalize the ubiquitous computing environments as a tree-structure of spatial regions based on Bittner [13]. A tree structure

[2]http://www.carc.aist.go.jp/consorts/2004/spatial-schema

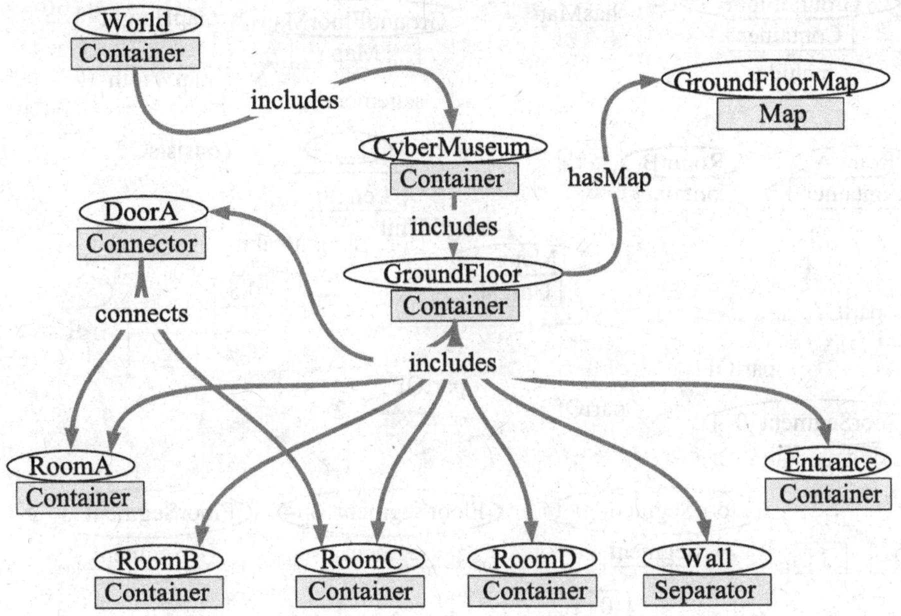

FIGURE 4. A part of tree-based spatial representation

of spatial regions is denoted as $G : G = (R, \subseteq)$, where $R : (r \in R)$ denotes a set of spatial regions, and denotes a part-of relation between two regions. The regions in have the following characteristics.

$$\exists r_i : \quad r_i \subseteq r_i \tag{3.1}$$

$$\exists r_i, r_j : \quad r_i \subseteq r_j \wedge r_j \subseteq r_i \Rightarrow r_j = r_i \tag{3.2}$$

$$\exists r_i, r_j, r_k : \quad r_i \subseteq r_j \wedge r_j \subseteq r_k \Rightarrow r_i \subseteq r_k \tag{3.3}$$

where $r_i, r_j, r_k$is a region.

We use a tree representation to show the relation of spatial regions and their properties in the spatial ontology that we have developed to describe the ubiquitous computing environments. Figure 4 shows an example of an ontological tree-representation (a structure of a museum) that we have developed. *includes* relations in the figure are the relations denoted by in the logical expressions above. When describing other buildings, one should describe the root node (top node of the world models) of the tree representation as *World*, a unique RDF resource.

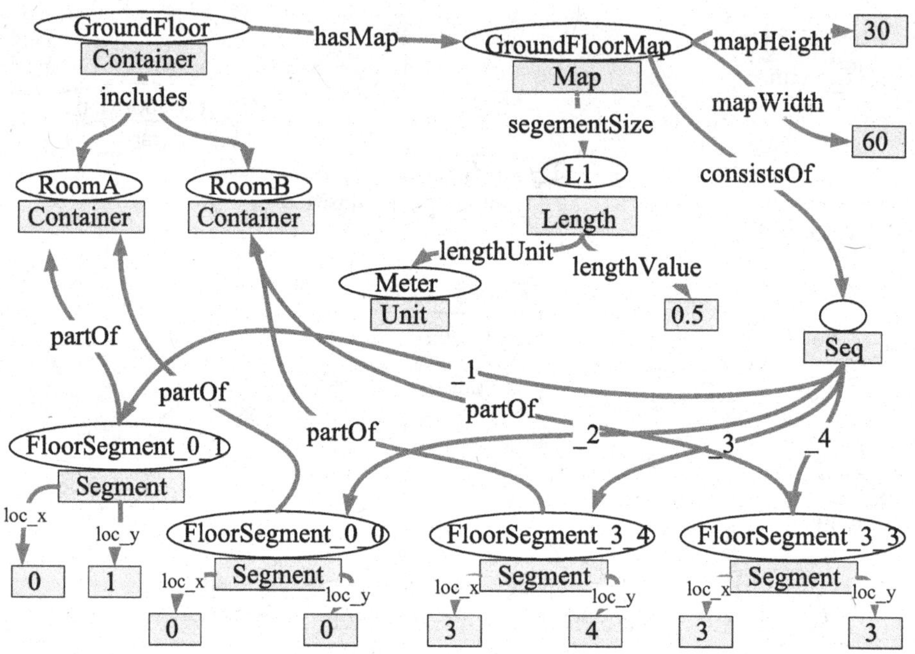

FIGURE 5. A part of grid-based spatial representation

TABLE 6. An example of a spatial representation

```
<space:Container rdf:about="#GroundFloor">
   <space:hasMap>
     <space:Map rdf:about="#GroundFloorMap">
        <space:segmentSize
                    rdf:about="#length-id1080288112486" />
        <space:consistsOf>
           <rdf:Seq>
              <rdf:li>
                 &lt;space:Segment rdf:about="#FloorSegment_0_0"
                    space:loc_y="0"    space:loc_x="0">
                    <space:partOf
                        rdf:resource="#RooomA" />
        ...
```

We also use a grid representation to show the shapes and locations of spatial regions in the spatial ontology that we have developed to describe the ubiquitous computing environments. Figure 5 shows an example of an ontological grid-representation (a structure of a museum) that we have developed. We define *Map* and *Segment* in the ontology. A *Map* is a set of *Segments*; A *Segment* is a primitive square segment referred by a 2-dimensional location on a *Map*. *partOf* relations represent that the segment is a part of a *Region* represented in a tree-representation. Table 6 shows a RDF description of an indoor space based on the grid representations.

4. Implementation

We have continued development of a scenario of context-aware information assist services in a museum. It is based on the location-mediated coordination framework. In that scenario, when a user is located near a painting, the user can receive information about the painting via the user's portable display device. We have implemented that framework using JADE [14], a software framework to develop an agent system that conforms to FIPA specifications.

We have implemented context-aware information assist systems in museums. In those systems, agents are aware of the distance between a user and the paintings in the museum[3]. When a user approaches a painting, the agents automatically provide information about the painting via a user's portable display device.

In the museum, when a user is located near a painting, the user can receive information from the agents about the painting via the user's portable display device. This service is possible because the painting information is derived from Internet resources. For example, if the user needs more information about the painting, the user should push the "tell me" button of the portable device. The agents notice the user's request, make a search query about the painting with the necessary information they have already had, e.g. the painting's name and user's preference, and access Web Services [15] on the Internet, e.g. Google Web Services [16], on behalf of the user.

Figure 6 shows an image of the monitor system of the information assist services in a museum. A museum map is visible in a main window in the lower right side of the figure; it has two information windows with a graphic image. In the map, human icons represent current locations of the users. Each zone surrounding a picture represents service zones of the museum service agents. Each line after the users represents users' trajectories. Information windows correspond to the screens of users' portable devices. In this application, the users casually roam around the museum. If a user enters the service zone, an information window pops up in the screen to display the picture information.

Figure 7 illustrates agent communication in the museum system. First, the service agent and the personal agents inform the middle agent of their profiles and request the middle agent to search for a matched agent based on their requirements. The requirements are described as some rules. The middle agent stores the rules and watches whether users who matched the rules are located in an environment. The device wrapper agent informs the middle agent where a user with a unique id is

[3]Currently, users, users' behaviors, and a museum in the system are simulated.

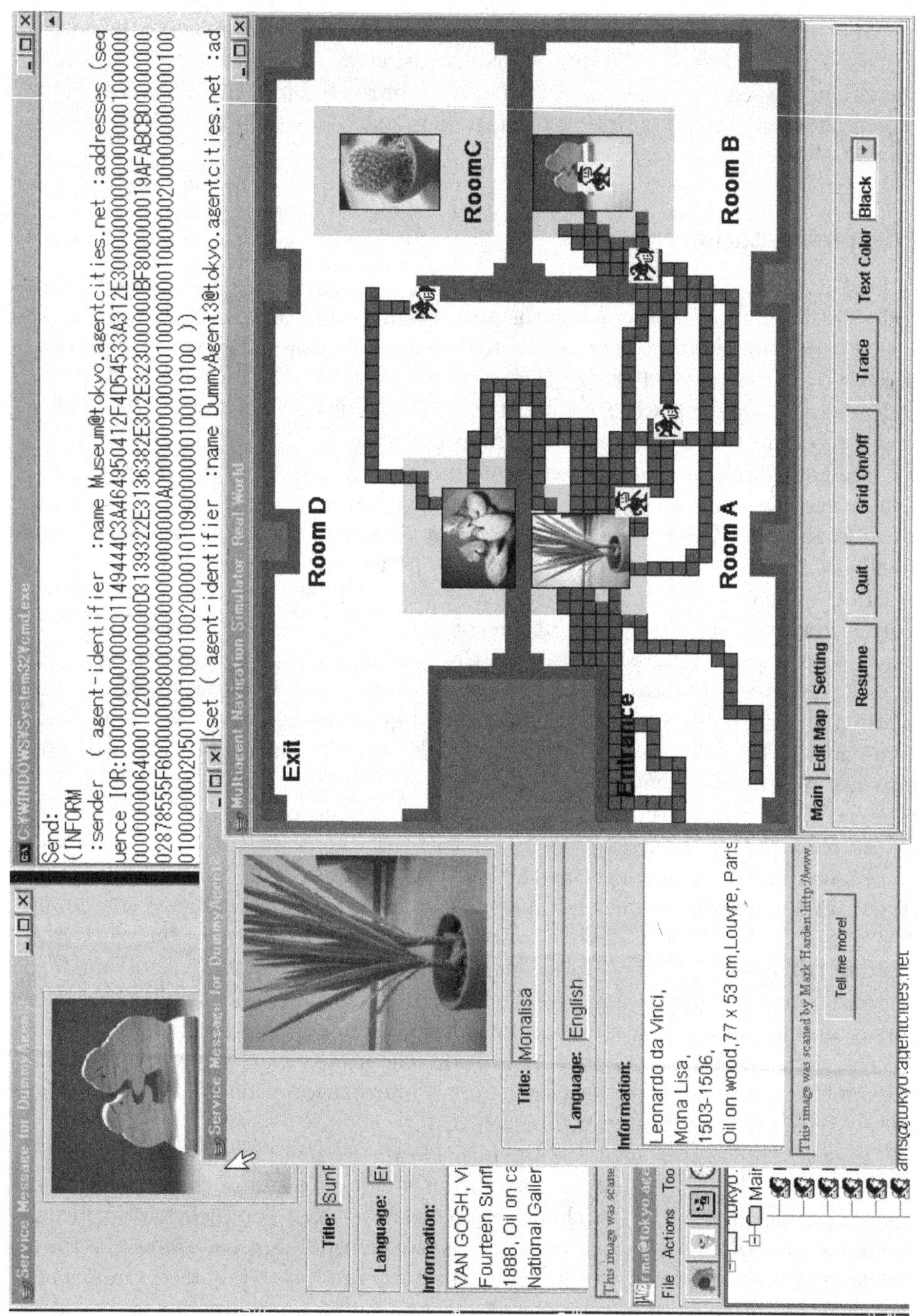

FIGURE 6. An image of a monitor system of context-aware information assist services in a museum

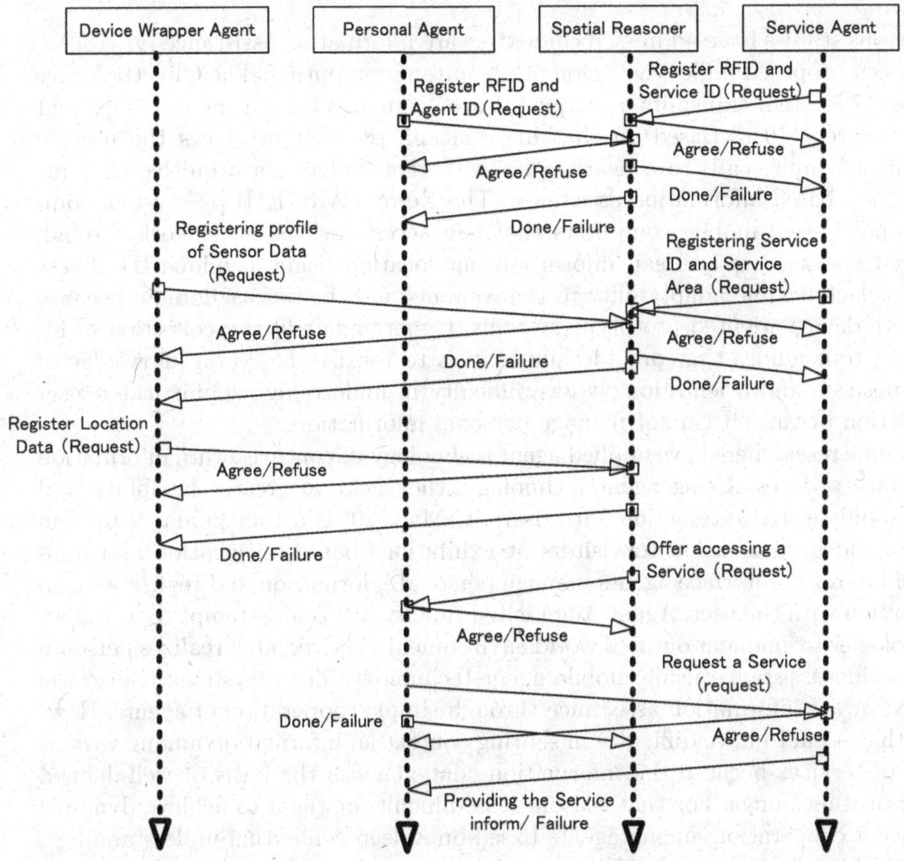

FIGURE 7. Message-flows in an assist system in a museum

located. When the middle agent notices that a user is located on a service region, the agent tells the personal agents the user available service name. Then, the personal agent requests a service based on the service name. Finally, the personal agent requests the device wrapper agent to show the service content on a user's portable display device.

In this system, we have confirmed the simplest framework of location-mediated coordination by applying agents to the context-aware information systems. Using the agent-based coordination framework, we have very rapidly developed context-aware information systems. New services can be added to the system by defining the service agents and their ontologies.

5. Related Work

Numerous studies have addressed context-aware information assistance [17][18][19] have been proposed under the vision of ubiquitous computing. The Olivetti Active Badge [17] system transmits a unique infrared signal to inform the user's current location every 10 s. Based on that information, the system allows the user to re-route incoming calls to a nearby phone. Active Badge is a primitive example of location-based information assistance. The Xerox PARCTAB [18] system comprises palm-sized mobile computers that can access local area network through infrared transceivers and can inform current location using a unique ID. These systems lack flexible adaptability to the contents and the service domain because they are device-oriented prototype systems. Cyberguide [19] is a collection of intelligent tour guides that provide information to tourists based on knowledge of their position and orientation. It has difficulty in undertaking sophisticated user interaction because it cannot manage personal information.

Some researchers have applied agent technology to context-aware information assistance services. Using agent technology, they achieve greater flexibility and more sophisticated interaction with users. C-Map [20] is a tour guidance system that provides information to visitors at exhibitions based on location and individual interests. Interface agents manage personal information and realize natural interaction with the user. Agent Augmented Reality [21] is an attempt to use agent technologies to augment our real world environment. The research realizes personal information assistance using mobile agent technology. These systems realize the context-aware information assistance through simple cooperation of agents. However, they seem to have difficulty in sharing contextual information among various kinds of services because the information context lacks the basis of well-defined ontological meanings. For that reason, it is difficult for them to achieve dynamic intelligent cooperation among agents based on a deep contextual understanding.

CoolAgent [22] CoBrA [23] are context-aware software agent systems. Agents can share contextual information described by RDF. However, these studies do not provide the implementation framework of agents' coordination to solve the coordination gaps. The present paper describes the location-mediated agent coordination as a coordination framework of ubiquitous agents and implements context-aware information assist systems in museums.

Finally, some studies for middle agents exist [5][6][7]. As mentioned previously, the work in this paper is an extension of work in ubiquitous computing. Hence, results from those studies, such as integration of DAML-S [11], must be useful for our future research.

6. Future Work

Section 2 described gaps between users' intentions and services in ubiquitous computing. However, we have presupposed that a user's intentions and behaviors do not affect other users' intentions and behaviors. Because we design services for multi users, we confront another gap concerning user intentions: the gap between mass users' intentions and limited service resources. The system must include a way of providing information to users that maintains overall system performance with limited service resources because serious conflicts among users may arise from poor resource allocation. Overall service performance will decrease in such a situation. In other words, user intentions may cause serious conflicts during access of limited service resources. For example, navigation systems for emergency fire evacuation must include a strategy for telling evacuees how to evacuate a building safely. If the systems simultaneously inform all users about the physically shortest path to an exit, users may crowd that path, creating a crushing panic.

To bridge the gaps between mass users' intentions and limited service resources, We plan to introduce the concept of "Social Coordination" [24][25]. "Social Coordination" aims to resolve conflicts arising from multiple users' requirements and to implicitly modify the provided information for each user to maintain overall system performance. We are implementing a facility using a market mechanism, called "user intention market" [26].

7. Conclusion

This paper presented discussion of intention and representation gaps in ubiquitous computing. It proposed a basic idea to bridge the gaps, called location-mediated agent coordination, inspired by Semantic Web agents.

In the framework, we have shown the potential of the distributed open agents in the real world. In the Semantic Web [2], an "agent" is defined as *"the program that collects information from diverse sources, processes the information and exchanges the results with other programs."* We have realized such agents in the context of the Ubiquitous computing, and extended application areas of the agents from the Internet to the real world.

Based on the proposed framework, we plan to apply more sophisticated AI techniques, such as qualitative reasoning, to the reasoning mechanism of the location-aware middle agents.

References

[1] M. Weiser. The computer for the 21st century. *Scientific American*, pages 94–104, 1991.

[2] T. Berners-Lee, J. Hendler, and O. Lassila. The semantic web. *Scientific American*, May 2001.

[3] Resource Description Framework (RDF). `http://www.w3.org/RDF/`, 2004.

[4] RDF vocabulary description language 1.0: RDF Schema (RDFS). `http://www.w3.org/TR/rdf-schema/`. 2004.

[5] K. Decker, K. Sycara, and M. Williamson. Middle-agents for the internet. In *Proceedings of the 15th International Joint Conference on Artificial Intelligence*, Nagoya, Japan, 1997.

[6] K. P. Sycara, M. Klusch, S. Widoff, and J. Lu. Dynamic service matchmaking among agents in open information environments. *SIGMOD Record*, 28(1):47–53, 1999.

[7] M. Paolucci, T. Kawmura, T. Payne, and K. P. Sycara. Semantic matching of web services capabilities. In *Proceedings of the 1st International Semantic Web Conference*, pages 333–347, 2002.

[8] The Foundation for Intelligent Physical Agents (FIPA). `http://www.fipa.org/`, 2004.

[9] Suggested upper merged ontology (SUMO). `http://ontology.teknowledge.com/`, 2004.

[10] OpenCyc. `http://www.opencyc.org/`, 2004.

[11] DAML Service (DAML-S). `http://www.daml.org/services/`, 2003.

[12] R. Casati and A. C. Varzi. *Parts and Places: The Structures of Spatial Representation.* The MIT Press, Cambridge, Massachusetts, 1999.

[13] T. Bittner. Reasoning about qualitative spatio-temporal relations at multiple levels of granularity. In F. van Harmelen, editor, *Proceedings of the 15th European Conference on Artificial Intelligence – ECAI 2002*, Amsterdam, 2002. IOS Press.

[14] Java Agent DEvelopment framework (jade). `http://sharon.cselt.it/projects/jade/`, 2004.

[15] Web Services Activity. `http://www.w3.org/2002/ws/`, 2004.

[16] Google Web APIs. `http://www.google.com/apis/`, 2004.

[17] R. Want, A. Hopper, V. Falcao, and J. Gibbons. The active badge location system. *ACM Trans. Inf. Syst.*, 10(1):91–102, 1992.

[18] R. Want, B. Schilit, N. Adams, R. Gold, K. Petersen, J. Ellis, D. Goldberg, and M. Weiser. The PARCTAB ubiquitous computing experiment. Technical Report CSL-95-1, Xerox Palo Alto Research Center, March 1995.

[19] G. D. Abowd, C. G. Atkeson, J. Hong, S. Long, R. Kooper, and M. Pinkerton. Cyberguide: a mobile context-aware tour guide. *Wirel. Netw.*, 3(5):421–433, 1997.

[20] Y. Sumi, T. Etani, S. Fels, N. Simonet, K. Kobayashi, and K. Mase. C-map: Building a context-aware mobile assistant for exhibition tours. In *Community Computing and Support Systems, Social Interaction in Networked Communities [the book is based on the Kyoto Meeting on Social Interaction and Communityware, held in Kyoto, Japan, in June 1998]*, pages 137–154. Springer-Verlag, 1998.

[21] K. Nagao and J. Rekimoto. Agent augmented reality: A software agent meets the real world. In *Proceedings of the Second International Conference on Multi-Agent Systems (ICMAS-96)*, pages 228–235, 1996.

[22] H. Chen and S. Tolia. Steps towards creating a context-aware agent system. Technical report, HP Labs, 2001.

[23] H. Chen, T. Finin, and A. Joshi. Semantic Web in in the Context Broker Architecture. In *Proceedings of PerCom 2004*, March 2004.

[24] K. Kurumatani. Social coordination in architecture for physically-grounding agents. In *Proceedings of Landscape Frontier International Symposium*, pages 57–62, 2002.

[25] K. Kurumatani. Mass user support by social coordination among citizens in a real environment. In *Multiagent for Mass User Support*, pages 1–19. Springer, 2004.

[26] K. Kurumatani. User intention market for multi-agent navigation - an artificial intelligent problem in engineering and economic context. In *Working Note of the AAAI-02 Workshop on Multi-Agent Modeling and Simulation of Economic Systems (MAMSES-02)*, pages 1–4. AAAI Press, 2002.

Acknowledgment

This work has been supported by Core Research for Evolutional Science and Technology (CREST) program of Japan Science and Technology Agency (JST).

Akio Sashima, Noriaki Izumi and Koichi Kurumatani
Cyber Assist Research Center
National Institute of Advanced Industrial Science and Technology (AIST)
2-41-6 Aomi, Koto-ku
Tokyo, 135-0064
Japan
e-mail: sashima@carc.aist.go.jp
niz@ni.aist.go.jp
k.kurumatani@aist.go.jp

An Ontology for Agent-Based Monitoring of Fulfillment Processes

Roland Zimmermann, S. Käs, Robert Butscher and Freimut Bodendorf

Abstract. An agent-based supply chain monitoring system for tracking orders and their related suborders is presented. To enable the necessary communication between the agents an ontology is introduced. The design of the ontology and the implementation are discussed in detail. The usage of the ontology for inter-agent communication is illustrated with the help of AUML models of the agent-interactions in the supply chain monitoring system. Concluding, two prototypes of the system are presented.

Keywords. Tracking, monitoring, supply chain, fulfillment.

1. Problem

Fulfillment processes in a supply chain show different kinds of irregularities and disruptions. Irregularities like delays in a production process are the result of variances in processing times and processing quality. Besides these "natural" irregularities disruptions caused by malfunctions of machines, failures in machine handling, incorrect picking in warehouses or external factors like traffic congestions have a serious impact on the fulfillment of orders within a supply chain (see fig. 1). The orders issued by different supply chain partners are often linked. In fig. 1 an order from the clothing manufacturer induces suborders for the dyer, the knitter and the thread manufacturer. The tighter integrated the supply chain partners' processes are the greater will be the impact of disruptions on the fulfillment processes.

Existing systems for order tracking typically generate standard messages for every order at certain intervals or milestones. As a result, large databases with information on orders are filled with data that is in most cases not concerned with the serious problems mentioned above. Only a small percentage of the orders encounters problems during fulfillment. Although information might be available it is generally communicated too late, the content will often not match the needs

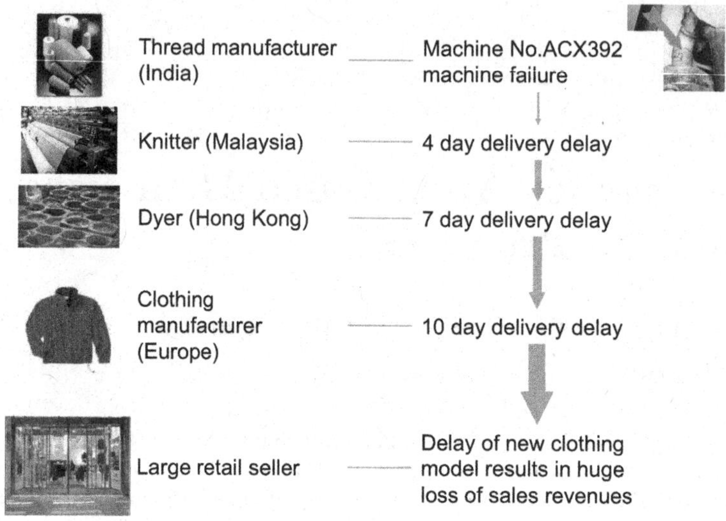

FIGURE 1. Example of a propagating disruption in a supply chain [1]

of a decision maker to react to the problem and it is lost in the large volumes of data. Such systems generate a huge amount of communication traffic between supply chain partners which is not offset by a similar huge benefit generated by this communication.

An innovative solution has to meet the following criteria [2]:

- *Consideration of interdependencies in supply chains* - The relationships between orders and suborders resulting from the division of labor have to be taken into account by an inter-organizational monitoring solution. Otherwise effects of events on the network cannot be reflected adequately.
- *Primacy of local data storage* - As a consequence of taking inter-organizational dependencies into account, the data sources that are available at each supply chain partner are not to be replicated unnecessarily elsewhere. Data between supply chain partners is only to be exchanged upon request or when critical situations call for an alert of affected partners.
- *Proactive monitoring* - Intensive monitoring of a large number of orders incurs cost that cannot be neglected. The detection of orders with a high probability of encountering events that threaten their proper fulfillment is needed. With this knowledge a more focused proactive monitoring is enabled optimizing the cost-benefit-relation of a supply chain monitoring solution.
- *Flexible monitoring* - The intensity of monitoring efforts has to correspond to the likelihood of disruptive events (see above). In dynamic supply chains error-prone order types may evolve over time into reliable ones that should not

be monitored as closely as newly evolving critical order types. Ideally a supply chain monitoring solution autonomously adapts to such new conditions in its environment.

- *Autonomous analysis of gathered information* - Data gathered from internal and external sources regarding the status of an order and its suborders has to be analyzed. The complex dependencies between orders and suborders have to be considered while aggregating the respective order information. Furthermore, an interpretation of the current situation of an order using the available data is needed to facilitate necessary management actions.
- *Intelligent generation of alerts* - Based on the analysis of monitoring data a supply chain monitoring system has to be able to communicate with intra- and inter-organizational systems and users to inform them of important developments, to trigger actions and to enable decision-making. Such alert generation facilitates operational fulfillment management across supply chains.

2. Supply Chain Monitoring

2.1. Supply Chain Model

Supply chain monitoring solutions for tracking orders need to be analyzed in the context of a domain. A typical logistics scenario consists of a variety of manufacturers, suppliers and logistics service providers. Figure 2 illustrates a scenario

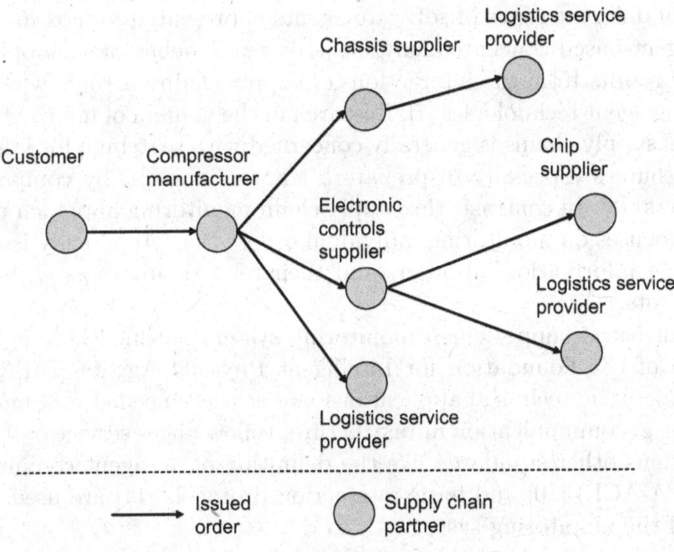

FIGURE 2. Order network in a supply chain

of a compressor supply chain. The links between the organizations represent the issued orders and suborders resulting from a customer's order. The example shows that the compressor manufacturer generates two orders for components (chassis and electronic controls) and one order placed with a logistics service provider to transport the finished product to the customer.

The linkage between incoming orders (these received by a company) and outgoing orders (those generated to fulfill the incoming orders) is of major importance. During the tracking process each enterprise has to check its suborders that correspond to a monitored incoming order. The information retrieved concerning these suborders is needed to derive the current status of the monitored incoming order. Matching the corresponding incoming and outgoing identifiers is one of the tasks that each partner is responsible for.

2.2. Agent-Based Concept

A concept for distributed supply chain monitoring has been developed. This approach differs from traditional isolated and centralized tracking systems that are widely implemented within logistics service provider networks [3] and similar approaches of production control [4]. However, an agent-based solution is better suited to meet the requirements defined above. It focuses on critical orders, allows for real-time tracking of orders across the supply-chain and offers the ability to react in a timely manner to unforeseen events during order fulfillment.

The use of software agents in the supply chain domain typically focuses on optimizing schedules through distributed coordination mechanisms (e.g. [5]). A general approach to supply chain management that covers planning and execution of actions with different types of software agents is presented by Fox [6].

Other agent-based concepts analyze the dynamic behavior of supply chains. This behavior results from the interactions of supply chain partners which can be simulated using agent technologies [7]. Research in the domain of information gathering agents in supply chains is generally concerned with searching for information in internet resources especially to prepare a transaction (e.g. by comparing and combining offers) [8]. In contrast, the supply chain monitoring approach presented in this paper focuses on monitoring individual orders that are already issued. The aim is to gather information on orders and their related suborders with the help of software agents.

The agent-based supply chain monitoring system outlined here is based on the standards of the Foundation for Intelligent Physical Agents (FIPA). These standards define basic technical applications and services needed in a multi-agent environment (e.g. communication infrastructure, yellow pages services) [9]. Besides these applications other standards like the definition of an agent communication language (FIPA-ACL) [10] and basic interaction protocols [11] are used to define the concept of the monitoring system.

Four agent types in three different application layers are proposed to realize the desired monitoring functionality (see fig. 3) [12]. The first layer is characterized as the external communication layer which is represented by the discourse agent of a company. It is concerned with the communication of monitoring information across the supply chain by interacting with the agent systems of other supply chain partners. This interaction is needed when information on suborders is gathered (pulled) and when important status information is proactively distributed (pushed) within the supply chain.

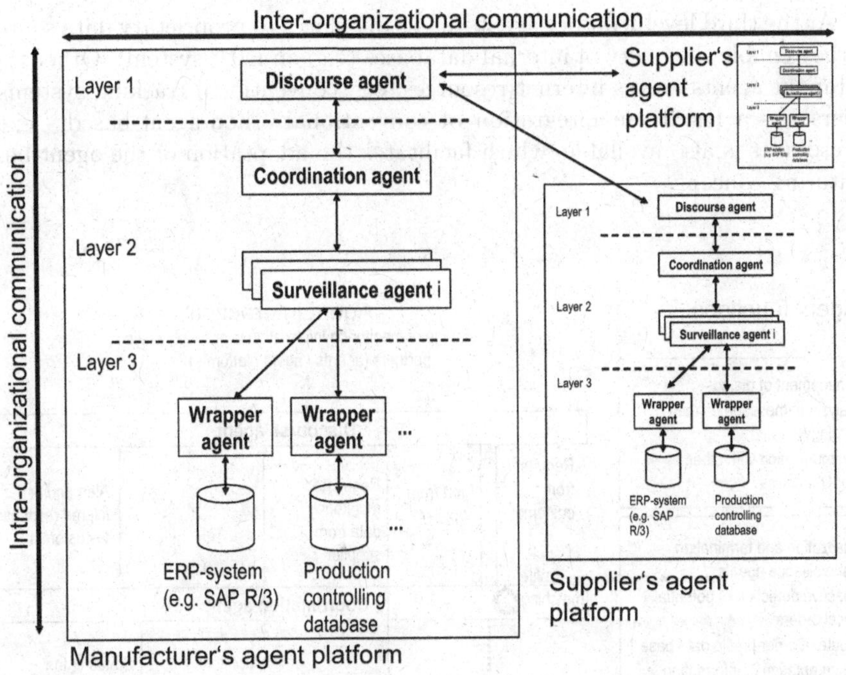

FIGURE 3. Agent architecture of the supply chain monitoring system

Layers two and three host the monitoring functions. They are responsible for gathering and analyzing the information available from internal and external sources. In the second layer the coordination agent hosts, besides others, an order profiling function and thereupon decides autonomously which orders are to be monitored. In addition, the request from a customer (respectively its agent) for monitoring information will also force the coordination agent to trigger the monitoring of an order as long as an order is not yet monitored (see also fig. 4).

For each monitored order of an enterprise a dedicated surveillance agent is started. It searches for desired status information within its company's resources (e.g. in a SAP R/3 system) by querying wrapper agents and it communicates with other enterprises. This external communication is facilitated through a cooperation with the discourse agent which is responsible for managing external communications. The surveillance agent transmits requests for status information regarding the suborders of its monitored order to the discourse agent which forwards these requests to the respective supply chain partners. In addition, the surveillance agent analyzes and interprets the gathered data. This information is transmitted to the coordination agent, which in turn decides on an appropriate action if the situation calls for an external alert to a customer or supplier.

At the third level wrapper agents act as interfaces to proprietary data sources, e.g. they enable the query of internal databases (e.g. an ERP system). Other types of wrapper agents access internet resources, e.g. conventional tracking systems of carriers. As a result, an integration of conventional - non-agent-based - external resources is also available, which facilitates the adaptation of the agent-based monitoring concept.

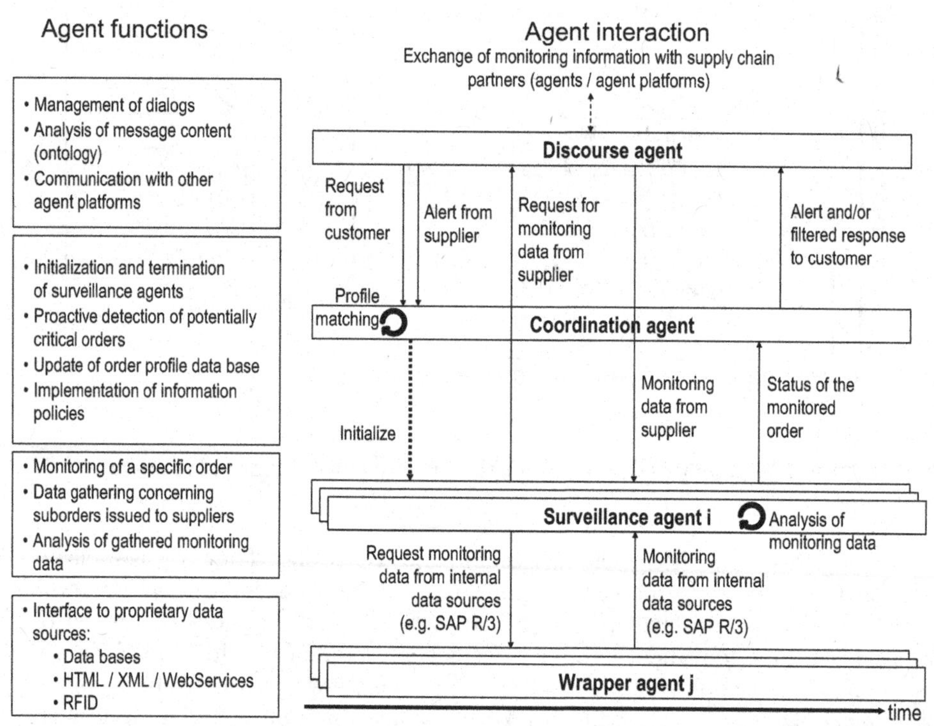

FIGURE 4. Agent interaction in a supply chain monitoring system

3. Ontology

An ontology is needed to enable the definition of content for the agent communication. Besides different types of monitoring data information on the environment of the software agents is needed to allow autonomous behavior of the agents. An ontology is an appropriate instrument to represent the relevant concepts of the environment (e.g. an enterprise) and tracking data related to a monitored order [13].

3.1. Methodological Approach

To design an ontology it is important to define the functions of the ontology and to characterize the users of the ontology [14]. The major role of the supply chain monitoring ontology is to act as the medium to define the content of the communication between the software agents in the proposed supply chain monitoring system. By providing a common understanding of the structure of the information needed for supply chain monitoring, the ontology enables the agents to extract relevant data from distributed data sources, to communicate with other agents and to cooperate. This implies that the supply chain monitoring ontology can represent all processes, organizational units and objects that are relevant within the supply chain environment. The relevant data is derived from the scenario described above as well as from the tracking data model (see next section).

Based on this, a rough first draft of the ontology can be derived that is iteratively refined step by step. There are several possibilities to derive this initial design. Holsapple and Joshi identify five basic approaches to ontology design: inspiration, induction, deduction, synthesis and collaboration [15]. Combinations of these approaches are possible.

For the design of the supply chain monitoring ontology a combination of the inductive and the synthetic approach is used. The inductive approach is characterized by *observing, examining, and analysing (a) specific case(s) in the domain of interest and applying this specific case to other cases in the same domain* [15]. For the synthetic approach, concepts from existing ontologies are adopted and integrated. The combination of these two approaches is relevant for this project as concepts from an existing ontology for the enterprise domain can be reused (synthesis) and, from an inductive perspective, the case of a business partner serves as a basic scenario. This basic scenario consists of one customer, one vendor and one logistics service provider. In a top-down process the most general concepts of this specific scenario were defined and subsequently refined. In a second step the ontology was enlarged to incorporate scenarios including multiple manufacturers, suppliers and logistics service providers.

Not all concepts of the ontology need to be defined in the design phase as the *Enterprise Ontology* [16] can partially be reused. It specifies a wide variety of concepts from the domain of enterprises. As the supply chain monitoring ontology belongs to the same domain, the *Enterprise Ontology* already provides some important general concepts. The main benefit of reusing the *Enterprise Ontology* is to allow different multi-agent systems that may be concerned with varying aspects of supply chain management (e.g. procurement planning vs. order tracking) to communicate on a generic level as long as they commit themselves to the same top-level-ontology (here the *Enterprise Ontology*). However, some important high-level concepts for the supply chain domain are missing and have been added, e.g. the concept of an order.

3.2. Tracking Data

The individual order is the main object that is tracked during supply chain monitoring. Orders are linked to other orders forming a network. During the tracking process attributes that characterize an order and its fulfillment are to be gathered [17]. To enable reactions to unforeseen events further information is needed, e.g. about the source of a disruption (see fig. 5).

To identify specific orders an *Order-ID* as well as references to other orders have to be provided to consider the interdependencies in the order network. The resulting data type is *basic data.*

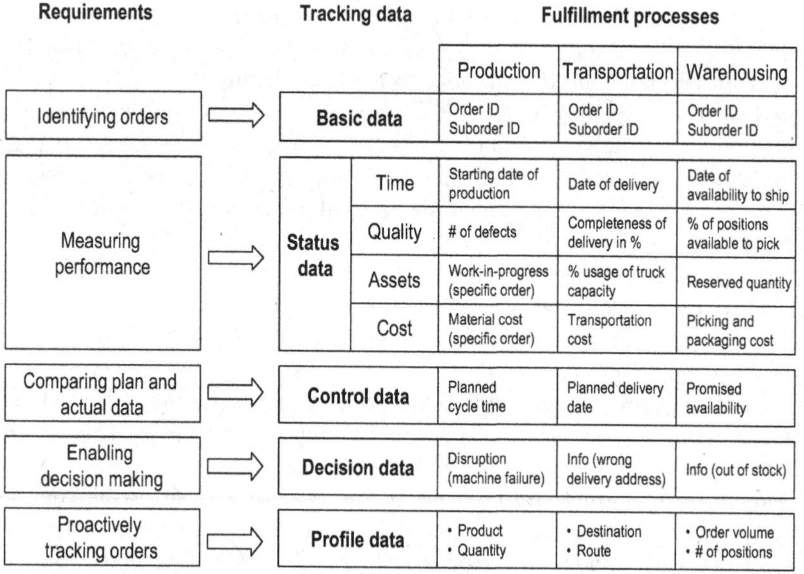

Requirements
Tracking data
Fulfillment processes
Production
Transportation
Warehousing
Identifying orders
Basic data
Order ID
Suborder ID
Order ID
Suborder ID
Order ID
Suborder ID
Measuring performance
Status data
Time
Starting date of production
Date of delivery
Date of availability to ship
Quality
# of defects
Completeness of delivery in %
% of positions available to pick
Assets
Work-in-progress (specific order)
% usage of truck capacity
Reserved quantity
Cost
Material cost (specific order)
Transportation cost
Picking and packaging cost
Comparing plan and actual data
Control data
Planned cycle time
Planned delivery date
Promised availability
Enabling decision making
Decision data
Disruption (machine failure)
Info (wrong delivery address)
Info (out of stock)
Proactively tracking orders
Profile data
• Product
• Quantity
• Destination
• Route
• Order volume
• # of positions

FIGURE 5. Examples of tracking data for supply chain monitoring

To characterize the fulfillment of a single order various performance criteria can be used such as cycle times or quality and cost measures. These measures are typically derived from attributes of an order. As an example the beginning and the end of production for a specific order are generally aggregated to the performance measure "cycle time". The requirement to calculate performance measures results in so called *status data*. This data covers the performance indicators of the Supply-Chain-Council's SCOR-model [18]. Therefore the status data types *time*, *quality*, *assets* and *cost* are defined.

Another requirement for tracking orders on a real-time basis is the ability to compare data on given events to data on planned events. Scheduled delivery dates, defined tolerances for product quality and target costs are examples of such information. The respective data type is *control data*.

For managing and optimizing the fulfillment of individual orders information concerning the actual status of an order and control data is not enough to make decisions. Special data is necessary to react to unforeseen events during fulfillment. For instance information on the causes of a disruption (e.g. a late delivery because of traffic congestion) is necessary to decide whether to issue another order (what makes sense, if the order is completely lost) or to accept the delay and adjust the plans. The relevant data for decision making is called *decision data*.

Supply chain monitoring focuses on critical orders. To identify these orders a profiling process is needed which requires attributes for the definition of order profiles. Based on these profiles proactive tracking of potentially critical orders is enabled. Attributes of an order profile do not change during order execution, e.g. the ordered product type and the quantity or the destination of an order. Attributes that can be used for defining an order profile are referred to as *profile data*.

3.3. Concepts

To represent a supply chain scenario the fulfilment process can be described as an interaction between three main concepts: *Actors, Activities/Processes* and *Orders* (see fig. 6). Different tracking data types are linked to the concept of an *Order*. An *Actor* issues an *Order* which is received by another *Actor* in the supply chain. More *Actors* can be involved in the fulfilment process if further *Orders* have to be issued to be able to fulfil the first *Order*. This is the case if a customer orders a product from a manufacturer who needs to order components from his suppliers for the assembly of this product.

By issuing an *Order* a sequence of *Activities/Processes* is triggered which has to be performed to fulfil the *Order*. These *Activities* are carried out by the respective *Actors*. As the fulfilment process is dynamic one more concept is relevant: *Time*. The time axis is needed for tracking the status of the fulfilment process as the *Activities* are carried out over a period of time. The majority of concepts of the supply chain monitoring ontology can be grouped into the four categories mentioned above: *Actors, Activities/Processes, Orders, Time*. The main concepts in each category are described in the following paragraphs. Subsequently a scenario illustrates the use of the concepts for the description of situations in the supply chain monitoring domain.

The central concept concerning *Actors* is *LegalEntity* (see fig. 7). A *LegalEntity* is recognized as having rights and responsibilities in the world by large and by

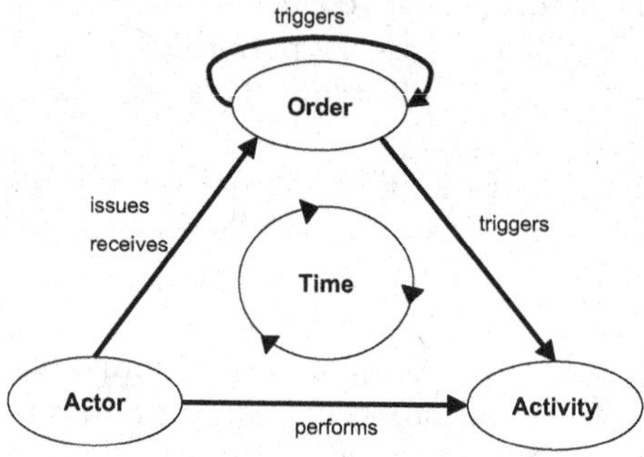

FIGURE 6. Basic concepts of the monitoring ontology

legal jurisdiction in particular [16]. *Customer*, *Vendor* and *Carrier* are *LegalEntities* that have relationships with each other.

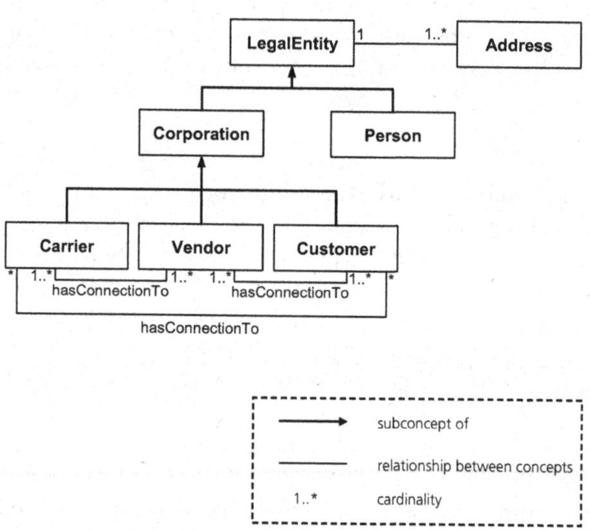

FIGURE 7. Actors in the supply chain

The central concept *Activity* (see fig. 8) represents the generalization of all actions that have to be executed within the fulfillment process. On the one hand *Activity* is needed to describe a specific scenario while on the other hand the fulfillment of an *Activity* can indicate the achievement of a *Milestone* (see below) and is therefore also important for representing tracking data.

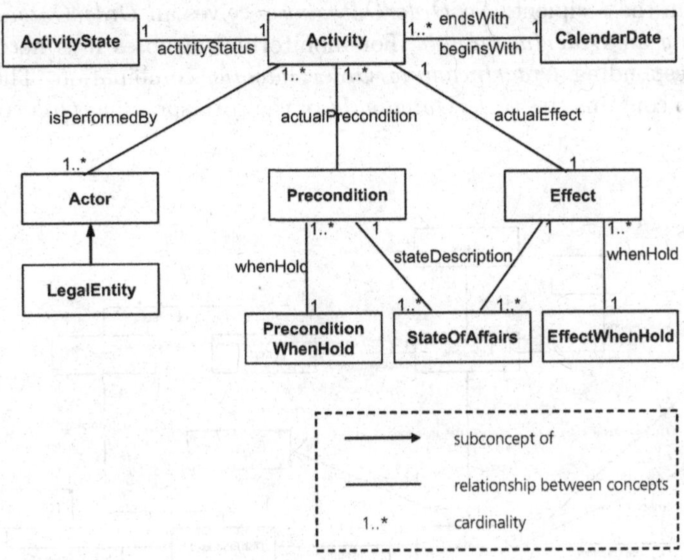

FIGURE 8. Activities in the fulfillment process

For the supply chain monitoring ontology fifteen specific activities have been identified: *ReceivingOrder, ConfirmationOfOrder, ProductionPlanning, IssueProductionOrder, Manufacturing, QualityAssurance, Picking, Packaging, DispatchGoods, PickingUpOrderFromSender, ReassignOrder, ArrivalAtHub, ArrivalAtCustoms, ClearingCustoms, Delivery.* These activities represent the major fulfillment processes in a supply chain on a generic modelling level. The execution of an *Activity* leads to a specific *Effect*, which consists of a *StateOfAffairs* that must hold true at a point of time (which is specified by the *EffectWhenHold* concept). An *Activity* has a *StartDate* and an *EndDate.* The status of an *Activity* at a certain point of time is described by the *ActivityState.* The fulfillment process is a sequence of *Activities* that are usually performed one after the other. Therefore, most *Activities* have as a *Precondition* the execution of another *Activity.* An *Activity* is performed by an *Actor.* A *LegalEntity* can be an *Actor.*

The concept of an *Order* is one of the basic concepts to model a supply chain scenario (see fig. 9). It is a legally binding contract concerning a transaction between *LegalEntities.* An *Order* thus defines relationships between partners in a supply chain. An *OrderIncoming* is an *Order* received by a *LegalEntity.* To fulfill this *Order* it might be necessary to place suborders (*OrderOutgoing*) with suppliers (e.g. a *Producer*) or a *Carrier* for distribution. This is denoted by the relation *triggers* (attribute of *OrderIncoming*) and the corresponding attribute *isTriggeredBy* of an *OrderOutgoing.* An *Order* consists of one or more *OrderItems* and it is identified by its *OrderId.* An *Order* receives an *OrderId* from its issuer as well as from the recipient: An *OrderOutgoing* receives an *OrderOutgoingId*, an *OrderIncoming* an *OrderIncomingId*. For monitoring purposes it is necessary to find the corresponding *OrderIncoming/OrderOutgoing* combination. The *OrderIncoming* also contains the *OrderOutgoingId* of the corresponding *OrderOutgoing*.

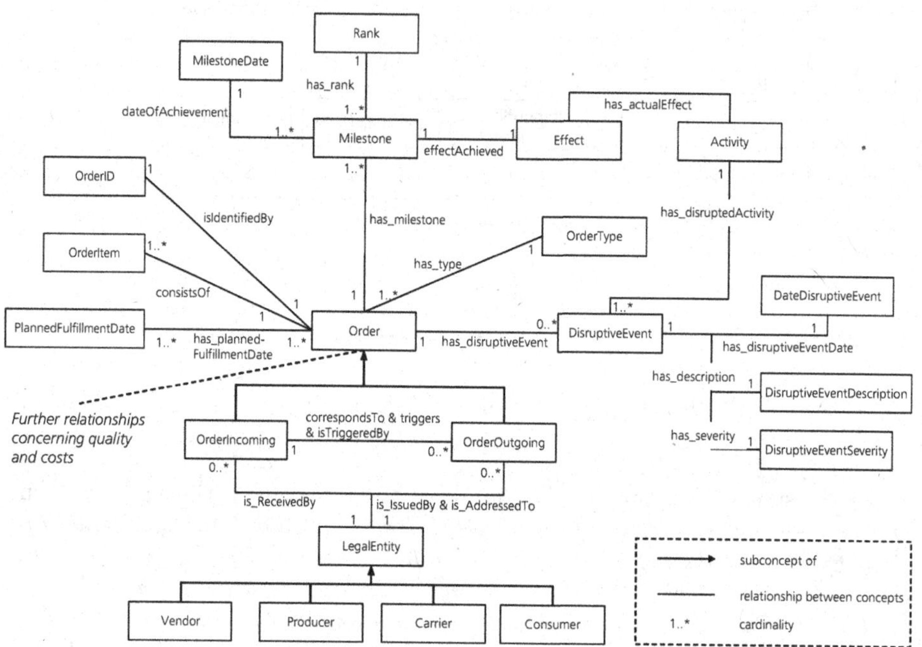

FIGURE 9. Orders in a supply chain

The *Activities* necessary to fulfill an *Order* depend on the respective *OrderType*. Three *OrderTypes* have been defined: *ProductionOrder*, *WarehousingOrder* and *TransportationOrder*. The concept of a *Milestone* is closely associated with *Activities*, since the *Effect* (that is the postcondition or output) of an *Activity* in combination with the date of achievement of the *Effect* (*MilestoneDate*) denotes a *Milestone*. To each *OrderType* only certain *Milestones* apply. Therefore *Milestones* are classified (according to the *OrderType*) into *ProductionMilestone*, *WarehousingMilestone* and *TransportationMilestone*. Since *Milestones* respectively *Activities* are achieved/conducted to fulfill an *Order* the concept *Rank* is introduced which helps to define the sequence of *Milestones*. For every *Milestone* planned dates of achievement and actual dates of achievement are defined to allow the calculation of deviations. Using the *Rank* concept the planned sequence of *Milestones* can be compared to the successively achieved *Milestones* and forecasts on the timeliness of an *Order* can be represented as well.

The third important group of concepts related to *Orders* are the *DisruptiveEvents* that cause the need for monitoring orders. They can be characterized by their date of occurrence (*DateDisruptiveEvent*) and by a severity measure that is defined in *DisruptiveEventSeverity*. For an assessment of a *DisruptiveEvent* a description of the event is needed which supports the decision making process by offering insight into details of the event. Other types of *status data* that are incorporated in the ontology but not explained here refer to the group of quality measures, e.g. the ratio of delivered to ordered quantity. The concept of *Time* plays an important role for tracking *Orders* along the supply chain. However, it is not specific for this environment. The *Enterprise Ontology* uses a *Time* concept imported from Allen's work [19]. This concept is also used for the supply chain monitoring ontology.

3.4. Supply Chain Scenario

Figure 10 shows a sample scenario for fulfillment processes in a supply chain. *Customer EnergyAlways* issues an order to the *Vendor CompressorManufacturer* which issues related suborders to a *Vendor (ChassisSupplier)* and a *Carrier (LogisticsServiceProvider)*.

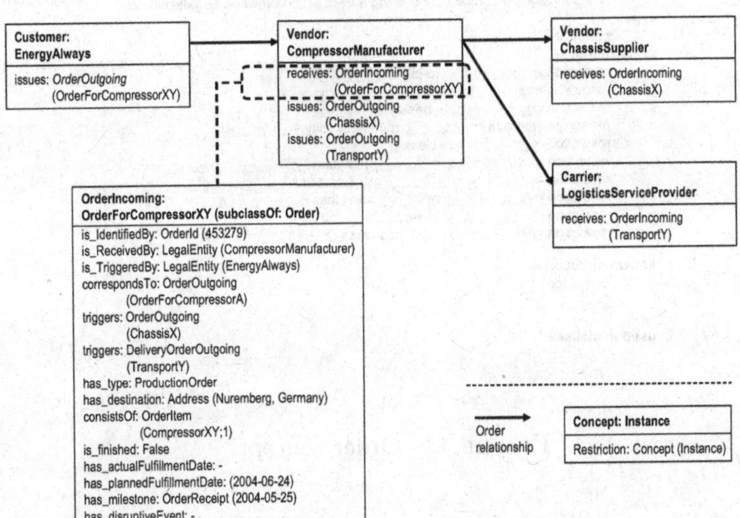

FIGURE 10. Supply chain scenario

The *Vendor CompressorManufacturer* receives an *OrderIncoming*. It corresponds to the *OrderOutgoing* issued by the *Customer* and has not yet been fulfilled (*ActualFulfillmentDate:* –). The *plannedFulfillmentDate* is a restriction (attribute) which refers to the general concept *CalendarDate* with the instance "2004-06-24". The *OrderIncoming* consists of the *OrderItem CompressorXY* and indicates an ordered quantity of "1". As *Vendor CompressorManufacturer* needs *ChassisX* to be able to produce *CompressorXY* for the *OrderIncoming* it has to trigger an *OrderOutgoing* for *ChassisX* addressed to *Vendor ChassisSupplier*. The finished product (*CompressorXY*) has to be delivered to the *deliveryPlace (Nuremberg)*. The delivery is not done by the *Vendor*. The *Vendor* issues a *DeliveryOrderOutgoing* addressed to the *Carrier LogisticsServiceProvider*.

4. Implementation

Different ontology description languages exist for the formal definition of ontologies. To facilitate interoperability within the priority research program "Intelligent Agents and Realistic Application Scenarios" of the *Deutsche Forschungsgemeinschaft (DFG)* [20] which this project is part of, OIL (Ontology Inference Layer) [21] and its further development into DAML+OIL has been agreed upon as the uniform ontology language.

class Order

documentation:
A legally binding contract concerning a transaction between LegalEntities.
type:
primitive
constraints:
restriction is_identifiedBy **to-class** OrderId
restriction has_type **to-class** OrderType
restriction has_destination **has-class** Address
property-constraint consists_Of **min-cardinality** 1 OrderItem
restriction is_finished **has-class** BooleanValue
restriction has_orderReceiptDate #1 **has-class** DateOrderReceipt #1
restriction has_plannedFulfillmentDate **has-class** FulfillmentDate
restriction has_dateOfAchievement **has-class** FulfillmentDate
restriction has_milestone **has-class** Milestone
restriction has_disruptiveEvent **has-class** DisruptiveEvent

known subclasses:
OrderIncoming
OrderOutgoing

used in classes:
OrderIncoming
OrderOutgoing

FIGURE 11. Order concept

OIL combines three important aspects provided by different communities: it inherits the formal semantics and reasoning support from Decision Logics, incorporates the essential modeling primitives of frame-based systems and uses existing Web standards by providing XML and RDF based syntax [22].

For the design of the supply chain monitoring ontology, the ontology editor OilEd has been used [23]. It provides an easy-to-use connection to the FaCT reasoner. The FaCT reasoner is a reasoning tool that checks the consistency of all class definitions in an ontology and discovers sub-class/super-class relationships that are implied by the definitions in the ontology but not explicitly stated [21]. The FaCT system includes one reasoner for the logic SHF and one for the logic SHIQ and is based on a CORBA client-server architecture. Within this project, the FaCT reasoner is used to validate the ontology. In addition, current versions of OilEd provide a DIG (DL Implementors Group) interface that allows to connect the Racer inference machine directly to OilEd [24].

OilEd supports various formats for exporting ontologies such as Simple RDFS, DAML+OIL, SHIQ, HTML, DIG, OWL and OWL RDF/XML. The flexible use of different formats allows to use the same ontology in different applications with a relatively small customizing effort. Since the standardized DAML+OIL syntax is machine-readable but inappropriate for illustration an HTML-export is used to present an excerpt of the ontology (see fig. 11).

Each class (concept) is documented in natural language. A class can have various restrictions applied to a property. For example, the class *Order* has a restriction attached to the property *has-orderReceiptDate* which has to be of the type (has-class) *FulfillmentDate*. There can be various subclasses of a class. The subclasses inherit all restrictions of the *Order* class and may define further properties in accordance with the specific characteristics of the subclasses (e.g. *OrderIncoming* has a restriction *is-ReceivedBy* which is not necessary for *OrderOutgoing*). The ontology currently consists of approximately 140 classes and 70 properties.

5. Ontology-Based Agent Communication

Supply chain monitoring focuses on the exchange of tracking data between companies. The information is used to optimize the fulfillment of individual orders. Therefore, agents engage in dialogs to gain insight into the status of orders and suborders. They use the ontology as the semantic hub for their communication activities. Generally *profile data* is not the main issue of the communicative acts as it is mainly stable and known to the partners concerned with an order. In fact, the dynamically changing *status data* and *decision data* are of interest during the monitoring process. In addition, control data is needed to compare the actual status of an order with the planned activities and to evaluate disruptive events in the light of the planned course of action. The behavior of a surveillance agent and the resulting interaction with other agents is depicted in fig. 12, fig. 13 and fig. 14.

After its initialization which is triggered by the coordination agent a surveillance agent gathers order details (e.g. the plannedFulfillmentDate) since it has only received an order identification number from the coordination agent. The order details are extracted from an internal data base (e.g. the Enterprise Resource Planning (ERP) system of a company) by a wrapper agent (see fig. 13)

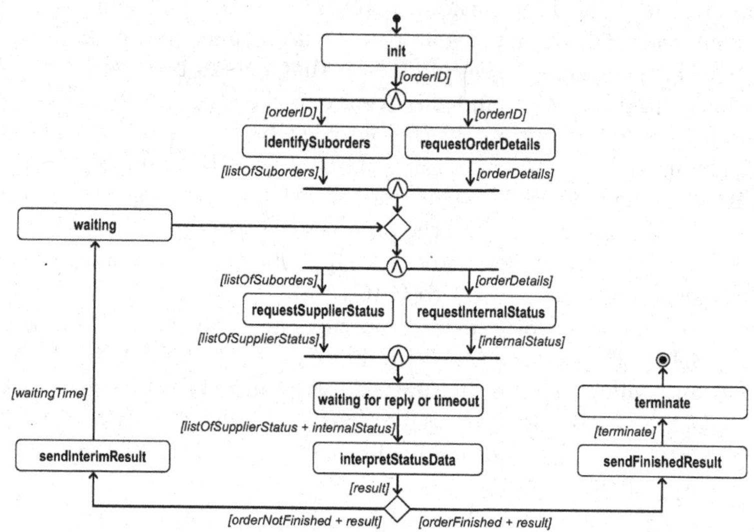

FIGURE 12. Behavior of a surveillance agent

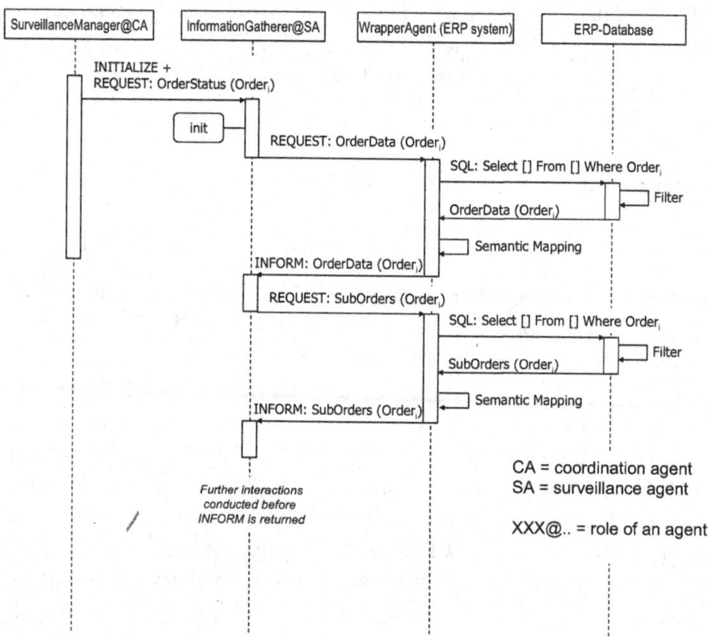

FIGURE 13. Agent interaction - *OrderDataRequest*

and the data is mapped to the terms defined within the ontology (see also fig. 10). The agents use the performatives of the FIPA agent communication language (FIPA-ACL) [10] while the content is defined based on the DAML+OIL ontology presented above. In addition, the surveillance agent identifies the relevant suborders. This information is needed to decide which external supply chain partners are to be queried for monitoring information.

Information on the current status of the monitored order and its external suborders is gathered in two ways:

- Internal resources (e.g. ERP, warehouse management or production control systems) are accessed via dedicated wrapper agents. In this case a similar interaction evolves as depicted in fig. 13.
- External supply chain partners are queried that have received a suborder. The request for tracking data to an external supply chain partner is communicated via the discourse agents of both companies that act as the technical and semantic gateways between the companies' agent systems (see fig. 14). Again, the information on the status of a suborder is defined in the terms of the ontology (e.g. information about milestones and disruptive events).

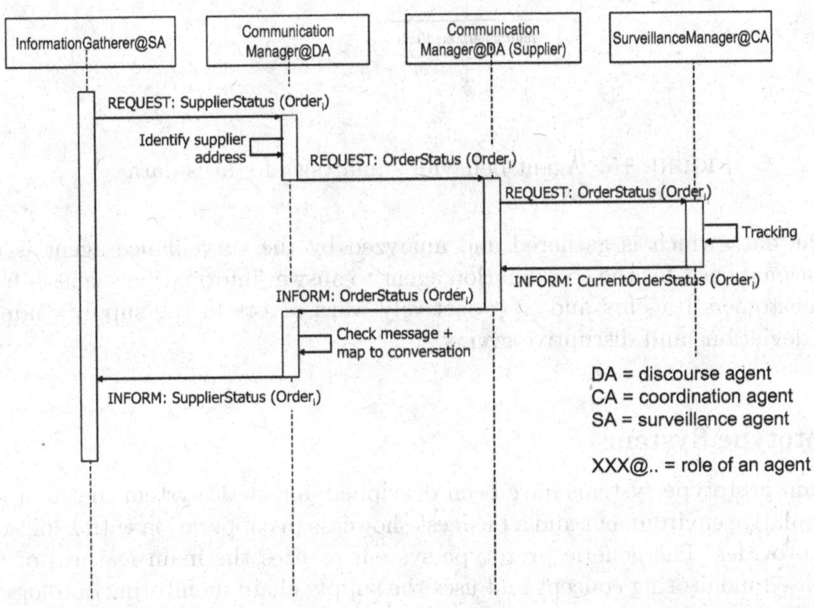

FIGURE 14. Agent interaction - *SupplierStatusRequest*

Based on the data which the surveillance agent receives from its various communication partners it is able to analyze the current status of the monitored order. The analysis considers various dimensions of *status data* (e.g. timeliness and completeness of an order or a suborder) and evaluates disruptive events that have been identified during the search for tracking data (see fig. 15). For the analysis of the data a fuzzy-based mechanism is used because it is suited to achieve realistic assessments of an order's fulfillment situation. Concluding, the surveillance agent checks the current plan for the achievement of the defined milestones and adjusts this plan if necessary.

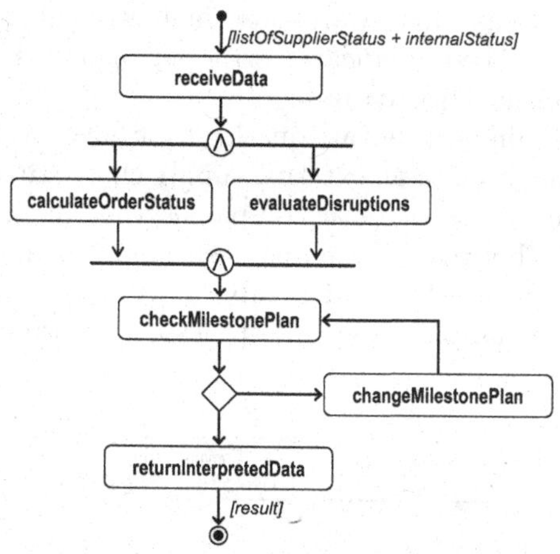

FIGURE 15. Agent behavior - analysis of status data

The data which is gathered and analyzed by the surveillance agent is the informational basis for the coordination agent to answer information requests from other (customers') agents and to proactively warn actors in the supply chain of serious deviations and disruptive events.

6. Prototype Systems

Two main prototype systems have been developed: a generic system that is based on a simulative environment and a business showcase in cooperation with a logistics service provider. The generic prototype system realizes the main features of the agent-based monitoring concept and uses the supply chain monitoring ontology to define the contents of agent communication. It is based on the FIPA compliant JADE platform. In fig. 16 the interaction between three companies in a simulative environment that are linked through order relations (orders and their suborders) is depicted. The interaction between the agent systems of the companies evolves during the search for monitoring data that characterizes the status of the related suborders.

In fig. 16 examples of the data analysis results are presented. The aggregated order status is an abstract but intuitive measure for the current fulfillment status of an order. It incorporates consequences of disruptive events such as delays and incomplete deliveries with the help of a Fuzzy-Logic module. Every time new monitoring data is gathered by the surveillance agent an update of the order status is made. In addition, the criticality of disruptive events is evaluated and if necessary an adjustment of milestones due to delays in the fulfillment processes is conducted.

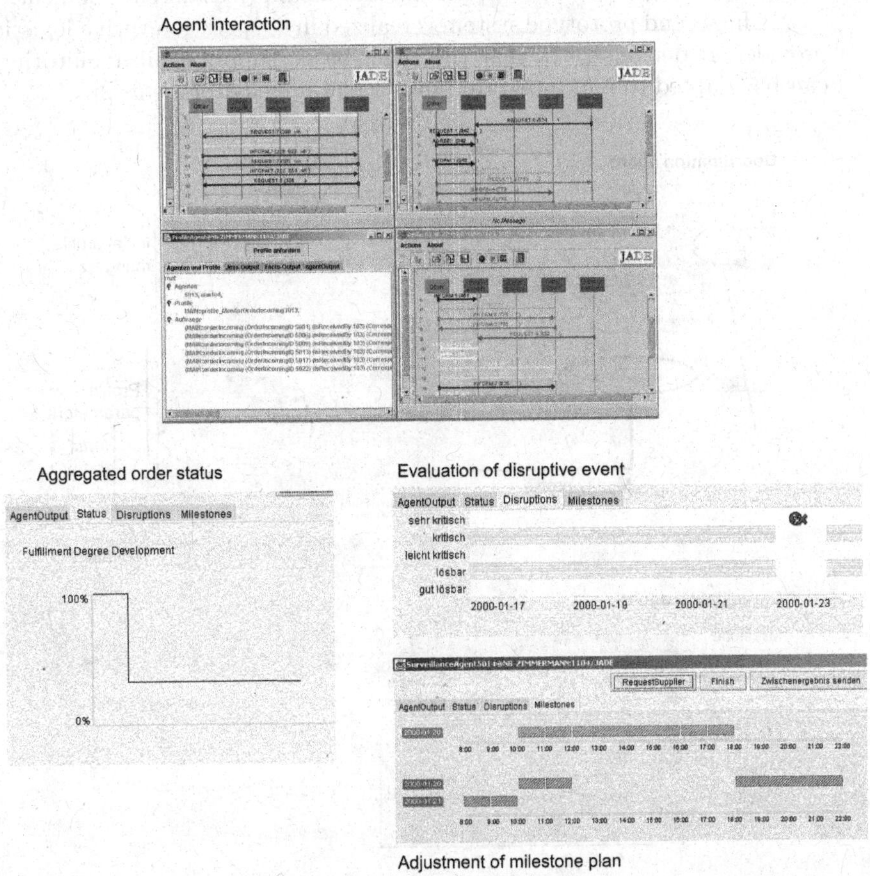

FIGURE 16. Generic prototype

The generic prototype is used to demonstrate the ability to realize the supply chain monitoring concept in a multi-stage supply chain environment. Besides the Fuzzy-Logic-based analysis mechanism it also realizes an efficient method to focus on potentially critical orders based on order profiles. This method is implemented based upon a rule-based expert system (Java Expert System Shell (JESS)) which is integrated into the coordination agent. As a result the use of order profiles allows to reduce the necessary amount of communicative interactions between the companies in a supply chain.

This prototype system is also integrated into a larger supply chain scenario that is based upon various multi agent systems which cover further aspects of supply chain management (e.g. production planning). The scenario called *Agent.Enterprise* [25], [26] is used to evaluate the performance of the monitoring concept in a realistic and complex simulated supply chain environment.

The second prototype system is realized in cooperation with a logistics service provider. It demonstrates that the agent-based supply chain monitoring concept can be adapted to and integrated into a real-life environment [2].

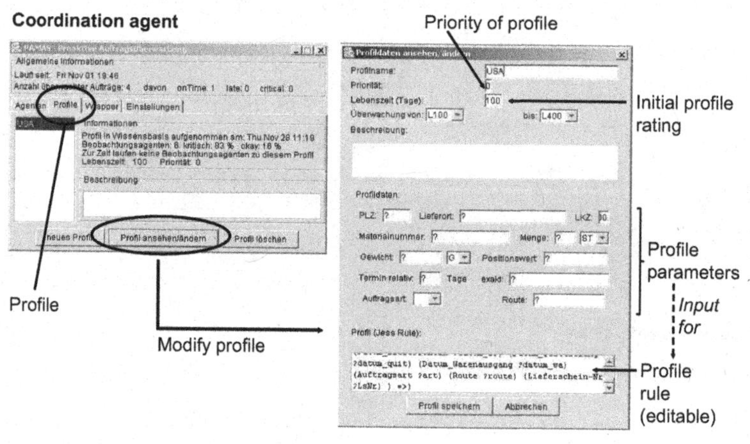

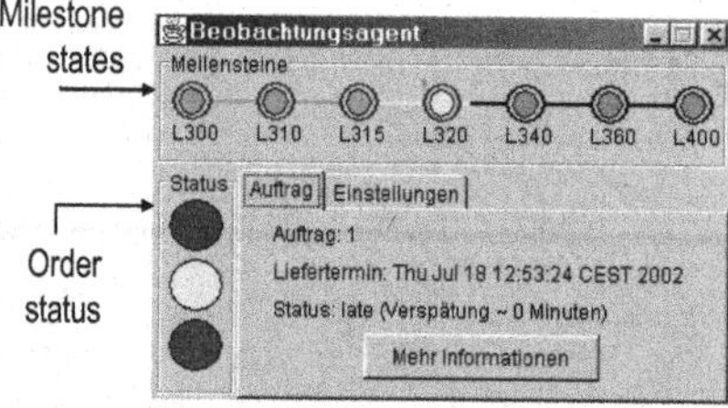

FIGURE 17. Business showcase

Specifically, it realizes the order profile mechanism of the coordination agent and provides an intuitive user interface to define and edit order profiles (see fig. 17). The ability to match the data types of the business partner to the supply chain monitoring ontology is a second important result of the business showcase. The

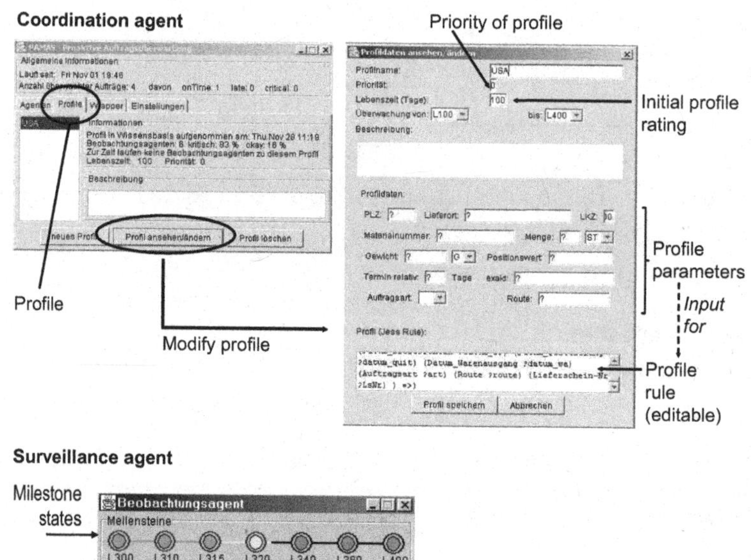

prototype system is able to query the internal SAP database of the logistics service provider as well as distributed tracking databases of different carriers via their web interfaces. In each case a dedicated wrapper agent is used which can access the data source and which converts the extracted data into the format required by the agent system and defined by the supply chain monitoring ontology.

Users are supported in their ability to react to identified problems by a graphical user interface of the surveillance agent (see fig. 17). It consists of two major graphical elements - the visualization of the different milestones (top) and an aggregated order status on the left both based on a traffic-light metaphor. Additional information on the order details and the details of the fulfillment process can be accessed manually by the user if necessary.

7. Conclusion

Irregularities and disruptive events in fulfillment processes have a major influence on supply chain performance. It is necessary to optimize the processes of gathering and communicating information related to such events. The agent-based concept presented for supply chain monitoring allows to speed up these processes and to focus on the monitoring of critical orders, thereby reducing the extent of communication in a supply chain. To enable the exchange of tracking information between software agents an ontology has been developed that comprises relevant tracking information and important concepts of a supply chain scenario. The formal model enables an efficient reuse of the ontology in different applications.

The ontology is used as the semantic basis for two prototype systems that demonstrate the applicability of the agent-based supply chain monitoring concept. Future developments will incorporate inferencing capabilities into the generic prototype system based on the RACER inference machine. The discourse agent which is responsible for managing ontology-related aspects of the inter-organizational communication will benefit from these inference mechanisms. Automatic checks of incoming and outgoing agent messages against the ontology will be one of the major benefits. Finally, further experiments to evaluate the supply chain monitoring concept in the *Agent.Enterprise* environment are on the roadmap.

References

[1] Radjou N., Orlov L.M., Nakashima T., *Adapting to Supply Network Change.* Cambridge (MA): Forrester Research Inc., 2002.

[2] Zimmermann R., Paschke A., *PAMAS - an agent-based supply chain event management system* Proceedings of AMCIS 2003, Mini-track on Intelligent Agents and Multi-Agent Systems, Tampa, 2003, 1892-1900.

[3] Stein A., Krieger W., Pflaum A., Dräger H., *Sendungsverfolgung zwischen Marketinginstrument und Produktionsunterstützungstool.* Nürnberg: GVB Schriftenreihe, Vol 40, 1998.

[4] Teufel T., Röhricht J., Willems P.; *SAP-Prozesse: Planung, Beschaffung und Produktion.* München: Addison-Wesley, 2000.

[5] Wagner T., Guralnik V., Phelps J., *Software Agents: Enabling Dynamic Supply Chain Management for a Build to Order Product Line.* Agents for Business Automation, 2002.

[6] Fox M.S., Barbuceanu M., Teigen R., *Agent-Oriented Supply-Chain Management.* International Journal of Flexible Manufacturing Systems **12**, No 2/3 (2000), 165-188.

[7] van Parunak D., Savitt R., Riolo R., Clark S., *DASCh: Dynamic Analysis of Supply Chains.* Http://www.erim.org/~vparunak/dasch99.pdf, download 2002-05-28.

[8] Wagner T., Phelps J., Qian Y., Albert E., Beane G., *A Modified Architecture for Constructing Real-Time Information Gathering Agents.* Agent Oriented Information Systems (AOIS), 2001.

[9] Foundation for Intelligent Physical Agents (FIPA), *Agent Message Transport Service Specification, Document number XC00067D.* Http://www.fipa.org, download 2002-03-28.

[10] Foundation for Intelligent Physical Agents (FIPA), *Communicative Act Repository Specification, Document number DC00038B.* Http://www.fipa.org, download 2002-03-28.

[11] Foundation for Intelligent Physical Agents (FIPA), *Interaction Protocol Library Specification, Document number XC00025E.* Http://www.fipa.org, download 2002-03-28.

[12] Zimmermann R., Butscher R., Bodendorf F., Huber A., Goerz G., *Generic agent architecture for supply chain tracking.* Proceedings of the 2nd IEEE International Symposium on Signal Processing and Information Technology ISSPIT 2002, Marrakesh: IEEE Press, 2002, 203-207.

[13] Gruber T. R., *A translation approach to portable ontologies.* Knowledge Acquisition **5** (1993), 199-220.

[14] Uschold M., King M., *Towards a Methodology for Building Ontologies.* Workshop on Basic Ontological Issues in Knowledge Sharing, IJCAI-95, 1995.

[15] Holsapple C.W., Joshi K.D., *A Collaborative Approach to Ontology Design.* Communications of the ACM **45**, No 2, 2002.

[16] Uschold M., King M., Moralee S., Zorgios Y., *The Enterprise Ontology.* Edinburgh, 1997, Http://www.aiai.ed.ac.uk/~entprise/enterprise/ontology.html-papers, download 2002-02-26.

[17] Zimmermann R., Butscher R., Bodendorf F. *An Ontology for Agent-Based Supply Chain Monitoring.* Workshop-Proceedings "Agent Technologies in Logistics", ECAI, Lyon, 2002, 65-78.

[18] Supply Chain Council *SCOR-Model, Version 2.0.* Http://www.supply-chain.org, 1997.

[19] Allen J.F., *Towards a general theory of action and time.* Artificial Intelligence **23** (1984), 123 -154.

[20] DFG Priority Research Program 1083 - http://www.realagents.org/

[21] Hurrocks I., Fensel D., Broekstra J., Decker S., Erdmann M., Goble C., van Harmelen F., Klein M., Staab S., Studer R., Motta E., *The Ontology Inference Layer OIL*. Http://www.ontoknowledge.org/oil/papers.shtml, download 2002-03-25.

[22] Fensel D., Ontologies: A Silver Bullet for Knowledge Management and Electronic Commerce. Berlin, 2001.

[23] OILED by Sean Bechhofer of the University of Manchester - http://oiled.man.ac.uk/

[24] DL Implementors Group - http://dl.kr.org/dig/

[25] Frey D., Stockheim T., Woelk P.O., Zimmermann R., *Integrated Multi-agent-based Supply Chain Management*. WETICE 2003, ACEC Workshop, Linz, 2003.

[26] Frey D., Mönch L., Stockheim T., Woelk P.O., Zimmermann R., *Agent.Enterprise - Integriertes Supply-Chain-Management mit hierarchisch vernetzten Multiagenten-Systemen*. Proceedings der GI Jahrestagung 2003, Frankfurt, 47-63.

Acknowledgment

This paper presents research results originating from a project sponsored by the Deutsche Forschungsgemeinschaft (DFG) within the priority research program "Intelligent Agents and Realistic Application Scenarios". The project "Agent-based Tracking and Tracing of Business Processes" is realized by the Department of Information Systems (Prof. Bodendorf) and the Department of Artificial Intelligence (Prof. Dr. Günter Görz) at the University of Erlangen-Nuremberg.

Roland Zimmermann, S. Käs, Robert Butscher and
Freimut Bodendorf
Lange Gasse 20
90403 Nürnberg
Germany
e-mail: roland.zimmermann@wiso.uni-erlangen.de
robert.butscher@wiso.uni-erlangen.de
freimut.bodendorf@wiso.uni-erlangen.de